THE
SWEDISH
ECONOMY

BARRY P. BOSWORTH and ALICE M. RIVLIN
Editors

THE
SWEDISH
ECONOMY

Barry P. Bosworth
Gary Burtless
Robert J. Flanagan
Edward M. Gramlich
Robert Z. Lawrence
Alice M. Rivlin
R. Kent Weaver

THE BROOKINGS INSTITUTION
Washington, D.C.

Library of Congress Cataloging-in-Publication data

The Swedish economy.

  Includes bibliographical references and index.
  1. Sweden—Economic conditions—1945–   .
2. Sweden—Economic policy. I. Bosworth, Barry,
1942–   . II. Rivlin, Alice M.
HC375.S977 1987   330.9485'058   86-29920
ISBN 0-8157-1042-9
ISBN 0-8157-1041-0 (pbk.)

9 8 7 6 5 4 3 2 1

THE BROOKINGS INSTITUTION is an independent organization devoted to nonpartisan research, education, and publication in economics, government, foreign policy, and the social sciences generally. Its principal purposes are to aid in the development of sound public policies and to promote public understanding of issues of national importance.

The Institution was founded on December 8, 1927, to merge the activities of the Institute for Government Research, founded in 1916, the Institute of Economics, founded in 1922, and the Robert Brookings Graduate School of Economics and Government, founded in 1924.

The Board of Trustees is responsible for the general administration of the Institution, while the immediate direction of the policies, program, and staff is vested in the President, assisted by an advisory committee of the officers and staff. The by-laws of the Institution state: "It is the function of the Trustees to make possible the conduct of scientific research, and publication, under the most favorable conditions, and to safeguard the independence of the research staff in the pursuit of their studies and in the publication of the results of such studies. It is not a part of their function to determine, control, or influence the conduct of particular investigations or the conclusions reached."

The President bears final responsibility for the decision to publish a manuscript as a Brookings book. In reaching his judgment on the competence, accuracy, and objectivity of each study, the President is advised by the director of the appropriate research program and weighs the views of a panel of expert outside readers who report to him in confidence on the quality of the work. Publication of a work signifies that it is deemed a competent treatment worthy of public consideration but does not imply endorsement of conclusions or recommendations.

The Institution maintains its position of neutrality on issues of public policy in order to safeguard the intellectual freedom of the staff. Hence interpretations or conclusions in Brookings publications should be understood to be solely those of the authors and should not be attributed to the Institution, to its trustees, officers, or other staff members, or to the organizations that support its research.

Foreword

SINCE the early 1970s the industrialized countries have experienced similar problems in economic performance—much slower economic growth accompanied by sharp increases in inflation and unemployment. Government policies to stem this economic deterioration have varied considerably, however, as have their degrees of success. Recent experience thus offers a comparative experiment in showing how market economies operate and respond to varying government policies. But simple comparisons can be highly misleading because of important differences in economic, political, and social institutions.

In this study a group of American social scientists examine the Swedish economy and its response to government policies that have varied as dramatically as those of the United States. In the 1970s Sweden followed a budget policy that foreshadowed U.S. policy in the 1980s: the government increased the budget deficit and borrowed abroad to maintain a domestic standard of living that was beyond the nation's means. In the 1980s Sweden decisively reversed this policy, cutting back the budget deficit and promoting exports as the key to expanding economic growth. At the same time, Sweden maintains a social welfare system with associated labor market policies and taxes far more comprehensive than those that have been so controversial in the United States. Thus many of the events in Sweden in the past decade offer comparisons and contrasts with the U.S. experience and serve as a reference for U.S. policy debates.

The American scholars hope that this study can also be of use in

Sweden. By offering an outside view unencumbered by involvement in internal policy debates, they may provoke new insights into the challenges and policy options that Sweden will face in the future.

The editors of this volume, Barry Bosworth and Alice M. Rivlin, are, respectively, a senior fellow in the Brookings Economic Studies program and the director of that program. The project could not have been undertaken without the assistance of many people in Sweden and the United States who were extremely generous of their time in providing guidance and assistance to the authors of these papers. The authors wish especially to thank Hans Tson Söderström of Studieförbundet Näringsliv och Samhälle (SNS) who helped obtain financial support and organized and chaired a conference on the Swedish economy held at Skokloster, Sweden, on June 3–4, 1986. He and the staff of SNS, including Gunilla Boström, Gunnar P. Eliasson, Agneta Granberg, Ingemund Hägg, and Torgny Wadensjö, helped make arrangements and appointments during the authors' research visits to Sweden. The authors also benefited from the hospitatility of the Industrial Institute for Economic and Social Research, the Institute for International Economics, and the Kommerskollegium.

In addition to the formal discussants whose comments are included in this volume, the authors profited from discussions with many individuals in Sweden and the United States. They are particularly grateful to N. Soren Blomquist, Anders Björklund, Peter Bohm, Paul Courant, Klaus Eklund, Karl Olaf Faxén, Siv Gustafsson, Eva Horwitz, Walter Korpi, Deborah Laren, John Martin, Rudolf Meidner, Per-Martin Meyerson, Robert Moffit, Richard Murray, Clas-Erik Ohdner, Pavel Pelikan, Mel Reder, Claes-Henric Siven, Roland Spant, Frank Stafford, Ann-Charlotte Stahlberg, Julie Sundquist, Steve Turner, Thomas Weisskopf, Bengt Christen Ysander, and Hans Zetterberg.

James Schneider, Jeanette Morrison, Brenda Szittya, and Theresa Walker edited the manuscript. Victor M. Alfaro and Almaz Zelleke verified the factual content. Tamara Giles, Sheila E. Murray, Mary S. Skinner, and Lori Wilson provided research assistance. Kathleen M. Bucholz, Judy Jackson, Valerie M. Owens, and Kathleen Elliott Yinug provided assistance in preparing the manuscript.

The conference on the Swedish economy was supported by grants from the Salén Foundation, the Jan Wallander Foundation for Social Science Research, the Marianne and Marcus Wallenberg Foundation, the National Swedish Industrial Board, the National Swedish Board for Technical Development, the National Swedish Board for Trade, and the Swedish Council of America.

The views expressed here are those of the authors and should not be ascribed to the individuals and organizations whose assistance is acknowledged above, or to the trustees, officers, or other staff members of the Brookings Institution.

Bruce K. MacLaury
President

December 1986
Washington, D.C.

Contents

Tables

Figures

1

Overview

ALICE M. RIVLIN

THIS IS A BOOK about the Swedish economy by a group of Americans. Although the authors have benefited enormously from information and insights provided by Swedish colleagues, they remain outsiders. They identify the apparent strengths and weaknesses of the Swedish economic situation and the major economic choices facing Sweden at the end of the 1980s. They offer, in all humility, some suggestions for the general directions that Swedish economic policy ought to take.

Economic analysis is difficult enough in the familiar setting of one's own country. Analyzing another economy, with barriers of language and culture and differences in economic and political institutions and traditions to surmount, is hazardous. And it is always presumptuous to offer advice in someone else's country. Nevertheless, the authors have undertaken this project for two reasons. First, they hope that the fresh viewpoint of outsiders will prove valuable in helping the Swedes to see their economic situation in new ways and that their proposals will stimulate constructive policy debate in Sweden.

Second, the authors hope this analysis will prove useful to Americans and others trying to grapple with the serious problems that have beset advanced economies since the early 1970s. After a long period of strong growth and sustained increases in productivity, all the advanced economies experienced sharp slowdowns in growth, largely attributable to a falling off of productivity increases. Part of the falling off can be explained by changes in energy prices, demographic shifts, increased regulation, and the like, but much remains a mystery. Even as their economies

1

recovered in the 1980s, the developed countries remained concerned about productivity growth, the health of many of their basic industries, and their ability to compete with newly industrializing nations. At the same time, and in varying degrees, all the advanced countries have been dealing with the growing demands of their citizens for public services and income transfers. These demands have meant higher taxes and worries about the effects of high taxes and benefits on incentives to work and save. Moreover, in most countries taxes have not risen as fast as expenditures, and large deficits have emerged in government budgets.

Economists and policymakers have been trying to learn from the experience of the 1970s and the early 1980s in their respective countries— to understand what went wrong, to assess the extent to which policy was at fault, and to design better mixes of policies. But analysts tend to be myopic, often ascribing their own country's failures to local mistakes in policy or political and economic institutions peculiar to their country. This book reflects the hope that countries can learn from each other's successes and failures in dealing with similar problems and can use that knowledge to design more effective policies.

At least until the early 1970s Sweden was known in the rest of the developed world for its success in merging a vigorous, competitive private sector with an egalitarian welfare state. But when the Swedish economy, like others, faltered in the 1970s, critics frequently blamed the excesses of the welfare state and Swedish government intervention in the private sector. Sweden came to be viewed as an example of an economy staggering under the weight of government commitments that were too expensive.

In this book the authors attempt to step back from the ideological fray and view the Swedish economic situation as dispassionately as possible. To what extent have Sweden's economic problems been caused by global forces that have had a similar impact on other countries with widely differing roles for government? How much have productivity and the ability to adjust to changed economic circumstances been improved or undermined by Sweden's commitment to equalizing incomes and maintaining full employment, especially its high levels of tax and government subsidies to businesses and individuals? Have macroeconomic decisions contributed positively or negatively to the health of the economy? Is Sweden living beyond its means and postponing hard choices?

What Strikes an American about the Swedish Economy?

First, of course, an American is struck by how small the Swedish economy is compared with the economies of the United States or the larger countries of Western Europe. In 1985 Sweden's gross domestic product was 3 percent of U.S. GDP, 16 percent of Germany's, and 20 percent of France's.

Sweden is an open economy, highly dependent on foreign trade and vulnerable to outside shocks. In 1985 exports accounted for 32 percent of GDP, compared with 10 percent for the United States and 35 percent for Germany. This dependence on foreign trade means that firms in Swedish export industries have to set their prices to stay competitive in world markets. Their profits decline when their costs rise more rapidly than those of their foreign competitors. While Sweden, unlike the United States, has long been conscious of its dependence on external trade, the recent integration of its capital markets with those of the rest of the world has increased Swedish vulnerability to world events.

The 8 million Swedes form a relatively homogenous population with a high level of education and skill. Swedes tend to be older than Americans: 17 percent were sixty-five years of age or older in 1984 compared with 12 percent in the United States. Sweden's postwar baby boom was smaller and occurred earlier than that of the United States, and the influx of young workers into the labor force was over by the mid-1960s.

Labor force participation is high in Sweden. In 1984, 83 percent of Swedes between the ages of fifteen and sixty-five were in the labor force, compared with 76 percent of Americans and 64 percent of Germans. The high labor force participation reflects the fact that most Swedish women work outside the home, even when they have small children. Many Swedish women and increasing numbers of men, however, work less than a full workweek. Hence despite the big increase in participation by Swedish women, total hours worked by the labor force have been declining.

Perhaps the most striking aspect of its economy is Sweden's high standard of living and absence of poverty. Current levels of income reflect a long period of sustained growth. From the end of World War II

4   THE SWEDISH ECONOMY

Table 1-1. *Swedish, U.S., and European Comparative Economic Indicators, Selected Periods, 1960–86*

Economic Indicators	1960–73	1974–82	1983–86
Average annual growth of GDP			
Sweden	4.1	1.4	2.6
Europe	4.7	1.8	2.3
United States	4.0	1.6	3.8
Average annual growth of GDP per worker			
Sweden	3.5	0.5	2.0
Europe	4.3	1.8	2.2
United States	2.1	0.0	1.4
Average unemployment rate			
Sweden	1.8	2.1	3.0
Europe	3.0	6.3	10.7
United States	4.8	7.1	7.8
Average inflation rate			
Sweden	4.9	10.4	7.3
Europe	4.9	10.3	7.1
United States	3.4	8.1	3.5
Gross saving as percent of GDP			
Sweden	24.7	18.8	17.2[a]
Europe	24.4	21.4	19.9[a]
United States	18.0	16.5	16.1[a]

Sources: Figures for 1960–73 calculated from data in Organization for Economic Cooperation and Development, *OECD Economic Outlook: Hisorical Statistics, 1960–1983* (Paris: OECD, 1985); figures for 1974–86 calculated from data in *OECD Economic Outlook*, vol. 39 (Paris: OECD, 1986), and background data from OECD.
a. Figures for 1983–84 only.

until 1973 the economy grew at rates comparable to the rest of Europe and higher than those of the United States. Saving was high, reflecting the decision of the government to run a surplus in the budget and make substantial public investments. Thus high national saving was effectively channeled into high rates of capital formation, both for public infrastructure and private plant and equipment.

After 1973 Sweden shared in the common experience of advanced industrial countries—its growth slowed sharply and inflation escalated (table 1-1.) The slowing of the growth in output was roughly comparable to that experienced by the United States and the rest of Europe, a drop from more than a 4 percent annual growth rate between 1960 and 1973 to less than 2 percent annually from 1974 to 1982. Thanks to devaluation of the krona and the general recovery of the world economy, however,

Swedish economic growth rebounded in the mid-1980s. Inflation has remained high—about the same as the average for Europe but substantially above Sweden's principal competitors, especially Germany. The high inflation reflects Sweden's unwillingness to permit the sharp rise in unemployment that Germany and some other countries tolerated in order to slow inflation.

The standard of living is still high, and unemployment, while substantial by past Swedish standards, is far below that in the rest of Europe. Hence economists are not concerned about the current standard of living and employment of the Swedes but rather about the future health and long-run competitiveness of the Swedish economy.

To outsiders, especially to Americans, the most striking feature of Swedish economic policy is the long-standing and pervasive commitment to economic equality. This commitment is carried out in policies for wage determination, taxation, and government spending programs.

Wage bargaining is highly centralized, and the number of bargainers is small. The Landsorganisationen (LO), which represents most blue-collar workers, and three coalitions of white-collar unions bargain for most salaried employees; the Svenska Arbetsgivareföreningen (SAF), which includes major employers, and the local and national governments bargain on behalf of employers. The centralization has enabled the blue-collar unions to maintain a "solidaristic" wage policy aimed at narrowing wage differentials. Differences in wages by occupation, industry, and level of skill have been consciously reduced. In recent years wage policy has attempted to erase wage differences between jobs held primarily by men and those held primarily by women.

The solidaristic wage policy was originally formulated in the 1950s as a way of improving both egalitarianism and economic growth. Compressing the wage scale by raising the lower end was expected to drive firms with low productivity out of business and shift industrial structure toward capital-intensive, high-productivity industries. As a result, differentials between high-wage and low-wage occupations and industries are small in Sweden and, while there is no statutory minimum wage, the central bargaining process effectively sets one at a higher level than in the United States.

The policy of equalizing wages between the sexes has been largely successful. Although Swedish women remain concentrated in particular occupations to an even greater extent than women in the United States, this occupational segregation has less impact on male-female earnings differentials in Sweden because wage differences among occupations are narrower than in the United States.

Sweden's progressive tax system makes a further contribution to equalizing incomes. By any standard, tax rates on income are high. After a modest personal exemption, Swedes pay a proportional tax on personal income to local governments and a progressive tax to the central government. The combined marginal rate payable by a full-time worker in the middle of the income distribution is between 50 and 64 percent.[1] Effective rates are somewhat lower than nominal rates and rise less steeply with income because, as in the United States, some deductions, such as those for interest on home mortgages, reduce effective rates more for higher-income than for lower-income people. Nevertheless, incomes after tax are not only much smaller than before tax, they are also more equally distributed.

The complex system of income transfers is an even more important mechanism for redistributing income in Sweden. The social security system, which is currently financed by a payroll tax of 36 percent paid by employers, provides retired workers with a basic benefit and an earnings-related pension that together replace a much higher fraction of preretirement income than does the U.S. social security system (see table 6-2). Disability benefits in Sweden are generous; sick pay replaces earnings for unlimited periods (longer than a day) and is paid by the government. Unemployment benefits are also generous, although low unemployment rates have held down the number of beneficiaries. Parents get allowances for children, paid child care leave, and subsidized day care. Other, often seemingly redundant, subsidies are available to families and individuals in amounts frequently based on income.

The net result of taxing and redistributing such massive amounts of income is that very little correlation remains between incomes before and after taxes and transfers. Differences in levels of living among upper- and lower-income Swedes are remarkably small.

In addition to the commitment to economic equality, Sweden is distinguished from other developed countries by the extraordinary lengths to which it has gone to hold down unemployment. In the high-growth period of 1960–73, unemployment averaged less than 2 percent

1. See chapter 6.

(see table 1-1). In the past few years Swedish unemployment has crept up only to 3 percent while rates in the rest of Europe have soared.

This remarkable record has been purchased at a substantial price, however. Large numbers of Swedish workers who would otherwise have been unemployed are enrolled in training programs or provided with jobs in the public sector. Potential unemployment has also been forestalled by providing subsidies to failing firms to enable them to continue operations.

The cost of these types of labor market programs has been extremely high. In the early 1980s Sweden was spending about 3 percent of its GDP to provide training and public employment opportunities for those who would otherwise have been unemployed and another 2 percent of its GDP for industrial subsidies. Some of these efforts enhanced the skills of the labor force and facilitated movement out of stagnating industries and into growing ones, but others merely disguised unemployment or postponed the shifting of resources into more productive uses. By refusing to allow unemployment to rise more rapidly, Sweden caused its rate of growth of output per worker to fall faster than it did in the United States or the rest of Europe as growth slowed in the 1970s.

The commitments to equality and full employment, as well as more general demands for such public services as education, transportation, and defense, have brought total government expenditures in Sweden to levels that strike Americans as astonishingly high. Spending at all levels of government in 1983 amounted to 61 percent of Swedish GDP, compared with 36 percent for the United States and 47 percent for Germany.[2]

Part of the reason that public spending is so much higher in Sweden is that almost all health and education spending is public, while in the United States large fractions of essentially similar services are financed privately. A more important reason, however, is that Sweden simply devotes a higher fraction of its GDP to income-equalizing transfer payments and subsidies to maintain employment.

The divergence between Sweden and the United States with respect to public spending is of relatively recent origin. In 1960, for example, public spending in Sweden was about 31 percent of GDP compared with

2. Calculated from data in Organization for Economic Cooperation and Development, *National Accounts, 1971–1983*, vol. 2: *Detailed Tables* (Paris: OECD, 1985).

28 percent for the United States.[3] Most of the increases in spending came in the 1970s when local government spending (which includes health), central government transfers to business and individuals, social security payments, and interest payments all rose rapidly.

Swedish tax levels also pulled away from those of Europe and the United States in this period. In 1960 Swedish tax levels were about equal to those in the United States. In the next two decades, however, Swedish taxes and social security contributions rose much more rapidly than comparable levies in the United States. By the early 1980s, Swedish government revenues as a percent of GDP exceeded U.S. levels by more than 20 percent.[4]

Although revenues rose in Sweden in the 1970s, spending rose faster, and deficits of worrisome proportions emerged. In 1982 the central government's financial deficit reached a high of 9.5 percent of GDP.[5]

One consequence of the massive Swedish budget deficits was a rapid increase in the interest burden of the public debt. The necessity of devoting increasing proportions of GDP simply to pay interest on the government debt in turn made it more and more difficult to cut the deficit.

The most serious impact of the high budget deficits, however, has been to reduce national saving and consequently capital formation. In the dynamic period of the 1950s and 1960s the Swedish economy was growing strongly because national saving and capital formation were high. The government made major contributions to capital formation both by investing directly, especially in housing, and by running a budget surplus. But in the 1970s the government contribution to capital formation dropped rapidly. The government's deficit overwhelmed its direct investments. This might not have mattered if private saving had risen to offset the government dissaving, but as Edward Gramlich makes clear in chapter 7, private saving did not rise. National saving dropped and with it capital formation. The Swedes were consuming more of their current income and investing less, to the detriment of their future well-being. It was not until after 1982 that strenuous efforts to get the deficit down raised the government's contribution to capital formation again, and total national investment began to recover.

A final point that strikes an outsider is the durability of political

3. Calculated from data in OECD, *National Accounts, 1960–1977*, vol. 2: *Detailed Tables* (Paris: OECD, 1979).
4. Calculated from data in OECD, *National Accounts, 1960–1977*, vol. 2; and *1971–1983*, vol. 2.
5. See table 7-1.

compromise in Sweden. Despite a wide spectrum of political parties—from communist to right wing—and despite sometimes strident political rhetoric, the basic outlines of the Swedish merger of welfare state with private sector have remained in place for several decades. Commitments to full employment, wage equalization, and high levels of public transfers and services are widely supported. Although the government programs implementing these commitments evolved during the long period of Social Democratic hegemony, they were maintained, even expanded, when the "bourgeois" parties came to power in the mid-1970s. Thus political debate focuses on incremental changes in Sweden, since political constraints preclude major departures from carefully worked out and long-standing compromises.

Why Be Concerned about Sweden?

Although Sweden has achieved remarkable progress toward economic equality and full employment, firm commitment to these goals also made adjusting to the economic slowdown of the 1970s more difficult than it was for other advanced economies. Clearly, the 1970s were a difficult time for all industrialized nations. After a long period of steadily rising productivity and low energy prices, the governments of these nations were accustomed to making political decisions about how to share the growth, which is the kind of decision democratic governments handle most easily. In the 1970s, however, rapidly rising energy costs and plummeting productivity growth forced the advanced economies to face more difficult decisions. The rise in standards of living could not continue at the accustomed pace. The pain of adjustment to slower income increases had to be shared, and major shifts in resources had to be made if growth were to pick up in the future. Most of the advanced economies reluctantly made the necessary adjustments by reducing real wage increases, accepting higher levels of unemployment, and accepting slower increases in consumption.

In Sweden the hard choices were postponed, and the postponement created still more serious dilemmas for the future. Private and public consumption continued to rise at a pace no longer justified by income increases. Indeed, public spending accelerated as the government endeavored to meet its commitments to egalitarian transfer programs and to full employment under conditions of slow economic growth. The resulting budget deficits reduced national saving. Moreover, productivity growth dropped off more precipitously than in countries that tolerated higher unemployment.

Thus Sweden responded to the 1970s by living beyond its means, sustaining public and private consumption by allowing investment to collapse and by borrowing from abroad. Both the drop in investment and the rising obligation to service domestic and foreign debt magnified the obstacles to restoring healthy growth.

By the early 1980s Swedish policymakers understood that the course chosen in the 1970s was not sustainable. They made major efforts to bring the public deficit down by cutting spending, especially industrial subsidies, to reduce foreign borrowing and improve industrial competitiveness. Devaluation improved the trade balance, and the Swedish economy shared in the economic revival of developed countries.

But inflation remains high in Sweden and is eroding the competitive advantages of devaluation. Productivity growth has not recovered. It seems possible that the current economic recovery is only a temporary respite from more fundamental deterioration in Sweden's competitiveness in world markets and its ability to sustain a rising standard of public and private consumption in the long run.

These concerns have touched off intense scrutiny of Swedish economic policies, scrutiny aimed at fixing blame for past failures and redesigning the nature and mix of economic policies to improve the performance of the economy. Two hypotheses and sets of associated remedies have emerged. One focuses on the impact of microeconomic policy—the influence of wage policy, regulation, taxes, transfers, and other subsidies on the decisions of individuals and businesses to work, produce, save, and invest. The hypothesis is that the commitments to equality and full employment have distorted Swedish economic incentives and introduced rigidities that retard adjustment to change. The remedies favor lowering tax rates, reducing transfers and subsidies, and generally eliminating interference with market outcomes.

The other view focuses on macroeconomic policy—the fiscal and monetary instruments that affect the overall level of economic activity, wages, prices, interest rates, and the exchange value of the krona. The macroeconomic hypothesis is that whatever the validity of the microeconomic hypothesis Sweden's macroeconomic policies have fostered consumption at the expense of saving and have accelerated domestic inflation to the detriment of the country's ability to compete in world markets. Remedies include retreating from the strong commitment to full employment to reduce the inflationary bias or allowing the exchange rate to adjust to keep exports competitive.

The Brookings team explores these hypotheses and finds truth in both. Sweden is undoubtedly paying a price for microeconomic policies that encourage short workweeks and discourage employers from hiring inexperienced workers. Nevertheless, in many respects the economy shows considerable flexibility and ability to adapt to change. The evidence is stronger that macroeconomic policy has impeded adjustment to change. Wages have risen too rapidly, necessitating devaluation to keep Swedish industry competitive in world markets, and the government's budget deficit has reduced national saving and undermined investment.

Microeconomic Policy

Economists would expect that Sweden's high marginal tax rates and numerous interventions in labor and capital markets would alter economic incentives to the detriment of economic growth. While it remains debatable whether on balance Sweden's microeconomic policies have aggravated or helped to alleviate the difficulties of adjusting to the shocks of the 1970s, there are clearly signs of some microeconomic distortions.

In chapter 6 Gary Burtless analyzes the response of Sweden's labor supply to high marginal tax rates and generous transfer payments and finds evidence that policies have encouraged the population as a whole to choose leisure over market work. In particular, Sweden's tax system, by reducing the value to individuals of working additional hours, is encouraging those in the labor force to work fewer hours a week. Furthermore, disability and unemployment benefits as well as partial retirement benefits enable older Swedish workers to drop out of the labor force or reduce their hours even before reaching normal retirement age. After examining cross-sectional and time series evidence for Sweden and comparing it with similar evidence from the United States, Burtless concludes that if tax and transfer growth in Sweden had been limited to the lower rates that occurred in the United States in the past two decades, Swedish labor supply in the early 1980s would have been 6 to 10 percent higher than it was.

Sweden's tax and transfer policy also has encouraged the substitution of wives' work for that of their husbands. Swedish married couples do not file joint tax returns, and, because Sweden's marginal tax rates rise steeply with income, couples have a strong incentive to substitute the work effort of the secondary earner for that of the primary earner. This incentive is reinforced by the fact that working parents receive generous parental leave and child care benefits. Thus there are strong incentives for Swedish wives to work at least a few hours a week if they have or expect to have children. To some extent the productivity of women workers may be increased by their staying in the labor force rather than dropping in and out. But there are costs to the economy as well. Even though the difference between women's and men's wages has been reduced, women continue to earn less. To the extent that the higher wages of men reflect a higher marginal productivity of men's labor, substituting women's labor for men's reduces efficiency.

By no means can all changes in working behavior in Sweden be attributed to changes in tax laws or transfer payments. Time series evidence shows that work effort has declined with increases in after-tax real wage rates. This evidence suggests that labor supply would have declined even if tax rates had not increased. Gary Burtless also points out that hours of work supplied by older men have been declining both in the United States and Sweden since long before either country had public pensions or high marginal tax rates. Similarly, the influx of married women into the labor force is occurring in all developed countries. Nevertheless, it seems clear that Swedish tax and spending policy has diminished Swedish work effort.

Other distortionary effects of the Swedish tax system are noted in chapter 7 by Edward Gramlich. High marginal tax rates create incentives for Swedes to perform services such as home and car repairs for themselves, rather than purchase them from more efficient sources, and to engage in barter and other forms of tax evasion. The tax system makes emigration attractive to high-income people. Moreover, taxation of capital income, while not a major source of revenue, distorts the allocation of capital. Effective tax rates on different forms of capital investment vary widely, especially in periods of inflation.

Swedish policies seem to have distorting effects that are not limited to the supply side of the labor market. In chapter 5 Robert Flanagan finds that Sweden's centralized wage determination process has skewed the hiring practice of employers. He concludes that the relatively high rates of unemployment and involuntary part-time employment among young people are attributable to the fact that the wage determination process effectively sets a minimum wage at too high a level for it to be attractive to employers to hire many inexperienced young workers.

Underemployment of youth is a current problem with longer-run consequences. Young people who fail to find a rung on a career ladder and gain experience in the workplace will be less productive workers in later years. Nevertheless, the dangers to Swedish youth should not be exaggerated. In comparison with other European countries Sweden's unemployment is low both for younger and older workers, and the damaging effects of unemployment on future productivity are undoubtedly mitigated by training programs.

Except for the impact on young workers, Flanagan finds little evidence that Swedish centralized wage determination introduces inefficiencies by limiting incentives for workers to seek education or move into more productive jobs. Swedes appear to quit jobs at about the same rates as Americans and to move among firms and areas in search of higher pay. Job search occurs mostly among those already employed, and job changes do not usually result in unemployment. Labor mobility declined in Sweden in the 1970s, but this probably reflects the decline in overall job opportunities rather than the effects of the wage structure. The rate of return to education declined in the 1970s, too. This might be a result of solidaristic wage compression undervaluing higher-skilled jobs, but Flanagan points out that in the same period the rate of return to education also declined in the United States, which has no centralized wage policy.

Part of the reason that solidaristic wage policy does not introduce more discernable rigidities into the Swedish labor market is that market forces actually influence the wages of workers more than would appear from examining the formal wage agreements. Between agreements, wages in particular firms tend to "drift" in response to supply and demand, and differentials among firms, skills, and areas tend to widen. Wage drift detracts from Sweden's ability to control labor costs (and hence inflation) through centralized bargaining, but it reduces the microeconomic costs of the wage determination system.

Aside from labor market distortions, another important question about Sweden's microeconomic policies is how have labor and industrial policies affected the economy's ability to adapt to structural change? In general, economists would expect Sweden's labor market policies to make the economy more adaptable. Low unemployment rates and generous benefits to the unemployed should enhance adjustment by making workers less fearful of unemployment and less resistant to economic change. The compression of Swedish wages is also likely to reduce worker resistance to change. Steel workers forced to accept other jobs, for example, would not face reductions in their standard of living comparable to those facing American steel workers, whose wages are much higher relative to average U.S. wages than Swedish steel workers' wages are relative to average Swedish wages. Training and public employment programs for the unemployed would also be expected to improve economic flexibility by avoiding atrophy and obsolescence of workers' skills and enhancing their productivity in new jobs. Unfortunately evidence is hard to come by. In chapter 5 Robert Flanagan examines the fragmentary information available and finds little to support the contention that Sweden has improved labor productivity appreciably by its massive spending for public employment and training, although it has clearly avoided much higher levels of measured unemployment.

On the negative side, Sweden's subsidies to declining industries might be expected to retard change; indeed they were designed to do so. Expansion of the public sector with its bureaucratic rigidities could also impede the economy's flexibility.

In chapter 3 Robert Lawrence and Barry Bosworth examine the net effect of all of these policy choices on the ability of the economy to adapt to change. They find that the Swedish manufacturing sector has proved remarkably adaptable despite the massive government efforts in the late 1970s to retard change with industrial subsidies. Only the nonmanufacturing sector, public and private, gives evidence of sclerosis.

Subsidies to declining industries are a relatively recent phenomenon in Sweden. Until the mid-1970s, industrial policy generally eschewed interference with market forces except to use solidaristic wage policy to ensure that low-productivity firms had little chance of survival. Sweden, like other advanced economies, has been experiencing major shifts in economic activities for several decades—from goods production to services and from lower to higher technology. Lawrence and Bosworth find no evidence, however, that the shift to a defensive industrial policy in the mid-1970s was a response to an acceleration of structural change in Swedish manufacturing. Shifts in output among manufacturing industries were no more rapid in the decade after 1973 than in the decade before. Rather, the explanation seems largely political: the industries in trouble in the late 1970s were historically important heavy industries like steel and shipbuilding with big plants and yards whose closing would have had serious local impacts. The industrial subsidies bought time but did not succeed in preventing rapid declines in employment in these industries. Training and public employment programs for the unemployed also bought time for adjustment and may have enhanced the skills of the labor force, although Flanagan concludes that evidence of discernable effects is not impressive.

Comparisons of structural adjustment in Swedish manufacturing with that in the supposedly more flexible economies of the United States and Japan are by no means unfavorable to Sweden (see table 3-11). There is no evidence that Sweden had a more difficult structural problem (that more of its resources were stuck in slow-growth industries) or that its goods-producing sector proved less adaptable. Substantial shifts in industrial employment from resource-intensive industries to higher technologies occurred between 1973 and 1982.

The goods-producing sector has been declining in importance in Sweden, as elsewhere, while services have been growing. In Sweden, unlike the United States, however, the shift to services has been strongly to public not private services. Lawrence and Bosworth consider whether the decline in manufacturing can be attributed to declining Swedish ability to compete in international markets and find that it cannot. Indeed, Sweden's surplus from merchandise trade has been rising faster than its total output. The growing relative size of the service sector reflects changes in the structure of domestic demand, especially the growth of government services.

The growing importance of services, however, may bode ill for the future flexibility of the Swedish economy. While structural change in Swedish manufacturing did not slow after 1973, that of nonmanufacturing slowed substantially (see table 3-10).

The shift to public services has meant rapid increases in the proportion of the work force that is employed by some level of government. This creates a major political constituency likely to be biased in favor of current government spending programs, a factor that may retard overall structural change. The growth in public employment also changes the nature of wage determination. As Robert Flanagan points out, competition between public-sector and private-sector unions has put upward pressure on wage levels in recent years. Rising money wage levels and consequent inflation are a serious threat to the development of a viable Swedish macroeconomic strategy.

Macroeconomic Policy

It is debatable whether on balance Swedish microeconomic policies alleviated or aggravated the difficulties of adjusting to the shocks of the

1970s. However, there is no doubt, at least with hindsight, that Swedish macroeconomic policy made a bad situation worse.

Productivity growth slowed dramatically in Sweden after 1973 as it did in other developed countries. The common nature of that slowdown in a broad range of countries with widely varying economic policies and conditions suggests that, whatever the causes of the slowdown, they were certainly not uniquely Swedish. The problem facing Swedish policymakers was the same one facing policymakers in other countries; since factors of production were no longer generating the increases in output that had come to be expected, anticipated increases in consumption would have to be reduced. Consuming capital or borrowing from abroad would only make future adjustment harder. In addition, the rapid rise in oil prices meant that Sweden, like other oil-importing countries, would have to give up more of its own product to pay for imported energy. Under these circumstances the appropriate macroeconomic policy was belt-tightening: restraining both public and private consumption and generating the domestic saving needed to get the economy growing again.

Yet Swedish macroeconomic policies in the middle and late 1970s were the reverse of what was needed. Instead of being constrained to the newly appropriate levels, public and private consumption went on rising rapidly. Government spending increases, spurred by efforts to stave off unemployment, resulted in escalating budget deficits. Domestic saving plummeted, and even a low level of investment could be maintained only by borrowing abroad. Sweden was living beyond its means.

Meanwhile, wages, which should have been limited to rates of growth consistent with the lower productivity increases, rose at far higher rates. It is vital that a small open economy like Sweden's not allow its production costs to get out of line with those of its competitors: it must keep inflation under control or countenance declines in the exchange value of its currency. Sweden, however, was unwilling to accept the unemployment increases tolerated by its competitors to hold down inflation. It relied on a peculiarly Nordic model of the inflation process that assumes workers in private firms will automatically moderate wage increases in deference to maintaining international competitiveness. When such a moderation failed to materialize, the government held to a fixed nominal exchange rate until the decline in competitiveness reached crisis proportions, ultimately forcing devaluations. Wage inflation reflected both the outcomes of the official wage negotiations with the private- and public-sector unions and increased wage drift, which was exacerbated by the government's commitment to disguise and avoid unemployment.

Sweden has undertaken a dramatic reversal of these policies in the 1980s. There is now general agreement that the budget deficit must be reduced, and substantial progress has been made since 1982. Second, a large devaluation in 1981–82 significantly improved Sweden's competitive position, and the surge of activity in the export industries and import-competing industries provided a stimulus to the domestic economy that more than offset the effects of the fiscal restraint. Sweden now enjoys a surplus on its trade account sufficient to finance the interest payments on the foreign debt it accumulated during the 1970s: the current account is in balance. The rate of inflation is also substantially below that of the beginning of the decade.

Essentially, the magnitude of the devaluation undertaken in 1981–82 freed the government from the constraint of a large external deficit and gave it time and room to adjust its domestic policies. In 1986 declining world interest rates and oil prices have further added to the government's breathing space.

There are, however, potential problems.

First, the budget deficit, while lower, is still far above the levels of the early 1970s. As a result Sweden's ability to finance higher rates of domestic investment is still limited by inadequate national saving. Investment is further constrained by a monetary policy that has held interest rates above international levels, promoting accumulation of financial assets at the expense of investment in productive capital.

Second, if Sweden's inflation continues to exceed that of its principal competitors, the competitive benefits of the 1981–82 devaluations will be largely lost by the end of the decade. A loss of competitiveness could reduce the stimulus from the trade balance and put pressure on the exchange rate. The use of higher interest rates to defend the currency would further reduce domestic investment. A recession led by the tradable-goods sector could ensue. The government budget deficit would come under severe strain as firms failing in international markets and workers displaced from the tradable-goods sector sought its assistance.

Many Swedes agree that this scenario is possible but argue that the inflation threat should be met by a strict commitment to defend the exchange rate. They ignore, however, the detrimental effect such a policy will have on the competitive position of the tradable-goods sector, investment, and the government budget.

We are wary of the commitment to defend the exchange rate as an indirect route to reducing inflation. The prospects of reduced competitiveness have been insufficient to persuade unions, particularly in the public sector, to reduce their wage demands. We are also skeptical that a government commitment not to accommodate inflationary agreements will rapidly improve the trade-off between inflation and unemployment. Given the government's historical record of accommodation, market participants will not readily take it at its word. Credibility will only be earned by experience. It implies a willingness of government to stand aside in the face of rising unemployment, a policy that is particularly un-Swedish.

Under a fixed nominal exchange rate, Sweden's competitive position is essentially determined by its success in matching the inflation rate of its competitors. It must adopt domestic economic policies that aim at following the ups and downs of the course of inflation in other countries with whom it competes in world markets. Frequent changes of policy in response to a changing international situation can disrupt the domestic economy.

Lawrence and Bosworth suggest a strategy that places the highest priority on restoring public saving by continued reductions in the government budget deficit. A restrictive fiscal policy should be accompanied by low interest rates to encourage the transfer of higher saving into domestic investment, a flexible exchange rate that preserves Swedish competitiveness in world markets, and continued efforts on the part of the government to persuade workers to moderate inflationary pressures. Robert Flanagan suggests that the government also take a firmer stance at the wage-bargaining table in its capacity as an employer in the public sector or adopt an incomes policy based on tax incentives.

If these policies succeed in bringing down inflation rapidly, Sweden's prospects should be good. If they fail, however, trade-offs must be made. Sweden will need to adopt even more costly measures to reduce inflation or allow its exchange rate to fall in order to maintain its competitive position. Commitment to a fixed nominal exchange rate, however, seems inappropriate regardless of the policy option that Sweden might choose.

One means of reducing inflation would be to adopt a more restrictive economic policy that allows unemployment to rise perhaps another 1 percent. Alternatively, Sweden could accept a higher inflation rate and allow the exchange rate to fall in an offsetting fashion. There is apparently little or no tendency for inflation in Sweden to accelerate, and it may be that with elimination of its impact on international competitiveness, continued inflation is less costly than the alternatives. The experience of the last decade, however, provides vivid evidence that the interaction of inflation with a fixed nominal exchange rate can impose extremely high costs in those industries that must compete in world markets. Lawrence and Bosworth point out that wage rates in Sweden, contrary to common perceptions, are very sensitive to labor market conditions, and that a relatively modest rise in unemployment would reduce inflation to rates prevalent in other countries. If Sweden opts for restraining the level of economic activity, the government should restrict domestic demand directly rather than indirectly through an overvalued real exchange rate, which concentrates the burden on the tradable-goods sector.

Conclusions

While the American team sees difficult economic and political choices to be made, it finds no evidence that Sweden cannot sustain domestic growth and international competitiveness if the economy is managed well. Despite the heavy commitments to wage equalization and high employment, the economy has proved responsive to the need for structural change. Lawrence and Bosworth's analysis does not provide evidence of any long-term decline in the competitiveness of Sweden's manufacturing sector. They conclude that unless the country is hit by future external shocks, like another large increase in oil prices, or allows new deterioration in its savings rate, it should be able to manage external balance without a real deterioration in its exchange rate.

Swedes are clearly choosing to take part of their potential rise in output in the form of increased leisure rather than goods and services. Numerous government policies reinforce the current tendency to work shorter hours. Reducing the high marginal tax rates inherent in the combined tax and transfer systems would likely increase work effort. Moving to a more neutral tax system would tend to channel resources into more productive investments at the margin. Relaxing the solidaristic wage policy to allow employers to offer lower wages to inexperienced workers would probably decrease youth unemployment.

More crucial decisions must ultimately be made about macroeconomic policy. Like the United States, Sweden has paid a heavy price for living beyond its means and has only partially redressed the errors of past unwillingness to bring public and private consumption into line with lower potential growth in income. The budget deficit should be reduced further and converted to a surplus in order to generate high levels of national saving. Moreover, some way must be found, either by incomes policy or allowing a rise in unemployment, to keep money wages from increasing more rapidly than warranted by Sweden's competitive position. If this cannot be done, Sweden should move to a flexible exchange rate. It is not sensible to penalize Swedish investment by using monetary policy to defend an exchange rate that wage increases are rendering untenable.

The real challenges, then, are to the Swedish political system. The ultimate question is whether the governing parties will take the responsible but risky course of imposing necessary losses in the common interest. Kent Weaver points out that the imposition of losses—never easy for an elected government—became necessary in the 1970s, just at a time when Sweden's political system was less equipped for the task than in the 1950s and 1960s. The long hegemony of the Social Democrats was breaking down. Voters were more volatile, and constitutional changes had made the Riksdag more sensitive to fluctuations in voter sentiment. The proliferation of white-collar workers was threatening the dominance of the blue-collar unions. Giving offense to workers and voters had become a riskier political proposition.

By the early 1980s, however, the necessity of retrenchment had become apparent. The current Social Democratic government has moved strongly in the required direction with its emphasis on wage restraint, austerity in social programs, increasing industrial competitiveness, and cutting wasteful subsidies to declining industries. Many more painful choices lie ahead. The pain can be disguised and delayed for a while— with increased long-term costs—as occurred in the 1970s. But it cannot be avoided. The vaunted ability of political and economic interests to arrive at compromise solutions has been sorely tested by the slower economic growth of the past fifteen years. But a revival of that ability— and its utilization to distribute the pain of adjustment in a politically acceptable manner—is the key to sustainable growth in the future.

Several lessons from the Swedish exprience could well be taken to heart by the United States and other developed countries. First is the simple principle that living beyond one's means is a short-sighted policy with heavy long-run costs. Sweden in the 1970s, like the United States in the 1980s, maintained consumption at unwarranted levels by running large government budget deficits and borrowing abroad. It paid a price not only in reduced domestic investment but in the continuing need to generate a trade surplus in order to service its foreign debt. Those in the United States who question the need to reduce the budget and trade deficits should examine the Swedish experience.

A more heartening lesson for the United States in the mid-1980s is that exchange rate devaluation can improve a country's competitive position substantially, especially if combined with growth in the world economy. Americans dismayed by the failure of the U.S. trade deficit to respond rapidly to the decline in the value of the dollar should find some encouragement in the improvement of the Swedish balance of trade after 1982.

Swedish efforts to combine growth with wage equality and full employment yield mixed lessons for other nations. The evidence from Sweden is consistent with that of other countries: equalization of incomes through tax and transfer policy can be successful but not without some reduction in work effort. The Swedish experience does not support the claims of those who believe that a large public sector and high tax rates necessarily lead to rigidities and stultification of the private economy. Indeed, Americans examining Sweden tend to be surprised that an economy with such high tax rates works so well. But the Swedish experience does not support the view that training, public employment, and other labor market policies can make it possible to enjoy both full employment and stable prices. In Sweden as elsewhere, public commitments to maintain full employment add to upward pressure on wage cost and hence to inflation. The Swedish experience in labor markets and other areas yields no magic solutions that make economic choices easier.

2

Adjusting to Slower Economic Growth: The Domestic Economy

BARRY P. BOSWORTH
and ROBERT Z. LAWRENCE

SWEDEN EXPERIENCED a severe deterioration of economic performance during the 1970s. The deterioration was not unique—all the major Western industrial economies did poorly—but its dimensions were unusually large. Between 1973 and 1982 economic growth fell to less than a third of the rate maintained during the prior decade. To sustain an expansion of domestic consumption in the face of little or no growth in income, Sweden allowed net national saving and investment to decline to extremely low levels, and by 1982 it was borrowing more than 4 percent of its income annually overseas. It became a nation living far beyond its means. The excess of consumption was most evident in the public sector, where the consolidated government budget balance fell from an average surplus equal to 10 percent of national income in 1963–73 to a deficit of 4.4 percent in 1982.[1]

1. Unless otherwise indicated, statistics cited in this chapter are authors' calculations based on Sveriges officiella statistik, *Nationalräkenskaper, 1970–1984* (Stockholm: Statistiska centralbyrån, 1985) [Official Statistics of Sweden, *National Accounts Annual Report, 1970–1984* (Stockholm: Statistics Sweden, 1985)]; and *Nationalräkenskaper, 1982–1985* (Stockholm, Statistics Sweden, March 1986). (Hereafter *National Accounts.*) Throughout this chapter the government surplus or deficit refers to the current spending balance (net saving of general government in the national accounts). The addition of the capital items yields the financial surplus or deficit, which is comparable to the budget concept in the United States.

In addition, production costs exploded in the mid-1970s: unit labor costs in manufacturing rose 52 percent between 1973 and 1976. And, in conjunction with efforts to maintain a fixed exchange rate, those cost increases sharply reduced the competitiveness of Swedish industry in world markets. The current account balance with other countries fell from a surplus equal to 2.7 percent of national income in 1973 to a deficit of 3.7 percent in 1982. Ultimately, the deteriorating competitive position forced Sweden to devalue its currency, only to find that continued large wage increases quickly eliminated any relative cost improvement.

Economic performance has improved in the 1980s; but because much of the change can be traced to the one-time gains from a large currency devaluation, some critics argue that the improvement is largely transitory and that serious fundamental problems remain. In Sweden, as throughout Europe, many explanations have been put forth to account for the falloff in economic performance since the early 1970s. While many of them complement one another, their emphases diverge sharply. The debate can be loosely characterized by distinguishing between broad microeconomic and macroeconomic explanations.

The microeconomic explanation emphasizes the changed nature of economic growth and the constraining influence of the welfare state that prevents adjustment to the new conditions. Before 1973, it argues, economic growth was predicated on growth in the traditional basic industries in which cheap raw materials were combined with high rates of capital formation that embodied new technologies. The removal of trade barriers and major improvements in transportation and communications promoted a rapid expansion of the international market and provided increased efficiency through economies of scale. The result was an export-led expansion with large gains in labor productivity and thus in standards of living.

After 1973 Sweden was faced with a far less attractive situation. It encountered intense competition in the basic industries from the developing nations of Asia, slow growth in its major markets for manufactured products, and depressed prices for exports of raw materials. It needed to deemphasize dependence on traditional industries and expand into new areas of high technology in which the requirements for growth are quite different. To compete at the frontiers of technology, firms must be flexible and willing to deal with risk and uncertainty.

It is argued, however, that the required adjustment was seriously limited by the structure of the Swedish welfare state. Low wage differentials and state welfare programs combined to discourage the movement of workers among industries and geographic regions. Thus labor market efficiency deteriorated. Other parts of the economy were also poorly organized to adapt to the changed economic environment. Entrepreneurs and the entry of new firms into the market are discouraged by the Swedish tax system and the structure of its capital markets, which encourage low-risk loans to established firms. The allocation of resources is controlled largely by a government bureaucracy and political votes rather than markets. The result is a system that shows signs of economic sclerosis and is incapable of adapting to a changing environment.

The macroeconomic explanation emphasizes the breakdown of the wage negotiation process and the government's inability to control inflation. The problem became particularly severe after 1973, the explanation goes, because of Sweden's efforts to bridge the 1974–75 recession in the world economy with a domestic program of fiscal stimulus and industrial subsidies aimed at maintaining employment. Coming on the heels of a domestic boom in the raw material industries, these accommodative policies supported workers' efforts to recover earlier losses in real wages caused by the rise in oil prices. The government also contributed directly to the escalation of costs through large increases in employment taxes.

The resulting cost explosion drastically reduced the competitiveness of Swedish industry in world markets; and because international competitive pressures inhibited the full passthrough of increased costs into higher prices, the share of income going to capital was greatly reduced. The result was sharply lower incentives for new investment. Weakening demand for exports and investment drove the government toward further fiscal stimulus—budget deficits—to support domestic employment; but the action was ineffective because it simply exacerbated the underlying wage inflation.

It is argued that the deterioration of the trade-off between wage inflation and unemployment has led to a situation in which the goals of internal and external balance of the economy have become incompatible with one another. Efforts to achieve announced targets for employment lead to wage increases in excess of the average experience in other countries, increases in the relative costs of Swedish industry, and an ever-growing current account deficit. The worsening performance of the current account in turn fuels a decline in domestic employment. The result has been a downward spiral of economic performance as weaknesses in the external account lead to domestic policy responses that cause further cost increases and loss of competitiveness.

Devaluing the currency provides temporary relief, but if domestic costs continue to rise more rapidly than costs abroad, or even worse, if the resulting rise of domestic prices causes wage increases to accelerate, the fundamental imbalance between domestic and foreign balance ultimately reemerges.

In this and the following chapter some of these explanations are examined in greater detail. In particular, we argue that discussion in Sweden emphasizes microeconomic structural imbalances too much and the importance of macroeconomic policies too little. Despite heavy regulation and high taxes, Sweden has allocated resources and adapted to changes in manufacturing at least as well as the United States and other industrial countries, and as well as it did before 1973. Most of the problems of the Swedish economy in the 1970s can be traced to excesses and basic conflicts in the conduct of such macroeconomic matters as budget policy, inflation, the exchange rate, and monetary policy.

The slowdown in Swedish economic growth since 1973 has primarily been the result of exogenous factors affecting all industrial countries, and it cannot be attributed to domestic economic policies. Sweden does stand out, however, in the extent of its failure to adjust to the slowdown, and that failure is most evident in its macroeconomic policies. Rapid growth had become crucial to a political and economic system that basically resolved conflicts by promising more to everyone. When growth slowed, the system lacked the mechanisms to scale back national consumption to conform to much slower increases in incomes. In other words, the political processes of government, not the economy, had the greatest difficulty adapting to changed economic circumstances.[2] The government's policies during the 1970s placed an especially heavy burden on the export industries and contributed in a major way to the erosion of Sweden's competitiveness in world markets.

The macroeconomic issues are the focus of the remainder of this chapter, which documents the sources and extent of the slump in economic growth after 1973 and then considers the problems of adjusting to that decline. While Swedish national disposable income remained virtually constant between 1973 and 1982, real national consumption rose 18 percent. That consumption was supported by large increases in the budget deficit as Sweden cut back investment and increased its

2. Throughout the 1970s the government ignored the evidence of slower long-term growth and continued to depend on rapid growth as the primary means of financing an ambitious expansion of its expenditure programs. See, for example, the tabulation of past projections in Ministry of Finance, *The 1984 Medium Term Survey of the Swedish Economy* (Stockholm, 1984), p. 28.

borrowing from abroad. The decline in investment was driven by a sharp fall in the rate of return to capital as industrial profits were squeezed by domestic costs that rose faster than international prices. While the rate of return on industrial capital has risen since 1982, investment continues to be held back by an increase in the inflation-adjusted rate of return on financial assets—the cost of funds.

The difficulty of adjusting to a slower rate of economic growth is also evident in the behavior of wages. Workers and firms did not adjust downward their goals for nominal wage increases to match the decline in productivity growth and the terms of trade. In the presence of fixed exchange rates, wage inflation squeezed profit margins and reduced the supply of traded goods. The result, by 1980, was an economy with little or no national saving, a low rate of domestic investment, and declining competitiveness in world markets as domestic cost increases outran those of foreign competitors. Again, however, government policy added to the inflationary pressures by maintaining very tight labor markets in support of large nominal wage increases and by sharply increasing employment taxes.

The Growth Slowdown

The dimensions of the slowdown in Swedish economic growth that began in the early 1970s are shown in table 2-1. The expansion of total industrial output slowed from an annual average of 3.3 percent between 1963 and 1973 to 1.3 percent between 1974 and 1984. The size of the slowdown was similar to that in the United States, about 2 percent annually; but its composition was very different. In the United States the slower growth could be attributed to a reduced rate of expansion of the labor force as well as smaller gains in productivity. In Sweden it was entirely due to smaller productivity gains.[3] Thus there was a more dramatic impact on the growth of real income per worker. Sweden's productivity slowdown was also concentrated in manufacturing, with a larger consequent impact on the country's competitive position in world markets.

3. After 1963 Sweden greatly reduced the number of hours worked in industry by reducing both employment and the average number of hours worked by each employee. The reduction in available hours moderated after 1973, but it was largely offset by a slower growth of capital services.

Table 2-1. *Output and Productivity Growth in Sweden and the United States, 1963–73 and 1974–84*
Annual Rates of Change

Category	Sweden			United States		
	1963–73	1974–84	Slowdown	1963–73	1974–84	Slowdown
Industry (excluding housing)						
Output	3.3	1.3	−2.0	4.5	2.6	−1.9
Capital and labor inputs	−0.2	−0.1	0.1	2.9	2.1	−0.8
Factor productivity	3.5	1.4	−2.1	1.6	0.5	−1.1
Capital/labor substitution	1.6	1.1	−0.5	0.8	0.5	−0.3
Labor productivity[a]	5.1	2.5	−2.6	2.4	1.0	−1.4
Manufacturing						
Output	4.8	1.0	−3.8	4.9	1.7	−3.2
Capital and labor inputs	−0.3	−0.9	−0.6	2.4	0.5	−1.9
Factor productivity	5.1	1.9	−3.2	2.4	1.2	−1.2
Capital/labor substitution	1.7	1.2	−0.5	0.6	0.8	0.2
Labor productivity[a]	6.8	3.1	−3.7	3.0	2.0	−1.0
Other						
Output	2.7	1.5	−1.2	4.3	3.0	−1.3
Capital and labor inputs	−0.1	0.3	0.5	3.1	2.9	−0.2
Factor productivity	2.8	1.2	−1.7	1.2	0.1	−1.1
Capital/labor substitution	1.6	1.0	−0.6	1.0	0.4	−0.6
Labor productivity[a]	4.4	2.2	−2.2	2.1	0.5	−1.6

Sources: *National Accounts;* and authors' estimates. The index of capital inputs is based on a simple average of the gross and net capital stock. The index of factor inputs is a geometric weighted average of capital and labor hours with weights of 0.25 and 0.75, respectively.
a. Labor productivity is the sum of factor productivity and capital/labor substitution.

The Swedish experience is also similar to that of the United States in that the precise causes of the slower growth of productivity remain pretty much a mystery.[4] It is possible, however, to account for some of the greater severity of Sweden's slowdown.

To begin with, capital formation played a much more important role in Sweden than in the United States. The rate of capital-labor substitution, shown in table 2-1, slowed substantially after 1973 and contributed 0.5 percentage point annually to the slowdown of output per labor hour

4. A useful discussion of the major explanations is presented in Assar Lindbeck, "The Recent Slowdown of Productivity Growth," *Economic Journal*, vol. 93 (March 1983), pp. 13–24. See also Edward F. Denison, *Accounting for Slower Economic Growth: The United States in the 1970s* (Brookings, 1979) and *Trends in American Economic Growth, 1929–1982* (Brookings, 1985). At present, research on the international decline in economic growth is stymied by the inability to evaluate the importance of some of the suggested hypotheses.

in industry and manufacturing.[5] The rate of capital-labor substitution in the United States, in the face of large increases in the labor force, was more modest; but it actually accelerated in manufacturing after 1973, and the decline in the total economy was smaller than that for Sweden.

The growth of productivity between 1973 and 1984 was also affected more sharply in Sweden than in the United States by purely cyclical factors. Because resource utilization in Sweden was very high in 1973 relative to both 1963 and 1984, it had a pronounced effect on the measurement of the slowdown between the two subperiods shown in table 2-1. If total factor productivity is adjusted for its historical relationship to the utilization rate, the estimated magnitude of the slowdown declines from 2.1 to 1.6 percent annually for all industry and from 3.2 to 2.4 percent for manufacturing.[6] A similar procedure for the United States alters the estimate of the productivity slowdown in manufacturing by only 0.2 percent annually. Adjusted for cyclical factors, the magnitude of the slowdown in total factor productivity within Sweden is about the same as in the United States at the level of the total economy, 1.0 to 1.5 percent annually, but it is larger within the manufacturing sector, in which Sweden had a phenomenally high rate of growth before 1973.

Surprisingly, given the emphasis in Sweden on structural explanations, shifts in the distribution of labor among high- or low-productivity industries have had no effect on the estimated growth rate.[7] As in the United States, the slowdown in productivity growth is evident among a wide variety of industries. Efforts to find a concentration of the slowdown

5. Much larger estimates of the impact of slower capital formation are posited in Swedish studies. Yngve Åberg, in particular, places the post-1973 effect at more than 1 percent annually. However, he uses a measure of capital services that reflects the actual returns to capital. Since the profit rate declined precipitously in the late 1970s, capital's contribution to output is assumed to fall in parallel fashion. In a subsequent section, this chapter argues that the low profit margin was primarily a reflection of an overvalued currency and did not represent the role of capital in production. Åberg's results may be interpreted as an upper limit on the combined effect of what we have identified as capital-labor substitution and cyclical factors. See Yngve Åberg, *Produktivitetsutvecklingen i industrin i olika OECD-länder, 1953–1980* (Stockholm: Industriens Utredningsinstitut [Industrial Institute for Economic and Social Research], 1984).

6. The method of adjustment requires measuring the utilization rate as the ratio of actual to normal output. Normal output is defined as a nine-year centered moving average of manufacturing value added. Normal output was projected beyond 1980 on the basis of surveys of manufacturing utilization. A regression that related total factor productivity to the utilization rate and a time trend was then estimated. The adjusted series is the actual effect less the estimated effect of the utilization variable.

7. Productivity growth was recomputed holding constant the distribution of hours among industries.

in export, capital-intensive, or energy-intensive industries were all unsuccessful.

While it is useful to analyze factors affecting growth in individual countries, the uniform nature of the slowdown in total factor productivity among nations should lead to skepticism about country-specific explanations. The slowdown seems more reflective of a decline in the underlying rate of technical change, which is not easily susceptible to government influence. Furthermore, continuing slow gains in productivity in countries such as the United States, where economic recovery has been strong, inflation is low, and structural barriers are largely absent, suggest that we should not anticipate an improvement in Swedish productivity very soon. Earlier arguments that oil price increases and other structural changes made much of the capital stock obsolete also seem less convincing today: most of the current capital stock is composed of investments made well after 1973. The precise explanation is important only to the extent that this chapter assumes the slowdown cannot be easily reversed soon. For the analysis of the policy options we assume that the more modest growth of total factor productivity will continue.[8]

Adjusting to Slower Growth

Although focusing on the business sector provides a vivid picture of deteriorating economic growth, it does not provide a complete picture of the extent of the decline in income available to support consumption in Sweden. First, 32 percent of the Swedish work force in 1984 was employed in government, compared to only 14 percent in 1963 and 24 percent in 1973.[9] If productivity of government workers is assumed to be constant, the decline in total GDP growth is less than that for industry alone.

But the growth of disposable income fell far more sharply than that of output. National disposable income differs from GDP by the net amount

8. An insightful theoretical and empirical analysis of the growth process in Sweden is provided in Pehr Wissén, *Wages and Growth in an Open Economy* (Stockholm: Economic Research Institute, Stockholm School of Economics, 1982). Wissén emphasizes the notion of economic slack—a gap between actual output and the steady-state growth path—in explaining the surge of growth in the 1960s and the consequent slowdown in the 1970s. The elimination of economic slack in the 1970s coincided with a cost crisis that drove real wages too high and held down capital formation.

9. A comparable figure for the United States is 15 percent in 1984.

Figure 2-1. *Indexes of Consumption and Disposable Income in Sweden, 1963–85*

Ratio scale (1963 = 1.0)

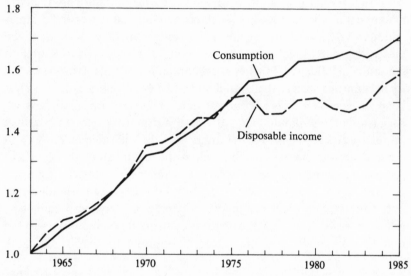

Source: *National Accounts.*

of income earned abroad, less capital consumption allowances (depreciation) of the current capital stock and gains or losses from changes in the terms of trade with other countries. All three factors had a negative effect on income growth in Sweden during 1973–82.[10] Sweden became a net borrower, paying more to foreigners than it earned abroad; capital consumption increased as a share of national output; and higher oil prices plus a real devaluation of the Swedish krona contributed to a major loss of terms of trade equal to 5.8 percent of GDP. The combined effect of these three factors reduced domestic income by 10 percent between 1973 and 1982.

As figure 2-1 shows, the net result of slower productivity growth and the other factors was essentially to eliminate any growth of real income after 1973. National disposable income, which had been rising 3.8 percent annually between 1963 and 1973, fell off to a paltry 0.2 percent increase

10. The 1973–82 period is used to highlight the decline in Swedish economic performance because the slowing of productivity growth becomes most evident after 1973, and 1982 marks a major change in the direction of economic policy.

Table 2-2. *Rates of Net Saving and Investment in Sweden,*
Selected Periods, 1963–85
Percent of net domestic product

Category	1963–73	1974–82	1982	1985
Net national saving and investment	16.3	8.7	2.7	7.1
Net private saving	6.1	6.2	7.0	8.9
Government saving	10.2	2.5	−4.4	−1.8
Net domestic investment	16.1	11.0	6.8	8.3
Private	10.6	7.5	3.9	6.3
Government	5.4	3.4	2.8	2.0
Net foreign investment	0.2	−2.3	−4.1	−1.2
Addendum: private saving				
Households	3.0	2.3	0.3	−0.1
Nonfinancial corporations	1.3	−0.7	1.5	2.9[a]
Financial corporations	1.8	4.1	5.2	6.1[a]

Source: *National Accounts.*
a. Estimates based on 1984 levels.

between 1973 and 1982 and was actually negative after 1976. If the slowdown had not occurred, real incomes of Swedes would have been 38 percent higher in 1982. A disruption of income growth of that magnitude is bound to create serious difficulties of adjustment, and it appears to have had a major effect on Swedish economic policy after 1973.

The adjustment problems were most evident in the failure of domestic consumption to moderate its growth in line with the slower growth of income. Consumption spending, both public and private, did slow after 1973, but the decline in the growth rate was only half that of income.[11] The moderation of spending was equal in both the public and private sectors; however, because public consumption had been rising more rapidly in prior years, its share of total consumption continued to expand. From 1973 to 1982 total consumption spending in Sweden rose by 18 percent in the face of almost no growth in income.

The imbalance of domestic income, saving, and consumption is highlighted from a different perspective in table 2-2, which shows trends in national saving and investment. The net national saving rate declined precipitously during the 1970s, from an average of 16.3 percent of net national product in 1963–73 to a low of 2.7 percent in 1982. The decline can be traced almost exclusively to the public budget, which fell from an

11. The growth of total consumption averaged 3.5 percent annually between 1963 and 1973 and 1.8 percent between 1973 and 1982.

average surplus equal to 10.2 percent of national output in 1963–73 to a deficit of 4.4 percent by 1982.

The deterioration of the public budget was particularly serious because government saving constituted such a major share of the national total in the years of rapid capital accumulation. Large surpluses in the social insurance funds were used to finance investment in the private sector. That policy was largely abandoned after 1973, however, as the growth of the social insurance surplus slowed and the central government began to run large deficits. If government saving is defined, as in the United States, as financial saving, including public investment in government expenditures, net national saving in Sweden was zero in 1982—no domestic resources were available for private capital formation.

Throughout the period private saving remained relatively constant, although the use of averages hides a sharp decline in 1976–78 when the business sector experienced large losses. There has also been a shift in composition as the household saving rate has declined and that of business has increased.[12]

On the investment side, Sweden has experienced a severe falling off of domestic capital formation. The share of output devoted to net domestic investment fell by 1982 to less than half that of the pre-1973 period. The decline was similarly large for both public and private investments, and it was most severe in the years after 1976.

The decline in domestic investment, while large, was still less than the decline in national saving, so that Sweden was forced to borrow increasing amounts abroad to finance what little investment was taking place domestically. By 1982 foreign borrowing was financing nearly two-thirds of net domestic investment (see table 2-2). The accumulating interest burden of that borrowing turned what had been a surplus on factor income from abroad to a deficit that contributed substantially to the erosion of disposable income. By 1982 net interest payments to foreigners absorbed more than 2 percent of the national income.

Thus far the picture that emerges of the Swedish economy in the 1970s is one of a nation living far beyond its means, reducing saving and investment, and borrowing overseas to sustain an ever-growing gap between current consumption and income. While aiding the current

12. A similar pattern is evident for the United States. It is thought to be related to the tax structure, because in both countries capital income is taxed very lightly at the corporate level and heavily under the individual income tax. Thus it makes sense for investors to hold any accumulated capital within corporations.

generation, the practice placed a large burden of reduced capital assets and heavy foreign debts on future generations. Throughout the 1973–82 period the Swedish government refused to accept the evidence of slower current growth as indicative of the future, instead anticipating a return to the growth rates of the 1960s.

In that sense the experience of Sweden in the 1970s is similar to that of the United States in the 1980s, and its current problems ought to give pause to Americans. After several decades of rapid growth, which public officials and private institutions had come to view as normal, Sweden was faced with the need to scale down expectations drastically. The failure to do so is most evident with respect to consumption; but, as we shall see in a subsequent section, the falloff in productivity growth was also a major force behind the acceleration of cost inflation in the mid-1970s.

The Collapse of Domestic Investment

The sharp decline in Sweden's domestic capital formation was particularly ominous because of its importance for economic growth. Cyclical factors plus a slower rate of technical change were the major factors behind the slowing of growth in total factor productivity. However, about one-third of the decline in labor productivity can be attributed to a slowing of the rate of capital-labor substitution. In the years before 1973 Sweden compensated for a shrinking labor supply (measured in labor hours) by a very rapid rate of capital accumulation. From 1963 to 1973 its overall rate of capital-labor substitution was twice that of the United States and nearly three times as high in the manufacturing sector (see table 2-1). If new technology is assumed to have been embodied in the capital stock, the estimated contribution of reduced capital formation to the growth slowdown would be even larger.

Major categories of net investment are shown as a share of net domestic product in table 2-3 for the pre- and post-1973 periods. The use of subperiods exaggerates the abruptness of the falloff in total investment, which extended over the whole 1963–82 period. Before 1973, however, most of the decline was concentrated in government and housing—the investment rate in manufacturing actually peaked in 1974. After 1973 all categories of net investment fell substantially. Of a decline of 7 percentage points in the investment share from the average of 1963–

Figure 2-2. *Real Rates of Return on Tangible and Financial Assets in Sweden, 1964–84*

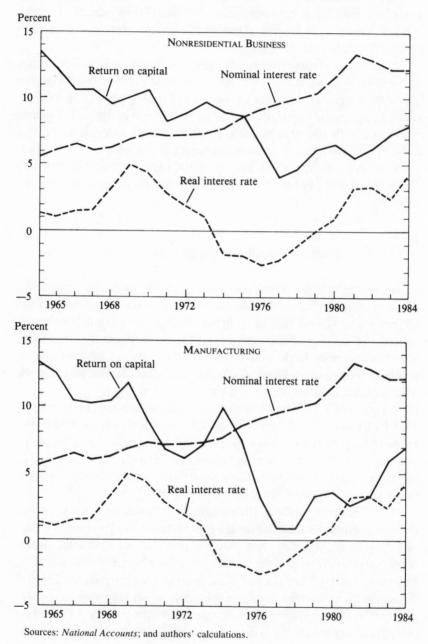

Sources: *National Accounts*; and authors' calculations.

Table 2-3. *Net Fixed Investment in Sweden as a Share of Net Domestic Product, Major Categories, 1963–84*

	Percent of net national product			
Category	1963–73	1973–82	1982	1984
Total fixed investment	15.1	10.4	7.9	7.6
General government	3.9	2.6	2.2	1.9
Business sector	11.2	7.8	5.7	5.8
Residential	4.2	2.1	1.6	1.4
Nonresidential business	7.0	5.7	4.0	4.3
Manufacturing	2.0	1.1	−0.1	0.1
Nonmanufacturing	5.0	4.6	4.1	4.2

Source: *National Accounts.*

73 to the low point in 1982, 4 percentage points were accounted for by government and housing. The decline in the nonresidential business sector was 3 percentage points. Net investment in manufacturing actually turned negative in 1982.

The major factors behind the reduced rate of investment include a sharp decline in the profit share, and thus the return on physical capital; the slow growth of demand, which led to excess capacity; and the decline in the underlying rate of technological change, which necessitated a slower rate of capital accumulation.

The net real rate of return on capital for nonresidential business and the manufacturing sector is shown in figure 2-2.[13] For nonresidential business, the rate of return fell gradually between 1964 and 1975 and then precipitously during the most severe period of cost pressures in 1975–77. The second half of the 1970s was also a period of generally low capacity utilization that contributed to the low rate of return. At its low point the return to capital was less than one-third that of the early 1960s.

A similar decline in the return to capital is evident for manufacturing, but in this case the return stayed high until after 1975. During the second half of the 1970s, however, the decline was more severe than that for business as a whole because of the competitive problems of the tradable goods sector. For many Swedish manufacturing firms, prices are essentially dictated by the world markets. Thus for those goods that are sold in world markets, costs cannot be simply passed on through higher

13. The actual level of the rate of return should not be emphasized because we did not have a measure of the value of land. The real rate of return is defined as net operating surplus divided by the midyear stock of reproducible capital. The latter is valued at its nominal replacement cost to eliminate the effects of inflation. The net capital stock and inventory data were obtained from Statistics Sweden.

prices. In the late 1970s the combination of high domestic cost increases and an overvalued exchange rate squeezed the profit share and, as a result, the return to capital. The low point was reached in 1977–78 when the rate of return to capital fell to only 1 percent. There has, however, been a major improvement in the profitability of manufacturing since the devaluations of 1981–82.[14]

The importance of international competitiveness for Swedish industry is readily illustrated by the following simple regression that relates the rate of return in nonresidential business (*RRBUS*) to an index of the real exchange rate based on the ratio of Swedish unit labor costs in manufacturing relative to the average of its competitors (*RCOST*), the ratio of the net capital stock to output (*K/O*), and the utilization rate (*UTIL*):[15]

$$RRBUS = -0.12\,RCOST - 12.18\,K/O + 14.59\,UTIL + 26.28.$$
$$\quad\quad\quad (6.4) \quad\quad\quad\quad (18.5) \quad\quad\quad (2.2) \quad\quad\quad\quad (4.2)$$

Standard error = 0.60; R^2 = 0.95; Durbin-Watson = 1.51

The rate of return declines by 0.1 percentage point for each 1 percent rise in Sweden's unit labor costs relative to its competitors.

A rise in the ratio of the capital stock to output also leads to a fall in the rate of return because it implies the progressive exploitation of more marginal investment projects—a declining marginal efficiency of capital schedule. If, as was argued earlier, the rate of labor-augmenting technical change did decline in Sweden and other countries after 1973, the rate of capital accumulation required to maintain balanced growth also should have declined. Thus, in part, the decline of investment within Sweden was a necessary adjustment to a slower rate of technical change as reflected in the slower growth of total factor productivity.

The investment decision is driven primarily by a comparison of the prospective return on physical capital with that on financial assets—the cost of funds. And, while the return on existing capital, as a proxy for the anticipated return on new investments, fell throughout the 1970s, its effect on investment was offset in some years by an equally large decline in the real return on financial assets. A rough measure of the real return

14. A similar pattern is evident if one focuses on capital's share in value added, but there is a greater decline in the rate of return because of the tendency for the capital-output ratio to rise over time.

15. The measure of relative unit labor costs is that of the International Monetary Fund. The utilization rate is the measure defined in note 5. *T*-statistics are shown in parentheses below the coefficients.

on financial assets can be obtained by subtracting an estimate of expected inflation from the nominal yield on long-term bonds.[16] Both the nominal and real rate of interest are shown in figure 2-2.

The nominal bond rate has moved upward since 1963, but the real rate of interest has followed a very different pattern. It was high in the late 1960s and then fell to a negative value in the mid-1970s as nominal interest rates failed to keep pace with an accelerating inflation of prices. Since 1980, however, higher nominal interest rates, combined with some slowing of inflation, has boosted the cost of funds back to a level above the average of the 1960s.

The comparison of the rate of return on physical capital with that for financial assets in figure 2-2 shows a substantial decline in the attractiveness of real versus financial investments in Sweden. The yield premium for physical investments in nonresidential business over the return on financial assets exceeded 10 percent in the mid-1960s, declined from then until 1973, rose temporarily in 1974–76, and then declined again. Within manufacturing the impact on investment incentives of the collapse of capital income in the mid-1970s was buffered for a time by an equally low return on financial capital, but by 1981 there was a negative spread between the yield on physical and financial investments. The most surprising result is that the relative return on physical capital was not particularly attractive in 1983–84 because a sharp rise in real interest rates negated much of the improvement in business profitability.

The importance of these factors for investment can be demonstrated with simple statistical equations that relate net investment as a percent of value added (I/VA) to the excess of the return on physical capital (RA) over the real rate of interest on financial assets ($RBOND$), and a measure of capacity utilization ($UTIL$).[17] The equation for business less housing for 1965–74 is

$$I/VA = 0.27\,(RA_{-1} - RBOND) + 0.26(UTIL_{-1}) + 0.10\,\text{time} - 12.0.$$

$$(3.8) \qquad\qquad\qquad (2.4) \qquad\qquad (2.4) \qquad\quad (1.2)$$

$$\text{Standard error} = 0.67;\ R^2 = 0.70$$

16. The expected rate of inflation is estimated with a weighted four-year average of the rate of change in capital goods prices. The weights for the current and prior three years are 0.4, 0.3, 0.2, and 0.1. They are arbitrary but in accord with the general pattern of adaptive expectations found in U.S. studies of expected inflation.

17. For manufacturing the utilization rate is based on a survey of business firms: it is a three-year average of the proportion of firms operating at capacity. For the total business sector the utilization rate is a two-year average ratio of actual to normal output, where normal output is a nine-year centered average of the actual.

The equation for manufacturing between 1966 and 1984 is

$$I/VA = 0.46\,(RA_{-1} - RBOND) + 0.04\,(UTIL) + 11.83.$$
$$\quad\;\;(5.4) \qquad\qquad\qquad\quad (1.7) \qquad\qquad (13.8)$$

Standard error $= 0.85; R^2 = 0.88$

These equations do not represent complete structural models of the investment process—in particular, they do not take account of taxes and other investment policies. They do, however, duplicate the major cyclical movements in the investment share and demonstrate the importance of the rate of return and financing cost.[18] For example, the equations imply that the rise in the rate of return on capital since 1982 should have increased the investment share of manufacturing by about 1.5 percentage points by 1984. The actual increase was only half as large because of an offsetting rise in the rate of return on financial assets.

There is no statistical evidence of a negative trend in the investment share. The inclusion of a trend variable resulted in an insignificant coefficient within manufacturing, and the trend for the business sector as a whole is slightly positive. That result is not in accord with the argument that the structure of growth in Sweden is shifting away from capital-intensive industries. As a check on this result, growth was also broken down within manufacturing into sixteen separate industries to see if the capital-intensive industries have been growing more or less rapidly than the average. A reweighting of growth in these industries using relative capital stock weights rather than output shares has no effect on the computed growth rate for manufacturing value added in either 1963–73 or 1973–84. Within manufacturing, at least, there appears to have been no shift in the composition of growth toward or away from capital-intensive industries.[19]

In summary, the decline of industrial investment in Sweden can be explained as the combined result of two phenomena: a sharp fall in the real return to capital and a rise during the 1980s in the inflation-adjusted

18. It is possible to estimate equations with separate coefficients on the two rate-of-return variables. Those equations were not significantly different from the ones shown above. The equations also perform better than an alternative accelerator-type model that emphasizes capacity utilization and the rate of growth of output. Many of those cyclical factors are captured above in the return on existing capital and the utilization rate.

19. A contrary argument is made in Det Okonomiske Rad [Danish Economic Council] and others, *Economic Growth in a Nordic Perspective* (Finland: DOR, 1984), p. 165.

rate of return on financial assets. While both rates of return have varied widely since 1963, the net yield spread has been unfavorable to physical investment since 1976, with only a modest improvement after 1982.

Inflation

Inflation has far more serious consequences in Sweden than in the United States. The United States has followed an essentially flexible exchange rate policy since 1971, and, in combination with the large size of its domestic markets, that policy allows for any excess of wage increases above the growth in productivity to be simply passed forward into higher prices.

In Sweden, however, prices of tradable goods are largely controlled by world market prices—producers are price-takers. Thus for the tradable goods sector, excessive nominal wage increases do translate into real wage gains but at the cost of squeezing profits and thus the incentives for new investment.

The acceptability of alternative strategies for controlling inflation also differs between the two countries. The United States reduced its inflation in the early 1980s at the cost of a severe recession with large increases in unemployment.[20] Since 1982 unemployment has declined in the United States, but it is being maintained at a level well above the rate, estimated at 6 percent of the work force, at which inflation might tend to accelerate. Essentially, a higher level of unemployment has been exchanged for lower inflation. Such a solution seems unacceptable in Sweden. There has been some increase in unemployment since the early 1970s, but it is much less than in other industrialized countries, and those who are unemployed are heavily compensated through a wide variety of job programs.

This section is concerned more with the question of whether there is anything different, in an economic sense, about the process of inflation in Sweden compared with that in the United States. Has the rate of inflation shifted upward at any given rate of resource utilization? How did wages respond in Sweden to the rise in the price of imported goods and the slowing of productivity growth? What role has government policy played in the inflation process?

20. It also benefited from a rising exchange rate that shifted some of the inflation abroad.

Figure 2-3. *Price Increases, the Composition of Wage Changes, and the Duration of Job Vacancies in Sweden, 1965–85*[a]

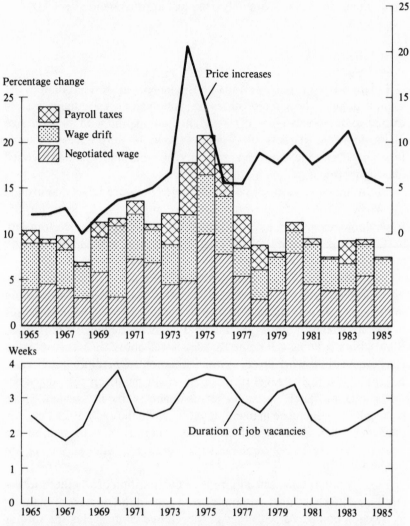

Sources: Swedish National Institute of Economic Research; and Nils Henrik Schager, "The Replacement of the UV-Curve with a New Measure of Hiring Efficiency," working paper 149 (Stockholm: Industrial Institute for Economic and Social Research, 1985).

a. Percentage wage increases for industrial workers are measured on a second-quarter over second-quarter basis. Price changes are those of the manufacturing value-added deflator.

The Inflation Record

The pattern of inflation in Sweden is summarized in figure 2-3. The surge of wage and price increases in the mid-1970s is clearly evident. The figure also breaks down the wage rate increases into three components: the negotiated increase, wage drift, and the contribution of higher employment taxes. Several features of the experience of the 1970s stand out. The first surge of inflation in 1974 seems to have been driven by excess demand: the acceleration is in prices, and negotiated wage increases make almost no contribution. However, wage drift, which might be associated with labor market conditions, and employment taxes both rose sharply.[21] Although negotiated wage increases did rise in 1975, wage drift and employment taxes continued to make up a large part of the cost acceleration between 1974 and 1976. In general, the formal spring negotiations account for a surprisingly small proportion of the year-to-year variations in the wage rate—hardly the situation one would expect for an economy dominated by large centralized unions.

Except during 1974–76, nominal wage rates have been strikingly constant despite a sharply higher rate of price increase. The average rise in nominal labor costs after 1977 has actually been less than it was before 1974, while the rate of price increase has been two to three times more rapid. A slower rate of productivity growth rather than higher nominal wage increases accounts for the more rapid rate of inflation in the 1980s.

Finally, there is little direct evidence of a strong response of nominal wage increases to price changes, even at times of major changes in the exchange rate, and thus the rate of *real* wage change has varied sharply over the past two decades.

Models of the Inflation Process

Much of the Swedish research on inflation has been done within the context of the Scandinavian model, which has the following basic characteristics: the economy is divided into two sectors, which produce tradable and nontradable goods and services, respectively. Within the tradables sector, firms are price-takers, setting prices in accord with

21. About one-third of the 1974 increase in employment taxes was the result of negotiations between the union and employers and might more correctly be associated with the negotiated increase. Wage drift is the amount by which actual wage rates rise in excess of the negotiated increase.

international markets. Thus with fixed exchange rates, changes in world market prices in combination with productivity growth in the tradables sector determine a warranted rate of nominal wage increase consistent with maintaining an unchanged competitive position and a constant distribution of income between capital and labor.

Within the nontradables sector, however, firms are price-setters, and prices are a simple markup over costs. The growth of wages is assumed to be the same as in the tradables sector. On the assumption that productivity growth between the two sectors is exogenous, inflation in the nontradables sector exceeds or falls short of that for tradables by the difference in productivity growth.[22]

The Scandinavian model can be contrasted with the analytical framework commonly used in the United States. Except for minor variables, the U.S. model relates the nominal rate of wage increase, $\dot{w}$, to unemployment, U, and the expected rate of price inflation, $\dot{p}$:

$$\dot{w} = f(U, \dot{p}).$$

If the coefficient on the price variable is unity, the rate of real wage change is solely a function of unemployment. Furthermore, in the United States, firms are taken to be price-setters, passing along all cost increases.[23]

What is conspicuously missing from the standard augmented Phillips curve used in the United States is any direct mechanism by which nominal wage changes adjust to reflect changes in labor productivity or the terms of trade. A decline in productivity growth increases unit labor costs and prices for any given rate of nominal wage increase. The escalation of prices in turn leads to a higher rate of nominal wage increase. In such a model the level of unemployment consistent with stable inflation is inversely related to the rate of productivity growth. If

22. This brief description is taken from Erik Lundberg, "The Rise and Fall of the Swedish Model," *Journal of Economic Literature,* vol. 23 (March 1985), pp. 21–22. A more detailed discussion is available in Odd Aukrust, "Inflation in the Open Economy: A Norwegian Model," in Lawrence B. Krause and Walter S. Salant, eds., *Worldwide Inflation: Theory and Recent Experience* (Brookings, 1977), pp. 107–53. An application of the model to Sweden is available in the same volume: see Lars Calmfors, "Inflation in Sweden," pp. 493–537.

23. There is some difference of views in U.S. research about the relative importance of producer prices (the demand for labor) and consumer prices (the supply of labor) in formulating the wage relationship. Because Swedish producers of tradable goods are largely price-takers, there is less relevance to the distinction between the two price indexes. A devaluation affects both by similar amounts. A commodity price shock, such as for oil, affects consumer prices but not value-added prices.

productivity growth slows, the upward spiral of wages and prices can only be contained by allowing unemployment to rise on a permanent basis, or, if wages do not fully adjust to price changes (a coefficient on the price term of less than unity), by allowing inflation to rise so as to erode the initial real wage gains.[24]

The Scandinavian model, in contrast, incorporates an additional term into the wage determination process, the warranted wage change required to maintain competitiveness. If the warranted rate plays a role in wage behavior in a positive rather than a normative sense, it offers a third way, other than higher unemployment or accelerating inflation, of bringing real wage increases in line with a lower rate of productivity growth.

An empirical measure of the warranted real wage rate in the manufacturing sector can be constructed as the product of four factors: labor productivity in manufacturing (adjusted for cyclical factors), labor's share of the losses on terms of trade and the costs of financing the foreign debt, the ratio of hourly earnings to labor compensation, and the ratio of producer to consumer prices. Symbolically,

$$wr = \pi \cdot \frac{NIA}{GDP} \cdot \frac{1}{1+s} \cdot \frac{P_{va}}{P_c},$$

where wr is the warranted real wage rate, π is an index of output per hour in manufacturing, NIA is national income adjusted for terms of trade, GDP is gross domestic product, s is the employment tax rate, P_c is the consumption expenditure deflator, and P_{va} is the value-added price deflator for manufacturing.[25]

The results of that computation together with an index of the actual real wage rate are shown in figure 2-4. The figure provides dramatic evidence of the wrenching change imposed on wage growth after 1973. After rising at an annual rate of 4 percent between 1964 and 1973, the

24. The latter option probably could not be sustained because workers and firms would come to anticipate the high rate of price increase. It is interesting to note that the argument for an inverse long-term relationship between unemployment and productivity growth is the opposite of the fear expressed in public discussion that increased productivity growth (automation) will add to unemployment.

25. Productivity growth is adjusted to exclude cyclical fluctuations. The measures of national income (adjusted) and gross domestic product are from the *National Accounts,* the third term adjusts for employment taxes, and the fourth term simply converts the wage rate from a product wage (producer prices) to a real wage (consumer prices). The employment tax rate is taken from Bertil Holmlund, "Payroll Taxes and Wage Inflation: The Swedish Experience," *Scandinavian Journal of Economics,* vol. 85, no. 1 (1983), p. 14.

Figure 2-4. *Indexes of the Actual and Warranted Real Wage in Sweden, 1964–84*

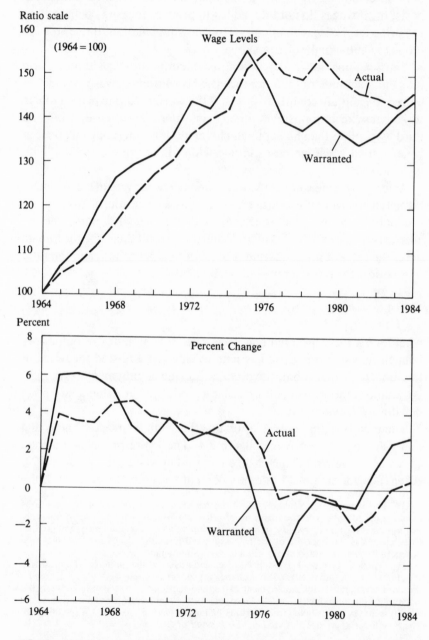

Sources: *National Accounts;* Bertil Holmlund, "Payroll Taxes and Wage Inflation: The Swedish Experience," *Scandinavian Journal of Economics,* vol. 85, no. 1 (1983), pp. 1–15; and authors' estimates.

Table 2-4. *Changes in the Warranted Wage Rate in Sweden,*
1964–73 and 1973–84
Percent

Components of warranted wage	Annual rate of change	
	1964–73	*1973–84*
Productivity growth	6.9	3.3
Employment taxes	−0.9	−1.9
Terms of trade[a]	0	−0.7
Relative prices[b]	−1.9	−0.4
Total	4.0	0.1

Source: Authors' calculations as discussed in the text.
a. Includes effects of foreign debt financing.
b. Change in the ratio of producer to consumer prices.

warranted rate of real wage growth shot up 9.5 percent in 1974–75 (due
to large increases in manufacturing prices relative to consumer prices)
and then actually fell until 1982.[26] The largest portion of this decline was
caused by slower productivity growth, but a significant contribution was
also made by the sharp increase in social insurance taxes. Between 1972
and 1976 the effective rate of employment tax doubled—from 15.9
percent to 34.6 percent—and was an astounding 49 percent of the wage
rate in 1984. If the change in the warranted wage rate between 1964–73
and 1973–84 is decomposed, one obtains the results shown in table 2-4.

Much of the discussion of Sweden's inflation process emphasizes the
deterioration in the trade-off between inflation and unemployment. But
a much larger contribution seems to have been made by the decline in
the rate of warranted wage increase and the difficulties of forcing an
adjustment to that new reality.

Empirical Analysis

The issues raised above can be examined by constructing a simple
empirical model of price and wage behavior in the manufacturing sector.

PRICES. The unique feature of price behavior by Swedish firms is
the extent to which they are limited in their ability to pass along
domestic cost increases into prices by the need to remain competitive with foreign producers. That point can be illustrated with a
statistical regression in which the value-added price deflator for

26. The decline in the product wage began after 1972 and reached its low in 1978.

manufacturing, P_{mfg}, is related to standardized unit labor costs, $SULC$, and foreign manufacturing prices, P_{for}, measured in Swedish kronor.[27] The results in logarithms for 1965–84 are

$$P_{mfg} = 0.98\,SULC + 0.23\,[P_{for}/\text{SULC}] + (0.28)\,[P_{for}/SULC]_{-1} + 4.72.$$
$$\quad\ (76.3) \qquad\qquad (2.5) \qquad\qquad\qquad (2.8) \qquad\qquad\qquad (239.4)$$

Standard error $= 0.024$; $R^2 = .997$; Durbin-Watson $= 1.2$

The basic coefficient on standard unit labor costs is close to unity, implying that cost increases are fully reflected in prices. As shown by the coefficients on the ratio of foreign manufacturing prices to domestic unit labor costs, however, foreign price changes either greater or less than those of domestic costs force a subsequent readjustment of prices. Collecting all the terms, the net coefficient on unit labor costs is 0.47 and that on foreign prices is 0.51.[28] Thus at a given level of foreign prices, only half of any increment in labor costs can be passed on in prices, the remainder being absorbed out of the profit margin. Similar estimates for U.S. manufacturing produce a coefficient of 0.15 or smaller on foreign prices.[29] On the price side, inflation in Sweden is heavily determined by foreign price developments and exchange rate policy, and domestic cost increases in excess of those abroad impose a heavy cost on profits and investment incentives.

WAGES. The major issue on the wage side is the extent to which workers' aspirations for wage increases have adjusted to a much slower rate of warranted wage growth. With a slower rate of productivity increase Sweden cannot generate the rapid gains in living standards that were achieved in the 1960s. If workers refuse to recognize that reality, increased nominal wages can only result in higher prices or reduced profits. The issue can be evaluated by estimating a statistical represen-

27. Standardized unit labor costs are defined as compensation per hour divided by an index of productivity that is adjusted to exclude cyclical fluctuations. The adjustment procedure is the same as that discussed in the prior section. The foreign price index is that used by the International Monetary Fund to measure relative competitiveness and uses bilateral trade weights.

28. The net coefficient on unit labor costs of 0.47 is obtained by adding the coefficients $(0.98 - 0.23 - 0.28)$. A correction for autocorrelation had no significant effect on the coefficients. In addition, there was no evidence that variations in the rate of domestic resource utilization influence the price-cost margin.

29. This form for the equation is estimated for the United States, Sweden, the United Kingdom, Germany, and Italy in Charles L. Schultze, *Other Times, Other Places: Macroeconomic Lessons from U.S. and European History* (Brookings, 1986), table 2-4. Schultze obtained coefficients on the foreign price term that varied from 0.78 for Sweden to 0.15 for the United States to 0.31 for Germany.

tation of the process by which nominal wage rates are established, and performing several tests to determine if changes in the warranted rate of wage growth are incorporated into wage negotiations. The most direct effort to construct an empirical version of the Scandinavian model, which implies that nominal wages will reflect changes in the competitive position of Swedish industry, is that of Lars Calmfors.[30] While he did not focus on the notion of the warranted wage rate, he did find a significant positive influence of productivity growth on nominal wage changes. The coefficient, however, was only 0.2.

More recently, Bertil Holmlund examined Swedish wage behavior with a particular emphasis on the effects of employment and income taxes on wage changes.[31] Holmlund found strong empirical evidence that about half of any employment tax increase is shifted backward directly in the form of smaller nominal increases in hourly earnings. He also concluded that a similar effect of smaller magnitude was evident for the income tax. Furthermore, he obtained large coefficients on changes in producer and consumer prices—the price coefficient was 0.77 in the unconstrained version of his model.

Although it was not formally treated in Holmlund's model, a decline in productivity growth should be similar in its impact on wage behavior to an increase in the employment tax. If workers are willing to moderate their wage demands, or are forced to do so by employers, to make room for increased employment taxes, they should be equally responsive to a change in labor productivity. Thus the results of Holmlund's study suggest that much of the decline in the warranted wage rate could have been accommodated through wage negotiations without the need for higher rates of inflation or unemployment.

Most other studies of Swedish wage behavior have focused on the appropriate measure of excess demand in labor markets.[32] Those studies have provided a list of potential measures of labor market conditions, including the unemployment rate, the job vacancy rate, and the duration of vacancies. We also experimented with several alternative series on wage rates, but the two most important were straight-time hourly

30. Calmfors, "Inflation in Sweden." See also the individual essays in Assar Lindbeck, ed., *Inflation and Employment in Open Economies* (Amsterdam: North Holland, 1979).

31. Holmlund, "Payroll Taxes and Wage Inflation."

32. See the summary with citations in Organization for Economic Cooperation and Development, *Economic Surveys: Sweden* (Paris: OECD, 1981), pp. 33–48, 55–59.

Table 2-5. *Regressions for Wage Inflation in Sweden, Selected Periods, 1951–84*[a]

Variable	1951–79	1951–84	1964–84	1964–84	1964–84
Constant	0.05	0.05	0.05	0.01	...
	(7.9)	(8.2)	(4.8)	(1.0)	...
$(1 + s)$	−0.57	−0.68	−0.54	−0.13	−0.50
	(−2.3)	(−2.7)	(−1.8)	(−0.5)	(−2.7)
$(1 - t)$	−0.22	−0.20	−0.22	−0.30	−0.16
	(−1.6)	(−1.4)	(−1.7)	(−2.2)	(−1.7)
Q/Q^*	0.06	0.11	0.13	...	0.09
	(1.9)	(4.2)	(4.6)	...	(4.5)
PPI	0.18	0.19	0.03	0.08	...
	(2.4)	(2.5)	(0.4)	(0.7)	...
PPI_{-1}	0.30	0.30	0.46	0.38	0.42
	(6.4)	(6.1)	(5.2)	(4.9)	(6.6)
CPI	0.29	0.17	0.18	−0.59	...
	(1.8)	(1.0)	(1.1)	(−2.6)	...
DV	...	...	...	0.01	0.01
	...	...	...	(1.5)	(3.5)
DV_{-1}	...	...	...	0.02	...
	...	...	...	(2.3)	...
$\bar{R}^2$	0.854	0.794	0.691	0.749	0.830
Standard error × 100	1.3	1.5	1.1	1.0	0.8
Durbin-Watson	1.6	1.3	1.8	1.2	1.7

Sources: Bertil Holmlund, "Payroll Taxes and Wage Inflation: The Swedish Experience," *Scandinavian Journal of Economics,* vol. 85, no. 1 (1983), p. 7; and Nils Henrik Schager, "The Replacement of the UV-Curve with a New Measure of Hiring Efficiency," working paper 149 (Stockholm: Industrial Institute for Economic and Social Research, 1985).

a. All variables are in change of the logarithm, except DV and Q/Q^*. The latter is measured in the level of the logarithm. T-statistics are shown in parentheses. Variables are payroll tax (s), average income tax rate (t), index of volume of production (Q/Q^*), producer price index (PPI), consumer price index (CPI), and duration of vacancies (DV).

earnings for adult male workers in mining and manufacturing and the sum of negotiated increases and wage drift for industrial workers as measured on a second-quarter to second-quarter basis.[33]

We began by updating Holmlund's equation because it is most supportive of the warranted wage approach. To make his results compatible with other available data, we extended his data period of 1951–79 to 1984 and then truncated the years before 1965. Those regression results are shown in the first three columns of table 2-5. The coefficients are nearly identical with those reported by Holmlund in his original study.

33. The first series is that of Holmlund extended to 1984. The second was supplied by Nils Henrik Schager of the Industrial Institute for Economic and Social Research, and it covers all workers in industry.

However, the conclusions are critically dependent on the measure of resource utilization. Holmlund used a measure based on the ratio of production in mining and manufacturing to its own exponential trend. Because of the slowing of economic growth after 1973, that measure implies a high level of excess demand for 1965–75, followed by a major shift toward economic slack. If we use, instead, a direct labor market measure such as the duration of job vacancies, as shown in table 2-5, row 4, the overall fit of the equation improves, but evidence of the backward shifting of employment taxes vanishes, and the rate of consumer price increase has a negative coefficient. If the consumer price variable is removed or constrained to be opposite in sign to the income tax, the income tax term also loses all significance in the equation.[34] Similar problems exist for the equations using the other available measures of labor market conditions.

However, if we include both an index of labor market conditions *and* Holmlund's resource utilization measure (table 2-5, row 5), there continues to be strong evidence of a backward shifting of taxes.[35] The coefficients on consumer prices and concurrent changes in producer prices become insignificant and are omitted. Finally, there is evidence of a direct backward shifting of taxes only for the equation that used straight-time hourly earnings of male workers; the results are inconclusive for the other wage-rate series. Thus the sensitivity of Holmlund's results to seemingly minor changes in the specification of the equations raises serious doubts about his conclusions. The role of his measure of resource utilization is difficult to interpret when more direct measures of labor market conditions are available.

As an alternative, we estimated an equation that related the annual wage change to the rate of price change, the profit rate in manufacturing, and different measures of labor market conditions. In those tests the duration of job vacancies consistently performed better than the vacancy rate, the unemployment rate, or a combination of the two. A simple regression of the duration rate on either the vacancy rate or unemployment, however, indicated a structural shift in the relationship after 1969.

34. The constraint is imposed in one version of Holmlund's equations.
35. The evidence of a backward shifting of taxes emerges only for equations that incorporate Holmlund's specific measure of resource utilization. Alternative measures that were tested included the survey of capacity utilization, the profit share in manufacturing, and a modification of Holmlund's variable to allow for a break in the trend of output growth after 1973. The results are also unaffected by inserting variables that distinguish between employment tax increases imposed by the government and those that arose out of the collective bargaining.

Table 2-6. *Swedish Wage Equation Using Various Labor Market Measures, 1965–84*[a]

Specific labor market variable	Price change	Profit	Labor Market			Constant	R²	Standard error	Durbin-Watson
			Current	Lagged	Shift Term				
(1) DV	0.19	23.43	1.24	1.66	...	-3.15	0.836	1.1	2.0
	(3.4)	(5.8)	(2.5)	(3.3)	...	(-2.2)			
(2) VR	0.28	22.84	1.26	3.18	2.85	-2.48	0.835	1.1	1.8
	(4.8)	(4.4)	(1.2)	(3.2)	(3.6)	(-1.9)			
(3) UR	0.25	26.8	-0.99	-1.28	4.0	5.72	0.827	1.1	1.6
	(4.2)	(5.3)	(-1.7)	(-2.2)	(4.9)	(3.3)			
(4) 1/UR	0.24	27.27	3.74	5.67	4.27	-4.10	0.779	1.2	1.4
	(3.6)	(4.7)	(1.4)	(2.1)	(4.4)	(-2.1)			
(5) VR − UR	0.26	25.36	0.59	0.98	3.62	3.03	0.834	1.1	1.7
	(4.4)	(4.9)	(1.4)	(2.5)	(4.2)	(2.1)			

Sources: Schager, "Replacement of the UV-Curve"; *National Accounts*; and the Swedish National Institute for Economic Research.
a. *T*-statistics are in parentheses. Variables are duration of vacancies (*DV*), vacancy rate (*VR*), and unemployment rate (*UR*).

If a dummy variable is included that is 1.0 in 1969 and thereafter, all the measures of labor market conditions work equally well.[36] Given the adjustment for 1969 and thereafter, we could find no further evidence of a structural shift in the wage equation.

A representative sample of the results for these different measures of the labor market is shown in table 2-6.[37] There is some trade-off between the price inflation and profit variables because including the latter reduces the size of the price coefficient. While this formulation works equally well with Holmlund's series on male wage rates, including the tax variables and his index of resource utilization in the equation leads to a reversion to equation 5 of table 2-5.[38]

Essentially, we are left with two alternative formulations of the wage process that differ depending on the specific measure of wage change used. For each of these versions, we attempted to insert the change in the warranted wage rate or its components, but all the coefficients were insignificant. There was no evidence that nominal wage changes do adjust to changes in the rate of productivity growth. Furthermore, the basic argument of the positive version of the Scandinavian model is that workers and firms will demonstrate a concern for international competitiveness in setting nominal wage rates. Thus the prior year's current account balance, as a share of GDP, was inserted into the above regressions to determine if the emergence of a trade imbalance affects wages. The resulting coefficient was negative and statistically insignificant.

As a final test, the annual rate of productivity growth was inserted into the original equation estimated by Holmlund for 1951–84 and a subperiod that ended in 1972. Again, the coefficient on the productivity term was small and statistically insignificant.

These empirical experiments lead to the conclusion that there is no

36. This includes the vacancy rate, the unemployment rate, the difference between vacancies and unemployment, the reciprocal of the unemployment rate, and the duration of vacancies. The reciprocal of the unemployment rate works somewhat less well.

37. The reported results are for the wage measure based on the percentage change from the second quarter of each year of hourly earnings (negotiated plus drift) for industrial workers. Holmlund's wage series gave similar results, except that the series he used yields a coefficient on the profit variable that is only half as large as the one reported in the table. We also experimented with different measures of price change, such as consumer and producer prices. The value-added deflator, which was lagged to reduce problems of equation bias, consistently worked better.

38. The results shown in table 2-6 were also far more stable for a dependent variable, defined as the sum of negotiated increases plus wage drift, than for either of the components.

endogenous element of Swedish wage behavior that causes a direct adjustment of actual wage increases to the warranted rate and that the Scandinavian model does not, in a behavioral sense, apply to the Swedish process of wage determination. Thus Sweden faces a situation similar to that of other countries in which the adjustment to a slower rate of productivity growth can only be made through higher inflation or higher unemployment.

What is surprising about the empirical results is the stability of the basic behavioral relationship. The errors during the period of high inflation in the mid-1970s are small and, if we accept the duration of job vacancies as a measure of labor market pressures, there is no evidence of a shift in the basic relationship.[39]

Furthermore, wages appear to be highly sensitive to labor market conditions in Sweden. After a lag of two years, a rise in the unemployment rate of 1 percent reduces annual wage inflation by 2.3 percent. And, if half of manufacturing is composed of price-setters who pass those wage changes on in prices, the long-term effect is a 2.6 percent annual reduction. In other words, a rise in unemployment of about 1 percentage point would reduce the rate of increase of unit labor costs to approximately the average of Sweden's trading partners.

At the same time, nominal wage rates do not appear to be particularly sensitive to prices in Sweden. The wage process looks more like that of the United States than that of the stylized view of the rest of Europe.[40] Nominal wage rates appear to be sticky and slow to adjust, while real wages are flexible. In fact, the whole period since 1964 is marked by a great deal of inertia in nominal wage changes.

In summary, it appears that the increased problem of cost inflation in Sweden during the 1970s was not the result of a breakdown in the nominal wage-setting process. There is some evidence of a deterioration in the trade-off between inflation and unemployment after 1968, but the deterioration appears small. Instead, the acceleration of unit labor costs can be traced to the collapse of productivity growth after 1973 that sharply reduced the potential for real wage gains. The response of nominal wages seems fully consistent with the historical experience. In addition, the

39. On this point, see Nils Henrik Schager, "The Replacement of the UV-Curve with a New Measure of Hiring Efficiency," working paper 149 (Stockholm: Industrial Institute for Economic and Social Research, 1985).

40. See, for example, Jeffrey D. Sachs, "Real Wages and Unemployment in the OECD Countries," *Brookings Papers on Economic Activity, 1:1983*, pp. 255–89.

problem was exacerbated by large employment tax increases that added to the cost pressures.

Thus the emergence of high inflation was primarily a reflection of the difficulties of adjusting workers' aspirations, as reflected in demands for nominal wage increases, to slower economic growth. Other countries, faced with the same deterioration in productivity growth, allowed unemployment to rise so as to force an offsetting downward adjustment of nominal wage increases. Sweden has been reluctant to follow this course and thus has experienced a smaller increase in unemployment at the cost of a larger acceleration of inflation.

Conclusion

Two major problems must be addressed by Swedish macroeconomic policy in the 1980s. The first is the need to cut back on the high level of domestic consumption, which can be supported only by drastic reductions in capital formation and extensive foreign borrowing. Second, nominal wage increases must be scaled back to a rate in line with the underlying rate of productivity growth.

Since 1980, but particularly since 1982, Sweden has made major progress toward addressing the first problem. Between 1982 and 1985 the government budget deficit was cut by an amount equal to 3 percent of national income. While the national saving rate remains far below the levels of the 1960s, it has been sufficient to finance a significant increase in domestic investment and nearly eliminate the prior current account deficit.

Far less progress has been made, however, in controlling inflation, and that failure threatens to unravel the gains made in other areas. Unit labor costs continue to rise at an annual rate 2 to 3 percentage points higher than that of Sweden's major competitors.[41]

The basic problem is illustrated by events since 1982. The devaluations of 1981–82 lowered manufacturing costs, relative to Sweden's competitors, by 24 percent. Fully 9 percentage points of that advantage has

---

41. The cost increases have been held down somewhat since the 1982 devaluation by strong cyclical gains in productivity, but such an effort cannot be sustained.

already been lost by excessive inflation of domestic costs in 1983–85.[42] A continuation of these trends will put the Swedish economy back into the condition of the 1970s. With a loss of relative competitiveness, the trade account will again deteriorate and the squeeze on profits will curtail investment. Sweden will be faced once more with a choice between another devaluation or larger budget deficits to prop up production in the domestic economy.

42. The cost calculations are based on unpublished data from the International Monetary Fund. The weighted average exchange rate fell 24 percent between the second quarter of 1981 and the first quarter of 1983. Between the first quarter of 1983 and the fourth quarter of 1985, unit labor cost increases exceeded those of Sweden's competitors by 9.3 percent when both indexes are measured in national currencies.

3

Adjusting to Slower Economic Growth: The External Sector

ROBERT Z. LAWRENCE
and BARRY P. BOSWORTH

MUCH of this volume seeks basic explanations and remedies for the disappointing aspects of Swedish economic performance in the 1970s and 1980s. Chapter 2 places the blame for many of Sweden's difficulties on inappropriate macroeconomic policies—budget deficits, foreign borrowing, and inflation-creating wage increases that Swedish policy, with its commitment to full employment, was unable to restrain.

This chapter continues the exploration in two directions. First, it focuses on the international side of Sweden's economic performance, especially its ability to compete in world markets. Why has Sweden been forced to devalue its currency and erode its standard of living to stay competitive, and is it likely to face those choices again? Second, the chapter shifts attention from macroeconomic to structural explanations. Was Swedish growth and competitiveness impeded by its peculiar industrial structure or by rigidities and government policies that slowed the adjustments of industry to changing demands?

Competitiveness and Economic Structure

Many Swedes are alarmed about their nation's perceived loss of competitiveness in international markets. First, they believe—erroneously, as we shall show—that Sweden's declining international competitiveness is responsible for the reduced importance of industry in the Swedish economy. Second, and more important, they see international competitiveness as a fundamental constraint on the improvement of Swedish living standards. If Sweden is required to sustain repeated real currency devaluations to maintain external balance, real income growth will suffer.

The relative size of the goods-producing sector of the Swedish economy has declined. Between 1973 and 1984, the value added in goods production (agriculture, minerals, and manufacturing) fell from 27.7 to 25.3 percent, measured in 1980 dollars. Most of this decline of 2.4 percentage points reflected the fall in the share of value added in manufacturing from 23.1 to 21.5 percent of GDP.[1]

Many Swedes attribute the erosion in the relative size of the goods-producing sector to a loss of international competitiveness. They urge a variety of supply-side (industrial) policies to stimulate the expansion of the industrial sector. Yet Sweden's surplus on merchandise trade has actually been growing more rapidly than GDP. This divergence of trends in the relative importance of total goods production and trade in goods can only be reconciled by reference to changes in the structure of demand within Sweden. In other words, domestic not international factors account for industry's declining importance.

Three factors in combination explain the shrinkage of the Swedish goods-producing sector during the previous decade. First, domestic consumption patterns shifted away from goods and toward government-produced services. Second, the net trade balance in services declined, thereby increasing the merchandise trade surplus required to achieve current account balance. And third, Sweden experienced a substantial decline in the terms of trade—the ratio of export to import prices—which entailed greater production of exports for any given quantity of imports.

Paradoxically, such negative external developments as the OPEC-induced oil shocks actually *increased* industry's share in the total economy. To be sure, in the short run the external shocks might have reduced industrial employment and output; but over the medium term, since they required a decline in Swedish terms of trade, achieved mainly

1. Unless otherwise indicated, statistics cited in this chapter are the authors' calculations based on Sveriges officiella statistik, *Nationalräkenskaper, 1970–1984* (Stockholm: Statistiska centralbyrån, 1985) [Official Statistics of Sweden, *National Accounts Annual Report, 1970–1984* (Stockholm: Statistics Sweden, 1985)], and appendixes 1–5. (Hereafter *National Accounts.*)

by exchange rate devaluations, the external elements increased the net production of manufactured products. Moreover, because Sweden borrowed heavily overseas during the 1970s, it must now generate a larger trade surplus to service that debt; and given its comparative advantage, that surplus is heavily concentrated in manufactures.

Our argument is best illustrated by considering the changing composition of the Swedish current account between 1970 and 1984. In 1970 Swedish trade was roughly in balance in each of the major categories: manufactured goods, other merchandise, services, and net factor payments. In 1978, when the current account was again roughly equal to zero, a surplus of almost 4 percent of GDP in trade in manufactures offset negative balances in the other components.[2] By 1984 the current account balance was associated with a manufactured goods surplus of 5.6 percent of GDP.

The upward trend in the manufactured goods trade balance reflected an adjustment to a decline in competitiveness. It was predicated on a series of real devaluations of the krona and associated declines in Sweden's terms of trade. By 1985, as estimated by the International Monetary Fund, the effective exchange rate of the krona was 26.3 percent less than its 1970 level.[3] In part the devaluations compensated for a relatively higher Swedish domestic inflation rate, but a variety of measures indicate that Sweden's terms of trade eroded by about 20 percent.[4]

Measured in 1980 dollars, the balance of trade in manufacturing increased by 5.1 percent of GDP between 1973 and 1984.[5] If each dollar of manufactured exports reflects about 66 cents of value added in Swedish

2. International Monetary Fund, *International Financial Statistics, 1985 Yearbook,* pp. 592–93.

3. Ibid., pp. 590–91; and IMF, *International Financial Statistics, July, 1986,* pp. 460–61.

4. Between 1970 and 1985, Swedish export prices increased 27 percent less than Swedish import prices; during the same period, export prices of manufactured goods rose 22 percent less than import prices of manufactured goods and 19.2 percent less than export prices of manufactured goods in other Organization for Economic Cooperation and Development countries. During the period there were five major devaluations of the krona. IMF, *International Financial Statistics, 1985 Yearbook,* pp. 592–93, and *July, 1986,* pp. 462–63; and *National Accounts.*

5. During the same period, the nominal balance of trade in manufacturing increased by only 2.6 percent of nominal GDP. In 1970, 1973, and 1984 manufactured exports had values equal to 15.8, 18.1, and 25.0 percent of GDP, while manufactured imports were equal to 15.5, 15.1, and 19.1 percent, respectively. *National Accounts;* and United Nations, *Yearbook of International Trade Statistics,* vol. 1: *Trade by Country* (New York: UN, annually).

manufacturing, a rough estimate would suggest that trade raised the share of manufacturing in total Swedish value added by about 3.4 percent of GDP between 1973 and 1984. This would imply a decline of 5.0 percentage points due to slower domestic use.

The declining importance of goods in domestic use reflects, in turn, the relative increase in government versus private consumption. Between 1973 and 1985, government consumption of goods and services increased from 26 to 29 percent of GDP (in 1980 prices), while private consumption fell from 53 to 50 percent. Most of this fall was in private consumption of goods; private consumption of services remained fairly constant—16.6 percent of real GDP in 1973 and 16.7 percent in 1985. If we assume that government consumption, exclusive of durable goods for the military, is composed only of services, total Swedish consumption of goods decreased from 43.4 percent of real GDP in 1973 to 37.7 percent in 1984. During the same period, the total consumption of services increased 3.5 percentage points, from 41.5 to 45.0 percent of GDP, and the government component accounted for 3.3 percentage points of the rise. This switch away from goods and toward services was due to the change in the composition of Swedish consumption toward the government, which is less intensive than the private sector in the use of manufactured products.

In sum, the shrinkage in the relative size of Swedish manufacturing output is mainly the result of expanded government programs rather than Swedish international trade performance.[6] Given the macroeconomic constraints of national saving and investment, which determine the size of the current account, and government spending, which plays an important role in determining the size of the service sector, industrial policies aimed at specific sectors are unlikely to greatly affect the overall structure of the economy. If successful, they might have the desirable effect of raising Swedish productivity growth and improving its terms of trade, but they could actually reduce rather than increase the size of the Swedish goods-producing sector.

<hr/>

6. According to Söderström, the switch toward government consumption was an induced response to the unemployment that resulted from the decline in competitiveness. We should note, however, that public consumption actually grew less rapidly after 1973 than before. See Hans Tson Söderström, "Exchange Rate Strategies and Real Adjustment after 1970: The Experience of Smaller European Economies" (Stockholm: Studieförbundet Näringsliv och Samhälle, February 1986), p. 18.

Figure 3-1. *Trends in Components of the Swedish Current Account Balance as a Share of Gross Domestic Product, 1970–84*

Current account surplus or deficit as a percent of GDP

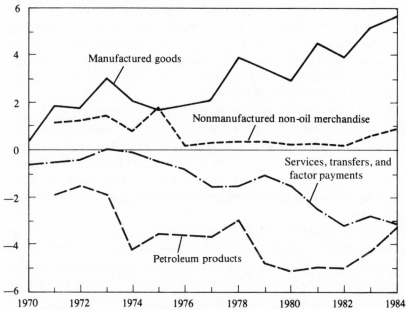

Sources: *National Accounts,* appendixes 1–5; United Nations, *Yearbook of International Trade Statistics,* vol. 1: *Trade by Country* (New York: UN, annually); and Sveriges officiella statistik, *Allmän månadsstatistik 1985: 11* (Stockholm: Statistiska centralbyrån, 1985) [Official Statistics of Sweden, *Monthly Digest of Swedish Statistics 1985: 11* (Stockholm: Statistics Sweden, 1985)].

Must the Terms of Trade Decline Continually?

The fall in Sweden's manufacturing terms of trade played a principal role in the growing trade balance in manufactured products. But why did the terms of trade decline? And are they likely to decline further? To analyze these questions, it is necessary to examine the components of the current account.

Figure 3-1 highlights the trends in the chief components of the current account in greater detail: the balance of trade in manufactured goods, which has sustained a continual upward improvement; the balance of trade in petroleum products, which eroded through 1982 and improved thereafter; the balance of trade in agricultural, forestry, and non-oil mineral merchandise, which experienced a major slump beginning in 1976 and some recovery after 1982; and the balance in services, transfers, and factor payments, which had a continual downward trend.

The slumps in the oil and services balances are easily explained. The deterioration of the balance on net factor income is a straightforward consequence of the buildup of a foreign debt. The balance in nonmanufactured goods primarily reflects changes in world demand for raw materials. The key questions about historical interpretation and the future relate to the rest of Swedish trade.

In the 1970s, was a real devaluation required, not simply to offset declines in the external balance because of higher oil prices and growing international indebtedness, but also to offset a decline that would otherwise have occurred in the rest of the trade balance? And in the future, if the Swedish terms of trade remain constant and Sweden and the rest of the world grow at long-run trend rates, will the trade balance tend to erode?

The *1984 Medium Term Survey of the Swedish Economy* offers pessimistic answers to both questions: "Terms of trade have deteriorated because relative prices in the exposed sector have had to be lowered continuously in order to contain the loss of shares for Swedish producers at home as well as abroad."[7] It also suggests that to achieve a current account surplus of 1 percent of GDP in 1990, relative prices must be cut about 18 percent during the 1980s.[8]

If such an analysis is accurate, its implications are serious both for Swedish living standards and for the choice of inflation objectives. Because non-oil imports constituted 22.8 percent of Swedish GDP in 1984,[9] a decline in the terms of trade of almost 2 percent a year would be a significant drag on improvements in economic welfare. In addition, even the ambitious objective of holding the rate of increase in unit costs equal to that of Sweden's chief trading partners would be insufficient; for the exchange rate to remain fixed, Swedish costs would have to rise less than those of its trading partners.

7. Ministry of Finance, *The 1984 Medium Term Survey of the Swedish Economy* (Stockholm, 1984), p. 58.
8. About 10 percent of this had been achieved by 1983. Ibid., p. 214.
9. Sveriges officiella statistik, *Statistisk årsbok för Sverige 1986* (Stockholm: Statistiska centralbyrån, 1985) [Official statistics of Sweden, *Statistical Abstract of Sweden, 1986* (Stockholm: Statistics Sweden, 1985)], pp. 128–29, 231. (Hereafter *Statistical Abstract of Sweden, 1986.*)

Trade Shares Analysis

There are some data to support this ominous interpretation. Between 1972 and 1984, Sweden's share of world trade tended to shrink when constant relative prices were maintained. Consider this regression in logarithms of the ratio of the volume of Swedish exports to the volume of world exports *(SX)* on a time trend *(t)* and the ratio of Swedish manufactured export prices to those of other developed countries *(RP)* from 1972 to 1984:[10]

$$SX = -0.009t - 0.22RP - 0.79RP(-1) + 5.00.$$
$$(1.9) \quad (0.59) \quad (2.40) \quad (3.9)$$

Standard error = .045; R^2 = 0.67; Durbin-Watson = 0.8

This equation suggests that with no change in relative prices, the Swedish share of world trade will erode 0.9 percent a year.

Among the factors believed to have hurt Swedish competitiveness in the 1970s and 1980s are a poor mix of products and markets, a profits squeeze in Swedish industry, and the crowding out of industrial capacity by expanding public-sector spending and policies.

PRODUCT MIX. According to several studies, Sweden has an unfavorable mix of exports in terms of commodity composition and geographic concentration. In particular, dependence on exports of iron ore, steel, forest products, metal products, and power machinery is seen as having been especially disadvantageous in the global marketplace of the 1970s. A concentration on slow-growing European markets has also hurt. For example, the *1984 Medium Term Survey* argues, "In the case of exports, part of the weaker growth for Swedish sales can be attributed to a commodity mix and a distribution by countries that have been disadvantageous in relation to overall market growth."[11] In the survey, about a third of the fall in Swedish market share is ascribed to an unfavorable commodity mix. Similarly, using constant-market-shares analysis, Hor-

10. *T*-ratios are in parentheses. *SX* is as estimated in UN, *Yearbook of International Trade Statistics,* vol. 1: *Trade by Country,* various issues. *RP* was obtained from IMF, *International Financial Statistics,* various issues.

11. Ministry of Finance, *1984 Medium Term Survey,* pp. 58–59. The survey reports that while world trade grew at an annual rate of 6.1 percent during the 1970s, Swedish exports increased only 3.3 percent a year. It ascribes an annual rate of −0.9 percent to unfavorable commodity composition and −1.7 percent to factors such as unfavorable relative price and profitability conditions. Ibid., p. 214.

62 THE SWEDISH ECONOMY

witz concluded that between 1970 and 1980 commodity and market mix together could account for almost 70 percent of the shrinkage in Swedish market shares.[12]

PROFITABILITY. Many Swedish firms trading in global markets are "price-takers" rather than "price-setters." Thus if Swedish unit labor costs increase more than those of their competitors, these firms experience a profit squeeze. Between 1969 and 1978 the share of profits in Swedish manufacturing declined from 30 percent to 15.2 percent of value added.[13] In total goods production—that is, agriculture and mining as well as manufacturing—the slump was 10 percentage points. By the late 1970s the solvency of many Swedish firms was seriously in question. Government subsidies for such capital-intensive sectors as shipbuilding, steel, and mining exploded. This poor profitability retarded growth of capacity in manufacturing and reduced the supply of Swedish manufactured goods in export and import-competing industries.

The large devaluation of the krona in 1981–82 translated into large gains in profitability. Indeed, in 1984 the profit share amounted to 33 percent of value added in manufacturing, a share higher than at any time since the 1960s.[14] Accordingly, if poor profitability explained the weak performance in the late 1970s, it ought not to have been a significant factor by the mid-1980s. But the adjustment in profitability levels through devaluation cannot be continually repeated.

THE EXPANSION OF THE GOVERNMENT SECTOR. The exploding relative share of the government sector is widely believed to have retarded Swedish competitiveness. The effects can operate both directly and indirectly. First, the government competes with industry for worker talent. Second, the expansion in government demand shifts the attention of firms away from producing tradables toward nontradables. Third, several government programs intended to aid industry may actually have retarded competitiveness. By increasing tax burdens, reducing work

12. Eva Christina Horwitz, "Export Performance of the Nordic Countries 1965–82: A Constant-Market-Shares Analysis," in Det Okonomiske Rad [Danish Economic Council] and others, *Economic Growth in a Nordic Perspective* (Finland: DOR, 1984), pp. 259–84. This is updated in Horwitz, "Marknadsandelar för Svensk Export 1978–1984" (Stockholm, Kommerskollegium [Swedish Board of Commerce], unpublished manuscript, February 25, 1986).

13. Organization for Economic Cooperation and Development, *National Accounts, 1971–1983*, vol. 2: *Detailed Tables* (Paris: OECD, 1985), pp. 49, 453; and *National Accounts*.

14. For an analysis of the distribution of profit shares across industry, see Swedish National Industrial Board (SIND), "Productivity and Gross Profits 1985: Towards Industrial Renewal?" (Stockholm: SIND, September 1985).

incentives, and undermining the work ethic, and by keeping assets and labor in slow-growing sectors, the programs may have delayed the reallocation of resources to high-growth activities.

These considerations suggest the insertion of three variables in addition to price into the trade-share equation: the share of profits in industrial value added *(SV);* an index of industrial capacity utilization *(CU),* and the ratio of government spending to GDP *(G/GDP).* These result in the following regression in logarithms:

$$SX = 0.003t - 0.46RP - 0.45G/GDP - 0.51SV - 0.027CU.$$
$$\quad (0.68) \quad\;\; (5.2) \qquad (2.4) \qquad\quad\; (3.9) \qquad\;\; (1.4)$$

Standard error = .014; R^2 = 0.98; Durbin-Watson = 2.65

This regression confirms that these other elements are crucial in explaining Swedish competitiveness. Once they are controlled for, the trend term is not statistically significant, and the remaining terms are highly significant with coefficients of the expected signs. We are thus able to explain the decline in Swedish shares. Each 1 percent rise in the price of Swedish manufactured products relative to those in other developed countries leads to a 0.5 percent decline in Swedish export volume; each 1 percent rise in labor's share in value added in Swedish manufacturing leads to a decline in volume of 0.5 percent. The expansion of the government sector also apparently detracts from overall compet-itiveness—an increase equal to 1 percent of GDP will lower exports 0.45 percent. Finally, other things being equal, the higher the level of capacity utilization, the lower the market share. Most important, the prior negative trend is now reversed in sign and statistically insignificant.

Trade Equations Analysis

The evidence that domestic factors have constrained exports need not imply Sweden's net trade position will deteriorate if terms of trade stay constant. An improvement in the trade balance is compatible with a declining share in foreign markets, provided imports expand more slowly than exports. To resolve this issue, we need estimates of the income elasticities of both imports and exports that can be applied to the trend rate of economic growth in Sweden and abroad. In what follows we obtain such estimates using standard econometric techniques. We use the variables reflecting costs, profits, capacity utilization, and the share of government in total GDP to explain the volumes of Swedish exports and non-oil imports. Estimates for both manufacturing and overall trade are provided.

In estimating our equations we assume that Swedish firms can be grouped into two polar types—price-takers and price-setters. Price-takers are concerned with the relation between the world price of their product and domestic costs, and an equation relating the quantity of exports (Q) to these variables will be a supply curve. We have attempted to capture this connection by relating exports of price-takers to the share of labor costs in domestic production (SVA), a measure of profitability:

$$Q_1 = f(SVA).$$

On the other hand, for price-setters, with constant markups over standard unit labor costs, exports depend on the relation between their prices (P_m) and those of foreign exporters (P_w), and the equation provides an estimate of the demand elasticity.[15] In addition, other factors such as world income (Y) and capacity utilization (designed to reflect delivery speed) might be included in such a system. Thus

$$Q_2 = f(P_m/P_w, CU, Y).$$

The overall equation for total exports is a weighted average of Q_1 and Q_2, where the weight is the share of each in total exports.

Thus the coefficients on export prices and standard unit labor costs should not be taken to be the overall price and supply elasticities for price-setters and price-takers, respectively, but rather those elasticities multiplied by the appropriate share in total trade.

We obtained an estimate of the relative importance of price-takers in Swedish exports by estimating an equation similar to that reported in chapter 2 for Swedish manufacturing prices, but with the export price as the dependent variable. That equation indicated that about 60 percent of Swedish export firms are price-takers and 40 percent are price-setters.[16]

In table 3-1 we report regressions for both manufacturing and overall

15. The assumption of infinitely elastic supply curves allows an equation relating the quantity of exports to the relative price of domestic and foreign products to be interpreted as a demand curve.

16. The specific equation in logarithms was

$$PX = -0.69 + 0.61\,PW + 0.42\,SULC,$$
$$(4.1)\quad(6.8)\qquad(4.3)$$

where PX is the manufactured export price; PW is the UN manufactured export world price index; and $SULC$ is the standard unit labor cost.

Table 3-1. *Regressions for Swedish Exports, Based on
Sample Period 1970–84*

	Dependent variable			
	Manufactured exports, QXM		All merchandise exports, QX	
Item	(1)	(2)	(3)	(4)
Variable				
QXW	0.94	0.99	0.90	1.16
	(27.5)	(19.4)	(12.7)	(16.1)
RP	−0.75	−0.75	−0.73	−0.46
	(8.2)	(10.7)	(3.9)	(4.9)
SVA	. . .	−0.21	. . .	−0.55
		(3.0)		(6.2)
CU	. . .	−0.095	. . .	−0.047
		(6.5)		(2.2)
G/GDP	. . .	−0.22	. . .	−0.56
		(2.1)		(3.8)
Summary statistic				
R^2	0.990	0.999	0.951	0.997
Standard error	0.021	0.009	0.044	0.013
Durbin-Watson	1.3	2.8	0.7	2.3

Sources: Based on annual data for 1970–84 in United Nations, *Yearbook of International Trade Statistics*, vol. 1: *Trade by Country*, various issues; and International Monetary Fund, *International Financial Statistics*, various issues. Numbers in parentheses are *t*-statistics. All variables are expressed in logarithmic form. Variables are volume of Swedish manufactured exports (*QXM*); volume of world trade, as measured by the United Nations (*QXW*); volume of all Swedish merchandise exports—manufactured and agricultural and mineral—(*QX*); ratio of Swedish export prices to those of its competitors (*RP*), as measured by the International Monetary Fund (reported coefficient is the sum of the current and lagged price terms); share of labor compensation in value added (*SVA*); index of capacity utilization (*CU*); and ratio of government spending to GDP (*G/GDP*).

trade that reflect these formulations. Equation 1 reports a conventional (demand) specification in which the quantity of manufactured exports is explained by the volume of world exports *(QXW)* and the relative export price of Swedish manufactured goods *(RP)* as measured by the International Monetary Fund. Because the variables are expressed in logarithms, the coefficients can be interpreted as elasticities. The equation has a standard error of 2.1 percent and a Durbin-Watson statistic that strongly suggests variables have been omitted.

The important contribution to the equation's explanatory power made by the inclusion of variables capturing the supply side is shown in equation 2. The complete specification tracks the volume of manufactured exports with a standard error of 0.9 percent—less than half that of the simple demand-side specification. The equation suggests that the demand for the products of Swedish price-setters has an elasticity of 1.8

(0.75/0.42). That estimate may be somewhat high, because we were forced to use the overall unit value index instead of the prices of just the price-setters. Similarly, it suggests that in price-taking sectors, supply has an elasticity of about 0.34 (0.21/0.61). The supply-side variables are each statistically significant and point to the contributions of domestic economic factors in determining export performances.

Equations 3 and 4 repeat the exercise with the total volume of Swedish exports. As might be expected, when the agricultural and minerals sectors are included, sectors that contain a greater share of price-takers, the importance of profitability increases. At the level of aggregate exports, the price elasticities and supply elasticities both seem to be fairly close to unity.

How well does an equation such as 4 estimated from a sample period of 1970–81 perform in tracking Swedish export performance after devaluation? An out-of-sample forecast provides errors of 1.3 percent in 1982, 0.95 percent in 1983, and −4.8 percent in 1984. Thus they suggest a relatively high degree of structural stability.

Equations for imports are reported in table 3-2. To measure the demand for imports we have used a data series of the Swedish National Institute of Economic Research that weighs the components of GDP by their import-intensity on the basis of an input-output table. We were unable to find a role for profit shares and capacity utilization in explaining import demand. There is some evidence that a rising share of government in GDP increases manufacturing imports. There is stronger evidence that a growing government sector increases imports of all merchandise. Although the aggregate import equation has a positive time trend, the addition of the government share of GDP to the equation eliminates the significance of the coefficient on the time trend, and G/GDP is positive and statistically significant. This result is particularly striking. Under normal circumstances, one would expect to see a negative coefficient on the G/GDP variable, since government spending on services is relatively less import-intensive than other components of GDP. The positive coefficient strongly suggests an expanding government sector is crowding out the domestic supply of tradables. The inclusion of nonmanufactured imports in the definition of the dependent variable, however, eliminates the previous incidence of a significant influence of relative prices. The out-of-sample forecast errors using the import equation are 0.04 percent for 1982, 2.6 percent for 1983, and −2.4 percent for 1984.

We have used equation 2 from table 3-1 and equation 2 from table 3-2 to decompose changes in the volume of trade of manufactured goods

Table 3-2. *Regressions for Swedish Imports, Based on*
Sample Period 1972–85

	Dependent variable			
	Manufactured imports, *QMM*		All merchandise imports, *QM*	
Item	*(1)*	*(2)*	*(3)*	*(4)*
Variable				
D^a	0.93	1.05	1.17	1.31
	(6.7)	(6.5)	(10.3)	(7.6)
t	. . .	. . .	. . .	-0.494×10^{-2}
				(1.03)
RPM	0.71	1.17	0.00	0.01
	(2.8)	(2.8)	(0.0)	(0.0)
G/GDP	. . .	0.19	0.25	0.35
		(1.3)	(2.5)	(2.5)
Summary statistic				
R^2	0.887	0.906	0.987	0.989
Standard error	0.028	0.027	0.019	0.019
Durbin-Watson	1.2	1.5	1.9	2.2

Sources: Based on annual data for 1972–85 from same sources as table 3-1. Numbers in parentheses are *t*-statistics. All variables, except the time variable, are expressed in logarithms. Variables are volume of Swedish manufactured imports (*QMM*); volume of all Swedish merchandise imports—manufactured and agricultural and mineral—(*QM*); weighted average of demand components (*D*); time trend (*t*); ratio of domestic manufactured goods wholesale prices to import price index for manufactured goods (*RPM*) (reported coefficient is the sum of the coefficients on the current and lagged price terms); and ratio of government spending to GDP (*G/GDP*).

a. Data from Swedish National Institute of Economic Research.

into their underlying components (see table 3-3). It is convenient to split the sample into two periods: 1972–78 and 1978–84. Thus arrayed, the periods exhibit striking differences in the forces driving their manufacturing trade balances.

In each period the volume of Swedish exports of manufactured goods increased by about the same proportion, 25.5 percent and 26.1 percent. Yet the composition of that growth was much different. In 1972–78 Sweden benefited from a relatively strong expansion of the world economy, adding 31.3 percent to exports. However, Swedish exports fell 5.0 percent because of a rise in relative prices, 2.1 percent because of squeezed profit margins in manufacturing, and 4.4 percent because expanded government spending crowded out exports. Only the low level of capacity utilization in Swedish industry added to export growth. At the same time, imports were held down by a recession within Sweden. Essentially, macroeconomic developments disguised deteriorating conditions in profits and relative prices.

In the second period, foreign economic growth was much slower—

Table 3-3. *Determinants of Change in the Swedish Trade Balance in Manufactured Goods, 1972–78 and 1978–84*
Percent change

Item	Actual change	Determinant of change					Standard error
		Market volume	Capacity utilization	Relative prices	Profit-ability	Government spending	
1972–78							
Exports	25.5	31.3	4.1	−5.0	−2.1	−4.4	1.6
Imports	7.4	13.5	. . .	−11.2	. . .	4.0	1.1
Net balance	18.1	17.8	4.1	6.2	−2.1	−8.4	0.5
1978–84							
Exports	26.1	13.7	−4.0	10.2	4.6	0.0	1.6
Imports	13.0	22.3	. . .	−8.3	. . .	0.0	−1.0
Net balance	13.1	−8.6	−4.0	18.5	4.6	0.0	2.6

Source: Authors' calculations as explained in text.

raising exports only 13.7 percent while domestic activity expanded more rapidly than before. However, the relative size of the government sector did not increase; the decline in the relative price of Swedish products boosted exports 10.2 percent; and the improvement in profit margins contributed an additional 4.6 percent.

In figure 3-2 the two equations are combined to show the determinants of the net change in the trade balance (expressed as the ratio of exports to imports). In turn, we can decompose the shift of the trade balance into its underlying components. First, differences in the rate of growth of the foreign and domestic markets held down the trade balance between 1972 and 1975, was a strong positive force up to 1978, and has remained relatively unchanged since then. Over the period as a whole, the growth of markets made a net positive contribution to the Swedish trade balance. Second, the contribution of price competitiveness fluctuated until 1977, but it has added greatly to the trade balance since then. Third, the principal source of decline in the Swedish trade balance is the growth of government in the domestic economy.

In sum, our analysis suggests that Swedish manufacturing does not suffer from a decline in competitiveness. Instead, higher oil prices and increased indebtedness required a *growing* surplus in Sweden's manufacturing trade balance, and that increase had to be supplied by real currency devaluations. The major lasting negative influence on competitiveness would seem to have been a crowding-out effect from growing government demand for services. In the absence of large shifts in its external terms of trade and in its national savings rate, Sweden should

Figure 3-2. *Determinants of Net Change in the Swedish Trade Balance in Manufactured Goods, 1972–84*

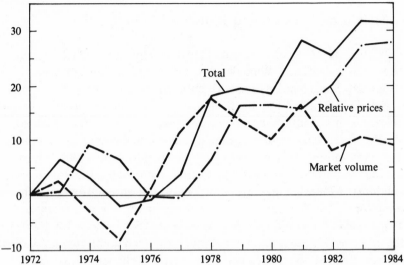

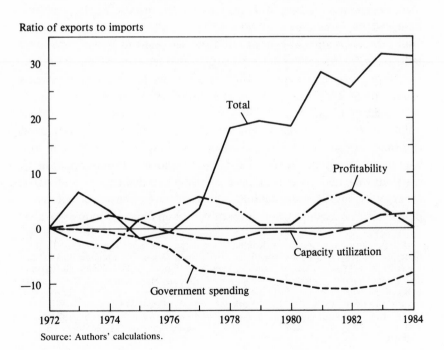

Source: Authors' calculations.

in the future be able to maintain external balance without real exchange rate depreciation.

Structural Change and Industrial Policy

We turn now to an assessment of the role of Swedish industrial policy. How has it worked? What have been its effects on adjustment to structural change and on Sweden's competitive position?

Swedish industry has been aided by a variety of broadly based programs that aim to improve performance in exports and to promote small corporations, underdeveloped regions, and energy conservation and exploration. As conceived and practiced in the 1960s, Swedish microeconomic policies stressed an activist approach to the labor market combined with a laissez-faire approach to the product market. These principles were laid out in a report presented to the Congress of the Trade Union Federation in 1961. The central theme was a firm belief in the efficiency of the market economy.[17] An open credit market was to finance efficient companies and to constrain inefficient firms. Government was to pursue free trade abroad and ensure the market was not hindered by monopolies at home. Above all, the state was not to "subsidize economically weak, and in the long run dying, firms and industries."[18] Indeed, by raising the relative wages of unskilled workers, the labor-market strategy of the trade unions sought deliberately to accelerate Sweden's move out of labor-intensive production.

The second half of the 1970s saw a qualitative shift in the Swedish policy approach to industry. The new thrust was to extend selective aid to firms in crisis (see figure 3-3). Roughly three quarters of industrial support paid out between fiscal 1976–77 and fiscal 1982–83 went to restructuring and reduction in crisis-ridden industries—a defensive strategy of subsidies to declining firms. The emphasis on defensive policies is also evident when support is broken down by industry (table

17. For an account of Swedish industrial policies, see Kjell Lundmark, "Welfare State and Employment Policy: Sweden," in Kenneth Dyson and Stephen Wilks, eds., *Industrial Crisis* (New York: St. Martin's Press, 1983), pp. 220–44; and Gunnar Eliasson and Bengt-Christer Ysander, "Sweden: Problems of Maintaining Efficiency under Political Pressure," in Brian Hindley, ed., *State Investment Companies in Western Europe,* (London: Macmillan; New York: St. Martin's Press, 1983), pp. 156–91.

18. LO Strukturutredningen, *Samordnad näringspolitik* (Stockholm: LO, 1961), p. 168, translated and quoted in Lundmark, "Welfare State and Employment Policy," p. 224.

Figure 3-3. *Swedish Government Support to Industry for Restructuring-Reduction versus Growth-Renewal, Fiscal Years 1975–84*

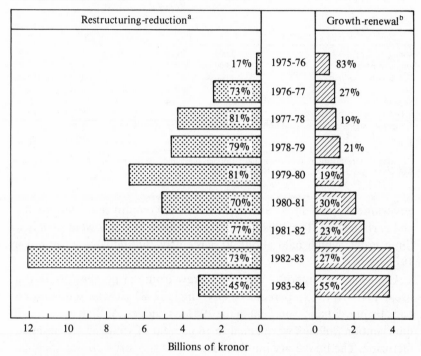

Billions of kronor

Source: Organization for Economic Cooperation and Development, *Economic Surveys, 1984–1985: Sweden* (Paris: OECD, 1985), diagram 16.
a. Temporary support plus sectoral support.
b. Includes support for R&D, regional policy, exports, and small businesses.

3-4). According to data of the Organization for Economic Cooperation and Development, the aid was remarkably concentrated and extremely expensive. Industries that accounted for 22.5 percent of manufacturing employment received 92.7 percent of the subsidies; and just two industries, steel and shipbuilding, representing only 8.8 percent of manufacturing employment, received 69 percent of the subsidies.[19] The magnitude of that support reached staggering proportions. Between 1977 and 1979 Swedish shipyards received subsidies equal to 120 percent of their total wage bill and 72.3 percent of value added. During this period the

19. See Bo Carlsson, "Industrial Subsidies in Sweden: Macro-Economic Effects and an International Comparison," *Journal of Industrial Economics,* vol. 32 (September 1983), pp. 11–12.

Table 3-4. *Swedish Government Support to Industry, Selected
Fiscal Years 1975–76 to 1981–82*
Billions of kronor, unless otherwise indicated

	Fiscal year			Total	Percent
Industry or policy objective	1975–76	1977–78	1981–82	1975–82	of total
Mining (LKAB)	0.000	0.000	2.148	4.210	13.8
Pulp and paper	0.000	0.039	0.300	1.505	4.9
Textiles and clothing	0.000	0.172	0.006	0.315	1.0
Steel	0.000	1.720	0.684	5.599	18.3
Shipbuilding	0.016	1.364	4.569	15.274	49.9
Schemes for crisis-ridden firms	0.000	0.247	0.027	0.472	1.5
Temporary support to individual firms	0.132	0.558	0.595	3.237	10.6
Total	0.148	4.101	8.329	30.611	100.0

Source: Organization for Economic Cooperation and Development, *Economic Surveys 1984–1985: Sweden* (Paris: OECD, 1985), table D4.

government spent about Skr 282,000 for each employee in shipbuilding and carbon steel. The subsidies in forest-based industry went mainly to three firms, which paid about 40 percent of the industry wage bill in 1977–79.[20]

Government support to industry grew from 0.3 percent of GNP in fiscal 1975–76 to 2.8 percent of GNP in 1982–83. It was suddenly cut back by more than 50 percent in the 1983–84 budget. At their peak, these intervention policies were equal to 16 percent of value added in manufacturing. The budgetary implications of this support were significant—between 1975 and 1982 the net costs of government support to industry averaged 20 percent of the budget deficit and 3.6 percent of the national budget.[21]

What accounted for the major reorientation of policy, especially between 1976 and 1983 when it was vastly expanded in scope and redirected in objective? One explanation might be that structural change in Swedish industry was much greater after 1973. To examine this question, we computed a simple index of structural shifts in Swedish industry, as measured by changes in the distribution of employment (see table 3-5). Surprisingly, shifts among industries within manufacturing were no greater after 1973 than in the previous decade.[22]

20. Ibid., p. 12.
21. Ministry of Industry, *Swedish Industry and Industrial Policy, 1985* (Stockholm, 1985), p. 16.
22. Indeed, the output measure suggests 28 percent less structural change in the 1973–82 period. Similarly, the structural change in U.S. manufacturing was no greater

Table 3-5. *Structural Change in Swedish Employment,*
1963–73 and 1973–83[a]

Source of employment	Structural change index
Manufacturing industries	
1963–73	8.44
1973–83	8.30
Nonmanufacturing industries	
1963–73	10.04
1973–83	6.95
All industries	
1963–73	9.49
1973–83	8.34

Sources: *National Accounts,* appendix 5; and authors' calculations.
a. The index is a summation of the absolute changes in each industry's share of total employment in the business sector, between 1963 and 1973, and between 1973 and 1983. $I = 100 \times 0.5 \, \Sigma_i \mid a_i1 - a_i2 \mid$, where a_i1 and a_i2 are the shares of sector i in periods 1 and 2. Employment is measured in millions of hours worked by entrepreneurs and employees, and the degree of industry detail is the maximum provided in the national accounts: nineteen industries in manufacturing and sixteen in nonmanufacturing.

A second hypothesis is that structural change was harder to accomplish after 1973 because it entailed greater dislocation and employment reduction. Yet the data also fail to confirm this hypothesis. Hours worked in manufacturing declined by similar amounts in the two periods, 17 percent between 1963 and 1973 and 21 percent between 1973 and 1983. For the total business sector, the rate of decline was actually slower after 1973, 9 percent versus 17 percent.

Finally, it might be argued there was a *need* for greater structural change after 1973, but the "inflexible" Swedish economy could not adjust rapidly enough. An international comparison, however, does not support the contention that the Swedish economy is incapable of change. In table 3-6 we show the index of structural change after 1973 for the manufacturing sectors of Sweden, Germany, the United States, and Japan. The latter two economies are widely viewed as largely free of the rigidities that inhibit change in Europe. Yet on the basis of both employment and output, the pace of resource reallocation in Sweden was as rapid as in the "flexible" economies.

Instead, to explain the industrial policies of the 1970s, one has to consider the interaction of political forces and the nature of the industries adversely affected.

before and after 1973. See Robert Z. Lawrence, *Can America Compete?* (Brookings, 1984), p. 52.

Table 3-6. *Comparison of Structural Change in Swedish, U.S., Japanese, and West German Manufacturing, 1973–82*[a]

Country	Value added	Employment
Sweden	7.67	7.08
United States[b]	6.70	5.38
Japan	8.79	5.81
West Germany	8.13	n.a.

Sources: United Nations, *Industrial Statistics Yearbook, 1983*, vol. 1: *General Industrial Statistics* (New York: UN, 1985), and *Yearbook of Industrial Statistics, 1978*, vol. 1: *General Industrial Statistics* (New York: UN, 1980); and authors' calculations.

a. The index is given by $I = 100 \times 0.5 \sum_i | a_i1 - a_i2 |$, where a_i1 and a_i2 are the shares of sector i in periods 1 and 2, respectively. The manufacturing sector is composed of twenty-eight three-digit sectors, based on sector categories according to the United Nations. Data for Germany were slightly more aggregated.

b. Figures for 1981.

In the 1970s several of the troubled industries were large, capital-intensive sectors in which high-wage, highly unionized workers were employed in large plants, often in relatively isolated regions. Worker dislocation in these industries was far more politically salient than the earlier shifts, which were more widely diffused among small production units. In the 1960s, for example, about 65 percent of the job losses came in sectors where establishments had fewer employees than the manufacturing average; in the 1970s these small establishments accounted for only about 45 percent of job losses.[23] The highly politicized nature of the policymaking in this area was reflected in the use of the Riksdag, or Parliament, rather than the traditional industrial policy agencies, to implement programs.

In large measure the industrial policies of the 1970s failed as an effort to thwart market forces. Because they were so narrowly focused, the policies did not greatly affect resource allocation. And over the medium term, the subsidies were unable to prevent large declines in employment in their targeted sectors. Their positive achievements lay rather in making change more socially acceptable by aiding and compensating those who were dislocated. By 1984, hours worked in shipyards and basic metals were 58.3 and 32.8 percent, respectively, below their 1973 levels.

23. These statements refer to the average number of employees per establishment in 1983, as reported in *Statistical Abstract of Sweden, 1986*, pp. 96–98. Sectors in which job losses increased after 1973 included shipbuilding (average establishment size of 194 in 1983), basic metals (average size 321), fabricated metals and nonelectric machinery (96), and rubber (109).

Ultimately, the budgetary costs of the subsidies forced their abandonment.

International Comparisons of Structural Change

Using the United States as a benchmark, Swedish industrial composition in 1973 was not particularly biased toward slow-growth sectors.
Between 1973 and 1984, for example, U.S. industrial production increased 31.6 percent. If the components of U.S. industrial production
had grown at the same rates, but initially been weighted according to
their shares in Swedish manufacturing, value added in 1973 (the total
growth) would have been 30.0 percent.

While the quantity of structural change in Swedish industries may
have been similar to that in the United States and Japan, what of the
quality? To what degree is the industrial labor force moving into the
high-technology industries of the future? To analyze this aspect of the
structural shifts within Swedish manufacturing, we have grouped the
data on employment and output of principal industries into four categories: high-technology, resource-intensive, basic industries, and transport equipment.[24] The results for Sweden, the United States, and Japan
are reported in table 3-7.

The composition of Swedish industrial employment has shifted dramatically. Although absolute employment declined in each main category of industry after 1973, the declines were largest in basic industries
(20 percent) and smallest in the high-technology sectors (4.2 percent).[25]
In 1973, 41 percent of Swedish industrial workers were employed in
high-technology industries and transportation equipment; by 1982, this
proportion had grown to 46 percent.[26]

24. While we have followed the traditional classification schemes of isolating high-
technology sectors, we report automobiles separately since, judged by the share of
research and development in Swedish value added in autos, they fall into the high-
technology group.

25. UN, *Industrial Statistics Yearbook, 1983,* vol. 1: *General Industrial Statistics.*
Between 1973 and 1983, employment fell sharply in shipbuilding (down 50 percent);
textiles and apparel (down 49 percent); rubber (down 39 percent); stone, clay, and glass
(down 30 percent); wood products (down 24 percent); and iron and steel (down 27
percent). In absolute numbers the largest declines were in wood products (down 22,100),
textiles and apparel (down 36,700); nonelectric machinery (down 19,500); shipbuilding
(down 17,400); iron and steel (down 15,000); and fabricated metals (down 13,800).

26. Judged by their 1983 ratio of R&D to value added, industries with above-average
R&D spending are pharmaceuticals (36.5 percent); instruments (22.5); electronics (22.4);
other transportation (19.4); chemicals (9.9); and machinery (9.6). *Statistical Abstract of
Sweden, 1986,* p. 371.

THE SWEDISH ECONOMY

Table 3-7. *Changes in Output and Employment Shares in Swedish,*
U.S., and Japanese Manufacturing, by Category of Industry,
1973 and 1982

	Share of value added			Share of employment		
Category of industry and year	Sweden	United States[a]	Japan	Sweden	United States[a]	Japan
High-technology industries[b]						
1973	27.60	34.35	34.92	28.75	30.36	32.42
1982	31.75	39.02	38.81	31.34	34.36	34.89
Percent change in share	15.04	13.60	11.14	9.00	13.80	7.62
Resource-intensive industries[c]						
1973	28.97	20.78	19.16	24.13	17.95	19.76
1982	28.04	21.08	18.50	24.52	17.22	19.87
Percent change in share	−3.2	1.44	−3.44	1.62	−4.07	0.56
Basic industries[d]						
1973	30.92	32.37	36.25	34.48	40.85	39.31
1982	26.93	29.37	32.43	29.75	38.46	36.57
Percent change in share	−12.9	−9.27	−10.54	−13.72	−5.85	−6.97
Transport equipment[e]						
1973	12.52	12.50	9.67	12.64	10.85	8.51
1982	13.28	10.54	10.27	14.43	9.97	8.67
Percent change in share	6.07	−15.68	6.20	14.16	−8.11	1.88

Sources: See table 3-6.

a. Figures for 1981 instead of 1982.

b. Industrial chemicals; other chemicals; plastic products; machinery; electrical machinery; and professional goods.

c. Food products; beverages; tobacco; leather products; wood products; paper and paper products; petroleum refineries; petroleum and coal products; pottery and chnia; nonferrous metal products.

d. Textiles; wearing apparel; furniture and fixtures; printing and publishing; rubber products; glass products; nonmetal products; iron and steel; metal products; and other.

e. Shipbuilding and repair; and motor vehicles.

The shifts in the composition of output are even greater, reflecting the relatively more rapid increase in output per employee in the high-technology sectors. The share of output by high-technology industries increased from 27.6 to 31.8 percent, while the share of basic industries declined from 30.9 to 26.9 percent.[27] The share of output devoted to resource-intensive and transport products remained fairly constant.

As shown in table 3-7, Sweden has maintained higher concentrations

27. These aggregate numbers understate the shift toward technology in Swedish industry. Increasingly, even so-called basic sectors are using more technology-intensive production methods. For example, Swedish industry has become a world leader in the use of robots for computer-aided manufacturing. According to the OECD, the use of robots per 10,000 workers rose from 1.3 in 1974 to 29.9 in 1981 (for Japan the figures are 1.9 and 13.9; for the United States, 0.8 and 4.0). OECD, *Economic Surveys, 1984-1985: Sweden,* p. 41.

of employment in transport equipment and natural-resource-based industries than either Japan or the United States throughout the period. Between 1973 and 1981, however, Sweden shifted its labor force into high technology more rapidly than Japan did, but somewhat more slowly than the United States. If transport equipment is considered a high-technology sector (which it is for Sweden), the Swedish performance looks even better. Under this definition, in 1973 high-technology industries held a similar share of the labor force in Sweden (41.4 percent), the United States (41.2 percent), and Japan (40.9 percent); by 1982 the share was largest in Sweden, 45.8 percent, versus 44.3 percent in the United States (1981 figure), and 43.6 percent in Japan.

At the same time, Sweden has been somewhat more successful than either the United States or Japan in moving out of basic industries—the employment share in basic industries has fallen relatively more in Sweden than in either the United States or Japan.[28]

In some specific high-technology industries, however, Sweden has done less well. For example, the share of manufacturing employment in the rapidly growing area of information technology—in particular, office computing machinery, electrical machinery, and professional goods—is low compared with other countries, and it has grown less rapidly than in the United States and Japan.[29]

The Role of Research and Development

As Swedish manufacturing as a whole shifts toward high-technology industries, expenditures on research and development are rapidly increasing. Although overall employment in mining and manufacturing fell by 12.4 percent between 1973 and 1983, during the same period the number of workyears expended on R&D increased from 19,300 to 25,400.[30] In 1973 Sweden devoted 1.6 percent of its gross domestic product to R&D, while the United States devoted 2.3 percent; in 1985

28. It is ironic that the relatively rapid reallocation of employment and output across Swedish industry may have been aided by distortions in the wage structure that were in turn a reflection of the solidaristic wage policy. See Harry Flam, "Equal Pay for Unequal Work," University of Stockholm, Institute for International Economic Studies, seminar paper 292, December 1985.

29. Robert Z. Lawrence, "The Employment Effects of the New Information Technologies: An Optimistic View," Brookings Discussion Papers in International Economics 20 (Brookings, 1984).

30. *Statistical Abstract of Sweden, 1986,* p. 370.

78   THE SWEDISH ECONOMY

both nations devoted about 2.6 percent of GDP to such expenditures.[31]
In 1983 R&D spending within mining and manufacturing in the two
countries was also similar—about 9 percent of value added.[32]

Swedish R&D spending is highly concentrated in large firms. Ninety-
five percent of spending occurs in those with more than 500 employees,
with the ten largest accounting for two-thirds of all R&D.[33]

Just as government industrial policies aided declining sectors but
ultimately did not greatly affect their size, government policies have had
a complementary but small direct role in stimulating the growth of R&D
spending. Although Sweden has a broad array of programs to promote
R&D, government funds for this purpose are primarily spent in the
higher-education sector. In 1983, while accounting for 39.5 percent of
total national R&D financing, the government contributed only 10.4
percent of the cost of research performed by business.[34]

The Influence of Trade on High Technology

Table 3-8 reports the ratio of exports to imports in four categories of
Swedish manufactured goods trade from 1973 to 1983. Sweden's comparative advantage in high-technology manufacturing does not appear
to have increased. While the ratio of total exports to total imports rose
from 1.19 to 1.26 between 1973 and 1983, the ratio of high-technology
exports to imports remained constant. Measured in current dollars, the
trade balance in high-technology products was almost zero in 1973, 1980,
and 1983. Although Sweden has increased its net exports of high-
technology goods in medicinal products, power-generating equipment,
and telecommunications equipment, these increases have been offset by
declines in office machines and other electrical machinery. Thus in the
aggregate, high technology's expanding share of total manufacturing
output must be attributable to growth in domestic demand.[35]

The switch of domestic demand toward high-technology products is

31. Ibid., p. 369; and U.S. Bureau of the Census, *Statistical Abstract of the United
States, 1986* (Washington, D.C.: Government Printing Office, 1986), table 994, p. 577.

32. *Statistical Abstract of Sweden, 1986*, p. 371; *Statistical Abstract of the United
States, 1986*, p. 580; and IMF, *International Financial Statistics, 1985 Yearbook*, pp.
646–47.

33. OECD, *Economic Surveys, 1984-1985: Sweden*, p. 42.

34. *Statistical Abstract of Sweden, 1986*, p. 369.

35. The positive impact of trade on Swedish manufacturing has thus occurred
primarily in the automotive and natural-resource parts of manufacturing—particularly
since 1980.

Table 3-8. *Composition of Swedish Manufactured Exports and Imports, by Category of Industry, 1973, 1980, 1983*
Percent of category total unless otherwise indicated

Category of industry	1973	1980	1983
		Exports	
High-technology	38.2	40.8	40.8
Resource-intensive	15.5	16.4	16.3
Basic	24.7	25.8	22.4
Transport equipment	21.5	17.1	20.5
Total value of exports (billions of Skr)	40.3	104.3	164.6
		Imports	
High-technology	44.8	47.7	51.6
Resource-intensive	7.3	7.2	6.3
Basic	34.4	34.5	30.4
Transport equipment	13.5	10.6	11.7
Total value of imports (billions of Skr)	33.9	90.1	130.5
	Trade balance (billions of Skr)		
High-technology	0.2	−0.4	−0.1
Resource-intensive	3.8	10.6	18.5
Basic	−1.7	−4.2	−2.7
Transport equipment	4.1	8.2	18.4
Total	6.4	14.2	34.1
		Export-import ratio	
High-technology	1.014	0.990	0.997
Resource-intensive	2.524	2.637	3.263
Basic	0.854	0.866	0.929
Transport equipment	1.893	1.867	2.210
Total	1.189	1.158	1.261

Sources: UN, *Yearbook of International Trade Statistics*, vol. 1: *Trade by Country*, 1975 and 1983 issues. See table 3-7 for category definitions.

to be expected in an economy with comparatively slow overall growth. Basic commodities for which the market is more or less saturated depend on increased income for higher sales. Demand for basic products also tends to be more sensitive to price competition than demand for novel products is, and Swedish firms have faced intense competitive pressures since 1973. By contrast, novel products are able to penetrate the market by displacing other products even when income is fairly constant. In addition, the shift toward the services sector moves demand away from heavy industrial products and away from basic commodities associated with construction.

Swedish domestic demand for products based on natural resources has also grown slowly. But because the devaluations of the early 1980s restored profitability in these sectors, although they accounted for only

16.3 percent of exports in 1983, they contributed more than half the overall surplus in manufactured goods trade.[36]

Nonmanufacturing: The Real Source of Sclerosis

While structural change within Swedish manufacturing was about the same in 1973–83 as it was in the previous decade, the nonmanufacturing sectors displayed less change in 1973–83 than earlier. And whereas between 1963 and 1973 structural change within nonmanufacturing industries was more rapid than in manufacturing, after 1973 it was much slower. This pattern of slower change within the nonmanufacturing parts of the private sector stands in sharp contrast to the experience of the United States, where the index of change in structural employment within services showed a 35 percent increase in 1973–83 over 1963–73.[37]

Although the structures of Swedish and U.S. manufacturing are similar, during the past ten years the structures of the rest of their economies have become increasingly different. As shown in table 3-9, both Sweden and the United States shifted out of goods production between 1973 and 1983. But Swedish employment moved into the public sector—the share of employment in private services actually fell slightly— while in the United States private services were the major source of employment growth. In 1983, private services accounted for only 23.4 percent of Swedish employment, compared with 40.2 percent in the United States. Especially striking were Swedish-U.S. differences in shares of employment in retail and wholesale trade (11.6 percent versus 21.6 percent), finance (1.5 versus 2.8), insurance (0.5 versus 1.8), and real estate and business services (3.7 versus 6.6).[38]

We have described how the Swedish policy of deliberately encour- aging structural change in the 1960s was transformed into one designed to stall such changes in the 1970s. However, the actual rate of resource reallocation within Swedish manufacturing, as measured by shifts in the distribution of labor and output among industries, was similar in the two periods. The amount of structural change within Swedish manufacturing also matched that in the United States and Japan, and Sweden moved

36. UN, *International Trade Statistics Yearbook, 1983*, vol. 1: *Trade by Country*, pp. 876–78.
37. Authors' calculations based on data from U.S. Department of Labor, *Monthly Labor Review*, various issues, and *Employment and Training Report of the President, 1982*, p. 239.
38. OECD, *National Accounts, 1971–1983*, vol. 2: *Detailed Tables*, pp. 50, 454.

Table 3-9. *Swedish and U.S. Employment Structures, 1973-83*
Percent

	1983 shares		Share change, 1973-83		Employment growth, 1973-83	
Employment activity	Sweden	United States	Sweden	United States	Sweden	United States
Goods[a]	33.2	26.8	−8.4	−5.5	−14.7	−4.1
Private services[b]	23.4	40.2	−0.2	4.5	6.0	30.2
Social services[c]	43.4	33.0	8.6	1.0	33.3	19.2
Total	100.0	100.0	0	0	6.9	15.6

Source: Calculated from employment data in OECD, *National Accounts, 1971-1983*, vol. 2: *Detailed Tables* (Paris: OECD, 1985), pp. 50, 454.
a. Includes agriculture, mining, manufacturing, and construction.
b. Includes trade, finance, insurance, real estate, and business, personal, household, recreational, and cultural services.
c. Includes transport and communications, utilities, education, medical, and government services.

into the high-technology industries about as rapidly as either the United States or Japan. Accordingly, the allegations that subsidy policies stifled change within manufacturing in the 1970s appear to be false. Change has been less rapid in the nonmanufacturing parts of the Swedish private sector, however.

Industrial Policies: Lessons for the Future

In this section we discuss Swedish industrial policy toward declining and expanding sectors in manufacturing. Although government policy on manufacturing has recently shifted in the right direction, increasing government commitments to firms in manufacturing must be avoided, and the general environment for smaller business and the nonmanufacturing sectors must be improved by both demand and supply-side measures.

Declining Industries

Industrial policies in Sweden and the United States have relied on different instruments, but they have one striking feature in common: neither has shaped the long-term evolution of economic structure. In the United States the primary instrument of defensive industrial policy has been trade protection. Because the economy is relatively closed, however, trade has been less important as a source of structural change than other factors, such as demand shifts and new technologies. Thus despite receiving protection, industries in the United States have undergone considerable adjustment.[39] In addition, the U.S. government has by and large avoided assuming responsibility for protecting specific jobs and firms, leaving the connection between protection and particular jobs saved implicit.[40] The costs of trade protection are generally hidden, so that in the United States, quotas have proved difficult to remove.

In contrast, most troubled Swedish industries have been in the export sector (for example, steel, shipbuilding, and forest products), and trade protection has not been an attractive mechanism for aid.[41] The Swedish government has, in addition, assumed obligations for saving particular jobs and firms, hence the need for a more precise instrument such as subsidies. Direct subsidies do have the advantage that by and large their costs are more transparent than those of trade restrictions.[42] And eventually, the cost of thwarting market forces becomes so burdensome that subsidies must be abandoned. This has clearly been the Swedish experience.

Industrial policy in the late 1970s placed a heavy emphasis on saving firms that would otherwise have gone bankrupt. Concerned about the unemployment impact of large closures, the Swedish government provided massive and concentrated support to a few firms. This strategy appears, particularly in retrospect, to have involved several errors. One was the source of the trouble. Many of the problems faced by troubled Swedish industries stemmed from macroeconomic imbalances in the economy, that is, the inappropriate configuration of saving and investment, and wages and profits. The use of subsidies for particular firms did not deal with the source of their problems. Indeed, subsidies may have exacerbated them: first by reducing the incentives for necessary wage adjustments, and second by inflicting a heavy cost on the budget

39. See, for example, Gary Clyde Hufbauer, Diane T. Berliner, and Kimberly Ann Elliott, *Trade Protection in the United States: Thirty-one Case Studies* (Washington, D.C.: Institute for International Economics, 1986).

40. The experiences with Chrysler and Lockheed are the exceptions. See Martin Edmonds, "Market Ideology and Corporate Power: The United States," in Dyson and Wilks, *Industrial Crisis*, pp. 67–101.

41. Textiles are the exception. See Carl Hamilton, "Swedish Trade Restrictions on Textiles and Clothing," *Skandinaviska Enskilda Banken Quarterly Review*, no. 4 (1984), pp. 104–11.

42. To be sure, there are many methods for hiding the true costs of subsidies—loan guarantees, for example.

deficit that in turn required more foreign borrowing and thus a stronger currency.

Another error was the government's equating of bankruptcy with the dissolution of all plants and unemployment of all workers. It therefore exhausted many resources in compensating owners for previous losses rather than taking the more appropriate approach of liquidating the companies through bankruptcy and reconstituting the viable components in new operations. And finally, the causes of injury were assumed to be transitory when in fact they were permanent.

In theory, selective subsidies to declining industries, if they are carefully designed, can perform better than a market in which wages adjust too slowly.[43] But the short-run benefits from utilizing economic resources more efficiently must be weighed against the long-term costs of resource misallocation. The longer such subsidies persist, and the larger they are, the more likely it is that the benefits from intervention will be less than the costs of market failure associated with laissez-faire. Because the government has typically been drawn to subsidizing large capital-intensive plants without first making creditors liquidate their claims, subsidies have been extremely expensive for each job saved.[44]

The government has now moved away from a defensive aid policy, and it has dramatically reduced its financial support for lame-duck sectors. A hands-off policy toward the closing of the Uddevalla shipyard and toward the bankruptcies of Salens, Sweden's largest shipowner, and of Consafes, a company involved in offshore construction, shows that the government is serious about changing course.

Nonetheless, a real test of its resolve will not come until the next recession. In the meantime, the government ought to prepare defenses against future entanglements. This requires, as a first step, making clear

43. Harry Flam, Torsten Persson, and Lars E. O. Svensson, "Optimal Subsidies to Declining Industries: Efficiency and Equity Considerations," *Journal of Public Economics,* vol. 22 (December 1983), pp. 327–45. See also Peter A. Diamond, "Protection, Trade Adjustment Assistance, and Income Distribution," in Jagdish N. Bhagwati, ed., *Import Competition and Response* (University of Chicago Press, 1982), pp. 123–45; and Harvey E. Lapan, "International Trade, Factor Market Distortions, and the Optimal Dynamic Subsidy," *American Economic Review,* vol. 66 (June 1976), pp. 335–46.

44. In his paper, which dramatically documents the size and waste in such subsidies, Carlsson nonetheless concludes, using simulations with the MOSES micro-macro model, that subsidies raise output over the long run relative to laissez-faire. Because the simulations fail to incorporate the impact of such subsidies on exchange rates, interest rates, wage bargaining incentives, and employment in sectors other than manufacturing, we remain skeptical of the policy implications of this approach. See Carlsson, "Industrial Subsidies in Sweden."

that subsidies to firms are an inappropriate policy tool that has been shown to be more inefficient in practice than relying on market forces. Precedents for allowing the bankruptcy of large firms must be established.

Second, the government must continue efforts to divest itself of state-held companies to reduce future pressures to expand subsidies. The government has direct ownership in a group of companies that accounted for only 8 percent of Swedish industrial employment but was responsible for about half the losses in Swedish industry in 1980–82.[45] The average return of these companies in 1984 was just 60 percent that of industry as a whole.[46] They occupy particularly low rankings in terms of their financial strength as evaluated by the Ministry of Industry.[47] Clearly, while the profitability of state-held companies has improved somewhat, they remain vulnerable to an economic downturn.

It is sometimes argued that government-owned firms can be more responsive to social concerns than their private counterparts. The state holding company, Statsföretag, has continually been torn between the conflicting objectives of its mandate: on the one hand, to achieve maximum expansion, subject to a minimum profitability constraint, and on the other hand, to fulfill a series of social objectives such as improving industrial structure, making the regional distribution of job opportunities more acceptable, and so forth.

The mixing of commercial and social objectives is likely, however, to result in poor performance on both counts. Industrial policy in France, where the objectives of national defense and prestige have been mingled with that of commercial success, appears to have been much less successful than in either the United States, where policy has emphasized the defense objective, or in Japan, where the goal has been commercial.[48] Accordingly, it would seem wise to confine industrial policy to correcting for market failures, providing public goods, and controlling monopolies, and to reject programs that try to supplant market forces. The emphasis on aiding displaced workers rather than preventing the displacement should continue.

---

45. Ministry of Industry, *Swedish Industry and Industrial Policy, 1985*, p. 68.

46. Ibid., p. 91. They had a nominal return on book values of 14 percent, compared with an estimate of 23 percent for total industry.

47. Ibid., p. 62. Eliasson and Ysander point out that this difference is largely due to the concentration of state-owned firms in crisis industries. See Eliasson and Ysander, "Problems of Maintaining Efficiency under Political Pressure."

48. See, for example, Richard R. Nelson, *High-Technology Policies: A Five-Nation Comparison* (Washington, D.C.: American Enterprise Institute, 1984).

Sunrise Industries

Recently, the emphasis of Swedish industrial policy has shifted. Financial aid has moved toward support for R&D, regional development, exports, and small businesses. The government also has established several programs to encourage industrial evolution by providing incentives for the diffusion of flexible manufacturing systems and other forms of advanced technology.

It seems appropriate that the government has concentrated on influencing the broad environment for industrial development and on programs to improve knowledge and technology, rather than investing heavily in specific ventures.[49] According to Eliasson and Ysander, past ventures in computers and nuclear technology in which the state took half interests (such as Data-Saab, Udd-Comb, and Asea-Atom) "cannot be judged as successful."[50]

Moreover, large firms do not require government assistance. The output, exports, and profits of Swedish industry seem increasingly concentrated in large firms.[51] Large Swedish firms have captured greater shares of the home market, while Swedish multinationals have retained their shares in global markets. The farther away from the home market (that is, the more important the role for large firms), the better Swedish firms appear to do.

The Swedish economy has a group of large firms (mostly in engineering) with great expertise, deep pockets, and a global perspective for whom government programs are unlikely to make more than a marginal difference. They are winners. Their performance depends to a much greater extent on the health of the economy as a whole than on particular subsidy programs. Given their dependence on trade, they have dramatically improved their market positions as a result of the overall policies since 1982.

Small Firms

By contrast, the weakness in the Swedish economy appears to lie in the fairly poor performance of small firms—an area in which the Swedish

49. Our philosophy is similar to that advocated in Assar Lindbeck, "Industrial Policy as an Issue in the Economic Environment," *World Economy*, vol. 4 (December 1981), pp. 391–405.

50. Eliasson and Ysander, "Problems of Maintaining Efficiency under Political Pressure," p. 162.

51. See, for example, Lars Oxelheim, "The Largest Nordic Manufacturing Companies," in Danish Economic Council and others, *Economic Growth in a Nordic Perspective*, pp. 192–95.

experience is opposite that of the United States. The Ministry of Industry reports that, as groups, small and medium-sized companies occupy the lowest ranks in terms of financial strength, together with state-owned companies and steel and minerals.[52]

Small firms have been particularly hurt by the evolution of Swedish demand patterns. Although many Swedes blame the erosion of the industrial sector on problems in international trade, this shrinkage stems principally from the pattern of domestic demand—the shift toward government consumption. Small firms are greatly dependent on the domestic market—in Sweden small firms account for a third of industrial employment but only 5 percent of direct exports.[53]

Small firms are best fostered by an environment that encourages entrepreneurship; specific breaks or subsidies are likely to have small marginal effects. It is a reasonable hypothesis that the difficulties of small firms in Sweden stem from the encompassing nature of the country's regulations and the efficacy of its government in enforcing them. By comparison, in Italy, another heavily regulated economy, the government's inability to police small firms seems to foster entrepreneurship. Small Swedish firms may also suffer, relative to large firms, from an inability to take full advantage of the Swedish tax system.

Other Recommendations

Instead of targeting "winners," policy measures might more appropriately try to stimulate competitive pressures and innovation throughout the economy.

To date, the focus of most structural policies toward product markets in Sweden has been the goods-producing sector. This emphasis seems misplaced; instead, Swedish policy should pay much more attention to services. If there is evidence of economic sclerosis in Sweden, it would appear to lie not in manufacturing but in the rest of the economy. Swedish sectors exposed to international competition have shown the greatest capacity for structural adjustment. That same environment should be re-created, as far as possible, in the domestic sector.

52. The rankings according to financial strength in 1983 were (1) chemicals and pharmaceuticals, (2) engineering firms, (3) foreign-owned firms, (4) large, family-owned firms, (5) forest enterprises, (6) other listed companies, (7) cooperative companies, (8) small, family-owned firms, (9) state-owned companies, (10) medium-sized, family-owned firms, (11) steel and minerals. Ministry of Industry, *Swedish Industry and Industrial Policy, 1985*, p. 62.
53. They are more important as suppliers of components to exporters.

Summary and Conclusions

Sweden's lapse into debtor nation status, and the decline in its terms of trade after 1973 caused by higher oil prices, required real devaluation to restore balance in the current account. This was achieved mainly by boosting the balance of trade in manufactured products. Over the medium term, therefore, trade made a positive contribution to manufacturing production. Responsibility for the manufacturing sector's decline as a percentage of the total Swedish economy lies with shifts in the composition of domestic, not international, demand. In particular, the rise in government services has displaced goods consumption.

Manufactured trade performance is well explained when price-taking and price-setting behavior are both modeled. The declining share of Swedish manufactured products in world trade can be explained by profitability, relative prices, and capacity utilization variables. In addition, the expansion of the government in GDP appears to have negatively affected the trade balance.

The sources of change in the trade balance have also shifted dramatically since 1973. Between 1973 and 1978 sluggish growth in the Swedish economy offset an erosion caused by the loss of price competitiveness and profitability and the expansion of the government sector. Between 1978 and 1984, however, improvements in competitiveness offset a decline in the trade balance induced by relatively rapid domestic growth.

Unlike several studies conducted in Sweden, we do not find that the Swedish manufacturing trade balance is subject to decline. The terms of trade losses during the last decade can be ascribed instead to the need to offset growing international indebtedness and higher oil prices.

Similarly, we are more optimistic than many Swedish commentators about the capacity of manufacturing to adapt to changing circumstances. Between 1973 and 1983 the amount of structural change in Swedish manufacturing employment was similar to that in the previous decade. The overall decline in manufacturing employment was also about the same in both decades. Furthermore, the shifts in the allocation of output and employment within manufacturing exceeded those in the United States and Japan. And Sweden has also been as successful in redistributing employment from basic to high-technology industries: by 1983 the share of manufacturing in high technology in Sweden was similar to that in the United States, as was the percentage of value added spent on research and development.

These changes occurred despite an industrial policy that was primarily defensive in nature. Although costly, the industrial policy programs were heavily concentrated in a few industries and did not affect most manufacturing firms. The dramatic shift in the 1970s to defensive strategies can be explained by the interaction of political forces and the nature of the industries adversely affected. Dislocation in large firms with large plants in isolated areas is more politically salient than similar dislocation in small firms that are even more widely dispersed.

At the outset of chapter 2, we contrasted two alternative explanations for the poor performance of the Swedish economy in the 1970s. The first emphasized macroeconomic imbalances in saving, investment, and the distribution of income. The second pointed to microeconomic rigidities resulting from a distorted wage structure, taxes, and excessive government intervention. We find some support for each of these interpretations—in particular, the microeconomic performance of the nontraded sector of the Swedish economy appears poor. On balance, however, priority for future policy lies in correcting the massive imbalances that developed in the macroeconomic economy in the 1970s. In that regard, major progress has been made in the 1980s.

Comments by Lars Werin

If one should speak of a special tendency in chapters 2 and 3, it is that traditional macroeconomic factors, especially those common to all countries, should be stressed more than is usually done in attempts to explain Sweden's poor performance, and microeconomic factors stressed less, in particular those consisting of rigidities in the production structure, but maybe also factors of taxation and wage formation. It is of course hard to draw clear and strict boundaries between macroeconomic and microeconomic explanations, and in microeconomics between rigidities and imbalances in the production structure, and tax and wage incentives. But it is a useful general classification, and I will stick to it.

The Bosworth-Lawrence thesis is cautiously presented, but still I feel a need to reemphasize the structural factors. I will only discuss imbalances of the production structure, not because they should be considered more important than distortion of incentives from taxes, transfers, and

wages, but only because the latter distortions are analyzed more extensively in other chapters and are therefore better discussed in connection
with them, while the production and trade structure in general is treated
mainly in these chapters.

In their analysis of the production and trade structure Bosworth and
Lawrence concentrate on manufacturing. It is desirable and even necessary to extend the perspective to the total production structure. But I
will start by extending the international and historical perspectives.

As for the international perspective, Bosworth and Lawrence mainly
compare Sweden and the United States. In itself this is a natural and
interesting thing to do because the two countries display similar problems
in some important respects. But slow growth has become perhaps the
key problem for Sweden, and the Swedish growth performance since
the middle of the 1970s has been clearly worse not only than that of the
United States but than that of practically all other members of the
Organization for Economic Cooperation and Development. New figures
show that Sweden will probably continue to lag this year and the next.
So even if the development since 1982 has been much more positive than
in 1975–82, Sweden should have been able to grow faster after two big
devaluations, and in a favorable world environment. In principle I agree
with Bosworth and Lawrence's point that because development of all
OECD countries has been parallel, we should be generally skeptical of
country-specific explanations. But Sweden is so much of an outlier that
we should not be too afraid of looking for such explanations.

The historical perspective runs into the structural. Generally this
makes me somewhat dubious about Bosworth and Lawrence's dominant
method of using 1973 as a more or less self-evident starting point of all
evils in Sweden, although admittedly this is the usual way of looking at
these things among Swedish economists as well. In my view 1973 is not
a perfect base year because the seeds of trouble were probably sown
earlier. A deficit on the current account appeared suddenly and unexpectedly as early as 1965 and proved difficult to get rid of. Although it
amounted to only about 1 percent of GDP—small compared to what was
to come later—the *Medium Term Survey* immediately sounded the alarm
bell. At the time, many economists found the alarm somewhat oversen-
sitive, but their concern has, of course, turned out to be a wise and
judicious assessment. It called forth the restrictive policies of the first
years of the 1970s, which led to a current account surplus in 1973. But
whether this result indicated the economy had once again been returned

to normal or whether the surplus was mainly a consequence of more restrictiveness in Sweden than abroad has never been satisfactorily determined—which is, of course, the fault of Swedish economists. Bosworth and Lawrence's analysis of this problem by means of an equation explaining the development of the manufacturing trade balance (see figure 3-1) points to 1973 as a year with somewhat stronger demand pressure abroad than in Sweden. But their analysis starts with 1971, and a longer time series is needed, at least for this particular problem.

If we now look at the years before 1973 and widen the structural perspective to cover not only the internal structure of manufacturing industry (for which Bosworth and Lawrence have some very interesting results to which I will return) but the production system as a whole, we find some interesting changes. Partly they had their counterparts in other countries, but they were more pronounced in Sweden.

First, there was a strong drawn-out boom in residential construction starting in the 1950s and reaching its peak in the late 1960s. This rather special time profile was only partly a result of macroeconomic forces and general movements of relative rates of return. It was mainly a political creation. Good comparative statistics are hard to put together, but it seems as if hardly any other country had a drawn-out boom of this kind; the United States certainly did not have it. This meant that a situation of strong demand lost much of its power in the late 1960s.

Second, and somewhat more speculatively, the automotive revolution, including a complete renewal of the road system, transport, movability, retail trade, and so forth, was somewhat more concentrated in time in Sweden than in most other countries. It started here in the early 1950s and was mainly completed by 1970. In saying this, I do not mean to be a stagnationist like Alvin Hansen but rather something of a Schumpeterian.

Third, and most important, the development of the Swedish production structure in the past two decades has been characterized by the rise in public production of services and the stagnating private production of services, at least outside of households. Looking at admittedly rather crude World Bank statistics, I find that private services in Sweden have a lower share of GDP than in practically any other country classified as an industrial market economy, and that Sweden's share has remained nearly unchanged during the past two decades, while it has grown in practically all the other countries. The major reason is that much service production in Sweden has not only been publicly financed but has also been reserved for production under public management to a higher extent than in most comparable countries. Has this holding back of private production had a negative indirect effect on growth of output and employment by diminishing the scope for entrepreneurial efforts? Theoretical argument and general observations strongly suggest such an effect, but it would of course be nice to see a strict empirical study. Lawrence and Bosworth in fact have some comments in this direction in chapter 3. The effect may be present as a part of the unspecified and rather mysterious crowding-out effect appearing in some of their equations.

So in addition to the first signs of a decline in competitiveness in the middle 1960s, certain other structural and to some extent country-specific components unfolded and contributed to lower growth in the 1970s. Thus the macroeconomic disturbances in the 1970s and the problems arising from taxation and wage formation during the 1970s and 1980s emerged in an environment that already contained structural disturbances.

Bosworth and Lawrence's analysis of structural problems is confined to manufacturing. Here they present some results that are both interesting and encouraging. They find that manufacturing output in Sweden has been as flexible and capable of change as that of the United States and Japan during the past dozen years and that the move out of basic industries into high technology has been at least as rapid.[1] Another result is of more doubtful value. Bosworth and Lawrence find that manufacturing was able to respond to negative external developments so efficiently that it generated trade surpluses in manufactured products. However, this response took place mainly via devaluations, which makes it less impressive. So the basic question remains whether Swedish manufacturing can adjust so as to generate stable trade surpluses at given exchange rates. Maybe Bosworth and Lawrence here softly prepare the readers for the proposal in chapter 4 that Sweden should adopt floating exchange rates.

To put the pieces together and add some new ones in a story told from the point of view of growth and composition of demand and output, I

1. Bosworth and Lawrence and I myself think in terms of traditional textbook trade-and-specialization theory based on easily defined industries and commodity groups. But perhaps this theory is less relevant today when value added has fallen to 32 percent of gross output on the average in Swedish manufacturing, and firms are growing more and more multinational. Clearly, the meaning of "industry" and the contents of imports and exports have changed dramatically.

arrive at the following, which is essentially the same story as Bosworth's and Lawrence's, although using a somewhat broader structural perspective:

—Growth-retarding factors that started to operate during the 1960s contributed to certain country-specific retarding factors already in force.

—Expectations kept perceived permanent incomes of both households and government high. Therefore both private and public consumption continued to rise.

—With given income levels and relative costs, households were confronted with a product mix containing too few goods and private services. This meant that demand spilled over into consumption goods with a high import content.

—The balance of trade in commodities other than oil was rather successfully adjusted by high adaptability in the manufacturing sector and by repeated devaluations.

The conclusion is that either the rate of growth has to be increased or the mix of goods and services produced has to be changed.

Comments by Per Magnus Wijkman

In their view of imbalances in the Swedish economy Bosworth and Lawrence claim that past macroeconomic policy choices rather than microeconomic or structural problems have caused Sweden's external and internal imbalances and therefore deserve the greater emphasis. They see these imbalances as caused largely by difficulties of adjusting to a collapse of economic growth. They argue that government encountered greater difficulty than private firms in adapting to change: the tradables sector remains competitive. They thus paint a stark picture of policy failure rather than of market failure. The implication is that Keynesian fine tuning can balance the Swedish economy. They find no need for supply-side (structural) policies.

This Gorbachevism—the doctrine that major improvements are possible without fundamental changes—should challenge any discussant. I shall concentrate on these challenges and bypass the many things I agree with.

The authors' key conclusion "suggests that Swedish manufacturing does not suffer from a decline in its competitiveness" and that the problems of external balances are caused by domestic rather than foreign factors. External imbalance arises mainly because the tradables sector is too small. And it is too small not because of noncompetitiveness but because of being crowded out by the expansion of government programs. Thus the authors conclude that a cutback in public spending is a sufficient policy option, and structural or micropolicies are superfluous.

By analyzing national accounting identities, the authors explain the reduction of the tradables sector's share of GDP by changes in domestic demand. I agree with this analysis and its stress on how an expanded public sector can crowd out other activities. However, I remain unconvinced by their evidence that the manufacturing sector is competitive. The authors interpret increased net exports of the manufacturing sector as testimony of that sector's competitiveness. I would accept that conclusion if the tradables sector had generated this level of net exports in the absence of policy measures. Instead, "competitiveness" appears to be the result of exceptional measures—five devaluations.

The authors dismiss Sweden's falling share of manufactured exports in world markets as evidence of deteriorating competitiveness. The negative trend that customarily appears in regressions of the Swedish market shares on relative export price disappears when the authors introduce three additional variables: the share of public expenditure in GNP, the level of capacity utilization, and the profit share. The last two are fairly traditional explanatory variables for competitiveness. The public-sector share is a novel variable. As a result of introducing it, the trend factor becomes insignificant. I think there are some problems of interpretation here.

The authors' regression does not determine causality. Is the expanding public sector crowding out the tradables sector, as the authors claim, or is a noncompetitive tradables sector attracting an expanded public sector? Some have argued that Swedish governments have yielded to pressures to use the public sector as an employer of last resort at given wage rates. Such a policy absorbs cyclical increases in unemployment into the public sector. Without a corresponding reduction of public-sector employment in boom periods, the policy will lead to the growth of the public sector. Furthermore, when the government acts as a residual employer, wages tend to respond less to competitive pressures in the tradables sector, making adjustments within that sector less likely.

I would like better proof that this correlation between the growth of government and the decline of the tradables sector is not nonsense. Any variable with a positive trend in it could have replaced time as an explanatory variable. Why not try the level of carbon dioxide in the atmosphere? Obviously because we lack good theoretical arguments for postulating a relationship between carbon dioxide and Sweden's market shares. But what are the theoretical arguments suggesting that an increase in the public sector will reduce Swedish market shares for manufactures? There is more here than meets the eye, and I feel it should be made explicit.

Finally, even if expansion of the public sector were the determining factor in reducing the tradables sector, expansion does this by reducing the sector's competitiveness. By bidding up wage rates, expansion of the public sector makes the tradables sector less able to retain factors of production. It makes little difference if the tradables sector becomes noncompetitive because of faster productivity growth abroad or increased government demand at home. In either case, there is a problem of maintaining competitiveness.

The authors' position that the public sector has not affected the competitiveness of the tradables sector but nevertheless should be reduced is ambiguous. If the public sector is expanding at the expense of the tradables sector without affecting its competitiveness, there is no need to reduce the size of the public sector—it reflects citizens' preferences. If an expanding public sector does affect the competitiveness of the tradables sector, we have a problem in competition. The crowding-out relationship between the public sector and the tradables sector is no doubt complex and deserves more attention. Has it become more costly to squeeze a given net export out of a smaller tradables sector because of reduced price elasticities or economies of scale?

A second major conclusion of Bosworth's and Lawrence's chapters is that structural rigidities do not significantly prevent the Swedish economy from making structural changes. This conclusion is based on measurements that suggest Sweden has changed the employment structure in its manufacturing sector at least as much as the United States and Japan, and at least as much after 1973 as before. Note in passing that the authors refer to structural change within manufacturing. Problems of shifting employment between public and private sectors, between services and goods, appear largely as problems of macroeconomic policy in the authors' presentation.

Now, does the structural change measured by the authors correspond to the need for structural change dictated by external imbalance? Horwitz has estimated, through an analysis of Sweden's share of world markets, that two-thirds of the registered fall in market shares for manufactures is caused by unfavorable commodity and country mix, leaving only one-third reflecting reduced competitiveness. If we are interested in the short-run competitiveness of Swedish industries, eliminating the negative effects of an unfavorable mix of commodities and countries is appropriate. If, however, we are interested in the long-run competitiveness of the country, it is less appropriate. External imbalance may well be caused by a failure to adjust to changes in the commodity and country composition of international trade. Structural rigidity implies precisely the inability to shift resources to serve growing markets—whether country markets or commodity markets.

Are large, closed economies like the United States and Japan appropriate norms for measuring structural change in Swedish manufacturing? Also, is 1983 an appropriate benchmark year?

Finally, the ability to change does not imply the absence of impediments to change. Impediments can be circumvented at a cost. The crucial question, therefore, is whether the cost of structural change is unnecessarily large. Regional and occupational mobility of labor in Sweden is stimulated by a broad range of government policies and is high compared with that in other countries. To the extent that rigidities are important, they probably consist of factors that prevent movements of labor and capital among firms. Thus the growth of conglomerates may in part be a response to government restrictions on interfirm movements. Conglomeration converts interfirm movements into intrafirm movements, and structural change is achieved, but at a cost.

Let me in conclusion mention some systemic aspects of the authors' approach. First, given that their analysis proceeds from national accounting identities, I am surprised that supply-side measures receive such scant attention. Balance-of-payments deficits can be cured not only by increasing public saving, as the authors argue, but also through increasing domestic production—that is, through growth. The authors assume that the root of the problem lies in the failure to choose the correct policy response to an exogenous collapse of growth. But could it not be the other way around? Could policies have contributed to the collapse? A number of structural factors may have reduced the economy's power to grow, which is precisely an ability to respond to external changes. These policy-induced structural or systemic factors may well be important also for solving short-run external imbalances.

A second surprise is the lack of microeconomic foundation for their macroeconomic analysis. I found it difficult to separate microeconomic and macroeconomic policy issues. Macroeconomic policy choices have microeconomic policy consequences. The taxes required to finance government expenditures distort wages and prices in markets. Clearly, the larger the public sector, the larger the wedges and the more acute the microeconomic problems. Is the macroeconomic or the microeconomic blade of the scissors doing the cutting? The authors' identification of the size of the budget as the culprit may be an oversimplification that reduces the number of options available to policymakers. Maybe it is not the amount of goods and services provided by the public sector that constitutes the problem but the way they are financed—through taxes rather than through user fees. It could be possible to provide the same volume of public services with fewer microeconomic distortions, and therefore less cost, if they were financed differently. Thus the size of the public sector is an issue only if its composition and funding is given; that is, only if one rules out the systemic issue.

Finally, have public expenditures increased simply as the result of errors of judgment on the part of well-intentioned ministers of finance? If so, it will be easy to correct now that Brookings has told the finance minister to reduce expenditures. But could it be that the public sector is too large because of systemic reasons? Is it characteristic of the Swedish model to provide services increasingly through the public sector, to charge citizens less than marginal costs for services and retain insufficient control over how much they consume, and to produce these services within government monopolies sheltered from competition? If so, then we should not be surprised to find that each citizen votes for a growing public sector and that the government must continually raise taxes to cover increasing unit costs of producing an increasing volume of services. It could be argued that those characteristics of the Swedish model *necessarily* generate a large public sector and that any finance minister who attempts to reduce the sector without changing these characteristics will be voted out of office. If so, the authors' policy recommendation to reduce the size of the public sector may be right, but surely implementing it would not be easy.

4

Economic Goals and the Policy Mix

BARRY P. BOSWORTH
and ROBERT Z. LAWRENCE

IN THE EARLY 1980s, the Swedish economy was in crisis. Growth had slowed to the point that the level of the nation's disposable income (adjusted for inflation) in 1981 and 1982 was below that of 1975. Inflation exceeded 10 percent annually. Unemployment was about 50 percent higher than in the early 1970s. Domestic investment was declining under the pressure of an intense cost squeeze that had driven down the profitability of business to extremely low levels. Combined spending at all levels of government had reached two-thirds of the nation's output; and the budget deficit of the central government had ballooned to more than 10 percent of national income, with much of the deficit reflecting the payment of subsidies to failing firms. A persistent current account deficit had swelled to 4.2 percent of the national income, and the foreign debt exceeded 20 percent of GDP.[1]

Previous chapters have documented these problems in greater detail. It is equally necessary, however, to recognize the extent to which the performance of the Swedish economy has turned around in the 1980s. Between 1982 and 1985 economic growth averaged 2.7 percent annually, slightly exceeding the average for Europe as a whole; the trade balance

1. For a pessimistic assessment of the Swedish economy at that time, see Eric Lundberg, "The Rise and Fall of the Swedish Economic Model," in Ralf Dahrendorf, ed., *Europe's Economy in Crisis* (New York: Holmes and Meier; and London: Weidenfeld and Nicolson, 1982), pp. 195–211.

moved into substantial surplus; and the rate of national saving and investment steadily increased as a share of domestic income.

The turnabout in economic performance reflects two major shifts in economic policy. First, the Swedish krona was devalued in 1981 and 1982 by a total of 24 percent against the currencies of its trading partners, sharply improving its competitive position in world markets and increasing exports. Second, the government has acted to reduce its financial deficit from 10.7 percent of net domestic product in 1982 to 6.4 percent in 1985.[2]

In providing the strong stimulus to the economy, the rise in net exports complemented efforts to reduce the budget deficit, offsetting what otherwise would have been a major shift toward fiscal restraint. Furthermore, the devaluation went a long way toward restoring the profitability of industry and thus incentives for new investment. By 1984 Sweden was able to finance a slowly rising rate of domestic investment entirely from domestic saving. While skeptics may point out that transitory factors dominated the early gains in reducing the budget deficit, a fundamental shift in fiscal policy is now evident, and much of it is reflected in a scaling back of government expenditures.

Although the Swedish economic situation has improved since 1982, several worrisome trends continue. First, the rate of cost inflation continues to exceed that of Sweden's trading partners. During 1984 and 1985, hourly earnings in Swedish manufacturing rose at an annual rate 2.2 percentage points above the average of the countries in the Organization for Economic Cooperation and Development (OECD). As shown in chapter 2, approximately one-third of the 24 percent gain in relative competitiveness supplied by the devaluations in 1981 and 1982 had been lost through excessive cost increases by the end of 1985. If that pattern is sustained, Sweden will find its competitiveness continuously eroding.[3]

Second, the recovery of investment spending since 1982 has been

2. Unless otherwise indicated, statistics cited in this chapter are authors' calculations based on Sveriges officiella statistik, *Nationalräkenskaper, 1970–1984* (Stockholm: Statistiska centralbyrån, 1985) [Official Statistics of Sweden, *National Accounts Annual Report, 1970–1984* (Stockholm: Statistics Sweden, 1985)]; and *Nationalräkenskaper, 1982–1985* (Stockholm, Statistics Sweden, March 1986). (Hereafter *National Accounts.*) The financial deficit includes the capital account items of general government.

3. The growth of hourly earnings in Swedish manufacturing did slow significantly during 1985—a 6.25 percent increase, compared with 3.75 percent in Germany, 3.0 percent in the United States, 3.25 percent in Japan, and 4.25 percent in the countries of the Organization for Economic Cooperation and Development as a whole. See *OECD Economic Outlook,* vol. 39 (Paris: OECD, 1986), p. 9, table 3.

fairly modest, despite a big improvement in profitability. One reason is that the high real interest rates required to defend the exchange rate have offset much of the incentive for new investment that should have followed from the rise in profitability of industry. In addition, business enterprises, caught between a fixed exchange rate and rising domestic costs, were subject to a profit squeeze during the late 1970s. Given that experience, they are understandably concerned that it is about to be repeated. Yet investment must play a critical role in sustaining future growth. The improvement of the trade balance was largely a one-shot response to devaluation. Unless investment spending rises in future years to replace the stimulus previously provided by an improved trade balance, the overall growth of the economy must slow.

Third, the improvement of the trade balance was achieved only at the cost of an enormous decline in Sweden's real exchange rate; in 1985 relative labor costs in Swedish manufacturing, compared with those of major competitors, were 17 percent below the level of 1980 and 12 percent below that of 1970.[4] While the evidence we present in chapter 3 suggests no long-term tendency for the Swedish trade balance in manu-facturing to decline further, many other observers are less sanguine. In 1985, for example, according to the OECD, the volume of Swedish manufactured exports grew 2.3 percent less than Swedish export markets did.[5] Sweden might have to sustain additional real devaluations to maintain equilibrium in the current account.

Finally, the cost of servicing a large foreign debt acquired during the 1970s seriously restricts Swedish economic policy. That debt totaled Skr 164 billion at the end of 1983, or 23 percent of GDP.[6] Since the debt is largely denominated in foreign currencies, declines in the exchange rate beyond those required by differential rates of domestic inflation impose an increased cost of debt service.

The Policy Debate

These developments have led to a debate in Sweden over the appro-priate goals for economic policy and the mix of policy tools that should

---

4. Data supplied by the staff of the International Monetary Fund.
5. *OECD Economic Outlook,* vol. 39, p. 155.
6. Nile Eric Persson, "External Assets and Liabilities," *Sveriges Riksbank Quarterly Review,* no. 2 (1984), p. 15.

be used to achieve them. Two approaches to economic policy, one followed by the government and one advocated by its "new classical" critics, define the argument.

Government Policy

The government has followed a strategy that emphasizes increasing domestic saving—eliminating the need to borrow overseas and providing increased domestic financing for investment. Thus the government has made serious efforts to reduce the budget deficit. To avoid the unemployment implied by a restrictive fiscal policy, the government acted first to promote export demand through the reduction in the exchange rate. It hoped to accelerate exports and private-sector employment growth, while avoiding either further fiscal stimulus that might generate inflation or a more restrictive policy that might increase unemployment.

Besides the primary goals of reducing the budget deficit, the Swedish government has set other ambitious objectives. It intends simultaneously to sustain growth, reduce inflation, "step up the fight for a fair income distribution," and from now on maintain a fixed exchange rate. The government's anti-inflationary policy instruments will be tight fiscal and monetary policies coupled with reforms of the process of setting wages. But it strongly emphasizes that higher unemployment would be unthinkable.

Given the unique circumstances associated with the one-time gains from the devaluation of the early 1980s, the government has been able to avoid making hard choices among goals. Indeed, appropriating a line from its critics, the government has vowed that "Another devaluation of the Swedish krona is absolutely out of the question."[7] In May 1985 Sweden reinforced this pledge by raising interest rates to defend the krona.

Unless Sweden reduces its inflation rate to that of its trading partners, however, it will eventually be forced to make some painful trade-offs. As competitiveness deteriorates, export growth, the force behind the prior expansion, will slow. If the government tries to use fiscal policy to stimulate domestic demand, it will be forced to yield on its goals for the budget deficit. If it turns to monetary expansion, it cannot defend the exchange rate. If, instead, the government opts to defend the currency

7. Ministry of Finance, *The Swedish Budget 1986–87* (Stockholm, 1986), p.12.

by a further tightening of monetary policy, it will be forced to accept slower domestic growth and higher unemployment.

While acknowledging that the economy faces problems in allocating resources, the government seeks to rely on special programs rather than market forces to enhance labor and capital mobility. It is true that credit policy has been liberalized by reducing regulation and increasing the role of open-market operations. The government has also shown a greater willingness to allow corporate bankruptcies. Nonetheless, an extensive apparatus to provide support to industry and to the labor market remains in place, and the government could be forced to provide additional support if many firms run into trouble. Moreover, many companies remain state owned, and a downturn in their profitability would place the government in an awkward position.

The government continues to support the solidaristic wage policy that systematically overrides the wage structure that would emerge from market forces. In addition, it retains extensive commitments to displaced and disadvantaged workers. Tools important to the labor market, such as job retraining, relief work, early retirement pensions, and special youth programs, account for about 4 percent of the GDP. Given the commitments to industry and labor, an erosion in competitiveness would trigger automatic and politically necessary expenditures that could seriously undermine the turn toward fiscal restraint.

In sum, the government's policies remain crucially dependent on investment and exports, which have been stimulated by improved competitiveness. An erosion in competitiveness, brought about by wage increases in Sweden exceeding those of competitors, would seriously expose the fragile nature of the expansion. If the government then tried to maintain its commitment to a fixed exchange rate, the job losses in export- and import-competing markets would trigger the budget-breaking responses that Sweden has sought so hard to avoid.

The New Classical Approach

An alternative is proposed by the advocates of a policy that would give greater priority to reducing inflation.[8] They would subordinate other goals of economic policy such as low unemployment and growth. They would make adherence to a fixed exchange rate the anchor of the policy

8. This view is articulated most fully in the reports of the Economic Policy Group of Studieförbundet Näringsliv och Samhälle (SNS).

on price stabilization. Importantly, they would eliminate the foreign exchange controls that limit capital transactions with other countries. Thus domestic monetary policy would have to be directed toward stabilization of the exchange rate and could not be part of a domestic policy of accommodation. Any tendency for Swedish industrial costs to rise faster than those abroad would, therefore, translate into a reduced trade balance, a lower rate of production, and rising unemployment. The threat of rising unemployment is expected to be the biggest moderating force on wage increases and thus on domestic inflation. By adhering to a fixed exchange rate the government could eventually force Sweden's inflation rate down to that of such trading partners as Germany. The government's unswerving commitment to avoid accommodating the economic disruptions of excessive cost inflation through offsetting domestic policies, however, is critical.

The critics charge that the government's anti-inflation stance lacks credibility since it is not coupled with a commitment to forswear the use of short-term stabilization policies. The government can impose the necessary discipline on wage negotiations only by abandoning the short-run policies of accommodating excessive wage increases by devaluation and fiscal-monetary inflation.

Just as government officials avoid thinking about the devaluation that will eventually be required should their anti-inflationary strategy fail, so proponents of abandoning discretionary policies avoid thinking about the unemployment that will eventually result if their policy should fail:

> An increased labor market responsibility for the short-run employment level does not mean that unemployment should be "used" to fight inflation. If the regime is credible, the inflation rate can be brought down without an increase in unemployment. Furthermore, credibility cannot be established unless the government refrains from giving short-run employment guarantees, regardless of the cost level.[9]

While a credible government commitment to avoid accommodating policies may improve the trade-off between inflation and unemployment, the experience of other countries suggests that such credibility is only achieved after considerable time and at a considerable cost to employment. If Sweden seeks to import the German inflation rate, it may also have to import the German unemployment rate.

9. Hans Tson Söderström, ed., *Sweden: The Road to Stability* (Stockholm: SNS Economic Policy Group, 1985), p. 41. See also Per-Martin Meyerson, *Eurosclerosis: The Case of Sweden,* trans. Victor J. Kayfetz (Stockholm: Federation of Swedish Industries, 1985), pp. 97–110.

Another concern raised by this view of the new classicists is that it will probably result in a major profit squeeze in the sector dealing in tradable goods. Indeed, squeezing profits is one way by which external discipline is supposed to operate to strengthen the backbone of employers in resisting inflationary demands. However, this effect will again weaken investment incentives, make the solvency of marginal firms precarious, and place burdens on the budget.

Nonaccommodation in microeconomic policies is a crucial complement to this macroeconomic program. Only by unleashing market forces it is argued, can growth be restored. The subsidies currently prevailing in housing, industry, and agriculture, as well as in the labor market, are to be radically reduced.

In addition, many see the need to reverse the solidaristic wage strategy and rely on a more flexible structure to allocate labor and encourage investment in human capital. The wage structure should become more "market-oriented and differentiated."[10] Relative wages, rather than labor market policies, should be the primary mechanism for allocating labor, with labor market policies concentrating on the relatively small groups in the labor market who have significant problems.[11] In general, the critics argue that the wedge introduced by taxes and transfers into the factor price system has become highly distortionary.

But the commitment to increase relative wage flexibility and to reduce the overall inflation rate simultaneously seems very ambitious. Unskilled workers would face wage cuts for several years if differentials were broadened in the face of an average wage inflation at German levels.

Both the government and its critics seek desirable goals. Both claim to place high priority on maintaining full employment, reducing the government's deficit, and lowering Sweden's inflation rate to that of its trading partners. Both would keep the exchange rate fixed and monetary and fiscal policies tight. But there are also different emphases on priorities and on the mix of policy instruments needed to achieve them.

Both programs face the same risk. If inflation undermines Swedish competitiveness, the government will have great difficulties in maintaining both budgetary targets and structural programs. In the face of continuing cost inflation, however, a policy of nonaccommodation is likely to yield high unemployment, a shift of industry out of tradable goods, and a thwarting of the effort to increase relative wage dispersions.

10. Meyerson, *Eurosclerosis*, p. 108.

11. See, for example, Industriens Utredningsinstitut [Industrial Institute for Economic and Social Research], *Evaluating the 1990s: IUI's Long-Term Survey, 1985* (Stockholm: IUI, 1985).

Advocates of both programs deny the need to choose among competing goals. Yet in an open economy subject to unforeseen events, contingency planning is crucial and choices must be made.

In the following sections, we will address these issues of choice in greater detail. We shall attempt to derive an explicit quantitative target for fiscal policy and examine the conditions necessary to ensure that increases in national saving translate into higher rates of investment. We conclude that, at a minimum, the consolidated general goverment budget balance, which was in deficit by an amount equal to 1.8 percent of net domestic product (NDP) in 1985, will have to be converted to a surplus of approximately 4 percent of NDP in future years. That is, despite the progress that has been made, Sweden still has a long way to go in reducing the budget deficit. The translation of this saving target into domestic capital formation, however, will require low interest rates and balance in the current account—conditions that may be incompatible with the goal for the fixed exchange rate in future years.

In discussing monetary policy, we shall focus on the issue of controlling inflation and, specifically, the role of the target for a fixed nominal exchange rate. Policymakers must decide the extent to which they are willing to adopt a nonaccommodative policy against inflation. Obviously, a fixed exchange rate cannot be maintained unless Sweden is determined to hold its inflation rate to that of trade competitors. That commitment in turn assumes that Swedish policymakers are willing to accept a higher rate of unemployment as the price for lower inflation.

In any case, however, monetary policy can be guided by either a nominal exchange rate target or a domestic aggregate, such as the rate of growth of nominal GDP. Regardless of its choice on the issue of accommodation, Sweden would benefit if it oriented monetary policy toward the domestic economy, adopting a goal for the growth of nominal GDP and allowing greater scope for market forces to determine the exchange rate.[12]

Macroeconomic Policies

The major issue facing economic policymakers is the priority of various economic goals and the choice of policies to promote them. In

12. It is not necessary to go so far as to consider a completely flexible exchange rate. A policy of short-term stabilization of the exchange rate, such as that suggested by proposals for a gradually changing rate, is not inconsistent with the following discussion of the advantages of allowing the exchange rate to adjust to market forces.

the past, Sweden emphasized full employment and directed fiscal policy toward that goal. At the same time, it articulated a commitment to a fixed exchange rate as the primary means of holding down inflation but was unable to meet that commitment.

The participants in the debate agree that the old policy mix has become untenable. As discussed in earlier chapters, the focus on short-run goals in fiscal policy ignored the longer-term consequences for capital formation. The budget deficit absorbed an increasing share of private saving and forced Sweden to borrow abroad. In addition, the commitment to a fixed exchange rate as a tool for restraining inflation lost force in the face of a fiscal policy that offset any domestic employment losses.

Some progress toward agreement on a new policy mix has been made. Both the government and its critics agree that a concern for saving and capital formation must play a greater role in the formation of fiscal policy. Thus continued reductions in the budget deficit are to be given priority over short-run stabilization of the economy.

There is less agreement about the remainder of the policy package. What measures, if any, will be taken to stabilize the domestic economy, and what are the implications of adherence to a fixed exchange rate—a goal on which all the parties agree?

In the 1970s monetary policy lacked a clear focus as its aims fluctuated among a defense of the exchange rate, support for the domestic economy, and assistance in the financing of the government deficit. That degree of autonomy for monetary policy will not be available in future years, however, because of two critical changes in the environment in which it operates: the elimination of controls on currency outflows and the government's commitment to finance future budget deficits in the domestic capital markets.

Sweden is dismantling a system of foreign exchange controls, in place since World War II, that sought to restrict capital transactions with other countries. In large measure, removal of the controls is simply a recognition of the reduced effectiveness of such restrictions in a world of multinational firms and sophisticated international capital markets.[13] The major effect of this change is to increase the potential for financial inflows and outflows from Sweden.

The intention to rely on domestic financing of future budget deficits is also a major change from past practice. Interest rates in Sweden during the 1970s were surprisingly low in view of government borrowing and

13. Lars Calmfors, "Exchange Controls Can Be Abolished!" *Skandinaviska Enskilda Banken Quarterly Review*, no. 3 (1985), pp. 90–95.

the general agreement that the krona was overvalued. The heavy deficit financing should have placed strong upward pressure on domestic interest rates to attract the required capital from abroad, or, in the absence of such inflows, to crowd out domestic borrowers.

Instead, the government camouflaged the domestic implications of borrowing by obtaining the funds directly in foreign capital markets and placing on itself any risk of a future exchange rate devaluation, obviating much of the upward pressure on domestic interest rates.[14] Between 1978 and 1984, for example, Sweden's net foreign liabilities rose by Skr 155.5 billion. Increased government indebtedness to foreigners accounted for Skr 111.4 billion of that change.[15] In effect, the method of debt financing was an important element of the policy used to stabilize the exchange rate.

Under the new regime Swedish capital markets will be much more integrated with those of the rest of the world. Continued adherence to a fixed nominal exchange rate, in this era of relatively unfettered capital markets, will require that monetary policy be directed toward offsetting pressure on the exchange rate, with little freedom to respond to domestic economic conditions. Some of the new restrictions on monetary policy were evident in 1985 when the reemergence of a current account deficit and a net outflow of currency put downward pressure on the exchange rate. The monetary authorities responded by raising domestic interest rates relative to those of other countries: at its peak the margin over the Eurodollar rate reached 8 percentage points before the current account improved in the second half of the year.[16]

The new macroeconomic strategy that is emerging is one in which fiscal policy is directed toward ensuring an adequate long-term rate of capital formation and monetary policy is targeted on maintaining a fixed exchange rate. Although the government's statements are less explicit than those of its critics, the policy actions imply an abandonment of short-term stabilization of the domestic economy. It resembles the

14. In more conventional terms the government's policy can be thought of as deficit financing in the domestic market, which would raise interest rates, combined with an intervention in the exchange market in which it borrowed foreign currencies to repurchase its own debt, reducing domestic interest rates. The costs of that policy became obvious in the 1980s when devaluation imposed a large capital loss on claims denominated in foreign currencies.

15. Persson, "External Assets and Liabilities," p. 15.

16. Erik Åsbrink and Lars Heikensten, "Currency Flows in 1985 and Swedish Economic Policy," *Skandinaviska Enskilda Banken Quarterly Review*, no. 1 (1986), p. 22.

strategy of the new classicists who believe that policy directed toward domestic stabilization is inherently destabilizing.[17] The only basic difference is rhetorical. The critics believe that government policy would gain credibility and have immediate impact on wage negotiations if the government were less ambivalent about its reponse to any future conflict between the policy on the exchange rate and goals for domestic employment. In the following two sections we will analyze this new strategy by examining the targets for fiscal and monetary policy.

Economic Growth and Targets for Fiscal Policy

Capital formation is critical for growth, and it is an area in which government has a strong role to play. The shift from substantial government surpluses to huge deficits has been primarily responsible for the decline in Swedish national saving since the 1970s and the sacrifice of investment to sustain the growth of consumption. Because economic research has cast doubt on the ability of government to alter private saving behavior through changes in taxes and other measures, the government must provide an adequate level of national saving through decisions on its own budget.[18] But what is the right saving rate? Is it the phenomenal 16 percent of national income that Sweden achieved before 1973, or is it closer to the 7 percent rate of the mid-1980s?

In a strictly private economy, the optimal rate of capital formation would emerge from market forces, and the national saving rate would reflect private decisions on the appropriate trade-off between current and future consumption. Domestic investment would, in turn, be based on comparing the return on domestic versus foreign investment.

In Sweden, however, most saving—particularly for retirement—is determined by public decisions, and policies on the exchange rate heavily influence the profitability of domestic investment. The link between exchange rates, profitability, and investment comes from the open nature of the Swedish economy where, at least for tradable goods, prices in the world market determine domestic prices.

One method of assessing the adequacy of Swedish investment is to estimate the rate of capital formation required to maintain steady growth. In the long term, an economy's growth rate can be defined as equal to

17. See, in particular, Calmfors, "Exchange Controls Can Be Abolished!" p. 91.
18. For a survey of that research see Barry P. Bosworth, *Tax Incentives and Economic Growth* (Brookings, 1984), pp. 67–94.

the growth of the labor supply plus the rate of labor-augmenting technical change. If the growth is to be balanced, the net capital stock must grow at the same rate as output. A higher level of output can be achieved by raising the investment share, but ultimately the rate of output growth must slow to that of the augmented labor supply. In effect, a whole family of parallel growth paths exists for output corresponding to different investment rates.

If this exercise is carried out for Sweden the following result for the nonresidential business sector is obtained:

	Annual growth rate	
	1963–73	*1973–84*
Total factor productivity (cyclically adjusted)	3.2	1.7
Labor-augmenting technical change	4.5	2.7
Labor supply (hours)	− 1.7	− 1.1
Warranted growth rate	2.8	1.4

The rate of factor productivity growth, reported in chapter 2, declined sharply after 1973 to a cyclically adjusted rate of 1.7 percent annually, compared with 3.2 percent from 1963 to 1973. If that slowdown truly reflects a lower rate of exogenous technical change, it would imply a sharply lower optimal rate of capital formation. For example, assuming a Cobb-Douglas production function with a labor share of 0.7, the associated annual rate of labor-augmenting technical change would be 4.5 percent and 2.7 percent from 1963 to 1973 and 1973 to 1984, respectively. Furthermore, Sweden did experience in both periods a substantial decline in the labor supply (workhours). Combining these two factors, the steady-state growth rate fell from 2.8 to 1.4 percent annually.

Thus the warranted growth of the capital stock in the nonresidential business sector should have fallen by half after 1973 simply because of changes on the supply side. In fact, the actual rate of growth of the capital stock substantially exceeded the warranted rate from 1963 to 1976 but was only slightly above it from 1977 to 1984. By implication, from 1963 to 1973 Sweden was, through high rates of capital formation, moving to progressively higher long-run growth paths; but since then it has been, at best, able to generate a rate of investment sufficient to maintain a lower steady-state growth path.

We should not anticipate a continued decline in the labor force as great as that experienced during the past two decades. *The 1984 Medium*

Table 4-1. *The Saving-Investment Balance in Sweden, 1963–73, 1974–84, 1985, and Projected*

Economic indicator	Percent of net national product			
	1963–73	*1974–84*	*1985*	*Projected*
Net national saving-investment	16.3	8.2	7.1	10.4
Net private saving	6.1	6.5	8.9	6.5
Government saving	10.2	1.7	−1.8	4.0
Domestic fixed capital	15.1	9.9	8.3	9.6
Inventory accumulation	1.1	0.3	−0.1	0.7
Net foreign investment	0.2	−1.9	−1.2	0.0

Sources: *National Accounts;* and authors' estimates. The private saving rate and inventory investment are projected at their trend averages.

Term Survey projects an essentially constant supply of workhours in the 1980s.[19] On that basis, a conservative assumption for the warranted growth of the net capital stock in the business sector in future years would be about 2.5 percent annually, the estimated rate of labor-augmented technical change.[20] This figure is about 20 percent higher than the actual rate of capital formation achieved in 1984, but it is far below the 5.2 percent average rate that occurred from 1963 to 1973.

Establishing appropriate levels of investment for government services and housing is more difficult—spending for these areas has been cut substantially in recent years. Sweden has most of its social infrastructure in place, and the lack of population growth means that there are few demands on net housing investment. In the absence of capital stock estimates for these two categories, we have assumed that the warranted rate can be approximated by the average net investment share that occurred from 1974 to 1984, 4.4 percent of net domestic product.

The combined estimate of this minimal, long-run investment rate for industry, government, and housing suggests a warranted share of net fixed investment in net domestic product of 9.6 percent compared with the actual 1985 share of 8.3 percent.[21] Such a target is well below the rate of investment achieved from 1963 to 1973, but it is about the same as the average from 1974 to 1984 (see table 4-1). If this investment target is

19. Ministry of Finance, *The 1984 Medium Term Survey of the Swedish Economy* (Stockholm, 1984), pp. 103–13.
20. The warranted growth rate would be higher if one anticipated an improvement in the underlying trend growth of technical change.
21. The warranted investment share was computed using the 1984 share of nonresidential business investment in net domestic product of 4.3 percent (9.6 = 4.3 * 1.2 + 4.4).

combined with a goal of balance in the current account, clearly Sweden must achieve a substantially higher national saving rate, an increase over the 1985 rate equal to 3.3 percent of net domestic product, if it hopes to sustain growth in future years.

In arriving at a specific estimate of the target for the budget surplus we have assumed that the private saving rate returns to the historical trend of 1963–84 and that the inventory-sales ratio is constant.[22] The target budget surplus of 4 percent is well above the − 1.8 percent of NDP achieved in 1985, but the required change is equal to that which occurred from 1982 to 1984.

The preceding calculations of the target for fiscal policy are only illustrative. In practice, fiscal policy would have to adjust to changes in the trend of private saving, domestic investment opportunities, and the current account. However, a framework that utilizes the national saving-investment balance can be a useful means of thinking about long-term objectives of fiscal policy. In particular, it implies that the current account balance becomes the primary indicator of the adequacy of the budget surplus or deficit: a current account deficit, such as reemerged in 1985, denotes a national saving rate insufficient to finance domestic investment.

Of course, a high rate of national saving alone is not enough. If growth is to be sustained, policymakers must ensure that those resources flow through to investment. That investment could be within the domestic economy or placed overseas—a repayment of debt. If the saving is invested overseas, the real exchange rate would depreciate, and the transfer of resources would be reflected in a larger surplus in the trade account.

In either case, the transfer of saving into investment requires a low level of domestic real interest rates. Chapter 2 showed business investment in Sweden to be sensitive to the real interest rate spread between tangible and financial assets. Low domestic interest rates are consistent with promoting investment in two ways: a low cost of borrowing and a weak real exchange rate that promotes a high return on tangible capital in the sector dealing in tradable goods. Thus from the perspective of maximizing long-term economic growth, the appropriate mix of policy

22. The historical trend in the private saving rate is very slightly positive but statistically insignificant. We assume that the high saving rate of 1984–85 was a transitory response to the devaluation and upsurge of profits, and we anticipate a return to the historical average in future years.

is one that emphasizes a tight budget policy and a relatively easy monetary policy.

Finally, the targets just set forth for capital formation only allow for a steady-state growth rate. They are not meant to imply that Sweden should not aim to do better. In the 1960s investment in Sweden proceeded at a more rapid pace, and the country was able to move to progressively higher growth paths. In the 1980s a 1.0 percentage point increase in the share of output devoted to industrial capital would raise the growth of net output by 0.06 percentage point annually during the first decade if technical change is not embodied, and about 0.12 percentage point if all the technological change is assumed to be embodied in new capital.[23] Such gains seem small on an annual basis, but when compounded over extended periods, the benefits in higher income levels are substantial.

Monetary Policy and Inflation

The historical review contained in earlier chapters demonstrates that the interaction of high rates of domestic inflation and a fixed exchange rate has been enormously costly to the Swedish economy. Cost increases in excess of those experienced abroad squeeze profits and lower investment. The deterioration of the trade balance results both from a rise in relative prices (loss of demand) and the reduction in profit margins that drives firms out of the industries dealing in tradable goods (reduced supply). Ultimately, a deterioration of competitiveness forces the industries that are highly dependent on trade to turn to the government for assistance. Breaking up this process is crucial to the long-term health of the Swedish economy.

Given this situation, Swedish policymakers face three options in dealing with inflation and its consequences: adopt a nonaccommodative policy that accepts higher unemployment to force nominal wage increases into line with the warranted rate; live with continuing inflation and a soft currency; or attempt to alter the institutional structure of wage setting by adopting an explicit incomes policy. Under any of these options, a fixed exchange is not desirable.

Several conclusions from the preceding chapters are important to this

---

23. These estimates are based on a simple Cobb-Douglas model with an initial net investment rate equal to 5 percent of output, a capital-output ratio of 2.0, capital depreciation at a geometric rate of 0.07 percent annually, an augmented labor supply growing at 2.5 percent annually, and the share of net capital at net output is 0.15. Such a model would seem to be closely representative of the Swedish situation.

review of policy options. First, in chapter 2 we could find no evidence in support of the notion, implicit in the Scandinavian model of wage determination, that nominal wage changes respond directly to changes in the international competitiveness of Swedish industry: neither changes in productivity nor in the current account balance seriously affect nominal wage rates. Instead, nominal wage behavior is well explained by a traditional model that relates nominal wage changes to variations in domestic labor market conditions; producer price changes, with a coefficient substantially less than unity; the profit rate; and, perhaps, employment taxes. Second, we could find no evidence of a major shift or breakdown of this process in the 1970s.[24] The acceleration of inflation since 1973 has primarily resulted from an inability to alter the determination of nominal wages to reflect the fact that there is less room for real wage increases—that is, slower productivity growth. Thus the major change has been in Sweden's ability to absorb nominal wage growth, not in the structure of wage determination.

We conclude that wage behavior in Sweden is not dissimilar to that in the United States. Changes in conditions in the labor market exert a strong effect on wage behavior, while the effect of price changes is relatively weak. The growth of real wages can be brought into line with a slower growth of productivity (or the warranted wage rate) only by increasing unemployment or by a higher rate of price inflation that erodes wage gains. Also, a rigidity of real wages is not the problem in Sweden that it is alleged to be in some European economies.

NONACCOMMODATIVE POLICIES. A policy of nonaccommodation would seem to mean a fairly straightforward decision to tighten up on monetary policy and to push the cost of excessive inflation back onto the private sector in the form of higher unemployment. The empirical analysis in chapter 2 suggests that a permanent increase in the unemployment rate of 1 percentage point would reduce the rate of inflation by 2 percentage points; and, as we shall see, that is about the amount by which inflation in Sweden exceeds that of its trading competitors.

It is suggested, however, that the government could avoid much of the unemployment cost by adopting a rigid rule for monetary policy that renounces any accommodation. If that position could be made credible, all parties to the negotiations on wage setting must be convinced that the

24. This assumes that the duration of job vacancies is the appropriate measure of labor market conditions. There has been a substantial deterioration since 1969 in the trade-off between inflation and the rate of open unemployment.

government will not ratify excessive cost increases by compensatory adjustments in its policies. The greater awareness of the costs of their actions—particularly in squeezing profits and reducing employment—is expected to lead the participants to change their behavior.[25]

It should be recognized, however, that an attempt to establish a new regime for wage determination will be costly in terms of a drawn-out period of high unemployment and low domestic investment. This seems particularly true given the history of Swedish politics and economic policies. Credibility will not come quickly. In fact, despite two deep recessions in the United States since the change in the monetary regime in 1979, strong disagreement among the empirical studies continues as to whether change in the basic process linking domestic inflation to resource utilization has occurred.[26]

The discussion of a monetary policy rule in the United States has normally been in terms of a target growth rate for various domestic monetary aggregates—a fixed growth of the money supply, for example. In Sweden, however, the instability of the relationship between money and income has led to the suggestion that the objectives of a nonaccommodative policy could be achieved by targeting a fixed nominal exchange rate—fixed relative to a market basket of foreign currencies.[27]

If Sweden adopted a target for a fixed exchange rate, the domestic rate of inflation would ultimately be forced into line with the average of its trading competitors. Such an inflation target is shown on a historical basis in figure 4-1. It is computed as a weighted average of the inflation rates in the the group of fifteen countries included in the Swedish Riksbank's currency index.[28] On average, inflation in Sweden has

25. For a detailed discussion of the potential effects of a nonaccommodation policy on expectations, see William Fellner, *Towards a Reconstruction of Macroeconomics: Problems of Theory and Policy* (Washington, D.C.: American Enterprise Institute, 1976), pp. 1–18; and Thomas J. Sargent, "Stopping Moderate Inflation: The Methods of Poincaré and Thatcher" (University of Minnesota and the Federal Reserve Bank of Minneapolis, 1981). See also the collection of essays in *American Economic Review*, vol. 72 (May 1982, *Papers and Proceedings, 1981*), pp. 77–91.

26. Marvin H. Kosters, "Disinflation in the Labor Market," in William Fellner, ed., *Essays in Contemporary Economic Problems: Disinflation* (Washington, D.C.: American Enterprise Institute, 1984), pp. 247–86; Robert J. Flanagan, "Wage Concessions and Long-Term Union Wage Flexibility," *Brookings Papers on Economic Activity (BPEA)*, *1:1984*, pp. 183–216; and Robert J. Gordon, "Understanding Inflation in the 1980s," *BPEA, 1:1985*, pp. 263–99. In the Swedish case a counterargument might be made that centralized bargaining might make it easier for the government to convince the participants that it has changed its policies and will not accommodate future inflation.

27. See Söderström, *Sweden: The Road to Stability*, pp. 16–22.

28. The currency index weights the exchange rate with each country by relative

Figure 4-1. *Rate of Consumer Price Inflation in Sweden Compared with an Average of Trade Competitors, 1965–86*

Percent change

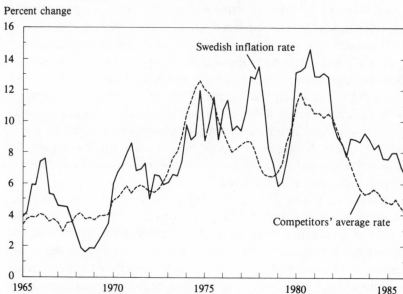

Source: Authors' calculations.

exceeded that of its competitors by about 2 percentage points annually. Thus adherence to the target should translate into a lower rate of domestic inflation. It is generally recognized, however, that the domestic costs of inflation derive from its variability. Surprisingly, the extent of variation in the average foreign inflation rate is not appreciably less than in the domestic rate. Given this result, from a strictly domestic perspective it is not clear why Sweden should prefer the foreign inflation rate to its own.

A target for a fixed exchange rate is not strictly speaking a nonaccommodation policy. Instead, it eliminates the discretion of policymakers. Sweden would simply abdicate control over domestic monetary conditions in favor of adapting to foreign ones. Someone else must take responsibility for determining the extent of accommodation for the group as a whole. The appropriate target for domestic wage and price increases would depend on policy decisions made in other countries.

importance in Sweden's external trade. The weights are those used in the Riksbank's index in 1984. That index doubles the relative importance of the U.S. dollar. The figure is based on consumer price changes over a four-quarter period, but a computation using wholesale prices yielded a similar inflation differential.

More important, a credible policy cannot be expected to emerge from its announcement alone. It will affect wages only as continued domestic inflation drives up the real exchange rate, reducing the trade balance, production, and employment. At that point, however, the required nominal rate of wage change is less than in the rest of the world. Starting from an initial equilibrium in the exchange rate, a period in which the cumulative rise of nominal wages exceeds that abroad must be followed by a period in which wage increases are less than those abroad to return the real exchange rate to its appropriate level.[29] Having achieved a domestic inflation rate in line with other countries, the government cannot correct the real exchange rate through a devaluation without destroying its policy. Thus the attainment of long-run control of inflation must be preceded by a period of overachievement. In the period of crisis the government is also likely to be faced with a serious problem of currency flight if there are any doubts about government intentions. There is no realistic interest rate that can compensate investors for the risk of an immediate large devaluation.

Alternatively, the government might set monetary targets in terms of domestic conditions and let market factors determine the exchange rate. The target might be stated in terms of a monetary aggregate; but, given the instability between the aggregates and economic activity, it seems preferable to turn directly to a focus on the growth of nominal GDP or inflation. In effect, the monetary authorities would tighten policy whenever domestic inflation showed evidence of exceeding the target rate. Such a target is inherently less specific than the exchange rate, which is observable on a day-to-day basis. However, the adoption of such a target would affect the economy immediately through higher interest rates rather than relying on the gradual buildup of restraint from an increasingly overvalued exchange rate.

The shift to a more restrictive monetary policy with higher domestic interest rates would initially depress production and employment, and the restrictive effect would be amplified by a rise in the exchange rate in response to higher interest rates. In fact, the sensitivity of the exchange rate to changes in interest rates would become a major means through

29. It is argued by some observers that Sweden is not starting from an initial equilibrium exchange rate but from one that is undervalued. However, even if it is initially undervalued, the rate would tend to overshoot in future years to demonstrate that the government will not give way—the simple announcement of a new policy will not be enough to reduce wage inflation as long as the exchange rate is undervalued. The domestic economy faces excess demand not unemployment.

which monetary policy would affect the economy, altering the level of real exports and imports. The initial tendency of the exchange rate to appreciate in response to the tightening of domestic monetary policy would reinforce the anti-inflation objective through lowering the domestic price of tradable goods. The impact on domestic employment would be the same as under an exchange rate rule; but it would occur earlier, and, having lowered domestic inflation to the desired rate, there would be no need for a subsequent period of overachievement.

With either a monetary or exchange rate rule, the costs of a nonaccommodative policy will be high politically as well as economically. There will be strong pressures to expand subsidies. The Social Democrats would find it hard to abandon accommodation in labor markets, and their bourgeois counterparts are prone to subsidize industry and agriculture. An unemployment rate increase of 1 percent would also automatically raise the budget deficit by approximately 2 percent of GDP.

In fact, however, higher unemployment has been the major means since the early 1970s of achieving a reconciliation of nominal wage increases with the slow growth in productivity. Since 1970, unemployment has increased by 1.0 percent to 1.5 percent of the labor force, and our empirical estimates suggest that the weaker labor market conditions have reduced annual wage increases by 2 percent to 3 percent—a sizable part of the 4 percentage point slowdown in warranted wage growth.[30]

Sweden might be able to avoid focusing directly on higher unemployment. Some evidence in our empirical work suggested that the policy option could be more accurately stated as a need to maintain a low average duration of job vacancies. For example, if workers with skills needed in the private sector could be released from public programs in a timely fashion, an expansion of private-sector employment might occur that would not add to inflation pressures.

LIVING WITH HIGH INFLATION. Sweden could continue to use price inflation as the primary means of scaling back nominal wage increases to the warranted rate and adjust other institutions to break the link between wage inflation and the structure of the real economy. To counter a tendency toward low investment incentives and the loss of international competitiveness, the government would simply engage in frequent devaluations of the currency.[31] Such a policy would eliminate the most

30. The 4 percentage point reduction of the warranted rate of wage increase is largely the result of slower productivity growth. The estimate is taken from the analysis in chapter 2.

31. Assar Lindbeck, "The Changing Role of the National State," *Kyklos*, vol. 28, no. 1 (1975), p. 41.

evident cost of excessive domestic inflation, the loss of international competitiveness. It would not, however, avoid the domestic costs.[32] Within the current wage-setting regime, however, with a weak influence of prices on nominal wage increases, such a policy should not generate an accelerating rate of inflation.

In the 1970s, Sweden appeared to use such a policy but, in fact, waited to make the adjustment to the exchange rate until damage to its real economy and fiscal stance became intolerable.[33]

Such a policy would deflect some of the pressures for direct government subsidies; and since workers would no longer be rewarded in real terms for excessive nominal wage increases through a rise in labor's share of the national income, the new regime might have a moderating effect on inflation. In a centralized negotiation it is easier for both parties to understand the consequences of their actions. In effect, real wage increases would become more independent of the negotiated nominal increase.

The policy, however, is not without risks. It is not clear how much employers' resistance to wage increases would be weakened by the knowledge that the increases could be passed through into prices. In a system of decentralized wage setting, domestic competition can be expected to create a concern for preventing one's own costs from moving out of line with those of competitors. Such restraint is not present in centralized negotiations, although wage drift, as we have seen, makes wage setting in Sweden far more decentralized in reality than it appears in principle.

In addition, there could be a change in the wage regime. As expectations of price inflation become incorporated to a greater extent into the process of wage setting, a shift toward greater real wage negotiation could occur. That is, the adoption of an explicit policy of living with inflation may cause a deterioration of the process.

INSTITUTIONAL CHANGE. It is often suggested that with an incomes policy, some form of active government involvement in wage setting is a less costly means of shifting the pattern of nominal wage determination. The structure of wage negotiations in Sweden, a highly centralized and highly unionized system of setting wages, seems ideally suited to such

32. It would become even more important to reform the income tax, which in its present form is not indexed for inflation. This issue is discussed more fully in chapter 7.

33. This policy is similar in some respects to that of Finland in the 1970s. See Lars Calmfors, "Sweden and Finland—A Comparison of Stabilisation-Policy Strategies," *Skandinaviska Enskilda Banken Quarterly Review*, no. 4 (1984), pp. 119–24.

efforts. However, there has been a strong tradition in Sweden against such programs, and past efforts to implement them have been quite unsuccessful.[34]

Part of the difficulty has been the competition between the major unions over relative wages and the fact that, for private-sector employees, wage drift introduces a substantial departure between actual and negotiated wage changes. The unions have also been opposed to incomes policies because, in conjunction with a fixed exchange rate, the restraint of nominal wages is not in their short-run interest since it implies a lower real wage. Again, accommodative government policies have effectively offset any loss of employment in tradable goods.

Given the history of government's role, an effective incomes policy would require nearly as dramatic a change of regime as is required for the explicitly nonaccommodative policy proposals. With incomes policy the government must be equally credible in convincing the private parties that it will not engage in the accommodative microeconomic and macroeconomic policies of the past. Incomes policies require a stick as well as a carrot. Again, flexible exchange rates, by breaking the link between average nominal and average real wage increases, are most supportive of this objective.

The best opportunity for changing the structure of the wage process seems to lie with reducing the competition among the major unions. In this regard the government must deal firmly with its public sector employees.

Overview

A substantial conflict between the goal of promoting economic growth and some of the options for controlling inflation exists. The optimal growth policy suggests a combination of a tight fiscal policy to raise national saving and an easy monetary policy to encourage the transfer of resources in investment. But most of the macroeconomic approaches to reducing inflation emphasize the need for a restrictive monetary

34. Robert J. Flanagan, David W. Soskice, and Lloyd Ulman, *Unionism, Economic Stabilization, and Incomes Policies: European Experience* (Brookings, 1983), pp. 301–62.

policy.[35] A strict nonaccommodative policy toward inflation conflicts in the short term with the objectives of growth and competitiveness.

Our analysis has emphasized the importance of not abandoning the goals of raising national saving and maintaining international competitiveness. Sweden could minimize the costs to growth and competitiveness by using fiscal policy to achieve the saving and allowing the exchange rate to adjust to market conditions. The choice between inflation and unemployment would then be resolved in the monetary arena. If the gains from lower inflation are worth the costs of higher unemployment, Sweden should make the adjustment in the most straightforward fashion—a tighter domestic monetary policy. If it is going to accommodate inflation, it should do so promptly with monetary policy and exchange rates, not with fiscal policy. What it should not do is deny that a choice must be made.

None of the options for controlling inflation is particularly attractive. Anti-inflation policies are a classic example of the problem of time inconsistency. Obviously, Sweden should make every reasonable effort to hold down inflation. It would be much better off if it would succeed. The real issue, however, is the cost the country should be willing to pay. The ideal policy would be to threaten a priori that strong measures will be taken, but the best ex post policy would be to devalue.

The devaluations of 1981 and 1982 have bought Sweden time before the cost squeeze again begins to seriously erode competitiveness. Lower oil prices also will reduce the domestic rate of inflation. Because other industrialized nations also benefited from the decline in oil prices, however, the decline should not affect Sweden's competitiveness. If anything, the effect of lower oil prices on wages seems less pronounced in Sweden than in other countries.

It is tempting to argue that because Sweden has used a combination of all three of the above anti-inflation policies (nonaccommodation, accommodation, and incomes policies) in the past, it is likely to continue to do so in the future. It is precisely such a circumstance, however, in which adherence to a fixed exchange rate target for monetary policy seems most dubious. Once the possibility of a future devaluation is introduced, a monetary policy directed toward a fixed exchange rate

35. It might be argued that a degree of price stability is a precondition for sustained growth, but that is largely a product of the distortions introduced by fixed exchange rates and an unindexed tax system. Certainly, the experience of the United States in the 1980s does not suggest that lower inflation translates into more growth.

target places a very heavy burden on the tradable goods sector of the economy. The costs of inflation are usually viewed as a trade-off against the costs of domestic unemployment, but with a fixed exchange rate there are additional real costs of a loss of competitiveness and greater instability of the economic environment in which the export industries must operate.

Comments by Villy Bergström

This chapter begins with an introduction that is positive analysis and follows it with a section on macroeconomic policy that is a mixture of positive analysis and normative prescriptions. There is hardly anything new for a Swedish follower of the economic debate, and much of the chapter could have been written about any small open economy. There are few mistakes, but the chapter suffers because the authors do not read Swedish. They have been excluded from original sources such as government proposals as well as from much of the policy discussion among economists and politicians. There is, for instance, very little in this chapter on labor market policy, which is an integral part of the policy mix and which plays a more important role in stabilization policy and growth policy than is indicated by Bosworth and Lawrence.

The Positive Analysis

The authors are right when they summarize government policy since 1982 as consisting of two main efforts: scaling back expenditures to improve the budget balance and devaluation to increase profitability and counteract stagnation in the manufacturing sector. They are also right when they stress two remaining "worrisome trends" that continue from the 1970s: a rate of cost inflation still higher than that of Sweden's trading partners, and the apparently short-lived recovery of investment spending, especially in manufacturing. The recovery started in 1984 and continued into 1985 but stopped without bringing the level of investment spending up to the 1975–76 peak in manufacturing, and bringing it only slightly above this peak in private business.

These last two trends are puzzling. There was a vigorous recovery in investment spending in manufacturing in 1984–85, once the devaluation had initiated a higher level of production and the slack capacity began to be absorbed. As the authors point out, the manufacturing sector is probably "structurally too small," and Sweden needs several years of investment spending at the rate of the preceding years, an increase of 15 percent. It seems that favorable conditions reign. Capacity utilization is high, liquidity is high, and opportunities for external financing of both equity capital and debt are excellent. Despite these facts, however, the latest forecast for 1986 points to a decrease of investment spending.

Bosworth and Lawrence discuss this. Their hypothesis is that the end of the investment boom is due to gloomy expectations on the part of business. They point to high real interest rates on financial investments and continued fast increases of nominal wage costs, which together with a fixed exchange rate may soon start to reduce profits.

But one need not turn to lack of confidence to see why investment spending is not continuing at the 1984–85 rate. A simple accelerator mechanism may provide part of the answer. The growth of production in manufacturing peaked in the first quarter of 1984. Since then the growth rate has been slowing down. Estimates of modified neoclassical investment functions with a flexible accelerator mechanism show long lags but a strong influence of output growth on investment demands. The mean lag on output is about ten quarters and the total lag is about eighteen. It may be that in the first half of 1986 the stimulus to investment spending in manufacturing, provided by the acceleration of growth in production from 1983 on, is tapering off and has been taken over by the deceleration of growth that has continued since the beginning of 1984.

Normative aspects

Bosworth and Lawrence regard the current economic policy mix, the combination of a relatively fast growth of wage costs with a fixed exchange rate, as very costly to Sweden. They recommend that fiscal policy should be used to secure a rate of saving compatible with optimal growth, and that monetary policy should be used for short-term stabilization policy. However, these recommendations should be implemented in combination with a flexible exchange rate to break the link between nominal wage inflation and short-term real rewards of workers. A monetary norm should be substituted for the norm of a fixed exchange rate.

I will not comment extensively on the proposal that Sweden should shift to a regime with a flexible exchange rate. However, I will raise two questions. First, doesn't this proposal suffer from the same problem as the proposal to implement a policy of nonaccommodation? It would take a long time until the new regime would be well understood and thereby credible. Shifting to nonaccommodation would risk a long period of high open unemployment; shifting to a flexible exchange rate would risk high inflation because it would not be well understood that the link between nominal wage increases and real wage increases had been broken.

Second, wouldn't a small open economy like Sweden's be vulnerable to heavy fluctuations of its exchange rate caused by shifts in the flow of financial capital? It has been demonstrated in the 1980s that even a large economy like that of the United States may have its currency value determined by financial flows quite independently of the competitiveness of its tradables sector.

Sweden's currency would probably be much more prone to swing because of decisions by investors in New York and London, possibly increased by bandwagon effects, disconnecting the value of the currency from Swedish productivity and wage costs.

Bosworth and Lawrence rather boldly calculate the optimal investment ratio by assuming a constant-return, Cobb-Douglas production function and a capital elasticity of that function of 0.3. They further assume zero growth of labor in natural units and growth of total productivity of 1.7 percent. This is then translated to a growth of augmented labor of roughly 2.5 percent, which in steady state calls for a growth of capital at that same rate. The required growth of the capital stock is used to calculate a warranted net investment ratio for the future of almost 10 percent, considerably higher than the present level.

This reasoning is fun, and I suppose it may say something about the direction of change of the investment ratio that Sweden should aim at. It is more doubtful whether it says something about the order of magnitude of that change: the authors argue that the present domestic investment ratio should be raised by about 1.5 percentage points, too small as a share of net domestic product. It is more difficult than usual to take seriously calculations based on "golden rule" concepts in the present situation, with Sweden far off any steady-state growth path.

Strategies for Stabilization

The authors draw on analyses from other chapters when they discuss policy strategies. Their main observation is that wage costs seem to be weakly influenced by price inflation but strongly influenced by labor market conditions. There are then three options: adopt a nonaccommodative policy and accept an increased level of unemployment to force down nominal wage increases; allow continuing relative inflation and a soft currency with, I reckon, discreet devaluations now and then; or implement an incomes policy by radically altering the mechanisms of wage setting.

Bosworth and Lawrence do not recommend the first strategy on the grounds that it depends heavily on credibility to avoid the social losses of drawn-out periods of high unemployment. "Credibility will not come quickly," they say. One could add that since the dominant political party is in close cooperation with at least one major trade union and has close connections with another, this policy would be very difficult to stick with even if it were announced beforehand. It would take a major shift of the electorate toward the right to implement this strategy effectively.

In the 1980s the Swedish government has incorporated elements of all three strategies in its policy. The 1982 devaluation was announced as "the last one" (it was the fifth since the autumn of 1976). The circumstances around its implementation gave some support to this claim, at least for the duration of the government's first term in office. Furthermore, the external balance was in huge deficit and so was the public sector. These conditions lent support to the government claims that there was no room for accommodation either by further devaluations or by reduced public spending, should the competitive situation get out of hand. So the government did announce a policy of nonaccommodation that was respected as a reality in the first half of the 1980s. For both the calendar years 1984 and 1985 the government announced norms for price increases and wage increases—4 percent and 3 percent respectively— something that I understand goes with nonaccommodation as a principle. Later, the norm of "no government foreign borrowing" was added.

Government policy also shows elements of the second strategy: the Swedish relative-cost position is constantly deteriorating between devaluations (and continues since the one in 1982). Presently, the construction of the weights of the index against which the Swedish krona is held constant leads on the average to a devaluation. The U.S. dollar is given excess weight in the construction of the index against which the krona is held constant. Thus the falling dollar leads to a depreciation against the German mark (and the Japanese yen), which is of special importance because Germany is Sweden's main competitor in third markets.

Finally, the government has tried many ways to influence wage costs: announcements of norms, persuasion of unions to scale down wage claims, roundtable talks involving all unions, and even a tax-based incomes policy. These efforts supplement its own large involvement in negotiations as a employer of public-sector employees. Therefore, current government strategy also includes elements of an incomes policy.

It is hard to say which strategy has been followed and which has not. This difficulty will probably continue. Government policy will combine all three strategies, with emphasis shifting as circumstances change.

5

Efficiency and Equality in Swedish Labor Markets

ROBERT J. FLANAGAN

FEW SOCIETIES have had as strong a commitment to economic equality as Sweden, and none has tried to implement so much of its commitment through the labor market. Over the years, Sweden has developed a unique set of labor market policies, involving both public and private institutions, intended to reduce earnings inequality, minimize unemployment, and increase the efficiency of the labor market. Throughout the 1950s and 1960s, when Sweden's economy was growing strongly, many of its labor market policies were widely praised and frequently emulated. Beginning in the 1970s, however, when Swedish growth slowed dramatically, questions arose about whether these policies might be contributing to the apparent loss of economic vitality.

Wage setting in Sweden is extremely centralized. Wages of public and private employees are set each year in a few national collective bargaining agreements. Swedish unions, which represent a much larger portion of the work force than do American unions, have a long history of adherence to a "solidaristic" wage policy that has greatly reduced the disparity of wages among firms, industries, and regions.

This chapter begins by examining the effect of that wage policy on the functioning of labor markets. Most economists would expect that a policy of narrowing wage differentials would reduce the effectiveness of the market in channeling workers into higher-productivity jobs. However, in most important respects the mobility of Swedish workers is not very different from that of U.S. workers. Swedish workers do, in fact, move from low-wage jobs and regions to better opportunities. The fall in mobility in the 1970s seems attributable more to lack of opportunity in a slower economy than to the inefficiency of the labor market. Other measures of market efficiency, such as rates of return on schooling, confirm that the Swedish labor market is sending appropriate signals to workers. The nation is, however, paying a high price in youth unemployment. In effect, the solidaristic wage policy sets a minimum wage that makes it uneconomic for employers to hire young workers. The result is that high rates of youth unemployment or involuntary part-time employment have the further effect of depriving young people of needed on-the-job experience. Surprisingly, however, the major efforts Sweden has made to reduce wage differentials between males and females have not led to substantial unemployment among women. At the same time, the gains in equity resulting from solidaristic wage policy appear small.

The chapter turns next to the effect of massive Swedish investment in training and, more recently, public employment opportunities for those who would otherwise be unemployed. These efforts, which absorb a far greater proportion of Swedish resources than comparable efforts in other countries, began during the 1960s in response to structural shifts in the Swedish economy, but have recently served mainly to counteract slack demand for labor and to disguise unemployment. There is disappointingly little evidence that these expenditures have improved the productivity of the Swedish work force.

The centralized nature of Swedish collective bargaining and the power of Swedish unions, combined with a policy to minimize unemployment, create the risk that real wages will be set too high for Sweden to compete in international markets and that the government will have to spend ever more to limit unemployment. Such was the case during the 1970s, when the historic restraint of the Swedish labor movement broke down as public-sector and white-collar unions grew in power and began competing with the blue-collar labor federation to raise wages. The remedy is not necessarily government-sanctioned increases in unemployment. The government could take a stronger bargaining position as a major employer, and it could build wage restraint incentives into income tax policies.

The chapter concludes with a discussion of the macroeconomic and microeconomic implications of wage earner funds—Sweden's most recent experiment in institutionalized capital sharing.

Labor Market Developments and Economic Growth

An important difference between the Swedish and U.S. economies is the growth of labor inputs. The past twenty years have seen no increase in the full-time Swedish labor force. Since 1965 the number of full-time employees has hovered around 3.2 million, with a small decline in full-time male employment just offset by an increase in full-time female employment. Virtually all of the employment growth during the past twenty years has come from part-time employment, which doubled between 1964 and 1985 and accounted for about 25 percent of Swedish employment in the early 1980s.[1] About two-thirds of the increase in the female labor force went into part-time employment, another 25 percent into full-time employment, and the remainder into unemployment. In addition, part of the statistical employment increase does not represent increased labor input, for under Sweden's generous parental leave policy, the proportion of women absent from their job for at least a week each year increased during the past twenty years. Total weekly hours worked dropped by 11 percent between 1965 and 1980 and by 1984 still remained below 1970 levels. Given the diminishing labor supply, the efficient allocation of labor resources is crucial to Swedish well-being.

While the labor force as a whole has not grown during the past twenty years, the public sector has expanded rapidly, both because of the Swedish investment in social welfare programs and because of the government's tendency to accomodate increases in labor costs with new expenditure programs. As in the United States, virtually all of the relative growth in public employment has occurred at the local government level (table 5-1). By 1985, 38 percent of all Swedes and 55 percent of Swedish women were government employees (indicating that many public jobs are part time). With most Swedish families now receiving at least part of their income through public employment, there is a significant lobby for the continuation of such programs.

Increased public-sector employment meant higher taxes. By the mid-1980s marginal income tax rates for salaried employees ranged up to 80 percent (but to 65 percent for most wage earners), and the payroll tax

1. About 18 percent of U.S. employment was part-time throughout the 1970s and early 1980s. U.S. Department of Labor, Bureau of Labor Statistics, *Employment and Earnings* (U.S. Government Printing Office, annual averages reported in 1970–84 January issues).

Table 5-1. *Public Employment in Sweden as a Percentage of Total Employment, by Sex, Selected Years, 1965–85*

Distribution	Central	Local	All government
Both sexes			
1965	9.9	10.3	20.2
1970	9.4	16.4	25.8
1975	9.7	20.6	30.3
1980	10.4	25.5	35.9
1985	9.9	28.3	38.2
Men			
1965	10.1	4.8	14.9
1970	10.0	7.4	17.4
1975	10.6	8.9	19.5
1980	11.7	10.8	22.5
1985	11.3	12.2	23.5
Women			
1965	9.6	19.9	29.5
1970	8.3	30.2	38.5
1975	8.5	36.6	45.1
1980	8.9	43.5	52.4
1985	8.4	46.4	54.8

Sources: Sverige officiella statistik *Arbetskraftsundersörkningarna* (Stockholm: Statistiska centralbyrån, 1978, 1981, 1985) [Official Statistics of Sweden, *The Labor Force Surveys* (Stockholm: Statistics Sweden, 1978, 1981, 1985)], *Am 1978:32; 1970–80,* and Am 1981–84 (manuscript copy).

rate on employers was 40 percent, up from 6 percent in 1950 and 14 percent in 1970. About 50 percent of the payroll tax is shifted back on workers, in the form of lower wage increases, within one year.[2] In the United States about 33 percent of payroll taxes is shifted back on workers.[3] Eventually the full burden of the payroll tax increases shifts to workers. With the rise in Sweden's public sector has also come a rise in the importance of public-sector unions. To understand the destabilizing effect of this development on collective bargaining, some background on the unusual institutional framework of Swedish collective bargaining is needed.[4]

2. Bertil Holmlund, "Payroll Taxes and Wage Inflation: The Swedish Experience," *Scandinavian Journal of Economics,* vol. 85, no. 1 (1983), pp. 1–15. One implication of the fact that the shifting of the tax is incomplete in the first year is that the collective bargaining system does not immediately provide full compensation for increases in payroll taxes.

3. Daniel S. Hamermesh, "New Estimates of the Incidence of the Payroll Tax," *Southern Economic Journal,* vol. 45 (April 1979), pp. 1208–19. Given the lags built into his model, Hamermesh apparently views this as an estimate of long-run shifting.

4. The historical development and postwar operation of this system has been studied

It is difficult to imagine a collective bargaining system more different from the decentralized bargaining arrangements of the United States than that of Sweden. Since the mid-1950s, wages for blue-collar workers have been set in negotiations between the Swedish Confederation of Trade Unions (Landsorganisationen i Sverige, or LO) and the Swedish Employers' Confederation (Svenska Arbetsgivareföreningen, or SAF)— the equivalent, in the United States, of wage negotiations between the AFL-CIO and the U.S. Chamber of Commerce. Unions representing most salaried white-collar workers in the private and public sectors are affiliated with the Central Organization of Salaried Employees (Tjänstemännens Centralorganisation, or TCO), which rarely bargains for its members. Instead, three major coalitions of national unions within the TCO—representing private, central government, and local government employees, respectively—conduct separate negotiations with SAF or the government. Salaried employees with university degrees are represented by the Swedish Confederation of Professional Associations (Sveriges Akademikers Centralorganisation, or SACO). While each of these central labor market organizations superficially resembles its rough counterpart in the United States, all have considerably more power over the national unions or industry-level employer associations that they represent. For example, SAF provides conflict insurance for its membership and has the authority to veto industry-level collective bargaining agreements and to determine whether employers can use a lockout in support of bargaining demands. SAF can also fine members who violate central directives. LO has indirect authority over the timing of strikes.

The potential economic power of the labor market organizations is also great. More than 90 percent of the blue-collar work force and 80 percent of the white-collar work force are represented by unions, and about 50 percent of Swedish employers (accounting for 85 to 90 percent of private-sector employment) are affiliated with SAF. Although such power could invite government intervention to restrain its use, the labor

extensively. See T. L. Johnston, *Collective Bargaining in Sweden: A Study of the Labour Market and Its Institutions* (London: Allen and Unwin, and Cambridge, Mass.: Harvard University Press, 1962); Gösta Edgren, Karl-Olof Faxén, and Clas-Erik Odhner, *Wage Formation and the Economy* (London: Allen and Unwin, 1973); Lloyd Ulman and Robert J. Flanagan, *Wage Restraint: A Study of Incomes Policies in Western Europe* (University of California Press, 1971), pp. 88–115; Robert J. Flanagan, David W. Soskice. and Lloyd Ulman. *Unionism, Economic Stabilization, and Incomes Policies: European Experience* (Brookings, 1983), chap. 6; and Karl-Olof Faxén and Hakan Lundgren, "Sweden," chap. 5, in Myron J. Roomkin, *The Changing Character of Managerial Employment: A Comparative View* (Oxford University Press, forthcoming).

market organizations have worked actively to avoid that possibility. Most of the rights and obligations governing labor relations were established by a mutual agreement between the major labor and management groups in 1938. (In the United States, many of these same rights and obligations are administered, subject to a large and growing volume of litigation, under the National Labor Relations Act.[5]) In addition, the parties have tried to develop bargaining methods and wage-growth objectives that would keep the government at arm's length. There has not been an official incomes policy in Sweden since a wage freeze in the late 1940s, largely because the labor market organizations have tried to exercise restraint in setting their bargaining objectives—effectively setting the parameters for a privately operated incomes policy. As the role of public-sector unions became an increasingly important element of collective bargaining in the late 1970s and 1980s, however, the line between the government's role as employer-negotiator and an official incomes policy has become rather fine.

There are two keys to successful voluntary pay restraint. The first is that negotiations must effectively determine the future growth of earnings. While this has generally been the case in decentralized collective bargaining systems, where wages are set close to the actual workplace, it has not been typical in Sweden or in other countries with centralized bargaining institutions. There, wage drift (a tendency for earnings to grow more rapidly than contractual rates permit) appears to result from revising compensation structures, local renegotiation of piece-rate systems, and, often, from the absence of centralized personnel policies within Swedish firms. The exact process by which wage drift is generated remains somewhat mysterious, and its interactions with negotiated wages are not fully understood. For example, bargaining over the local implementation of a central agreement can produce drift, but some drift also arises in periods lacking such implementation. Whatever its sources, drift drives a wedge not only between the objectives and effects of bargaining, but also between central trade unions and their members as the negotiated wage increases resulting from central bargaining come to represent a smaller fraction of earnings.

A second key to successful voluntary pay restraint is limiting the number of negotiators. Until the late 1960s, the Swedish bargaining system stayed small. Since then the number of negotiators has increased,

5. See Robert J. Flanagan, "NLRA Litigation and Union Representation," *Stanford Law Review*, vol. 38 (April 1986), pp. 957–89.

as the public-sector unions within LO and TCO have become more militant in response to their memberships' growing discontent with the terms negotiated for their private-sector counterparts. The public-sector unions' fight for an independent role in negotiations created conflict among the organizations in the early 1980s and led to a deterioration of Sweden's hitherto enviable record of industrial peace. In addition, bargaining within the private sector became more contentious as salaried workers facing relatively high marginal income tax rates were increasingly less inclined to accept patterns established in LO-SAF negotiations.

At the center of Swedish trade union efforts to produce greater equality in the labor market is the "solidaristic wage policy." Initially conceived in 1936 as a policy to narrow pay and productivity differentials between firms, the policy was more fully developed by LO economists in the early 1950s and became a part of wage settlements for blue-collar workers—the only workers represented by LO—beginning in 1957–58.[6] Developed along with government labor market programs subsidizing training and labor mobility, the solidaristic wage policy that emerged in the 1950s had both growth and equity objectives. The basic principle was equal pay for equal work: workers performing the same job should receive the same wage, irrespective of interfirm or interindustry differences in productivity and profitability. The principle was implemented by raising the relative wages of workers in low-productivity, usually labor-intensive, firms, and by not fully exercising bargaining power at firms with the greatest ability to pay. (The self-interest of unions at those firms was curbed by the centralized collective bargaining arrangements.) The resulting cost pressures on low-productivity sectors were expected to weed out the least efficient firms and shift employment, with the assistance of government labor market programs, to high-productivity, capital-intensive sectors.[7] In the absence of exact criteria for comparing jobs in different industries, the growth-oriented version of solidaristic wage policy gave way by 1960 to a more strictly egalitarian version that sought to narrow pay differences between workers in different occupations.[8]

Solidaristic wage policy appears to have realized its wage objectives. There has been considerable compression of virtually all dimensions of

6. LO, *Trade Unions and Full Employment* (Stockholm: LO, 1951).

7. Erik Lundberg, "The Rise and Fall of the Swedish Model," *Journal of Economic Literature,* vol. 23 (March 1985), pp. 18–19.

8. Edgren, Faxén, and Odhner, *Wage Formation,* pp. 40–44; Derek Robinson, *Solidaristic Wage Policy in Sweden* (Paris: OECD, 1974), pp. 17–24.

Figure 5-1. *Wage Dispersion for Swedish Blue-Collar Workers as Measured by the Coefficient of Variation, 1957–84*

Index (1972 = 100)

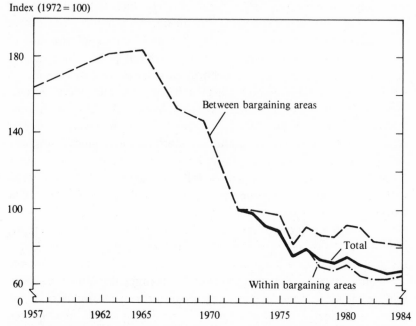

Source: Lennart Jonsson and Claes-Henric Siven, *Varför Löneskillnader?* (Stockholm: Svenska Arbetsgivareföreningen, 1986), p. 2.

the wage structure since the mid-1960s. The compression is most notable for blue-collar workers, for whom solidaristic wage policy has been an explicit bargaining objective (see figure 5-1). The wage dispersion between bargaining areas (generally industries) peaked in 1965 and then declined precipitously until 1972. Since 1978 it has followed no distinct trend. However, wage dispersion has fallen even more rapidly among individuals than among industries since 1972, when figures for individuals were first available. More generally, wage dispersion by skill, sex, and age has declined in virtually every industry.

Two facts—that smaller reductions in wage dispersion also occurred for white-collar workers, whose unions never adopted the solidaristic wage policy (figure 5-2), and that interindustry wage gaps narrowed in many countries without explicit solidaristic wage policies[9]—suggest that

9. See "Relative Wages, Industrial Structure and Employment Performance," *OECD Employment Outlook* (Paris: OECD, 1985), pp. 83–98.

Figure 5-2. *Wage Dispersion for Swedish White-Collar Workers as Measured by the Coefficient of Variation, 1958–83*

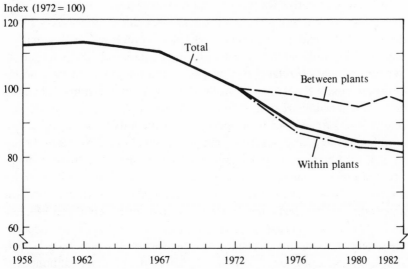

Index (1972 = 100)

Source: See figure 5-1.

not all of the blue-collar wage compression should be attributed to LO's wage policy. As will become apparent, however, much of the Swedish compression appears to be institutionally driven.

To the extent that this is true and therefore reflects equal pay for unequal work, distortions in the allocation of labor might be expected. The next two sections of the chapter explore the issues of labor market efficiency raised by both the premises and results of solidaristic wage policy.

Economic Incentives and Labor Mobility

The intellectual foundation of postwar Swedish labor market policy has been the idea that wage differentials do not reallocate labor efficiently enough to accommodate the structural changes inherent in an open economy. That argument provided the case for institutional action to reduce wage differentials and for government programs to allocate labor. Now that wage differentials have been successfully compressed, however, concern has arisen that the work force has become immobile. The evidence is that this concern is not well-founded.

The original "evidence" in support of an immobile Swedish labor force apparently consisted of statistically insignificant simple correlations between relative wage and employment changes. It is now widely recognized that inferences based on such evidence are shaky. First, there are the standard simultaneity problems presented by any market experiencing shifts in both the supply and demand schedules for labor. Second, simple correlations of wages and employment ignore the investment character of most important labor market decisions. When the costs of a decision are concentrated in one period of a person's life and returns are spread over many periods, the incentives (to change jobs, enroll in training, and so forth) facing groups that differ by age and even by sex may vary radically. Aggregation into simple industrywide or occupationwide employment and wage changes tends to obscure the influence of wages on rational labor market choices, given the investment character of these decisions. Ignoring the investment character of labor market choices tends to lead to empirical strategies that do not focus on the groups making the decisions and the incentives they face. Third, simple wage-employment correlations ignore the influence of nonpecuniary compensation on labor market choices.

At a simple descriptive level, with quit rates in industry taken as a measure of voluntary mobility, the mobility rate in Sweden is essentially the same as the rate in the United States. From 1970 to 1982 the monthly quit rate for blue-collar workers in Swedish industry averaged just under 2 percent.[10] During the 1970s, the quit rate for production workers in U.S. manufacturing also averaged 2 percent.[11] At this level of generality, little interpretation is possible, although the data may challenge some preconceptions about the comparative level of labor mobility in Swedish labor markets.[12]

Although virtually all measures of labor mobility and migration in Sweden have declined during the 1970s and early 1980s, the decline does

10. Bertil Holmlund, *Labor Mobility: Studies of Labor Turnover and Migration in the Swedish Labor Market* (Stockholm: Industrial Institute for Economic and Social Research, 1984), p. 26.

11. *Employment and Training Report of the President 1982* (Government Printing Office, 1983), p. 252. Although some changes in employment status denoted as "other separations" in the U.S. data are counted as quits in Sweden, adjusting the U.S. data for this factor would add at most 0.5 percent to the monthly quit rate, leaving a difference between the countries that is well within the range of sampling error.

12. The total separation rate is lower in Sweden than in the United States, but this reflects the lower overall layoff rate in Sweden, which results almost entirely from the relatively low level of temporary layoffs there.

not reflect a change in workers' propensity to move. It appears, instead, to be almost entirely the result of a decline in job vacancies (and thus a lower probability of receiving a job offer), longer average job tenure (given the lower new hire rates of the period), and a gradual increase in average plant size.[13]

Is the mobility of the Swedish work force efficient? One way to pose this question is to ask whether workers tend to move from relatively low-productivity to relatively high-productivity jobs. The evidence suggests that they do. Both the quit behavior and the quit intentions of Swedish workers are inversely related to their relative wage position. That is, Swedish workers with relatively low wages are more likely to quit than those whose wages are higher. Moreover, estimates of the response of quits to relative wages in Sweden appear to fall into the same range as parallel estimates for U.S. workers.[14] The sensitivity of quit intentions to relative wage position appears to have increased in Sweden during the 1970s, largely because of the increase in the number of women workers, whose quits are more responsive to wages than are men's (as they are in the United States) and have grown more responsive more rapidly.[15] In short, Swedish workers seem no less likely than their American counterparts to pursue wage increases. Further evidence on the efficiency of Swedish job changing can be gathered by examining the wage returns realized by those who change jobs, and in fact workers do increase their wages by moving, whether to a new job or a new region. Moreover, the wage increases associated with moving are two to three times larger than the returns on spending one more year in school.[16]

It is obvious from the small contribution of quits to Swedish unemployment that many workers search for and find new jobs before leaving their old ones. Some 20 to 25 percent of Swedish employees reported

13. Holmlund, *Labor Mobility*, chaps. 2, 4.
14. Holmlund reports wage elasticities in the range of -0.5 to -1.0 from an analysis of quit behavior in the Swedish engineering industry. Holmlund, *Labor Mobility*, pp. 88–90. U.S. estimates from both interindustry and individual data fall toward the upper end of that range. In an analysis of interindustry data from 1960, Pencavel found wage elasticities ranging between -0.8 and -0.9. John H. Pencavel, *An Analysis of the Quit Rate in American Manufacturing Industry* (Princeton, N.J.: Princeton University, Department of Economics, Industrial Relations Section, 1970), chap. 3. In an analysis of the Michigan Panel Study of Income Dynamics, Viscusi found that the wage elasticity of quitting a 1975 job was -0.9 for men and -1.0 for women. W. Kip Viscusi, "Sex Differences in Worker Quitting," *Review of Economics and Statistics*, vol. 62 (August 1980), pp. 388–98.
15. Holmlund, *Labor Mobility*, pp. 102–08.
16. Ibid., chaps. 6, 7. The returns on mobility (and on schooling, as will be discussed) did decrease between 1968 and 1974, however.

that they were searching for work in the 1970s.[17] That such workers seek
new jobs in a distinctly procyclical pattern shows that their search is
sensitive to market opportunities.[18] Because job search is costly, however, it is a type of labor market investment that would rationally be
concentrated early in worklife, when the expected returns are highest.
On-the-job search activity in Sweden follows such an age profile, peaking
in the late twenties for most workers and gradually tapering off. While it
may be possible to improve the efficiency of the job search process in
Sweden, it is difficult to argue that this is a society that is not searching
for and responding to better labor market opportunities. The problem
during the 1970s and early 1980s was a shortage of opportunities.

Another way to examine the question of labor market efficiency is to
look at the results, as Adam Smith suggested more than 200 years ago.[19]
If workers move so as to maximize their net advantage, the labor market
should produce wage differentials that compensate for differences between jobs in other monetary and nonmonetary benefits and costs.
Arguably the operation of the solidaristic wage policy could produce
something different from a compensating structure. Thus one way to
assess the functioning of the Swedish labor market is to ask whether the
outcome appears distorted by comparison with the wage structures of
economies that do not share Sweden's particular institutional characteristics.

One of the most common applications of Smith's theory has been the
estimation of rates of return on schooling. Analyses of Swedish data
using essentially the same methodologies applied in the United States
produce two general findings. First, there is a highly significant and
positive rate of return to schooling, although the rates of return estimated
for the late 1960s—about 7 to 8 percent in Sweden—are lower than the
10 to 12 percent rates estimated for that period in the United States.[20]
Second, the rate of return to schooling in Sweden dropped during the
early 1970s to about 5 percent. Although this reduction is sometimes
casually associated with the effects of solidaristic wage policy, it may
be significant that the United States experienced a similar decline in the

17. Sverige officiella statistik, *Arbetskraftsundersörkningarna* (Stockholm: Statistiska centralbyrån, various issues) [Official Statistics of Sweden, *The Labor Force
Surveys* (Stockholm: Statistics Sweden, various issues)].

18. Holmlund, *Labor Mobility*, pp. 74–76.

19. Adam Smith, *An Inquiry into the Nature and Causes of the Wealth of Nations*
(Modern Library, 1937), book I, chap. 10.

20. Holmlund, *Labor Mobility*, pp. 152, 156.

rate of return on schooling at about the same time.[21] The U.S. decline has been associated with changes in industrial structure that reduced the relative demand for college-educated workers at the same time that students who had enrolled in response to earlier market signals completed their education. The U.S. decline in the return on schooling is thus interpreted as the response of flexible relative wages to a disequilibrium in the labor market. But in Sweden the decline tends to be viewed as an institutionally driven change in relative labor prices that is likely to provoke labor market disequilibrium (for example, a skill shortage). Given the significant extension of compulsory schooling in Sweden in the late 1960s, however, it would seem useful to ask how much of the decline in the Swedish rate of return on schooling simply reflects an increase in the relative supply of educated workers.

There are also significant, although apparently declining, returns on job tenure and labor force experience. On average, a year of experience raised the hourly wage at the beginning of a career by 3 percent in 1968 but only 2 percent in 1974. For a worker who had spent ten years in the labor force, an additional year of experience raised the hourly wage by 2 percent in 1968 but by half that in 1974.[22] These experience-earnings profiles, which include returns on investments in training made after graduation, appear to be flatter than those measured in the United States where, for example, in 1959 a year of labor-force experience was worth about 8 percent at the beginning of a career and 5.5 percent ten years later.[23]

The Swedish profile, however, more nearly resembles those for unionized workers in the United States, which are considerably flatter than those estimated for nonunion workers. Studies of U.S. data for white males in the early 1970s find that an additional year of experience raised the hourly wage of union workers by 1 percent, that of nonunion workers by 2.3 percent.[24] Unfortunately, these returns cannot be com-

21. Richard B. Freeman estimates that the private internal rate of return on schooling in the United States fell from 11.5 percent in 1969 to 8.5 percent in 1974. See "Overinvestment in College Training?" *Journal of Human Resources*, vol. 10 (Summer 1975), pp. 287–311.

22. Holmlund, *Labor Mobility*, p. 152.

23. Jacob Mincer, *Schooling, Experience, and Earnings* (New York: National Bureau of Economic Research, 1974), p. 92.

24. Farrell E. Bloch and Mark S. Kuskin, "Wage Determination in the Union and Nonunion Sectors," *Industrial and Labor Relations Review*, vol. 31 (January 1978), pp. 183–92. See also Gregory M. Duncan and Duane E. Leigh, "Wage Determination in the Union and Nonunion Sectors: A Sample Selectivity Approach," *Industrial and Labor Relations Review*, vol. 34 (October 1980), pp. 24–34.

pared directly with those in the previous paragraph, because the regressions from which they are estimated control for occupation and industry. That is, they do not include the returns from moving between occupations and industries. These same studies also indicate that union workers in the United States earn a lower return on schooling than nonunion workers.

The general differences between the two countries in the returns for schooling and experience appear to reflect differences in the degree of union representation more than differences in market behavior. While U.S. unions do not have a formal solidaristic wage policy, they have traditionally sought to "take wages out of competition" and appear to have had considerable success in narrowing wage differentials within the union sector.[25] Indeed, the important contrast appears to be less between an economy that operates under a solidaristic wage policy and one that does not, than between an economy in which equity objectives are implemented in nationwide wage policies and one in which wage policy is essentially firm-oriented. Returns on schooling and experience in Japan, where both union and nonunion wage policies are oriented toward firm performance, are greater than those in either Sweden or the United States, for example.[26]

The main consequence of relatively low returns on experience is a suppression of performance incentives within organizations. If steeper earnings-tenure profiles reflect greater investment in specific human capital, fewer such investments will be made when the returns are reduced by institutional actions. Alternatively, earnings profiles may reflect efforts by firms to avoid the loss of experienced workers by "bonding" workers to firms.[27] According to this view, low wages early in a worker's career are a type of performance bond posted in the expectation that good performance will lead to continued employment, wage increases, and rather high wages later in the career. Whichever theory one subscribes to, the development of better incentives within

25. Richard B. Freeman, "Unionism and the Dispersion of Wages," *Industrial and Labor Relations Review,* vol. 34 (October 1980), pp. 3–23; and Freeman, "Union Wage Practices and Wage Dispersion Within Establishments," *Industrial and Labor Relations Review,* vol. 36 (October 1982), pp. 3–21.

26. Masanori Hashimoto and John Raisian, "Employment Tenure and Earnings Profiles in Japan and the United States," *American Economic Review,* vol. 75 (September 1985), pp. 721–35.

27. Edward P. Lazear, "Agency, Earnings Profiles, Productivity, and Hours Restrictions," *American Economic Review,* vol. 71 (September 1981), pp. 606–20.

firms is likely to reduce mobility among them, because there is more to lose.[28]

A more subtle question is whether Swedish wages tend to offset the nonpecuniary conditions of employment. In the United States, wages tend to compensate for the risk of death but not necessarily for risk of job injury or onerous job conditions.[29] In Sweden, whatever the institutional vagaries of the labor market, there is a distinct tendency for workers to receive relatively higher wages for relatively undesirable working conditions (and conversely).[30]

Costs of Solidaristic Wage Policy

Solidaristic wage policy was gradually implemented in some industries by means of low-wage "kitties" under the central agreement permitting a plant to receive an extra amount to be paid to low-wage workers, and by negotiating higher minimum pay for all workers.[31] Since 1966, wage increases have been set in absolute terms (as in most U.S. collective bargaining agreements). The scope of application of the special low-wage kitties broadened rapidly. In the late 1960s, kitty size was based on the number of workers receiving less than 96 percent of the mean industrial wage. But by 1981–82, contributions were based on the number of workers earning less than 200 percent of the industry average. The distribution of the kitties was left to local negotiations. Only after 1982 is there any evidence of a relaxation in the thrust of solidaristic wage policy.[32]

The narrowing of the wage structure that has occurred since the early

28. Again, Japan, where earnings profiles are steeper and job tenure much longer than in the United States, provides an interesting data point. See Hashimoto and Raisian, "Employment Tenure and Earnings Profiles."

29. Robert S. Smith, "Compensating Wage Differentials and Public Policy: A Review," *Industrial and Labor Relations Review*, vol. 32 (April 1979), pp. 339–52.

30. Greg J. Duncan and Bertil Holmlund, "Was Adam Smith Right After All? Another Test of the Theory of Compensating Wage Differentials," *Journal of Labor Economics*, vol. 1 (October 1983), pp. 366–79.

31. For a discussion of the technical aspects of this method of implementation, see Karl-Olof Faxén, "From National Level to Plant Level: Agreement and Calculation Technique in the Application of a Central Framework Agreement," in *On Incomes Policy: Papers and Proceedings from a Conference in Honour of Erik Lundberg* (Stockholm: Industrial Council for Social and Economic Studies, 1969), pp. 245–58.

32. In 1983, the low-wage benchmark dropped to 140 percent of the industry average wage. Data are from LO, *De Centrala Överenskommelserna Mellan LO och SAF, 1952–83* (Stockholm: LO, 1983).

1960s appears to be largely the result of the minimum wage provisions of the central agreements rather than of the low-wage kitties. During the 1970s the dispersion of wages declined most rapidly in industries in which *only* negotiated minimum wage increases were operative. Moreover, studies of the aggregate relationship between negotiated wage increases, wage drift, and wage dispersion for six-month periods find that in periods when the central agreement was applied, the wage dispersion narrowed (largely as a result of increased minimum wages). In intervening periods, wage drift increased and wage dispersion was partially restored.[33] Another study used the details of the low-wage provisions of central agreements to estimate the changes in the wage structure desired by LO over the contract period (assuming the low-wage provisions were implemented exactly). When this "objective" is compared with actual changes in the wage structure, it turns out that unions achieved about one-third of their goal between 1964 and 1982, the remaining two-thirds being undone by wage drift.[34]

Economists instinctively doubt that institutionally driven changes in the wage structure that produce equal pay for unequal work are likely to be obtained without cost. This section analyzes Sweden's experience in narrowing the two sets of wage differentials—that between young workers and adults and that between male and female workers.

The Labor Market for Swedish Youth

By all indications job opportunities for young Swedish workers have deteriorated substantially since 1970. Although employment has grown, relative unemployment figures are only the tip of an iceberg. There is also substantial underemployment in the form of involuntary part-time work. In a survey taken in February 1984, for example, almost half of the sixteen- to twenty-four-year-old women, and about 39 percent of the young men working part time would have preferred an increase in working hours. (Twenty-two percent of all part-time employees preferred longer hours.) Most seemed to be looking for full-time work.[35]

33. Lennart A. Jonsson and Claes-Henric Siven, *Varför Löneskillnader?* (Stockholm: SAF, 1986); and Jonsson and Siven, "Lönespridningens Örsaksfaktorer inom Verkstadsforeningens Omrade," unpublished manuscript, March 22, 1982.

34. Christian Nilsson, "De Regionala Arbetsmarknadsproblemen och den Fackliga Lönepolitiken," unpublished manuscript, September 4, 1986, p. 49.

35. DELFA [Committee for the Study of Working Hours], *Preferred Working Hours,* DELFA debate report 3 (Stockholm, June 1984), p. 4.

What explains the apparent excess of young workers? Sweden, along with many other countries, experienced an increase in the relative supply of such workers in the 1960s. This demographic effect, however, peaked in the late 1960s and early 1970s and was over by the time the youth unemployment problem began to develop. During the 1970s and 1980s the labor force participation rate of teenagers declined as years of schooling increased, and their share of the labor force declined from the mid-1960s. Participation rates for twenty- to twenty-four-year-olds increased, but their share of the labor force peaked around 1970. During the 1970s, the labor force failed to accommodate new teenagers despite the fact that their raw numbers were no larger than in the 1960s.

Persistent excess supply of a labor resource implies inflexible relative wages. In the United States, for example, there is considerable evidence that the federal minimum wage has reduced job opportunities for youth. Its major impact has not been to increase the measured unemployment of youth, but rather to lower labor force participation rates.[36] There are also more subtle effects: since the minimum wage law covers only part of the U.S. economy, there has been a reallocation of the least productive (usually the least experienced) workers toward the uncovered sectors. The youth fraction of employment in manufacturing and other covered industries has declined substantially since the passage of the law in 1938.[37] Moreover, increases in the minimum wage are associated with a shift from full-time to part-time (largely uncovered) employment for youth.[38]

Sweden has no statutory minimum wage, but the solidaristic wage policy has tended to narrow wage differences between less-skilled and more-skilled workers and between younger and older workers. While labor agreements permit a "subminimum" wage for workers under eighteen years of age, the full adult rate is paid to all workers at eighteen years of age. During the 1970s, the minimum contractual wage for eighteen-year-olds increased relative to the median wage for LO workers, and age-earnings profiles were virtually flat.[39] It appears likely that

36. Jacob Mincer, "Unemployment Effects of Minimum Wages," *Journal of Political Economy*, vol. 84 (August 1976, part 2), pp. S87–S104; and Edward M. Gramlich, "Impact of Minimum Wages on Other Wages, Employment, and Family Incomes," *Brookings Papers on Economic Activity, 2:1976*, pp. 409–51.

37. Finis Welch, *Minimum Wages: Issues and Evidence* (Washington, D.C.: American Enterprise Institute, 1978), pp. 29–32.

38. Gramlich, "Impact of Minimum Wages."

39. Claes-Henric Siven, "The Wage Structure and the Functioning of the Labor Market," unpublished manuscript, September 9, 1985, p. 23.

Table 5-2. *Hourly Earnings of Swedish Youth Relative to Adults, by Sex and Years of Schooling, Selected Years, 1960–81*
Ratio

Distribution	1960	1968	1974	1980	1981
By age and sex					
Males					
Blue-collar[a]	0.56	0.58	0.65	0.72	n.a.
White-collar[b]	n.a.	n.a.	0.30	0.39	n.a.
All employees[c]	n.a.	0.46	0.58	n.a.	n.a.
Females					
Blue-collar[a]	0.69	0.71	0.74	0.81	n.a.
White-collar[b]	n.a.	n.a.	0.49	0.58	n.a.
All employees[c]	n.a.	0.51	0.53	n.a.	n.a.
By years of schooling					
All employees[d]					
9 years	n.a.	0.43	0.53	n.a.	0.71
10 years	n.a.	0.50	0.57	n.a.	0.59
11 years	n.a.	0.44	0.59	n.a.	0.68

Sources: Age and sex data from Anders Björklund and Inga Persson-Tanimura, "Youth Employment in Sweden," in Beatrice G. Reubens, ed., *Youth at Work: An International Survey* (Totowa, N.J.: Rowman and Allanheld, 1983), p. 258; years of schooling data from Level of Living Survey.
n.a. Not available.
a. Ratio of earnings of workers aged 16–17 to those of workers aged 18 and older.
b. Ratio of earnings of workers aged 16–17 to those of workers aged 20 and older.
c. Ratio of earnings of workers aged 16–19 to those of workers aged 25 and older.
d. Ratio of earnings of workers aged 16–19 to those of workers aged 20 and older.

the solidaristic wage policy operates as a de facto national minimum wage for youth. Indeed, during periods of sustained effort to narrow the wage structure in sequential collective bargaining negotiations, the impact may be much stronger than that of the statutory version in the United States, for the latter is altered infrequently, only to be repealed by the forces of inflation until the next statutory action.

Certainly there has been a substantial narrowing of the youth-adult gap in relative wages in Sweden, both in the aggregate and by years of schooling (table 5-2). The wage of male and female blue-collar workers aged sixteen to eighteen rose, relative to the wage of workers eighteen and over, only 2 percentage points between 1960 and 1968, but then rose 5 percentage points (4 for young women) in the next two years and another 9 points (6 for women) during the 1970s. By 1980, wages for male and female teenage blue-collar workers were respectively 29 and 17 percent higher, relative to workers eighteen and older, than they had been in 1960. Measurements for white-collar workers go back less far, but during the 1970s the teenage-adult relative wages in these jobs also increased by 11 to 12 percentage points.[40] Such increases could, of course, reflect increasing productivity among youth, and in fact the years of schooling completed by successive cohorts of young workers did increase steadily into the 1970s. Nevertheless, the relative wages of youth and adults with the same amount of schooling also narrowed substantially during the period—a fact that is more likely to be attributable to the effects of the solidaristic wage policy.

The relative wage effect on young workers is serious for two reasons. First, elasticities of substitution for young workers are quite large, so that institutionally driven increases in the relative wage of youth reduce immediate employment prospects.[41] Second, increasing the unemployment and involuntary part-time employment of youth tends to lower the long-run earnings profiles of today's youth by excluding them from the early employment experiences that provide substantial on-the-job training investments. Perhaps this long-run effect is less important in a country where wage profiles are relatively flat than it would be in the United States, but the fact that there are trade-offs between immediate and long-term equality should not be ignored.

Male-Female Wage Differentials

Since the 1960s, both Sweden and the United States have attempted to reduce labor market discrimination against women. In the United States the thrust has been mainly statutory and has given rise to considerable litigation. In Sweden the lead came from the labor market organizations, which until 1960 maintained separate wage scales for male and female workers. In 1960 LO and SAF agreed to phase out the separate scales by 1965. Subsequently, a narrowing of male-female wage differentials was an element of the general solidaristic wage policy of reducing all wage inequalities in society.

Since the early 1960s, the hourly wage of women relative to men appears to have changed more rapidly and moved much closer to equality

40. Data are from Statistics Sweden as reported in Anders Björklund and Inga Persson-Tanimura, "Youth Unemployment in Sweden," in Beatrice G. Reubens, ed., *Youth at Work: An International Survey* (Totowa, N.J.: Rowman and Allanheld, 1983), p. 258.

41. Using a constant-elasticity-of-substitution production function specification, Nilsson estimates elasticities of substitition of about three and five respectively for men and women under age eighteen. Christian Nilsson, "Ungdomsarbetslöshet och facklig lönepolitik," unpublished manuscript, March 19, 1984. For a review of the elasticities estimated for other countries, see *OECD Employment Outlook* (Paris: OECD, 1984), pp. 81–83.

Figure 5-3. *Relative Swedish Female-Male Wage, 1947–83, and Salary, 1963–83*

Percent

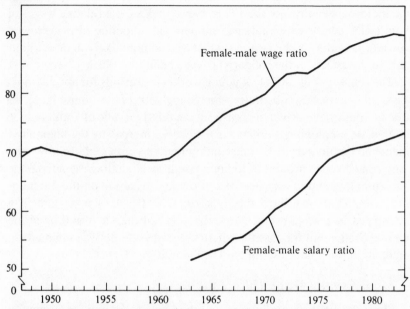

Source: Official Statistics of Sweden, *Löner* (Stockholm: Statistics Sweden, various issues), as reported in Anders Björklund and Inga Persson-Tanimura, "Youth Employment in Sweden," in *Youth at Work: An International Survey* (Totowa, N.J.: Rowman and Allanheld, 1983.)

in Sweden than it has in any other advanced country.[42] From the late 1940s until the early 1960s, the hourly wage of women in manufacturing seemed stuck at just under 70 percent of the male wage. Beginning in 1962, the midpoint of the period in which the labor market organizations had agreed to eliminate sex differentials, the relative wage of women in manufacturing began to rise by a percentage point a year, reaching 90 percent of the male wage in the early 1980s (figure 5-3). Much the same picture emerges for salaries. Salaried women received 50 percent of the monthly pay of salaried men throughout the late 1940s and 1950s. Beginning in 1962, however, relative salaries of women also began to

42. The United States appears to be an exception among modern industrial nations in this respect. In a recent twelve-country comparison, it was one of only two countries in which the female relative wage did not increase between 1960 and 1980. The other country was the Soviet Union. Jacob Mincer, "Intercountry Comparisons of Labor Force Trends and of Related Developments: An Overview," *Journal of Labor Economics,* vol. 3 (January 1985), pt. 2, p. S6, table 3.

rise at about a percentage point per year, reaching 73 percent of the male salaries in the early 1980s (see figure 5-3). Differences were even smaller in the public sector, where salaries received by women equaled 85 to 90 percent of those received by men in the early 1980s.[43] Not all of the increase can be attributed to the policies of the labor market organizations, however. The relative schooling of women increased substantially during this period, and the fact that the female relative wage ranged from near equality for workers twenty-four years old and under to approximately 63 percent for workers forty-five to sixty-four suggests that increasing relative productivity is part of the story.[44]

One way to estimate the effect of discrimination and other institutional influences on both the level and the change in the female relative wage is to use standard regression techniques to decompose overall male-female wage differences into differences in productivity, such as schooling and work experience; differences in the measured returns to productivity; and differences in the constant terms, which reflect the effects of unmeasured influences. To the extent that labor market discrimination exists, it will be reflected in the last two sources of male-female wage differentials. In a decomposition analysis of the Level of Living Survey sample, it appears that less than 25 percent of the gross male-female wage differential from 1968 to 1981 can be attributed to productivity differences.[45] Although the overall male-female wage differential is relatively small in Sweden, productivity differences appear to play a smaller role in "accounting" for the differential than they do in the United States. The fraction of the narrowing gross differential accounted for by productivity variables increased between 1968 and 1981 (from 16 to 25 percent), indicating some scope for institutional factors, including solidaristic wage policy, in producing greater wage equality between men and women. Measured returns on human capital investments are about the same for Swedish men and women. When these returns have

43. In a broader sample of the Swedish labor force, the Level of Living Survey, the relative wage was somewhat larger, but rose from 72 percent in 1968 to 85 percent in 1981. Siv Gustafsson and Roger Jacobsson, "Trends in Female Labor Force Participation in Sweden," *Journal of Labor Economics,* vol. 3 (January 1985), pt. 2, p. S263. Survey measures of labor force experience for this purpose are crude. They do not, for example, reflect male-female differences in weekly hours—a factor of potential importance in an economy in which part-time work by women is so common.

44. Siv Gustafsson and Petra Lantz, *Arbete och Löner* (Stockholm: Almqvist and Wiksell, 1985), p. 226, table 36.

45. Gustafsson and Jacobsson, "Trends in Female Labor Force Participation," p. S 263.

changed, as in the falling rate of return to schooling in the 1970s, they have changed for both sexes. The narrowing of the total male-female wage differential during the period has come largely from a reduction in the difference between constant terms in the regressions for men and women and from some narrowing of productivity differences. Constant terms aside, earnings profiles, which are so different for the sexes in the United States, were essentially identical for Swedish men and women by the mid-1970s.[46]

Equal Employment Opportunity Policies

The government commitment to equalize the treatment of women and men in the labor market emerged in the United States at about the time that LO and SAF were eliminating the separate wage scales for men and women in Sweden. Like the action taken by the Swedish labor market organizations, the initial U.S. statute, the Equal Pay Act of 1963, sought to eliminate unequal pay for identical work. Subsequent federal action, notably Title VII of the Civil Rights Act of 1964 and executive orders establishing affirmative action requirements for federal government contractors and subcontractors, mounted a much broader attack against discriminatory practices.

In Sweden statutory efforts to eliminate labor market discrimination against women came later. When they did, LO, TCO, and SAF opposed them on the grounds that collective bargaining provided a better forum for addressing those issues. Changes in the Swedish constitution in 1974 forbade discrimination by sex except in cases involving military service or efforts to promote equality—the latter exception enabling Sweden to avoid the conflict between the nondiscrimination and affirmative action standards that has developed with the implementation of equal opportunity policy in the United States.[47] Nevertheless, until 1980, Sweden

46. Holmlund, *Labor Mobility*, pp. 155–57.
47. Siv Gustafsson, "Equal Opportunity Policies in Sweden," in Günther Schmid and Renate Weitzel, eds., *Sex Discrimination and Equal Opportunity* (New York: St. Martin's Press, 1984), p. 144. Under Title VII of the Civil Rights Act of 1964, most firms in the United States are held to a general nondiscrimination standard. In implementing this standard, the courts have emphasized the results, rather than the intent, of an organization's personnel policies. In addition to this general nondiscrimination standard, firms that happen to be government contractors are subject also to special requirements to take affirmative action, which seems to imply more than even-handed treatment of minority groups. Some personnel policies formulated out of a

had no agency monitoring compliance with the nondiscrimination stand-ard or inducing affirmative action efforts.

In 1980 the Act of Equality between Men and Women at Work went into effect. The act, which covers the entire economy, bars discrimina-tion, requires employers to promote equality in the workplace actively, and establishes enforcement procedures. The ban on discrimination applies to both unequal pay for equal work (a provision widely viewed as superfluous in view of collective bargaining actions taken in the early 1960s) and unequal pay for work of equal value. The latter concept is essentially the standard advanced by "comparable worth" advocates in the United States, but Swedes have been no more successful than Americans in developing an operational approach to this standard. Under affirmative action, the Swedish law contemplates that specific goals and timetables to produce equality will be set in collective bargaining, and the enforcement mechanism established for this aspect of the law has not been invoked thus far. In the United States, where discrimination in unionized settings often reflected joint decisions by labor and manage-ment, an outside body, such as a regulatory agency or the courts, was seen as necessary to produce real change.

There are three steps to the enforcement of the Swedish ban on discrimination. A plaintiff first brings the problem to the union for resolution with the employer. If the first step fails, the plaintiff can take the matter to a uniquely Swedish institution, the equality ombudsman. If the ombudsman is unable to negotiate a settlement with the employer, the case can be taken to the Labor Court, a special body handling litigation that arises out of the employment relationship. Two restrictions on cases brought before the Labor Court limit the likely role of litigation in producing changes in the employment and earnings of women. First, although technically permitted, class actions are not envisaged, given the emphasis on voluntary solutions to be worked out by the parties to the labor market. Second, punitive damages awarded to a plaintiff are limited to Skr 20,000 (about $2,300 in mid-1985), although full back pay can be awarded if a charge is proved. Given the lack of incentives for lawyers and potential plaintiffs, Sweden is unlikely to have either the volume of litigation or the results associated with U.S. equal opportunity policy. A disproportionately large number of cases brought to the

---

sensitivity to affirmative action requirements have generated Title VII litigation alleging discrimination against nonminority workers.

ombudsman have been against public employers, apparently because the cost of proving a charge is relatively low since public-sector employers are required to reveal the names and qualifications of applicants for jobs or promotions.[48]

Whether by the action of the labor market organizations or by government policy, some of the narrowing in the male-female wage differential in Sweden appears to be institutionally driven. There seems, however, to be no offsetting drop in job opportunities for women workers.[49] During the period of narrowing wage differentials, there has been no increase in the relative unemployment rate of women, for example. There are two possible explanations. First, much of the growth of female employment has been in the public sector, where the sex differentials are relatively narrow. On its face, this is consistent with the general equilibrium predictions of the neoclassical models of labor market discrimination (that wage equality would tend to produce greater employment segregation).[50] While it is tempting to suggest that the effect of raising the female relative wage has been to foreclose private-sector job opportunities and force women into part-time work in the public sector, women, unlike youth, do not appear to be hours-constrained. The growth of part-time employment appears to reflect the preferences of the female labor force.[51]

The second possibility may surprise Americans used to thinking of Sweden as a pioneer in equality between the sexes. Occupational concentration, the tendency of men and women to be distributed disproportionately among occupations, is at least as great in Sweden as in the United States.[52] In 1960, 74.5 percent of the women in the Swedish

---

48. The enforcement experience is reviewed in Anita Dahlberg, *Om Jämställdhet* (Stockholm: Arbetslivscentrum, 1983).

49. This is similar to experience in Australia, where it has also been difficult to find offsetting losses in job opportunities as a result of a substantial institutionally driven increase in the female relative wage in the 1970s. See OECD, *The Integration of Women into the Economy* (Paris: OECD, 1985), chaps. 2, 3; and R. G. Gregory, P. McMahan, and B. Whittingham, "Women in the Australian Labor Force: Trends, Causes, and Consequences," *Journal of Labor Economics*, vol. 3 (January 1985), pt. 2, pp. S293–S309.

50. Gary S. Becker, *The Economics of Discrimination*, 2d ed. (University of Chicago Press, 1971); and Kenneth J. Arrow, "Models of Job Discrimination," in Anthony H. Pascal, ed., *Racial Discrimination in Economic Life* (Lexington, Mass.: Lexington Books, 1972), pp. 83–102.

51. DELFA, *Preferred Working Hours*, p. 2.

52. The dissimilarity index, *D*, measures male-female differences in the occupational

labor force would have had to change occupation in order to obtain the same occupational distribution as men. By 1975 that percentage had dropped only to 70.3, and close to two-thirds of that small change resulted from the increasing representation of men in female occupations.[53]

As in the United States, the reduction in occupational dissimilarity was concentrated among young workers. Very little change occurred for workers older than thirty-five years of age. Since the index is not standardized for productivity, the change may in large measure be attributable to the increased schooling of younger women. For the United States 70.7 percent of women workers in 1970 would have had to change jobs to have the same occupational distribution as men. By 1980, the percentage had fallen to 63.5.[54] There thus appears to be more occupational separation of men and women in Sweden than in the United States.

It may seem paradoxical that women earn a higher relative wage in a society in which the occupational segregation of men and women is relatively great. The key to the paradox appears to be that the solidaristic wage policy has narrowed occupational wage differentials without affecting job segregation. In purely economic terms, occupational segregation is not as costly to women in Sweden as to women in other countries.

Evaluation of Solidaristic Wage Policy

The solidaristic wage policy, initially proposed in 1936 as a mechanism for achieving greater equality by altering labor market rewards, evolved

---

distribution of employment. It is defined as

$$D = \frac{1}{2} \sum_{i=1}^{n} \left| \frac{W_i}{W} - \frac{M_i}{M} \right| \cdot 100,$$

where W_i and M_i indicate respectively the number of women and men employed in occupation i, and W and M indicate the total number of women and men in the labor force. Complete segregation exists when $D = 100$. See Christina Jonung, "Patterns of Occupational Segregation by Sex in the Labor Market," in Schmid and Weitzel, *Sex Discrimination and Equal Opportunity*, pp. 46, 52.

53. Ibid., p. 58.

54. Francine D. Blau and Wallace E. Hendricks, "Occupational Segregation by Sex: Trends and Prospects," *Journal of Human Resources*, vol. 14 (Spring 1979), pp. 197–210; and June O'Neill and Rachel Braun, *Women and the Labor Market: A Survey of Issues and Policies in the United States* (Washington, D.C.: Urban Institute, 1981).

during the 1950s into a policy that was also intended to facilitate growth and economic change in Sweden. By 1960 the emphasis had shifted again, to simply narrowing pay differences. This objective has been largely achieved, at some cost to the efficiency of the economy. It is hard to find strong evidence of widespread misallocations among experienced workers, although there is some evidence that in narrowing wage differentials by skills, the policy has contributed to some skills shortages as individuals who might have trained for high-skilled blue-collar work have moved into salaried employment instead. Since wage compression is the policy of the blue-collar workers' federation (LO), but not of the salaried workers' federation (TCO), one consequence is that graduates of technical colleges increasingly choose salaried white-collar jobs in TCO jurisdiction instead of skilled blue-collar jobs that are subject to pay compression. The pay compression policy thus has implications for the institutional security of some LO unions.

One may infer from the behavior of the employers' confederation (SAF), however, that the costs of misallocation among experienced workers are modest and concentrated in a minority of firms. SAF has never made a major issue of the solidaristic wage policy in collective bargaining, primarily because the policy raises the labor costs of low-wage firms only. The management of large, capital-intensive firms, whose wage structure generally does not reach into low-pay regions, cares as little about this issue as the managements of major American corporations care about the federal minimum wage. For most SAF members, the costs of taking on this issue in collective bargaining exceed the meager benefits. (In contrast, SAF has vehemently opposed the creation of Wage Earner Funds, discussed later in this chapter, which would tax the profits of virtually all employers.)

The one large group that does appear to bear serious costs from the solidaristic wage policy, youth, does not get to vote on the bargaining policy of the labor market organizations. Since the deterioration of job prospects early in life will reduce on-the-job-training, the cost is not transitory. Lifetime earnings profiles are lowered, as is the general productivity of the economy. In a very real sense, a side effect of the solidaristic wage policy may be the squandering of a valuable human capital asset.

Are the efficiency costs of the solidaristic wage policy a reasonable price to pay for the gains in equity? At the core of this fundamentally subjective question is the further question of how much equity Sweden

Table 5-3. *Relative Hourly Earnings Position of Swedish Males Employed in 1968 and 1974*
Percent

| | Worker position in 1974 | | | | |
| | Lowest quartile | Second | Third | Highest | Total |
Position in 1968					
Workers aged 16 to 24					
Lowest quartile	41	21	19	19	100
Second	27	30	27	16	100
Third	24	27	33	16	100
Highest	8	20	25	48	100
Workers aged 25 and older					
Lowest quartile	58	28	9	6	100
Second	25	43	28	4	100
Third	11	23	49	17	100
Highest	6	6	14	73	100

Source: Computed from data from Level of Living Survey tapes reported in Björklund and Persson-Tanimura, "Youth Employment in Sweden." Components may not add to 100 because of rounding.

would lose by abandoning the solidaristic wage policy. For three reasons, the answer may be "not much." First, Sweden has more effective ways to change the distribution of income than changing the distribution of wages. Despite the success of wage compression, wages are, in fact, the most unevenly-distributed component of income in Sweden. The force that substantially offsets the inequality is government taxes and transfers.[55]

Second, while the solidaristic policy has narrowed differences in wages, it has been undermined partially by other labor market developments. Over a contract cycle, for example, wage drift tends to undo efforts to reduce wage inequality through collective bargaining. Third, the effect of collective bargaining on the structure of earnings by job is to a considerable extent undone by the mobility of individuals through the earnings structure. Negotiated reductions in the inequality of the earnings structure will lower individual inequality only to the extent that individuals maintain their relative position in the earnings structure. But the relative earnings of individuals are in fact quite volatile. Change of employers, promotions, layoffs, and variation in effort under payment-by-results systems all tend to rearrange relative earnings. Table 5-3

55. Assar Lindbeck, "Interpreting Income Distributions in a Welfare State," *European Economic Review*, vol. 21 (July 1983), pp. 227–56.

Table 5-4. *Relative Hourly Earnings Position of Swedish Blue-Collar Workers in 1984 and 1985*[a]
Percent

| Percentile | 1984 | 1985 | | | | | | | | | | |
| | Separated during year | Distribution of Those with Same Employer | | | | | | | | | | |
		Lowest percentile	Second	Third	Fourth	Fifth	Sixth	Seventh	Eighth	Ninth	Highest	Total
Lowest	39.0	30.8	14.4	6.2	3.7	2.2	1.2	0.9	0.6	0.5	0.5	100
Second	26.6	5.1	38.8	16.9	6.2	2.6	1.5	0.9	0.6	0.4	0.4	100
Third	22.3	1.8	9.8	37.6	15.9	6.1	2.9	1.7	1.0	0.6	0.4	100
Fourth	22.1	1.1	2.5	11.5	30.3	18.0	7.1	3.7	1.9	1.1	0.7	100
Fifth	19.0	0.7	0.9	2.7	15.8	28.9	18.3	7.4	3.5	1.7	1.0	100
Sixth	17.3	0.4	0.5	1.1	4.0	15.7	29.0	18.6	8.1	3.4	1.9	100
Seventh	16.3	0.4	0.3	0.6	1.3	4.7	17.4	30.7	18.7	6.6	2.9	100
Eighth	15.8	0.3	0.3	0.4	0.7	1.6	4.7	17.6	35.0	18.1	5.5	100
Ninth	14.8	0.2	0.2	0.3	0.5	0.9	1.5	4.2	16.3	44.3	16.7	100
Highest	17.4	0.2	0.2	0.3	0.4	0.7	1.1	1.7	3.3	14.3	60.3	100

Source: Lennart Jonsson and Claes-Henric Siven, *Varför Löneskillnader?* (Stockholm: Svenska Arbetsgivareföreningen, 1986), p. 19.
a. Data are for the second quarter of each year.

shows how Swedish males moved through the earnings structure between 1968 and 1974. Each number shows the percentage of males in the row quartile of the earnings distribution in 1968 who were in the column quartile of the distribution in 1974. If there were no mobility between these rather broad sections of the earnings distribution over the six-year period, all numbers would fall on the principal diagonal and would equal 100 percent. As the table shows, there is considerable mobility in both directions through the earnings distribution. Not surprisingly, the relative earnings of youth are most volatile, with only a third to a half maintaining their position over the six-year period. While there is greater stability for adult males, only about 55 percent on average retain their relative position over the six-year period.

Even within periods as short as a year and for workers who remain in the same plant, there is substantial earnings mobility. This can be seen in table 5-4, which is set up like table 5-3, except that the earnings distribution is divided into deciles rather than quartiles. The second column indicates the overall level of mobility—that is, the percentage of workers who leave their plant. Separations (largely quits) are inversely related to wages. About 40 percent of the workers in the lowest decile of the earnings distribution left their firms in the course of one year. The relative change in earnings among workers who are not part of these turnover flows is also great. The interpretation of the main body of table 5-4 is as follows, using row 1 as an example: 30.8 percent of workers who remained with their firm and were in the bottom decile of the earnings distribution in the second quarter of 1984 remained there one year later; 14.4 percent moved into the second decile, and so on. The other rows can be interpreted accordingly. The relative earnings of about 40 percent of all workers were changed simply by developments at their place of work within the course of a year. (More than half of the workers remained at the same plant for the year.)

With so many workers changing their relative earnings position during even short periods of time, it is doubtful that changes in the earnings structure can be regarded as a powerful influence on overall equality, particularly in a society that uses taxes and transfers triggered directly by an individual's realized earnings to redistribute income. Given that the allocational costs yield rather small distributional benefits, a reconsideration of the value of the solidaristic wage policy to the modern Swedish economy would seem to be in order.

Unemployment and Labor Market Policy

Swedish unemployment experience and labor market policy has been widely discussed over the past twenty-five years, and this section will not attempt a review of that discussion. Instead, it will focus on a few characteristics of unemployment and related policies pertinent to the efficient operation of the labor market in the 1980s. In terms of structure, Swedish unemployment reflects comparatively long durations of joblessness and comparatively low flows into unemployment. Moreover, unemployment durations in Sweden appear to be growing. Studies of the labor market experience of the unemployed over time find evidence of scarring; long durations of unemployment are associated with lower wages in subsequent employment for a given vector of human capital characteristics.[56] In a human capital setting, some depreciation occurs. There is also evidence that participation in a government training program or (less certainly) a relief work program tends to reverse that depreciation.[57]

Active Labor Market Policy

The broad facts of the Swedish commitment to active labor market policies have been widely reported.[58] We have seen how policies stressing labor supply adjustments became an essential complement to solidaristic wage policy in the Swedish strategy for adjusting to structural change as early as the 1950s. Since the late 1960s, however, nominal and real expenditures on selective policies have mushroomed, reaching over

56. Anders Björklund, "Studies in the Dynamics of Unemployment" (Ph.D. dissertation, Stockholm School of Economics, October 1981), chap. 5.
57. Bertil Holmlund, "Determinants and Characteristics of Unemployment in Sweden: The Role of Labor Market Policy," in Gunnar Eliasson, Bertil Holmlund, and Frank P. Stafford, eds., *Studies in Labor Market Behavior: Sweden and the United States* (Stockholm: Almqvist and Wiksell, 1981), pp. 97–137.
58. See, for example, Jan Johannesson, "On the Composition of Swedish Labor Market Policy," in Eliasson, Holmlund, and Stafford, eds., *Studies in Labor Market Behavior,* pp. 67–95; Jan Johannesson and Inga Persson-Tanimura, *Labour Market Policy under Reconsideration* (Stockholm: Arbetsmarknadsdepartementet, 1984), p. 44; Gösta Rehn, "Swedish Active Labor Market Policy: Retrospect and Prospect," *Industrial Relations,* vol. 24 (Winter 1985), pp. 62–89; and Frank P. Stafford, "Unemployment and Labor Market Policy in Sweden and the United States," in Eliasson, Holmlund, and Stafford, eds., *Studies in Labor Market Behavior,* pp. 21–65.

7 percent of government expenditure and over 3 percent of gross national product by 1983–84. In every year since 1973, the number of persons in labor market programs has exceeded the number of officially unemployed persons, and the comparatively low official unemployment rates are understated because of the scale of government labor market programs.[59]

Not all of these people have been in supply adjustment programs (for example, to improve job matching, influence geographic and occupational mobility, and rehabilitate hard-to-place labor). Indeed, the original growth-oriented policy rationale for the policies was to a large extent lost in the early 1970s, as Sweden's growth and international competitiveness declined. Mounting employment problems led to a shift in emphasis toward demand-oriented programs, including temporary jobs, policies to maintain the regional distribution of employment, temporary employment subsidies, on-the-job training to avoid layoffs, and subsidies for stockpiling.

What conclusions can be drawn from these massive (by international standards) investments? For over twenty-five years many countries have looked to "the Swedish experience" when seeking a model for their own labor market policies. Here I shall reverse this process and explore whether Swedish policy has avoided some of the problems encountered in the process of pursuing labor market policy on a much smaller scale in the United States.

Like the early Swedish labor market policies on which they were modeled, the aim of the initial manpower policies in the United States was to facilitate adjustment to factors producing "structural" unemployment. Beginning in 1965, however, U.S. labor market policies were increasingly targeted on specific groups (such as minorities, welfare recipients, and youth) that seemed to suffer from above-average poverty or unemployment. During the late 1960s and 1970s, the emphasis shifted from training and job skills to varieties of wage subsidies ranging from public service employment to hiring subsidies for private-sector firms.

Program evaluations do not provide grounds for excessive optimism regarding the effects of the U.S. programs on the employment prospects of their clients. At the most aggregate level, the relationship between unemployment and vacancies appears to have shifted out during the 1970s, despite the increased investment in labor market programs. Whatever the exact effects of the programs, they were not sufficient to

59. Johannesson and Persson-Tanimura, *Labour Market Policy under Reconsideration*, pp. 44, 47.

offset forces leading to a mismatch of workers and jobs.[60] In contrast, the relationship between unemployment and vacancies in Sweden appears to have shifted inward during the massive labor market investments of the late 1970s (after having shifted outward in 1969–74).[61] Given the shifting mix of Swedish policy during this period, however, participation in many of the labor market programs of the period appears to have been a form of disguised unemployment.

Manpower program evaluations seek to determine whether program participants subsequently have more favorable labor market outcomes, particularly with respect to wages and hours of work, than identical nonparticipants. Many U.S. studies have foundered on the control-group problem, but those that have not found that program effects have been modest, restricted to participants with little work experience, and limited to raising the annual worktime, rather than the wage, of the participants. Moreover, earnings differences between target and control groups seem to narrow and disappear within five years of training.[62] These results may reflect an inability of public agencies to make judgments about where the jobs are (and hence what the training should be) or an inability to raise the productivity of participants. (The initial returns to trainees may reflect a "placement effect" that dissipates as on-the-job performance reveals true post-training abilities.)

In the mid-1970s the shift in emphasis from training to temporary public service employment, which in theory would provide experience that would improve the private-sector job prospects of enrollees, was accompanied by the familiar problem of fiscal substitution, which has been estimated to range between 50 and 100 percent. In addition, enrollees experienced difficulty in finding subsequent private-sector jobs. Fiscal substitution has been a feature of Swedish relief-work programs as well.[63]

Economists have long argued the advantages of wage subsidies for employment creation, and by the late 1970s, experimental programs began to emerge as a part of U.S. labor market policy, targeted on

60. James L. Medoff and Katharine G. Abraham, "Unemployment, Unsatisfied Demand for Labor, and Compensation Growth, 1956–80," in Martin Neil Baily, ed., *Workers, Jobs, and Inflation* (Brookings, 1982), pp 49–88.

61. Björklund, "Studies in the Dynamics of Unemployment," p. 214.

62. Orley Ashenfelter, "Estimating the Effects of Training Programs on Earnings," *Review of Economics and Statistics*, vol. 60 (February 1978), pp. 47–57.

63. Edward M. Gramlich and Bengt-Christer Ysander, "Relief Work and Grant Displacement in Sweden," in Eliasson, Holmlund, and Stafford, *Studies in Labor Market Behavior*, pp. 139–66.

particular disadvantaged groups. Despite the theoretical advantages, employer participation in these programs has been disappointingly low. "The number of workers whose wages are subsidized by the programs is far below the number of workers who are technically eligible to be covered. . . . Employers appear to be passing up opportunities to collect tax credits for employment decisions they are making anyway."[64]

There may well be a fundamental barrier facing all efforts at targeted manpower policy in the United States. In a revealing experiment in 1981, the clients of a manpower agency in an urban area were randomly divided into three groups: participants in one group were given vouchers informing employers that the applicants were eligible for a tax credit; participants in the second were given vouchers informing employers that the applicants were covered by a cash subsidy (equal in value to the tax credit); participants in the third received no voucher and were not subsidized. The third group was more successful in finding jobs than either of the vouchered groups. Moreover, few of the firms that hired vouchered workers bothered to apply for the subsidy.[65] The suspicion emerges that in the United States membership in a group targeted by labor market policy is interpreted as a signal of low productivity by employers, and the resulting stigma tends to undermine the objectives of such programs independently of their design.

To what extent have these problems been encountered in Swedish labor market policies? Much more appears to be known about program expenditures and enrollments than about the economic effects of individual programs in Sweden. The massive expansion in Swedish labor market policies since the late 1960s has not been accompanied by the growth of a cottage industry in benefit-cost analyses of the programs. Analyses of the effect of training programs in the 1960s find that training provided a return of 5 to 10 percent for two to three years after completion of training. There is considerable uncertainty concerning social benefits and costs because of the short follow-up periods.[66] A more recent study

64. Gary Burtless, "Manpower Policies for the Disadvantaged: What Works?" *Brookings Review*, vol. 3 (Fall 1984), p 21.

65. It is not known whether those workers informed prospective employers of the vouchers. The experiment is described in Gary Burtless, "Are Targeted Wage Subsidies Harmful? Evidence from a Wage Voucher Experiment," *Industrial and Labor Relations Review*, vol. 39 (October 1985), pp. 105–14.

66. Åke Dahlberg, *Arbetsmarknadsutbildning—Verkningar for den enskilde och samhallet*, Studier i Nationalekonomi No. 3 (University of Umea, 1972); and Dahlberg, *Geographical Mobility: Social and Economic Effects*: SOU 1978:60 (Stockholm, 1978).

of a small group of trainees over 1976–80 indicates an average wage return of around 11 percent, but a negative effect for the marginal participant in training programs.[67] With respect to mobility grants, a study of about 1,500 migrants who received relocation subsidies from the National Labor Market Board found that the earnings gains (relative to control groups) associated with migration disappeared about four years after changing location.[68]

There has also been some analysis of the relationship between program participation and subsequent unemployment experience for the 1968–73 period. Participation in a training program tends to reduce the probability of incurring unemployment—but only for those who experienced previous unemployment. Indeed, for those people training appears to have completely offset the "scarring" effects of earlier unemployment. The data suggest that work relief programs had a similar effect, but it is smaller and measured much less precisely.[69] For those without previous unemployment experience, however, participation in training and, particularly, work relief programs actually raised the probability of unemployment. The open question at this juncture is whether this suggestion of stigma conferred by participation in government labor market programs has grown any stronger since the early 1970s.

There is remarkably little solid information on what Sweden has obtained from its large public investments in labor market policy. Certainly the old model of mobility-oriented policies cum solidaristic wage policy as a method of maintaining competitiveness in the face of structural change largely disappeared during the 1970s. Devaluations rather than labor market adjustments have become the source of profits for Swedish industry. Many of the newer government programs for youth appear to be a form of disguised unemployment. For the purposes of long-run growth, a return to greater emphasis on supply-oriented programs that assist workers in adjusting to the market signals that they already appear to recognize is a preferable strategy.

Within this strategy, there is a case for according greater attention to the distinction between government financing and government produc-

67. Anders Björklund and Robert Moffitt, "Estimation of Wage Gains and Welfare Gains from Self-Selection Models," discussion paper 735–83 (University of Wisconsin-Madison, Institute for Research on Poverty, August 1983).
68. Åke Dahlberg, "Effects of Migration on the Incomes of Unemployed People," British Journal of Industrial Relations, vol. 16 (March 1978), pp. 86–94.
69. Holmlund, "Determinants and Characteristics of Unemployment in Sweden," pp. 102–110.

tion. When government does both, choice—particularly with regard to the type of training or job search assistance—may be unnecessarily limited. The evidence reviewed earlier indicates that workers are generally responsive to market opportunities. Therefore a model in which the government role was limited to financing supply-oriented policies— by the provision of vouchers for training or job-search services, for example—but production was left to the private or nonprofit sectors could increase the returns to these public investments. Implementation of this approach to delivering training services has already begun. In the area of labor market information, however, private dealers are now forbidden by Swedish law (with the exception of the Employment Security Council run jointly by SAF and the union for white-collar workers in the private sector).[70]

Collective Bargaining and Aggregate Wage Determination

In the United States, with less than 20 percent of the labor force unionized, the ultimate restraint on union power is the existence of the nonunion sector. The early 1980s offered dramatic examples of this in the high incidence of concession bargaining by unionized workers in industries with substantial nonunion competition.[71] The pattern of union-nonunion wage differentials in the United States also confirms the restraining effect of nonunion competition. As a general rule, differentials appear to be largest in sectors where the barriers to new nonunion entrants are greatest, and smallest, even to the point of disappearing, where the barriers to entry are negligible.[72] Although collective bargaining in Sweden occurs in a very different setting, some of the lessons learned from thinking about unions in a largely nonunion economy remain pertinent.

The setting, of course, is one in which any real restraint on union

70. Anders Björklund, "Policies for Labor Market Adjustment in Sweden," in Gary C. Hufbauer and Howard F. Rosen, eds., *Domestic Adjustment and International Trade* (Washington, D.C.: Institute for International Economics, forthcoming).

71. Robert J. Flanagan, "Wage Concessions and Long-Term Union Wage Flexibility," *BPEA, 1:1984*, pp. 183–216.

72. A number of studies are summarized in H. Gregg Lewis, *Unionism and Relative Wages in the United States* (University of Chicago Press, 1963); and Lewis, *Union Relative Wage Effects: A Survey* (University of Chicago Press, 1986).

behavior will come not from the decentralized decisions of thousands of nonunion agents, but from the one institution in Swedish society that is more centralized than a union federation—the government. The government has many choices, including some that might expose Swedish unions to some of the same risks faced by their American counterparts. But the Swedish setting involves bargaining among three central institutions, and the key issues are somewhat different from the issues in standard U.S. labor-management bargaining.

. During a period that arguably extended into the early 1970s, the central union (LO) and central employer federation (SAF) effectively negotiated wage increases consistent with the government's employment objectives, and the government used stabilization policy—always in the form of fiscal policy, given fixed exchange rates—to stabilize employment in the face of temporary disturbances. This general scenario was formalized in the Scandinavian model of inflation developed by the Norwegian economist, Odd Aukrust, and extended to the Swedish economy in 1968 in a collaborative study by the chief economists of the main Swedish labor market orgnizations.[73] The model, known as the EFO model from the initials of the Swedish authors' last names, was used to calculate the "room" for increases in wages, salaries, and profits, given existing trends in world prices and productivity. The collaboration effectively preempted a government initiative and established a relatively narrow range for bargaining before negotiations began. According to the model, trade union behavior was not responsible for inflation, which was basically determined by the path of world prices and differences in productivity trends in the sectors of the economy producing tradable and nontradable goods. What union wage setting could determine was profitability and international competitiveness. The government was responsible for the employment level. A consequence of this division of responsibilities is a tendency toward growth of public employment, assuming that fiscal policy accommodates economic disturbances by means of increased government employment.

More recent Scandinavian models of the interaction between centralized labor federations and national governments stress that such public employment growth is likely to be temporary.[74] But a general government

73. Odd Aukrust, "Inflation in the Open Economy: A Norwegian Model," in Lawrence B. Krause and Walter S. Salant, eds., *Worldwide Inflation: Theory and Recent Experience* (Brookings, 1977), pp. 107–53; and Edgren, Faxén, and Odhner, *Wage Formation.*
74. See, for example, Lars Calmfors, "Employment Policies, Wage Formation and

policy of accommodation may come to be recognized as a more or less automatic government response to any disturbance—including a real wage increase—that drives employment below the government's target. As such, an accommodation policy effectively lowers the elasticity of the labor demand curve facing the union, so that the maximizing response of the union is to increase the real wage further. The benefit in terms of additional income to employed union members more than offsets whatever losses occur through reduced employment, at least initially. An immediate consequence is an expansion in the public sector that is now related to a permanent union real wage strategy rather than a temporary macroeconomic disturbance. In such a situation the public sector grows even more rapidly—as it did in Sweden during the 1970s. Unions that believed the public sector should be larger as a matter of social policy might even provoke its growth with their wage policy when facing an accommodating government.[75]

The general scenario sketched by these more recent models fits the Swedish experience in many respects. In a country known for its fiscal accommodation to employment objectives, real wages were too high for employment targets during the 1970s. Unable or unwilling to bear the political costs of an investment in credible nonaccommodation, the government ultimately chose to devalue the currency but found that a sequence of devaluations was necessary to restore profitability. Contrary to the EFO model, by the early 1980s Swedish employers looked to government exchange rate policy rather than union wage restraint as the source of profits. Does the broad fit between the Scandinavian models and the Swedish experience during the 1970s and early 1980s lead inevitably to the conclusion that the only live policy option to restrain real wage pressure is some increase in unemployment? My provisional answer is "no." A closer look at the Swedish labor market shows that

Trade Union Behavior in a Small Open Economy," *Scandinavian Journal of Economics*, vol. 84, no. 2 (1982), pp. 345–73; Lars Calmfors and Henrik Horn, "Employment Policies and Centralized Wage-Setting," *Economica*, vol. 53 (August 1986), pp. 281–302; and Lars Calmfors and Henrik Horn, "Classical Unemployment, Accommodation Policies and the Adjustment of Real Wages," *Scandinavian Journal of Economics*, vol. 87, no. 2 (1985), pp. 234–61. For a clear, nontechnical summary of this model and an analysis of alternative policy implications, see Calmfors, "Stabilization Policy and Wage Formation in Economies with Strong Trade Unions," in Michael Emerson, ed., *Europe's Stagflation* (Oxford University Press, 1984) pp. 104–18.

75. One theoretical difficulty with these models is that they adopt the assumption (shared by most other models of union behavior) that the union can impose whatever wage it wishes, and the employer chooses the employment level given by the labor demand schedule.

there are other alternatives. The broad similarity between the models and the Swedish economy breaks down in three areas: the growth of the public sector, the structure of collective bargaining, and the interpretation of wage drift.

The Public Sector

According to the models, fiscal accommodation will mean growth in the public sector. Sweden's experience bears the models out. But with growth in the Swedish public sector has also come growth in public-sector unions, and increased restiveness among unions of salaried workers as rising tax rates have reduced the relative disposable wage of many white-collar workers. And with additional union players have come wage demands that are not closely related to government employment objectives. As unions of both local and central government employees grew in relative strength within LO and TCO during the 1970s, they managed to develop considerable bargaining autonomy, in large measure because their employer was not represented by the SAF. Unions of private salaried workers, whose members generally face higher tax rates and experience less wage drift than blue-collar workers, were less and less willing to follow bargaining frames established by LO and often were unable to agree on salary relationships with white-collar workers in the public sector.

The conflict between public and private employees stems from differences in wage drift between the two sectors and from the fact that wage structures are more compressed in the public than in the private sectors. Wage drift is generally greater in the private sector, and public unions have argued that under the solidaristic wage principle, they merit larger negotiated wage increases to maintain overall equality in earnings growth between the private and public sectors. Private-sector unions, noting that the lowest-paid workers in the public sector receive a higher wage than the lowest-paid private employees, do not find that solidaristic principles call for drift compensation for all public employees. In addition, public employees have so far enjoyed lifetime job protection. LO's traditional role of leader in bargaining has effectively been undermined by agreements negotiated between the government and the public-sector unions. Negotiations between LO and SAF over private-sector wages have increasingly been dominated by considerations of equality with public-sector and salaried employees rather than national economic targets or the bargaining range suggested by the older EFO model.[76] The result of the negotiations has been that LO's blue-collar industrial members received smaller negotiated increases than did government workers throughout the 1970s and 1980s. (Between 1973 and 1980 industrial blue-collar workers also received smaller increases than did industrial white-collar workers.)

There is no evidence that LO responded to the government's fiscal accommodation by unilaterally raising its real wage during the period in which it dominated the union side of collective bargaining. The individual bargaining rounds instead show considerable evidence of disagreements between unions concerning the appropriate wage or wage-change relationships between private- and public-sector workers and, within the private sector, between blue-collar and white-collar unions. But the outcome of this process does not square well with the idea that LO raised the real wage in response to government accommodation. Instead, the fiscal accommodation that produced the growth of the public sector also increased the extent of competition between unions at the national level, which had already begun with the increasing autonomy of professional groups in the 1960s. This in turn appears to have set off a prisoner's dilemma relationship among the major unions, in which each is reluctant to risk the wrath of members by accepting a relatively modest wage increase that may not be accepted by the other unions. To the extent that the rise in the Swedish real wage can be traced to union behavior, the pressure stems less from adjusting goals to an accommodating fiscal policy than from rivalries and emulation.

Nonaccommodation—and the unemployment that would result—is not the only policy option in this setting. To the extent that the public-sector unions have become or aspire to become the wage leaders in bargaining, for example, the government holds an extra card—as employer. Once public employees become wage leaders, a government may effectively establish an incomes policy by bargaining as a tough employer, at a cost of increased strike activity. (Something like this appears to have occurred in 1985 and 1986, when the government accepted strikes in support of its bargaining position, but it is not yet clear that these episodes were the beginning of a sustained labor policy initiative by the government.) The willingness of government to accept

76. For a review of the growing conflicts on the union side of negotiations, see Flanagan, Soskice, and Ulman, *Unionism, Economic Stabilization, and Incomes Policy*, pp. 301–62.

such strikes is a key aspect of establishing the credibility of its bargaining position. Claims that public opinion will undermine the ability of public employers to resist demands by public-sector unions were once common in the United States, as they now are in Sweden. Such claims presume a remarkable naivete among voters concerning the connection between increased wages for public employees and increased taxes. American experience with public-sector bargaining at the state and local government levels indicates that such naivete is short-lived, if it exists at all.

A second way to reduce negotiated wage pressures would be to alter the nature of compensation systems, so that unions negotiate over a share of the profits (or revenues or product prices) of a firm.[77] Two objections are likely. The first is that under Swedish last-in, first-out seniority systems, profit sharing would reduce the income security of the median union voter. A less accommodative fiscal policy might weaken such an objection, however. The second is that any system that indexes compensation to a firm's performance conflicts in a fundamental way with the solidaristic wage policy of the unions, which on its face can accommodate only collective profit-sharing arrangements. The real question at this stage is how far solidarity goes. Recently, many firms have introduced their own profit-sharing plans, apparently with the active participation and negotiation of local unions. However, these private plans have little relevance to the behavior of the public-sector unions that have become the wage leaders of the 1980s.

Decentralization of Negotiations

Recent Scandinavian models of collective bargaining also diverge from the Swedish experience by giving wage equality no explicit role in a union's objectives. But wage equality has been a key feature of centralized bargaining in Sweden. We have seen how Swedish efforts to apply solidaristic wage policy are accompanied, and partially countered, by wage drift, with the result that efforts to alter the wage structure are associated (weakly) with general wage growth. This linkage has inspired several proposals to decentralize the collective bargaining structure in order to reduce institutional pressures on real wages.

The first proposal, currently advocated by SAF, is really a return to

77. See, for example, Martin L. Weitzman, *The Share Economy* (Harvard University Press, 1984); and Weitzman, "The Simple Macroeconomics of Profit Sharing," *American Economic Review,* vol. 75 (December 1985), pp. 937–53.

bargaining arrangements of the 1960s in which the central labor market organizations negotiated a central "frame" for wage increases but left determination of the structure of wages within that frame to negotiations at the industry or plant level. During the 1970s the central organizations gradually departed from this arrangement as LO pressed to address more and more issues of wage structure in the central negotiations.[78] A return to the earlier form of decentralized bargaining seems sensible, for while a centralized approach may be necessary to implement notions of solidaristic wage policy, centralized determination of the wage structure is likely to encounter the same problems that confront central price determination in planned economies. Given my earlier conclusions about the balance between the equity gains and efficiency losses associated with solidaristic wage policy, a return to the traditional division of responsibilities among different levels of bargaining is likely to improve efficiency with very little loss of equity.

A more radical decentralization proposal would move all bargaining over wages to the industry or plant level without any guiding framework established in central negotiations. This approach would move the authority to use the leverage of conflict, currently vested in the central union and employer federations, to their affiliates at the industry or local level. Proponents offer this decentralized bargaining structure as an alternative to nonaccommodation in securing wage restraint on the theory that unions would be restrained by the knowledge that the government could not easily accommodate wage increases negotiated at the industry or plant level. They will effectively face a more elastic demand curve than in centralized negotiations. The great risk in this form of decentralization is that it may result in a much broader version of the prisoner's-dilemma interaction that Sweden has already experienced with relatively centralized bargaining arrangements.[79] To the extent that emulation comes to dominate collective bargaining, the pressure for government accommodation of the pattern established by negotiations in a particular industry will be equivalent to the pressure to accommodate a central bargain.

78. The fact that SAF supports this type of decentralization implies that whatever the effects of wage drift in countering the application of solidaristic wage provisions during the 1970s and early 1980s, the resulting wage structure was not viewed as efficient by employers.

79. Society will be worse off from noncooperative interactions between unions when the workers represented by the unions are complements, as seems to be the case with Swedish unions. If workers were substitutes, society would be better off with a noncooperative solution.

Explosive interactions like this are not unknown in either the United States or Sweden. Wage developments in the U.S. construction industry in the late 1960s and early 1970s are an example, although in that, as in all other cases, wages were ultimately controlled by the existence of a nonunion sector. Under decentralized bargaining arrangements prevailing in Sweden in the early 1950s, SAF was unable to restrain the wage increases offered by members facing labor shortages. These increases spread rapidly to other sectors through a combination of competitive responses and emulation by LO. SAF entered salary negotiations with unions of white-collar employees after World War II for the same reason; competition between member firms for scarce salaried personnel resulted in salary increases that made it difficult for employers to resist the wage claims of LO. For its part, LO sought to restrain the wage demands of the unions in shortage sectors to prevent the pursuit of wage equality by unions in other sectors from causing general inflation and a loss of competitiveness. It is sobering to recall that the centralization of collective bargaining thirty years ago was motivated more by the need of LO and SAF to develop greater internal control over their competitive members than by a desire for greater economic power.

The key point here is that Sweden, unlike the United States, has no domestic nonunion sector to exert ultimate control on decentralized bargainers. A growing market share of imports could establish an equivalent pressure on union wage objectives, but during the late 1970s and early 1980s, international disparities in the growth of labor costs were offset by government exchange rate policies. Unlike the situation in the United States, government policy choices are crucial for establishing market pressures that might modify bargaining objectives. Unless the government establishes a credible policy of nonaccommodation, decentralized bargainers face no real restraint on their action, once the prisoner's dilemma interaction begins. Decentralized bargaining over the level as well as the structure of wages is likely to be a destabilizing influence in the general development of Swedish wages rather than an effective substitute for nonaccommodation.

Wage Drift

Although both analytical models and general policy discussions of wage determination in Sweden focus on the central collective bargaining negotiations, between 40 and 50 percent of the hourly earnings increases of blue-collar workers and 20 to 50 percent of the increases of white-

Table 5-5. *Industrial-Sector Wage Drift as a Percentage of Hourly Earnings Increases and of Hourly Labor Costs in Sweden, 1971–84*

	Blue-collar workers		White-collar workers	
Year	Earnings	Labor costs	Earnings	Labor costs
1971	40	36	30	27
1972	36	35	20	20
1973	49	35	21	17
1974	58	39	15	10
1975	42	33	13	11
1976	41	32	18	14
1977	49	32	20	15
1978	40	30	28	22
1979	46	44	24	21
1980	34	31	28	24
1981	42	39	39	40
1982	46	45	45	45
1983	43	31	48	38
1984	40	40	61	61
1971–84 average	43	36	29	26

Source: Konjunkturinstitutet [National Institute of Economic Research], *The Swedish Economy* (Stockholm: NIER, Fall 1985), table 24d.

collar workers in private industry continue to come from wage drift (table 5-5). In fact, drift has become an increasingly large fraction of labor cost increases during the 1980s, with the diminished importance of new payroll taxes. In the public sector, drift has been much smaller, representing perhaps 10 to 15 percent of earnings increases in an average year.

When wage drift is such an important part of the total increase in earnings and labor costs, it seems odd to claim that excessive real wages are being established in official collective bargaining negotiations. These two components of earnings are determined in inherently different ways. Central collective bargaining establishes a "frame" increase that is applied through industry and local negotiations. In contrast, decisions resulting in wage drift are decentralized.

Research into the determinants of wage drift confirms the strong influence of market forces at the macroeconomic level.[80] Overall, drift

80. Nils Henrik Schager, "The Duration of Vacancies as a Measure of the State of Demand in the Labor Market: The Swedish Wage Drift Equation Reconsidered," in

includes elements of market forces (for example, adjustments in wage structure that increase a firm's wage bill beyond the central frame amount established in collective negotiations) and elements of institutional pressure (for example, through local applications of the low-wage provisions established in the central frame agreement). A deemphasis of, or withdrawal from, solidaristic wage policy by LO should reduce the wage drift that results from local efforts to offset centrally negotiated wage compression. It would hardly eliminate wage drift, however, as is evident from the data in table 5-5 for white-collar workers, who have never adopted a solidaristic wage policy.

If the remaining drift does not bear a strictly compensatory relationship to negotiated wage increases, it may be possible to reduce the real wage by reducing drift rather than focusing on negotiated wages. Such a policy would offer an effective alternative to nonaccommodation. Wage drift has not only increased wage cost pressures in the private sector, but has also helped to destabilize the demands of public-sector unions, and to a lesser extent the private white-collar unions, who seek to negotiate compensation for the drift that they do not receive. Thus control of drift could also create more stability in the determination of negotiated wages.

Like most wage determination in the United States, decisions over wage drift in Sweden are inherently decentralized. Since they are likely to result from both market and institutional pressures, the objective is to find a policy that serves to discourage the latter without interfering extensively with the former.[81] To an American outsider, a tax-incentive policy (TIP) would seem to be just such a policy.[82] A tax on firms whose wage bill increased more than the frame increase would provide employers and workers an incentive to stay within the frame agreement, while permitting local adjustments, largely issues of wage structure. (If the solidaristic wage policy were not relaxed, there could also be a modest allowance for wage drift required for wage-structure flexibility.) Focusing on the wage bill rather than on individual wages preserves the

Eliasson, Holmlund, and Stafford, eds., *Studies in Labor Market Behavior*, pp. 393–442; and Lars Jacobsson and Assar Lindbeck, "On the Transmission Mechanism of Wage Change," *Swedish Journal of Economics*, vol. 73 (September 1971), pp. 273–93.

81. From evidence presented earlier on the interaction of negotiated wage rates and wage drift, it may be inferred that decentralized negotiations over the wage structure may reduce wage drift, but drift was also evident in the 1960s, when wage structure decisions were left to industries and plants.

82. There is by now a large literature on TIPs. Most of the issues are covered in Arthur M. Okun and George L. Perry, eds., *Curing Chronic Inflation* (Brookings, 1978).

freedom to alter the wage structure. Structural changes that increase the wage bill beyond the central frame amount would be permitted, but only at the cost of higher taxes.

The major Swedish counterargument appears to be that a TIP would raise severe administrative difficulties in Sweden because the implications of a central agreement for plant-level wage increases are more difficult to determine than the requirements of most incomes policies. If the plant-level implications of central agreements could have been determined with reasonable precision, SAF would have run a de facto TIP by using its powers to fine members for excessive wage drift, but in the event, this was not possible. Most of the ambiguity about what central agreements imply for individual plants results from provisions for implementing solidaristic wage policy; this may be one more argument for deemphasizing the policy in the future. Once the implications of central frame agreements for wages at the plant were clear, a TIP would be easier to implement.

Wage Earner Funds

One of the most controversial policy debates in postwar Sweden, made as early as 1975, concerned proposals to tax profits and use the revenues to establish a fund, to be controlled by employee representatives, for investing in Swedish industry. A nationwide profit-sharing arrangement is of interest in modern economic policy discussions for several reasons. First, a number of economists have argued that "share economy" compensation systems that index pay to firm performance—that is, pay arrangements that lower pay for each worker as more workers are hired—would tend to reverse the inherent inflationary tendency of economies dominated by fixed-wage payment systems.[83] A nationwide profit-sharing plan embodying these characteristics could serve as a demonstration program to show whether the idea merits more widespread application. Second, a Wage Earner Fund or similar capital-sharing policy could be part of a compensatory incomes policy: unions would modify demands for fixed base wages as a quid pro quo for the profit-sharing component of compensation. Third, a policy that bases pay on the performance of the firm is of particular interest in a period of

83. Weitzman, *The Share Economy;* and James E. Meade, *Stagflation,* vol. 1: *Wage Fixing* (London: Allen and Unwin, 1982).

declining productivity growth. In addition, capital-sharing arrangements may be a way of altering the distribution of income or of securing specific social objectives, such as investments in declining industries and regions.

Early fund proposals would have given workers significant power over Swedish industry.[84] The Wage Earner Fund legislation passed by the Swedish Parliament in 1982 did not.[85] Rather than creating one fund, the legislation established five regionally based funds, apparently to disperse whatever economic power (to purchase a controlling interest in companies) might accrue to a single fund. This objective is reinforced by limiting each fund's holdings to shares representing 8 percent of voting rights. Hypothetically the five funds together could acquire a 40 percent interest in a company, but by law each fund is limited to Skr 400 million a year (about $45 million at mid-1985 exchange rates). Barring changes in the funding arrangements, the five funds will control a total of about Skr 14 billion, or 5 to 6 percent of the value of all listed shares, by 1990 when the program will be reviewed. Clearly, the present funds will not provide the potential economic leverage on Swedish industry that some of the original proponents may have envisaged.

The funds are also limited in their ability to pursue social objectives by the statutory requirement that they earn a real rate of return of 3 percent—a goal that leaves little room for investments yielding mainly nonpecuniary returns. Each year the funds transfer the returns on their investments to the National Pension Fund, which merges these funds with general pension funds and invests in fixed-income securities. It seems clear that the ultimate legislation produced a capital-sharing plan that was not well suited to the social and distributional goals of some original proponents of the approach.

Neither did the fund, as finally set up, make compensation significantly contingent on firm performance. By law the funds are financed by a combination of an increase of 0.2 percent in the payroll tax plus a profits tax equal to 20 percent of real profits over a minimum exempted amount.[86]

84. An early proposal is in Rudolf Meidner, Anna Hedborg, and Gunnar Fond, *Kollektiv Kapitalbildning Genom Löntagarfonder* (Stockholm: Tidens Förlag, 1975). See also Berndt Öhman, "The Debate on Wage-Earner Funds in Scandinavia," in Colin Crouch and Frank A. Heller, eds., *International Yearbook of Organizational Democracy*, vol. 1: *Organizational Democracy and Political Processes*, (New York: John Wiley and Sons, 1983), pp. 35–52; and Lundberg, "The Rise and Fall of the Swedish Model," pp. 30–32.

85. Indeed, general support for the legislation by the Social Democratic Party was motivated mainly by the need to gain political acceptance of the profits that developed following a 20 percent devaluation of the krona in 1982.

86. The actual computation—particularly the adjustment of capital asset values for

The returns on fund investments, once transferred to the national pension funds, may comprise about 3 percent of the total pension funds by 1990. (Upon retirement, Swedish workers receive a defined pension benefit from these funds equal to 65 percent of the wage earned during the highest-paid fifteen years of their work experience.)

These bare facts show how weak the incentives for performance are under the Wage Earner Funds. Even if all of the resources of the fund came from the profits tax, the returns would represent a trivial fraction of pension benefits at some remote future time for most workers. Moreover, the Swedish Wage Earner Fund could not be expected to restrain wages for the simple reason that the workers' ultimate compensation depends on the performance of Swedish industry generally rather than the performance of their firm. Over the time horizon that is relevant for employment and output decisions, the crucial feature of share economy compensation systems is missing; the pay of each employee does not fall in response to an increase in the number of workers hired.

In fact, the profit-sharing impact of the funds has been very limited in practice. The Wage Earner Fund legislation has become something of a full-employment act for Swedish accountants. In 1985, one of the most profitable postwar years in Swedish industry, Volvo and many other major firms paid no profit-sharing tax into the funds. Less than a third of the Skr 330 million that went into one fund in 1984, also one of the best years for Swedish industry, came from the profits component of the funds. In practice, the Wage Earner Fund legislation has become little more than another increase in payroll taxes.

While avoiding taxes on profits might make sense for Swedish industry for the short term, it is a less obviously rational long-term strategy, for future wage pressure may depend on the extent to which current profits are shared. One unabashed purpose of the funds has been to "secure acceptance for a high level of profits in industry and commerce."[87] If the policy fails to tap profits, an agrument for wage restraint is removed. Why should industry follow a policy that tempts fate?

One answer may be that business doubts that profit-sharing will result in any moderation of wage claims.[88] But many of the accounting

inflation is somewhat complicated. The profit-sharing base consists of real profit minus appropriations to investment reserves, annual tax expense, and the exempt amount (the larger of Skr 500,000 ($55,600) or 6 percent of the wage bill.). For additional details, see Ministry of Finance, *Employee Investment Funds* (Stockholm, 1984), pp. 24–25.

87. Ibid., p. 7.

88. If traditional elasticities hold, half of the 0.2 percent increase in the payroll tax increase will be shifted back on workers, however. See Holmlund, "Payroll Taxes and Wage Inflation."

maneuvers could not be repeated indefinitely. Why provoke the unions for a short-term gain? In part, the business community expected a removal or simplification of the profit-sharing element, irrespective of who won the national election in autumn of 1985. In part, however, companies face the kind of prisoner's dilemma often encountered by unions considering compliance with a government incomes policy. If all companies desist from accounting maneuvers, the profit contributions will be relatively high and the likelihood of union wage restraint will be maximized. If all companies avoid profits taxes, they are likely to face union wage demands that imply substantial increases in labor costs. Why doesn't the cooperative solution dominate? Any one company will do even better if it alone avoids taxes, thereby gaining the benefits of the wage restraint resulting from the "compliance" of other companies in addition to its tax savings. When all companies make this calculation the system defaults to the noncooperative solution. Thus even in the absence of doubts about the effects of the funds on union wage restraint or about legislative revisions, decentralized company decisionmaking is likely to result in systematic avoidance of the profit-sharing component of a wage earner fund.

Conclusion

When an outside economist first views the Swedish labor market, with its compressed wage differentials, comparatively high marginal tax rates, and numerous government-financed alternatives to work, the first reaction tends to be amazement that the labor market works at all. Yet work it does. Contrary to Swedish oral tradition, labor mobility is comparatively high and responsive to wage differentials. To the extent that aggregate mobility has fallen since 1970, it has been the result of slack markets and the compression of the wage structure.

The remarkable compression of the Swedish wage distribution during the 1960s and 1970s has resulted in surprisingly few allocational distortions, foremost among which is the deterioration in the labor market for youth. Incentives for job changing have also declined, although the responsiveness of workers, particularly women, to the wage incentives that exist has if anything increased. There may also have been a decline in investment in skill, although evidence on this point is elusive. Certainly the declining earnings profiles reduce performance incentives for career employees *within* private and public organizations. On the other hand, it is less clear that the remarkable increase in the relative wage of women has been accompanied by a decline in the number of job opportunities, although this may in part reflect the fact that government has been the dominant employer of women.

Although the allocational costs of solidaristic wage policy are comparatively small, there is still room for criticism of the policy. First, while allocation costs may not be widespread, those that have developed are important, particularly in the case of youth. Second, the contribution of wage-structure policy to income equality is small in comparison to the role of taxes and transfers. Third, the implementation of the policy contributes modestly to general wage growth, first from wage drift (largely among private blue-collar workers) as the effects of central agreements on the wage structure are partially offset by local action and later from "compensating" wage claims by public and salaried employees who receive less drift. Whatever the original case for solidaristic wage policy, it no longer appears to contribute to the growth and equity objectives that Swedes set for themselves.

Swedish collective bargaining provides a fascinating study of the limitations of centralized representation in the face of increasing membership heterogeneity.[89] Much of the fragmentation in Swedish bargaining arrangements is traceable to the social policies of the labor movement—particularly its support of public redistributive policies and of full employment policies that resulted in the growth of public employment and high marginal tax rates. The basic tensions in the bargaining system are well in place and can be influenced only marginally by changes in bargaining structure or shifting coalitions between union federations, SAF, and the government.

In the area of aggregate wage determination, the surprise for an outsider is that so much policy and intellectual attention is devoted to collective bargaining activities in a country where between one-third and one-half of earnings growth consists of wage drift. This is reminiscent of the tendency of the American press and, at times, public policy to focus on a few highly visible collective bargaining settlements, when the real action in the United States is in the 70 percent of the national wage bill determined by nonunion pay decisions. Drift is not completely

---

89. For a discussion of the tension between power and representational factors in choice of bargaining structure, see Robert J. Flanagan, "Workplace Public Goods and Union Organization," *Industrial Relations*, vol. 22 (Spring 1983), pp. 224–37.

independent of decisions made in Swedish collective bargaining, any more than nonunion wages in the United States are completely independent of union wages. In Sweden the links between negotiated rates and drift seem weak, however. Even given those links, it seems that the most appropriate policy stance is to accept negotiated wage increases as a floor on earnings growth that can be influenced modestly in either direction by structural changes in bargaining arrangements and to focus attention on wage drift.

Comments by Lars Calmfors

This chapter consists of two parts. The first deals with relative wages and the allocative efficiency of the labor market. The second deals with the aggregate wage level and macroeconomic stability. I shall concentrate on the latter, which I find the more controversial. As to the first part, I shall only make a few minor comments.

Relative Wages and Allocative Efficiency

Robert Flanagan argues convincingly that equalizing the wage structure is an inefficient way of promoting economic equality. The only major aspect I miss is a thorough discussion of the wage structure in the public sector. Do low salaries for employees with higher education (relative to the private sector) threaten to cause a drastic and increasing lack of competence in the public sector? Do high relative wages for less-skilled workers make employment in the public sector more attractive for such workers than employment in the private sector? It is not possible to assess properly the welfare costs of the deviations from a market-clearing wage structure without considering these imbalances. Moreover, the overall relative wage developments in the economy cannot be understood without recognizing public employers' active support in the past for the equalization of the wage structure.

I should also have liked a clearer distinction between different phases of the solidaristic wage policy.[90] The aim of the original Rehn-Meidner model was not to interfere with the long-run wage structure consistent with market equilibrium but rather to speed up the adjustment to it

90. This point has been made especially in Lennart Jonsson and Claes-Henric Siven, *Varför Löneskillnader?* (Stockholm: SAF, 1985).

by reducing wage differentials among regions and sectors already in the short run. Such a wage policy causes transitory unemployment, but when it comes to mobility of labor, it mainly substitutes one form of adjustment for another. Reallocations will take place not as voluntary supply responses to relative wage changes but instead as forced movements of unemployed workers from declining sectors and regions to vacancies in expanding ones.

It is quite another thing to compress long-run wage differentials between various age and skill groups, as has been done in recent years. There is obviously no mechanism through which young workers who are too expensive to employ can be transformed into middle-aged ones who are in demand. As to wage differentials between more- and less-skilled workers, vacancies for the former and unemployment for the latter do, of course, constitute incentives for acquiring skills. But the method is not likely to be efficient: the unskilled workers becoming unemployed are probably the ones that will raise their productivity the least through more education. The welfare costs of later stages of the solidaristic wage policy are thus likely to be far more harmful than those of the earlier stages.

The conclusion that stands out most clearly to me is, however, how little we still know quantitatively about the welfare effects of compressing wage differentials. The reason is not that we should expect these costs to be small, but that they are much harder to quantify than, for example, the effects of various macroeconomic policies. This asymmetry of knowledge may impart a bias to the whole public discussion of economic policy and wage setting, which tends to become focused on macroeconomic rather than microeconomic issues.

Aggregate Wage Setting and Macroeconomic Stability

In the section on aggregate wage setting and macroeconomic stability Flanagan discusses various ways of coping with inflationary wage increases. His conclusions can be summarized as follows: he is skeptical about a nonaccommodative policy stance; he favors a tougher government attitude in public-sector wage bargaining; he wants to focus on curbing wage drift instead of negotiated wage increases; and he is in favor of centralized wage bargaining.

These conclusions are based on an analysis of the causes of excessive wage increases. Two common explanations are considered.

Figure 5-4. *Union Wage Behavior under Accommodation and Nonaccommodation Government Policies*

a. Accommodation policy and trade union wage-setting

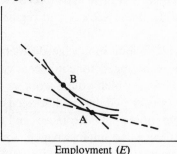

Employment (*E*)

b. The union-union game: negative externality

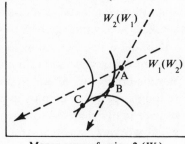

Money wage of union 2 (*W*₂)

c. Accommodation policies and the wage-wage spiral

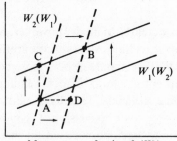

Money wage of union 2 (*W*₂)

d. The union-union game: positive externality

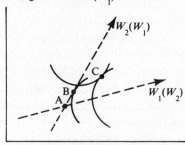

Money wage of union 2 (*W*₂)

According to the first one, accommodative government policies have weakened the incentives for wage restraint. This can be illustrated in terms of a model of a utility-maximizing trade union.[91] In such a framework, policies aiming at stabilizing employment at some target value lower the elasticity of labor demand and thus create an incentive for a union that cares about both the real wage and employment to substitute a higher real wage for lower rates of employment. The flavor of the argument is given in figure 5-4a, which shows labor demand

91. See Andrew J. Oswald, "The Economic Theory of Trade Unions: An Introductory Survey," *Scandinavian Journal of Economics,* vol. 87, no. 2 (1985), pp. 160–93, for a survey of such models.

schedules (the straight lines) and indifference curves showing the union's evaluation of real wages and employment. Employment policies that steepen the labor demand schedule in the way indicated will induce a trade union to choose a point like *B* instead of *A*.[92]

The second explanation stresses that increased rivalry has made it harder for unions to take account of macroeconomic conditions. Flanagan points to increased controversy about relative wages between blue-collar and white-collar workers and between public-sector and private-sector employees. White-collar workers and public-sector employees no longer seem content to let agreements between the Swedish Confederation of Trade Unions (LO) and the Swedish Employers' Confederation (SAF) set the pace for the whole labor market as they did in the 1950s and 1960s.

This explanation can also be illustrated in a model similar to that of figure 5-4a.[93] In figure 5-4b this is done for two unions that could be either blue-collar and white-collar in the private sector, or private-sector and public-sector unions. The straight lines are reaction functions showing that the real wage for one union depends positively on the wage for the other. The curves are indifference curves showing combinations of the two wage rates that keep each union's utility constant. They will look as depicted, and utility for the individual union will increase, as indicated by the arrows, if a wage increase for one union decreases the utility of the other.[94] This may have several causes. One possibility is a direct "jealousy" effect. Another is that price increases (or in the case of wage increases in the public sector, tax increases) reduce the purchasing power of the other union's members. In addition, employment of the other union's members will fall if the two groups of employees are complementary.[95]

92. This point was originally made in Lars Calmfors, "Employment Policies, Wage Formation and Trade Union Behavior in a Small Open Economy," *Scandinavian Journal of Economics,* vol. 84, no. 2 (1982). See also Calmfors and Henrik Horn, "Employment Policies and Centralized Wage-setting," *Economica,* vol. 53 (August 1986), pp. 281–302.

93. The diagram is based on work in progress with John Driffill extending the models in Andrew J. Oswald, "Wage Determination in an Economy with Many Trade Unions," *Oxford Economic Papers,* vol. 31 (November 1979), pp. 369–85; and Thorvaldur Gylfason and Assar Lindbeck, "Competing Wage Claims, Cost Inflation, and Capacity Utilization," *European Economic Review,* vol. 24 (February 1984), pp. 1–21.

94. Along the reaction function the particular union's wage is chosen so that utility is maximized given the other union's wage. A change of the wage in either direction thus causes utility to fall and hence must be compensated by a wage reduction for the other union to keep utility constant.

95. According to J. Ekberg, "Översikt av forskning kring arbetskraftsefterfrågan," in *Arbetsmarknadspolitik under omprövning,* Sou 1984:31 (Stockholm, 1984), there is some weak support for complementarity between blue-collar and white-collar workers in Swedish manufacturing. Estimated cross-elasticities of demand are of the order of magnitude of 0.15–0.25.

The diagram serves to illustrate several possible outcomes. Point *A* is a noncooperative Nash equilibrium, in which each union acts in isolation. Point *B* is a Stackelberg equilibrium in which union 1 acts as leader and sets its wage by taking into account the response of union 2, which acts as a follower. Wage rates will be lower and the utility of both unions higher in the Stackelberg equilibrium because the leader takes into account that raising its own wage triggers a wage increase for the other union, which affects its own utility negatively. Point *C* is one possible cooperative outcome (the set of such outcomes is given by the tangency points between the two sets of indifference curves). As can be seen, wage rates are even lower and the utility of both unions higher with cooperative solutions than in *B*, because the negative welfare effects of the first union's wage increases on the other are fully internalized. The way to interpret increased union rivalry in terms of the diagram would be as a movement from a Stackelberg equilibrium such as *B* when one union (LO) is the wage leader, or from a cooperative solution like *C*, to a Nash equilibrium like *A*.

Flanagan finds the union rivalry hypothesis more plausible than the accommodation hypothesis. My main objection is that he regards the two explanations as mutually exclusive. In my view they are complementary.

Flanagan's criticism of the accommodation hypothesis is based on too literal an interpretation. The formal models have focused on the interaction between a government and *one* dominating private-sector union. But this has mainly been a presentational device. Accommodation policies produce basically the same results in models with several unions. It is true, of course, that the accommodative effect on each union is diluted: the members of an individual union contemplating a wage increase can expect to receive only a share of an offsetting increase in the government demand for labor. Hence the incentive created for each union to raise its wage is smaller than in the one-union case, provided that other wages stay constant. But they will not. Accommodation policies create incentives for *all* unions to raise wages. Once this occurs, a wage-wage spiral is triggered. The process is illustrated for the Nash equilibrium in figure 5-4c, in which accommodation policies are assumed

in *Arbetsmarknadspolitik under omprövning*, Sou 1984:31 (Stockholm, 1984), there is some weak support for complementarity between blue-collar and white-collar workers in Swedish manufacturing. Estimated cross-elasticities of demand are of the order of magnitude of 0.15–0.25.

to shift the reaction functions. The new equilibrium will not be at points like C or D, but at B, where wage increases for the two unions have reinforced each other. The final effect may be as large as in the one-union case. What may look like interunion competition may thus only be the mechanism through which accommodation policies work.

I do not want to deny the importance of genuinely increased union rivalry as illustrated in figure 5-4b. I also agree that the growing numbers of white-collar workers and public-sector employees are crucial to explaining why their organizations strive for a more active role. But a movement to less cooperative outcomes may also have something to do with the costs for unions of moving there. These costs will be lessened to the extent that accommodation policies reduce the employment losses resulting from higher wage increases.

Thus I do not share the view that the importance of union rivalry weakens the case for nonaccommodation. As to Flanagan's alternative policy suggestions, I want to emphasize a number of complications that are not discussed.

Although a tougher stance by the government in bargaining is in principle an attractive option, Swedish experience shows that it is not easy to implement. Previous attempts seem to have failed because politicians and the public simply are not willing to accept prolonged interruptions of public services. One problem in this context is that bargaining on the employers' part is conducted by special central negotiating bodies without operative responsibility for government services. This seems to have led to a tendency to misjudge the consequences of conflicts with a resulting pressure from the public on the employers to give in.

As to the suggestion to limit wage drift through an extra tax on wage increases in excess of the centrally negotiated ones, I find two problems. First, to the extent that wage drift is anticipated by central negotiators, it may just be one institutional form for centrally determined wage increases. If so, lower wage drift only results in higher central wage increases. Empirical studies showing the responsiveness of wage drift to excess demand in the labor market do not really tell us anything about this issue. Second, if an extra tax on wage increases is successful in restraining wage drift, this may not be a good thing. Here I find Flanagan self-contradictory. In the section on allocative efficiency he argues for greater flexibility of relative wages, yet he proposes macroeconomic policies that would curb the market-determined part of wage increases.

However, as pointed out earlier, we know too little about the effects of relative-wage rigidities to be able to compare the allocative costs of a TIP with the likely costs of transitory unemployment with nonaccommodation.

Finally, I would like to address the issue of centralization versus decentralization. It has been discussed mainly in connection with the tendency toward sectorwide bargaining between LO and SAF. This development is the result of deliberate influence from private employers, who see bargaining as a means of increasing relative-wage flexibility.

How does the degree of centralization affect the aggregate wage level? If we assume that centralized bargaining results in cooperative outcomes between the unions involved and decentralized bargaining in noncooperative Stackelberg or Nash equilibria, we can apply the same analysis as before. If the picture is as in figure 5-4b, centralization is obviously to be preferred from the point of view of aggregate wage determination. But suppose instead that the picture is as in figure 5-4d. It corresponds to the case when the utility of each union *increases* when the other union's wage rises. Such a positive externality may exist if the labor organized by the two unions produces goods that are substitutes for each other, so that a wage increase for one union, by affecting relative prices of the goods, causes demand to spill over to the other sector and thus raises employment there. If this effect is strong enough, it may outweigh jealousy and the negative effects of purchasing power.[96] Then decentralization produces a lower aggregate wage level than centralization.

It is not immediately evident which case is the relevant one when comparing sectorwide bargaining with centralization in the LO-SAF area. Positive spillover effects on employment in other sectors may be important among many nontradables sectors, but such effects are not likely to be strong between tradables sectors; the main spillover effects will be to foreign competitors.[97]

In general, spillover effects on employment will be much stronger between firms within the same sector than between sectors. This raises the possibility that from the point of view of aggregate wage determination, sectorwide bargaining may be inferior both to complete

96. It may also be the case that wage increases in one sector increase utility of union members in a second sector to the extent that they consider employment in the first sector as an alternative opportunity in case of unemployment.

97. Indeed, in the extreme case of tradables sectors for which prices are determined in the world market, there will be no employment spillover effects at all, nor any price effects affecting other unions.

centralization and decentralization to the firm level. A possible conclusion is that if we want to decentralize wage bargaining in order to enhance relative-wage flexibility, it may be better to go all the way to the firm level rather than to stop halfway.

But the centralization-decentralization issue does not have only one dimension. It is certainly possible to combine decentralization of wage negotiations at the level of the individual firm with more cooperation between blue-collar and white-collar workers within firms. Likewise one can conceive of more cooperation between public and private employers on lower levels.

The degree of centralization is not, however, a policy parameter of the government, except to the extent that as an employer, the government can affect the form of bargaining. The labor market organizations can facilitate economic policy by choosing appropriate forms of negotiation; but if this is not done, the government's only option is to affect the incentives of wage setters through traditional policy tools.

Comments by Bertil Holmlund

The main section of this chapter deals with the solidaristic wage policy, and this is perhaps also the most controversial part. Robert Flanagan proposes that the solidaristic wage policy should be abandoned, although he is not very explicit about how that could be done or what policy should replace it. My comments will focus on this issue.

Flanagan's discussion of solidaristic wage policy is based on a fundamental assumption, more or less explicitly stated, that institutionally driven wage changes are distortionary compared to market-driven changes. A fall in labor mobility as a response to compressed wage differentials is regarded as evidence of allocational costs.

I will argue against the general validity of these presumptions. A basic problem here is to specify a reference case, the labor market that would exist in the absence of a solidaristic wage policy. Critics of union wage policies are seldom explicit on this point, but a frequent implicit hypothesis seems to be that abandoning the solidaristic wage policy would move the economy closer to a competitive Walrasian world, with market-clearing wages in all submarkets. This may or may not be true, but it is not something that should be taken for granted. Let me give a few theoretical and empirical examples.

Suppose that unions give up their solidaristic wage policy and that wages instead are set by individual firms competing for labor in a market with turnover costs and imperfect information. Such an economy may entail involuntary unemployment, and it may also entail artificial wage dispersion, that is, unequal pay for equal work.[98] This kind of wage dispersion has no allocative function; on the contrary, it induces socially wasteful search and turnover. A social planner—or a union—that enforces equal pay for equal work could increase net output in the society. This has been pointed out in recent theoretical papers, but it was also pointed out thirty or more years ago in the Swedish discussion on centralized wage setting.

There is thus a case for solidaristic wage policy, not because workers do not respond to economic incentives, but because they do. A reduction in wage dispersion concomitant with a decline in mobility provides in itself no evidence of a less efficient labor market; it may well indicate a more efficiently functioning market.

Let me now turn to empirical examples. Flanagan's discussion includes figures confirming the absence of any correlation between wages and average labor productivity in firms. And this is as it should be according to the solidaristic wage policy. But it is also consistent with a model of a competitive Walrasian labor market, in which the wage structure is determined primarily by skill differentials.

How does this Swedish pattern compare to the U.S. labor market? A recent NBER study by L. A. Bell and R. B. Freeman shows that relative wage movements among industries are to an important degree influenced by industry-specific price and productivity factors.[99] If a sector's relative prices go up, there is a strong tendency for its relative wages to increase as well. This would not occur in a competitive labor market, except perhaps in the very short run. The kind of flexibility in industry wages that we have seen in the United States may well reflect such inherent imperfections of the labor market as lack of information or other barriers to mobility between sectors.

My comments so far may seem a nonselective defense of the solidaristic wage policy. They are not meant to be, however. I would like to offer only a selective defense: the basic principle of equal pay for equal

98. See, for example, Joseph E. Stiglitz, "Equilibrium Wage Distributions," *Economic Journal*, vol. 95 (September 1985), pp. 595–618.

99. Linda A. Bell and Richard B. Freeman, "Does a Flexible Industry Wage Structure Increase Employment? The U.S. Experience," working paper 1604 (NBER, April 1985).

work is sound, and it is not obvious that it would be achieved without the assistance of wage-setting institutions like unions.

In practice solidaristic wage policy has also had egalitarian objectives, probably with adverse effects on youth employment as a result. I do not question Flanagan's interpretation in this respect. In fact, I think that his point could be strengthened by noting that a rapidly growing number of Swedish youths are found in labor market programs. However, very little is known about the relevant elasticities of substitution in the Swedish economy. Economists do not know whether youth labor is a substitute or complement to adult labor, and it is also highly unlikely that wage-setters have a precise knowledge of the elasticities. Whether lower wages for youth will involve hiring sons and firing fathers is, unfortunately, still an open question.

A reasonable position is to accept the efficiency-oriented objectives of the solidaristic policy, but at the same time to reconsider the application of its egalitarian goals. It seems obvious that employment considerations must be taken more seriously. How that can be achieved in practice—given that unions determine their own wage policies—is an interesting and difficult question that is not addressed in this chapter or in others in this volume that are also critical of the solidaristic wage policy. The Swedish discussion on this point has not been very constructive either. There have been a lot of complaints about the wage structure but few suggestions about how desirable changes could be induced by government policies.

Before finishing my comments, I cannot resist the temptation to present some interesting results from a recent paper of the London School of Economics, written by C. R. Bean, P. R. G. Layard, and S. J. Nickell.[100] The paper focuses on labor market behavior in eighteen OECD countries. The same labor market model is estimated on data for each of those countries. The model consists of a labor-demand equation and a real-wage equation; the exogenous variables include taxes, import prices, and proxies for labor market mismatch and search effort.

The estimated equations allow comparisons of how labor markets in the different countries respond to shocks. The paper looks at how quickly temporary shocks are erased from the system, events that are captured by the lag structure of the equations. This is one conceivable operational definition of the widely used but rather vague term "flexibility."

100. C. R. Bean, P. R. G. Layard, and S. J. Nickell, "The Rise in Unemployment: A Multi-Country Study," discussion paper 239 (London School of Economics, Centre for Labour Economics, 1985; forthcoming in *Economica*).

Of the eighteen, which has the most flexible labor market? Sweden. The least flexible labor market is found not in Britain but in the United States.

As usual, one can raise a number of questions about the model and the data and so forth. A general finding, however, is that labor markets in more centralized or corporatist systems adjust more quickly to shocks. This result, along with similar findings in other studies, should moderate the enthusiasm for decentralized wage negotiations. This is also a conclusion of Flanagan's chapter.

It seems, then, that the Swedish labor market performs rather poorly by the high standards set by the Swedes. But compared to the labor markets of other countries, it seems to work reasonably well.

6

Taxes, Transfers, and Swedish Labor Supply

GARY BURTLESS

TAXES, TRANSFER PAYMENTS, and public spending are high in Sweden compared with levels elsewhere in the industrialized world. The high level of government spending finances income redistribution programs unrivaled in scope and generosity. Although there is broad public consensus within Sweden on the need for most of these programs, their cost has aroused intense interest, particularly among economists.

A number of scholars have argued that tax levels in Sweden are now so high that the government could actually increase revenue by reducing tax rates on marginal income. This argument rests largely on the belief that workers would substantially increase their taxable earnings by working more hours if rates were lowered. The concern about the impact of taxes on Swedish labor supply may seem odd. Sweden already enjoys one of the world's highest rates of labor force participation. Observers from countries with lower participation rates might wonder whether the high Swedish rate is not actually due to public spending on programs, such as day care and worker retraining, that are aimed at raising employment. Generous spending on these programs requires high taxes.

This chapter analyzes the principal tax and transfer incentives that affect Swedish labor supply. Its goal is to determine whether and how much labor supply has fallen in response to heavy taxes and generous redistribution policies. Because the chapter is aimed at audiences outside as well as inside Sweden, it compares Swedish incentives and behavior with those observed in the United States. This comparison is interesting because the United States has adopted policies nearly the opposite of those in Sweden. American tax burdens are comparatively low, and the government engages in far less income redistribution on behalf of working-age people and their children.

The opening two sections describe the major Swedish tax and transfer programs that affect adult labor supply. Where appropriate, they are compared with similar ones in the United States. Readers already familiar with Swedish programs may wish to skip these two sections. The next section analyzes the theoretical incentives of the Swedish tax-transfer system. It is followed by detailed time-series evidence about comparative labor supply trends in Sweden and the United States. The final substantive section reviews the published empirical research on Swedish labor supply and presents a simple econometric analysis of the aggregate time-series evidence. The chapter concludes with a brief summary.

Taxes

Tax rates on Swedish labor income are high. According to estimates by the Organization for Economic Cooperation and Development, income and payroll taxes for typical wage earners are higher in Sweden than in any other OECD country.[1] Hansson and Stuart have attempted to measure the average and marginal tax rates on Swedish labor earnings in 1979. The marginal rate is computed as the tax that would be levied on an added krona of wages in the Swedish economy, taking account of the distribution of tax rates faced by all wage earners. The two economists estimate that the 1979 marginal and average rates were 73 percent and 55 percent, respectively,[2] far above comparable rates in the United States. Stuart estimates that the marginal U.S. rate in 1976 was 43 percent and the average rate only 27 percent.[3] U.S. taxes are thus nearly 30 percentage points below equivalent rates in Sweden.

Not only are Swedish tax rates high, but they have risen steeply over

1. Organization for Economic Cooperation and Development, Committee on Fiscal Affairs, *The Tax/Benefit Position of Selected Income Groups in OECD Member Countries, 1974–78* (Paris: OECD, 1980), pp. 20–24.

2. Ingemar Hansson and Charles Stuart, "Tax Revenue and the Marginal Cost of Public Funds in Sweden," *Journal of Public Economics*, vol. 27 (August 1985), p. 343. This estimate includes the effect of the Swedish value-added tax (VAT), since most of the burden of this tax is borne by wage earners.

3. Charles Stuart, "Welfare Costs per Dollar of Additional Tax Revenue in the United States," *American Economic Review*, vol. 74 (June 1984), p. 356.

Table 6-1. *Swedish and U.S. Taxes on Wage Earners,*
Selected Years, 1960–82
Receipts as percent of gross domestic product

Source	1960	1965	1970	1975	1980	1982
Individual income taxes						
Sweden	14.3	17.4	20.2	20.2	20.3	20.5
United States	8.7	8.1	10.6	10.0	11.3	11.5
Social security contributions						
Sweden	1.2	4.3	6.1	8.6	14.2	14.0
United States	3.8	4.4	5.8	7.4	8.1	8.4
General consumption taxes						
Sweden	0.5	3.7	4.2	5.3	6.6	6.6
United States	1.0	1.2	1.7	2.0	2.0	2.0
Sum of the above						
Sweden	16.0	25.4	30.5	34.1	41.1	41.1
United States	13.5	13.7	18.1	19.4	21.4	21.9
All taxes						
Sweden	27.2	35.9	40.7	44.1	49.6	50.3
United States	26.6	26.5	30.1	30.2	30.7	30.5

Sources: Data for 1960 from Organization for Economic Cooperation and Development, *Long-Term Trends in Tax Revenues of OECD Member Countries, 1955–1980* (Paris: OECD, 1981), pp. 14–15. Data for 1965–82 from Enrique Rodriguez and Sven Steinmo, "The American and the Swedish Tax System: A Comparison" (University of Uppsala, Department of Economic History, May 1984), pp. 3–6.

time, although the rate of rise has slowed in recent years. Hansson and Stuart suggest that the marginal tax on added labor earnings was 58 percent and the average rate 43.5 percent in 1965.[4] By implication, the marginal tax rose 15 percentage points (or 26 percent) and the average rate 12 points (or 26 percent) in the fourteen years after 1965.

Table 6-1 shows some of the sources of the growing tax burden on Swedish wage earners. The burden of individual income taxes, social security contributions, and general consumption taxes, such as the value-added tax, is believed by economists to be borne disproportionately, if not exclusively, by labor. Each of these sources of revenue has become more important over the past quarter century. As a share of gross domestic product, income taxes rose more than a third, social security contributions nearly twelvefold, and general consumption taxes more than thirteenfold between 1960 and 1980. These types of taxes have of course risen in other OECD nations also, but in few other countries has the rate of increase been so spectacular. The United States

4. Hansson and Stuart, "Tax Revenue and the Marginal Cost of Public Funds," p. 343.

has a relatively small—and slow-growing—tax burden, but its situation is closer to the average of OECD nations than is Sweden's. While the United States and Sweden had reasonably similar tax burdens at the start of the 1960s, by the end of the 1970s the difference between the two was wide (see table 6-1).

To determine whether this difference in tax burdens affects labor supply in the two countries it is necessary to examine differences in the structure as well as the level of labor taxes. The remainder of this section describes some major features of the Swedish system.

Individual Income Taxation

Sweden has an integrated system of central and local government income taxes. For that reason, the overall treatment of labor income is comparatively straightforward. The local (*kommunal*) tax is the simplest to understand. Local jurisdictions impose a strictly proportional tax on incomes above a modest exempt amount (Skr 7,500 in 1985, or roughly one month's salary for an average production worker). This local tax is not deductible in computing income taxes owed to the central government. In 1985 local rates ranged from 25 to 34 percent, with an average rate of just over 30 percent. Between 1965 and 1980, local income tax rates jumped from 17 to 29 percent, but they have grown much more slowly since 1980.[5] By contrast, local income tax rates in the United States are modest, and U.S. state income taxes are also somewhat more progressive than the kommunal income tax. In 1984 the top marginal rates in American states with an income tax ranged from 2.2 percent to 17.6 percent. Because state taxes are deductible in computing federal taxes, the effective marginal state tax rate faced by workers in the top tax brackets ranged from only 1.1 percent to 7.3 percent.[6]

The central government income tax in Sweden is nominally strongly progressive. Taxable income below Skr 70,200 a year is subject to a very low marginal rate (4 percent), but above that income level the rate rises rapidly, reaching 25 percent at Skr 124,800 and 50 percent—the top marginal rate—at Skr 351,000.[7] A full-time employee near the middle of

5. Svenska Arbetsgivareföreningen (SAF), *Fakta om Sveriges Skatter, '85* (Stockholm: SAF, 1985), p. 7.

6. Joseph A. Pechman, *Federal Tax Policy,* 4th ed. (Brookings, 1983), pp. 382–83. In a few U.S. cities an additional tax is levied on income, but the resulting effect on marginal rates is relatively small.

7. Krister Andersson, "The Swedish Tax System," (University of Lund, 1986), p. 13. This paper provides an excellent overview of the entire Swedish tax system.

the earnings distribution could expect to face a nominal marginal tax rate ranging from 20 to 34 percent on added earned income. Combined with the local rate, this yields a total marginal income tax rate between 50 and 64 percent. This rate is applied on wages actually received by earners. Social security contributions are paid by employers, and hence are not subject to individual income taxes (see the discussion below).

Effective tax rates are reduced because of deductions allowed in computing taxable income. The most significant deduction is the one for housing. Taxpayers are permitted a special deduction for an owner-occupied home (Skr 1,500) and are also allowed to deduct interest payments on home mortgages.[8] On the other hand, a low assessment of the imputed rental value of a home is counted as income and subject to income tax. Nonetheless, home ownership is highly favored in the Swedish tax system, as it is in the American. The tax treatment of housing is especially advantageous to upper-income families who are subject to the highest marginal tax rates.[9] Because the true incomes of these families are not fully taxed, the effective tax rate on earnings is below the nominal rate. For example, if tax-favored housing expenditures rise more or less in proportion to a family's permanent income, a one krona rise in earnings will result in a proportional rise in tax deductions and hence in a rise in taxable income that is less than one krona. In making long-run labor supply decisions, wage earners presumably respond to the effective tax rates rather than nominal rates imposed on earned income.

A notable feature of the Swedish tax system is its treatment of earned income in husband-wife families with two earners. Each wage earner is taxed separately, rather than jointly as in the United States.[10] This provision was introduced on a limited basis for high-income couples in 1965 and for all two-earner couples in 1971. In comparison with joint taxation, the current Swedish system imposes a much lighter tax burden on families in which both spouses work. Under a joint tax system, such as the one in the United States, the first dollar earned by the second wage earner is subject to the same marginal tax as the last dollar earned by the primary wage earner. Under a system of separate taxation, the

8. Ibid., p. 6.

9. The advantage to high-income taxpayers has been limited in recent years by changes in the tax code. Under certain circumstances, the taxpayer is not permitted to fully deduct interest payments on a mortgage. Ibid., p. 11.

10. However, capital income in excess of an exempt amount is taxed at the marginal rate applicable on the earnings of the more highly taxed spouse.

first dollar earned by the second wage earner is subject to a much lower marginal tax rate.

Separate taxation of husbands' and wives' earnings can strongly influence family labor supply decisions. In 1978 the full-time wage of an average production worker in Sweden was about Skr 57,000 a year. The marginal income tax rate at this level of earnings was 61 percent for a married couple with two children. If the spouse of the average production worker contemplated entering employment under a system of joint taxation, the 61 percent marginal tax rate would apply to his or her initial earnings. But under a system of separate taxation, the tax burden on the second earner is lower. A spouse entering part-time employment and earning one-third the average production wage faced a 1978 tax liability of only 27 percent of earnings, far below the rate levied on the full-time worker's marginal income. The Swedish family's tax situation contrasts with that of an identical American family. In 1978 the average U.S. production worker with a nonworking spouse and two children faced a 24 percent marginal income tax rate. If the nonworking spouse found a part-time job paying one-third of average earnings, the average tax on those earnings would have been 23 percent—virtually the same rate imposed on the full-time worker's marginal income.

Swedish families are given a strong tax incentive to substitute the wife's market work for the husband's in supplying labor. American families do not have this incentive. The point is demonstrated by considering the different tax liabilities of a family under alternative patterns of earnings. The hypothetical family consisting of a husband, a wife, and two children earns 1.66 times the annual wage of an average production worker. If all this income were earned by a single breadwinner, the family's 1978 income tax liability in Sweden would have been 48 percent of total earnings; if 40 percent of the family's income had been contributed by the wife, the family's tax liability would have been only 32 percent of total earnings. That is, a Swedish family with a single earner would owe half again as much income tax as a family with two earners. In the United States the two families would have virtually the same income tax liability regardless of the distribution of earnings between husband and wife.[11]

11. The average U.S. income tax rate on the one-earner family would have been 18.5 percent in 1978; the average tax on the two-earner family would have been 17.7 percent. All computations are based on statistics reported by the OECD Committee on Fiscal Affairs, *Tax/Benefit Position*, pp. 24, 82–85.

Figure 6-1. *Swedish Income Tax Rates on Full-Time and Part-Time Married Workers, 1963–82*

Tax rate (percent)

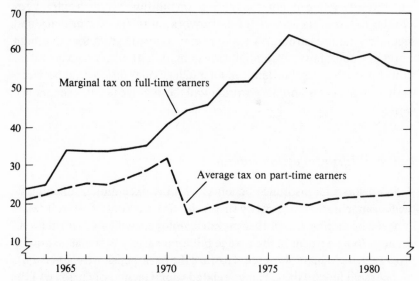

Source: Data from Stig Tegle, *Part-Time Employment: An Economic Analysis of Weekly Working Hours in Sweden, 1963–1982* (University of Lund, Department of Economics, 1985), pp. 76–77.

Trends in Swedish income tax rates are displayed in figure 6-1. The higher line shows the trend in the *marginal* income tax rate on the earnings of a full-time worker being paid the average hourly wage for males. The lower line shows the trend in the *average* tax rate on the earnings of a 20-hour-a-week worker who is paid the average hourly wage for Swedish women and is married to a full-time worker paid the average male wage. This comparison between the marginal tax on full-time workers and the average tax on part-time spouses is meaningful for many families. Such families are faced with the choice of marginally changing the hours of the full-time worker or changing the work status of the secondary or part-time worker. Marginal tax rates on full-time workers rose sharply from 1963 through 1976 and have declined somewhat since then as the central government's income tax formula has been reformed. The trend in average tax rates on secondary, part-time earners is strikingly different. The average tax rate rose 11 percentage points between 1963 and 1970 (from 21 to 32 percent), but then fell 15 points in 1971 when the tax system was reformed to permit separate

rather than joint taxation of earnings. The average tax on part-time
earnings has since risen very slowly and remains less than half the rate
on marginal earnings of a full-time worker. Figure 6-1 dramatically
illustrates the rising income tax burdens on full-time Swedish employees
and the different incentives for extra work on the part of primary and
secondary family earners. A similar time-series diagram for American
workers would show substantially lower marginal and average tax rates,
slower growth in tax burdens, and a much smaller differential between
the marginal tax on a primary worker and the average tax on a secondary
earner.

Social Insurance Contributions

Swedish social insurance benefits, with the exception of unemployment compensation, are partly or wholly financed out of payroll taxes
imposed on employers. In 1986 private employers will pay contributions
equal to 36.65 percent of their wage bill for a variety of social insurance
programs, including 9.45 percent toward the basic pension (*folkpension*),
10.2 percent toward the earnings-related supplementary pension (ATP),
and 9.3 percent for sickness insurance.[12] The Swedish contribution rate
is twice the comparable social security tax rate in the United States. The
1986 combined tax rate for the American old-age, survivors, disability,
and health insurance (OASDHI) programs is 14.3 percent, with half the
rate paid by employers and half by employees. The U.S. social security
tax is paid on wages and self-employment income below a taxable
maximum, currently equal to about two and one-half times the annual
earnings of an average production worker. Figure 6-2 shows the trends
in Swedish and U.S. payroll tax rates as a percentage of gross earnings
(including the employer's tax contribution). The graph understates the
tax burden on wages in Sweden compared with the United States because
American wages are partially exempt from social security contributions,
whereas all Swedish wages are taxed. In particular, highly paid American
workers face no social security tax on marginal earnings.

Economists generally believe there is no difference in incidence
between the payroll taxes legally imposed on employers and those
imposed on employees. Most if not all of the burden of the tax is probably

12. Andersson, "Swedish Tax System," p. 19.

Figure 6-2. *Swedish and U.S. Social Insurance Tax Rates, 1965–85*

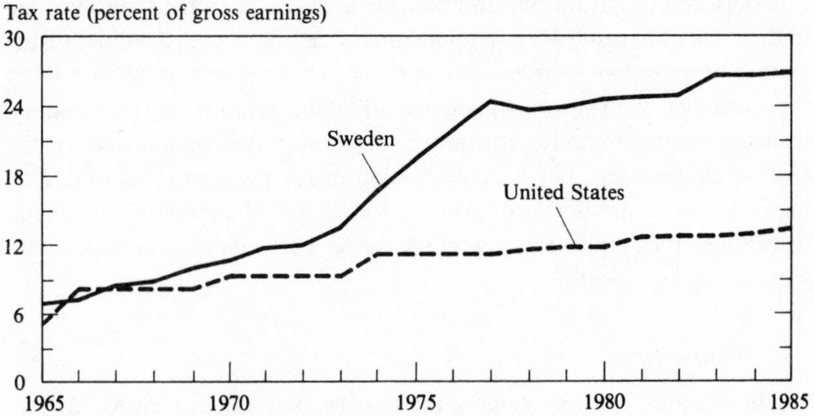

Tax rate (percent of gross earnings)

Sources: Svenska Arbetsgivareföreningen (SAF), *Fakta om Sveriges Skatter, '85* (Stockholm: SAF, 1985); and U.S. Department of Health and Human Services, Social Security Administration, *Social Security Bulletin, Annual Statistical Supplement, 1984/85* (Washington, D.C.: U.S. Government Printing Office, 1985).

borne by employees in the form of lower real wages.[13] It does not follow, however, that social insurance taxes distort labor supply behavior in the same way as other taxes on labor. Workers covered by social insurance expect that some of their own and their employer's current tax contributions will be returned to them in the form of pensions, disability pay, or health benefits. Viewed in this light, social insurance is simply a form of delayed compensation and should cause no more labor supply distortion than private nonwage compensation (for example, private pension and health benefits). If workers expect to receive discounted social insurance benefits exactly equal in value to tax contributions paid in their behalf, there might be almost no distortion arising out of social insurance taxes.[14] In neither Sweden nor the United States is the relation between contributions and benefits especially close, however. In both countries, health insurance benefits depend on a person's medical bills, not on his or her prior tax contributions. Public pension benefits are related to a worker's previous tax payments, but in both countries the

13. For a summary of the arguments, see Pechman, *Federal Tax Policy*, pp. 215–17, and the citations mentioned in Joseph A. Pechman, *Who Paid the Taxes, 1966–85?* (Brookings, 1985), p. 31.

14. A small distortion would remain because workers are compelled to accept compensation in a form they might not otherwise choose themselves. For example, they might prefer to receive more in money wages and less in pensions or health insurance.

retirement and disability formulas are very redistributive. The connection between contributions and benefits is thus somewhat tenuous even in the case of earnings-related pensions. Because Swedish social insurance is more redistributive—particularly in the upper and lower tails of the earnings distribution—I suspect that the relation between social insurance benefits and contributions is weaker in Sweden than in the United States (see the discussion of transfer programs below). This implies that a greater proportion of Swedish than American social insurance taxes represents a genuine wedge between worker output and worker compensation.

Consumption taxes

The present Swedish value-added tax (*mervärdeskatt,* or MOMS) is a successor to the retail sales tax, first levied in 1960. Originally set at 4 percent, the sales tax doubled during the 1960s. In 1969 it was converted to a value-added tax, with a rate initially set at 10 percent. The rate has nearly doubled since then, and now stands at 19 percent. The tax covers 70 to 80 percent of private consumption. Although the rate is nominally uniform, the existence of partial and total exemptions implies some differentiation in effective rates among various goods and services.[15] There is no equivalent national-level tax in the United States. However, nearly all American states, as well as numerous cities and counties, impose retail sales taxes. In most states, food and drugs are exempt from taxation to reduce the tax burdens on lower-income families. State sales tax rates ranged between 2 percent and 7.5 percent in 1983.

Besides general consumption taxes, both Sweden and the United States impose excise and other taxes on specific goods and services, including tobacco products, alcoholic beverages, and energy. Over time, this source of revenue has declined in importance and now accounts for less than 10 percent of tax receipts in both countries. The burden of specific taxes in Sweden, however, is about twice that in the United States—4.9 percent of gross domestic product in Sweden versus only 2.6 percent in the United States.[16] Some portion of this tax burden is borne by wage earners in their capacity as consumers, although it is unknown precisely how much of a burden they bear.

15. This discussion is based on Andersson, "Swedish Tax System," p. 21.
16. These figures refer to 1982. Enrique Rodriguez and Sven Steinmo, "The American and the Swedish Tax System: A Comparison" (University of Uppsala, Department of Economic History, May 1984), p. 7.

Figure 6-3. *Total Marginal and Average Tax Rates on Full-Time Male Swedish Workers, 1965–82*

Tax rate (percent)

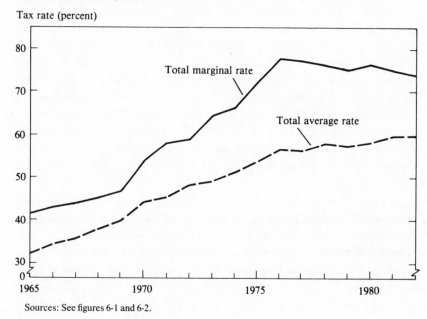

Sources: See figures 6-1 and 6-2.

Trends in Taxation

The recent trends in overall Swedish tax rates are shown in figure 6-3. The top line shows the trend in the total marginal tax rate on a full-time male worker; the lower line shows the trend in the total average tax rate on the same worker. For simplicity, only the effects of changing income tax rates, social insurance contribution rates, and value-added tax rates are taken into account. The income tax rate is based on computations for a full-time male production worker earning the average hourly wage. It is assumed that the worker is married to a nonworking spouse and has at least one child under 16. (The marginal rate on the same worker with a working spouse would be even higher.) I assume that the burden of the social insurance tax is entirely borne by the worker and is perceived by the worker as a pure tax. Finally, I assume that the value-added tax is paid on 75 percent of the worker's final consumption.[17]

Marginal and average tax burdens may be understated because the

17. This estimate is based on Andersson, "Swedish Tax System," p. 21.

computations ignore certain taxes, such as excises, that may be partly borne by labor. However, tax burdens are overstated by the naive treatment of social insurance contributions. As mentioned above, wage earners should expect that part of the social insurance taxes paid on their marginal earnings will be repaid to them in the form of sickness pay and pensions. If workers expect that a third of their contributions will be returned to them in eventual benefits, the social insurance tax rate would be reduced by a third, or about 2 percentage points in 1965 and 8 percentage points in 1982. Moreover, to the extent that worker compensation has included a growing amount of untaxed noncash benefits, the rise in tax rates on total compensation is overstated in the graph, which reflects the rate of taxation only on money wages and social security contributions.

Even with adjustments, however, the 1965–82 rise in Swedish tax rates would remain impressive. The average tax on a full-time male production worker has climbed almost without interruption since 1965, although the rate of increase has slowed since 1976. The marginal tax rate rose 36 percentage points—or 86 percent—between 1965 and 1976, but fell slightly in the late 1970s and early 1980s. A similar graph for average American production workers would show a much more gradual rise in marginal and average tax rates, although upper-income U.S. workers have experienced relatively large increases in marginal tax rates.[18] Nonetheless, by the mid-1980s, average and marginal tax rates on U.S. workers were substantially below those on their Swedish counterparts.

Transfer Programs

This section describes five transfer programs that provide substantial benefits to working-age adults in Sweden. Two of the programs, unemployment and sickness pay, might influence labor supply decisions throughout a person's working career. One program, paid leave for bearing and rearing children, disproportionately affects younger women. The last two programs, old-age pensions and disability pay, naturally

18. For time-series data on the tax position of representative U.S. workers, see Barry P. Bosworth, *Tax Incentives and Economic Growth* (Brookings, 1984), pp. 133–38.

have their largest effects on older, experienced workers. Where relevant, the programs are compared with similar American programs.

Unemployment Insurance

Swedish unemployment benefits are generous but relatively unused by current European standards, mainly because unemployment is so low. Most coverage is provided by unemployment insurance societies, many of them connected with labor unions. Membership in such societies is in principle voluntary, but most of the labor force belongs. In 1980, 72 percent of workers were covered, up from 56 percent in 1970 and 64 percent in 1975.[19] In addition to the insurance societies, the government provides insurance protection under the cash benefit (KAS) program. This program is intended to cover workers who choose not to belong to the insurance societies, workers who belong but have not yet become eligible for benefits, new labor market entrants, and unemployed workers more than sixty years old who have exhausted insurance society benefits.[20] Weekly KAS benefits are substantially lower than insurance society payments and are limited to thirty weeks.

The Swedish system of unemployment compensation evolved significantly over the past two decades as unemployment rose from the extremely low rates prevailing in the 1960s. Government subsidies now play a much larger role in financing the voluntary insurance societies. In the early 1960s subsidies financed half of insurance society outlays, but today pay more than 90 percent of outlays.[21] Thus the incentives for the societies to limit outlays in order to maintain low contribution rates are now much weaker than they were twenty years ago. As mentioned above, participation in the insurance societies has risen. Benefit levels for the insured unemployed have gone up as well. Björklund and Holmlund calculate that the real, after-tax benefit for a worker receiving the average payment rose nearly 60 percent between 1965 and the late 1970s, although real benefits have fallen slightly in the 1980s. The average after-tax replacement rate of insurance benefits now ranges between 65

19. Anders Björklund and Bertil Holmlund, "Unemployment Compensation in Sweden" (Stockholm: Industrial Institute for Economic and Social Research, May 1984), p. 12.
20. Ibid., p. 16. New labor market entrants are required to seek employment for three months before becoming eligible to draw KAS benefits.
21. Ibid., p. 13.

and 75 percent, with higher rates for low-wage workers.[22] These replacement ratios are somewhat higher than the rates in the United States. Since 1968 unemployed Swedish workers have been permitted to draw insurance society benefits for up to sixty weeks, or ninety weeks in the case of jobless workers aged 55 and older. Before 1968 the maximum benefit duration was thirty weeks irrespective of a worker's age. By comparison, the U.S. unemployment insurance system limits benefits to twenty-six weeks in most states and to thirty-nine weeks in a few states with exceptionally high cyclical unemployment.

Swedish insurance societies impose eligibility requirements on newly unemployed members that are similar to those imposed by state systems in the United States. A jobless worker must have worked a minimum of five months in the twelve months preceding the onset of unemployment. In the United States there is no backup system of insurance for unemployed workers who fail to meet this type of work experience requirement. In Sweden, many jobless workers failing to qualify for insurance society benefits are eligible to receive KAS payments. Introduced in 1974, these payments provide about a third as much weekly income as insurance society benefits. Roughly 40 to 50 percent of the unemployed collect insurance society benefits, and another 20 to 22 percent collect KAS payments.[23] Far fewer—less than one-third—of the unemployed collect benefits in the United States. Most of the American unemployed not collecting payments are ineligible because they lack recent work experience or because they have exhausted benefits.

Relative to an unemployed American worker, a jobless worker in Sweden is more likely to collect unemployment insurance benefits and for roughly twice as long. The benefit received typically replaces a greater fraction of lost wages. Despite the potential work disincentives created by the Swedish system, it is not obvious that the insurance payments cause significant work reductions, except perhaps among older jobholders. Sweden has historically maintained a very low unemployment rate. Thus not many labor force participants are directly affected by the work disincentives arising from the unemployment insurance program. As Robert Flanagan argues in chapter 5, Swedish employers are legally constrained in their ability to lay off experienced

22. Ibid., updated version, February 1986, figs. 2 and 4. Unemployment benefits have been treated as taxable income since 1974.
23. The figures refer to the period 1977–81. Ibid., pp. 22–23.

employees. Hence the workers who would potentially qualify for the most generous unemployment benefits tend to be laid off relatively infrequently.

The Swedish employment service is also reasonably effective in referring unemployed workers to vacant positions. Employers are required to register job openings, so the service enjoys a strong advantage over its U.S. counterpart in making the insured unemployed actively seek work. In addition, Sweden's active labor market policy ensures there will usually be training and public service job opportunities to which unemployed workers can be referred. Government labor market authorities can actually compel insured jobless workers to undertake some constructive action that will remove them from unemployment. Those unemployed who prefer not to work can be taken off the unemployment benefit rolls. Because these labor market options are not available to American unemployment insurance officials, they usually cannot enforce the requirement that insured unemployed workers use their best efforts to find jobs.[24]

The generous Swedish unemployment benefits can, however, sometimes affect employment decisions. Despite low overall unemployment, regional joblessness is sometimes high and local opportunities for training and public service jobs too few. Under these circumstances, generous unemployment benefits can deter effective job search. In an area of persistently high unemployment, the best route to a job might be the road out of town; high jobless pay might deter insured workers from taking that road.

Sickness Pay

Swedish citizens are well insured by their government against loss of income resulting from sickness. In addition, they are substantially reimbursed for medical and dental expenses and given virtually free hospital care.

Cash benefits during sickness might have a major impact on the effective labor supply of Swedish workers. Since 1974 these benefits have replaced 90 percent of the gross earnings lost because of illness, up

24. For a related discussion, see Martin Neil Baily, "Unemployment Insurance as Insurance for Workers," *Industrial and Labor Relations Review*, vol. 30 (July 1977), pp. 497–98.

to a weekly earnings loss of 7.5 times the base amount, or about 1.8 times the average worker's weekly wage.[25] These benefits are taxable. In principle they can last indefinitely, though a doctor's certificate is needed for absences longer than a week.[26] On average, nineteen sick days are claimed yearly for each covered person.[27] Although the government's program does not cover the first day of an illness, white-collar workers can collect sickness pay for the first day under a collective bargaining agreement with employers.

At first glance the Swedish system of sickness pay does not seem especially generous compared with typical benefits in the United States. Wage and salary employees of most U.S. companies are fully paid for days lost because of illness, instead of being limited to 90 percent of lost earnings. Nor is there a one-day waiting period. But the Swedish system is open to greater abuse than its American counterpart. First, most U.S. employers limit the number of sick days that can be claimed for each year of employment and do not compensate absences in excess of this limit. Second, because the cost of sick pay is directly borne by the affected employer in the United States, there is a strong incentive for each employer to monitor sick leave claims carefully. Most of the cost of Swedish sick pay is picked up by the state, and the incentive for employers to police sick leave is thus weak.[28] In fact, since neither the worker nor the employer in Sweden bears the direct costs of an additional day of paid sick leave, there is a clear incentive for the worker and firm to collude against the government to raise the share of total compensation paid in sick benefits. The adverse incentives for total labor supply could conceivably be large.[29]

25. The base amount itself is calculated to reflect the cost of a minimally adequate living standard for one person, conceptually equivalent to the poverty line for a one-person family in the United States. At the exchange rate prevailing in 1985, the U.S. poverty line for a single-person family was twice the Swedish base amount.

26. Sven E. Olsson, "Welfare Programs in Sweden" (University of Stockholm, Swedish Institute for Social Research, June 1983), pp. 20–21.

27. Ministry of Finance, *The Swedish Budget, 1986–87* (Stockholm, 1986), p. 83.

28. Sickness pay is financed under the social insurance payroll tax described above. All employers pay the same tax rate on earnings; the tax is not "experience rated" to reflect each employer's experience of paid sick leave.

29. The adverse incentives are larger today than they were at the beginning of the 1960s, when the waiting period for sickness benefits was longer and the replacement rate was lower. The program was liberalized in 1968, when waiting days were reduced and the replacement rate raised to 80 percent of lost earnings. It was liberalized again in 1974, when the replacement rate reached its present level of 90 percent. See Olsson, "Welfare Programs in Sweden," p. 26.

Child-Rearing Benefits

The Swedish state provides a variety of benefits and guarantees to families with or expecting children. Parental insurance protects families against loss of earnings arising from a child's birth or illness. The basic parental benefit is payable to mothers who worked in the nine months before a child's birth or adoption, and it lasts one year. The daily benefit is the same as the parent's sickness benefit for nine months, then drops to Skr 48 a day for the remaining three months of eligibility. Since 1975 parents have been able to claim paid leave for the care of sick children under twelve years of age. This payment is equal to the normal cash sickness benefit and can now last up to sixty days a year for each child.[30] In addition, parents are eligible for two paid "contact days" a year for visiting the day nursery or school of their children between four and twelve years old.[31] Paid leave can be taken by either parent, but mothers claim most of the benefits. In 1982 an average of 0.2 percent of employed men and 3.2 percent of employed women were absent as a result of paid parental leave.[32]

Swedish protections for childbearing are not a recent phenomenon. Women have been protected since 1939 from dismissal because of pregnancy. In 1962 a maternity allowance was introduced giving new mothers six months' paid leave. Parental insurance replaced the maternity allowance in 1974. For families with two parents in the labor force, one parent is permitted by law to work shorter hours until the youngest child attains the age of eight.

The generous provisions for bearing and rearing children among the working population do not end with income protection and job guarantees. Swedish workers with children also receive extremely large subsidies for child care. Child care centers are built and maintained by local communities, although small fees are levied on participating families according to their ability to pay. In addition, subsidized child care is provided by so-called day care mothers. Child care in the government-

30. When the benefit was introduced in 1975, leave was limited to ten days a year. Siv Gustafsson, "Equal Opportunity Policies in Sweden," in Günther Schmid and Renate Weitzel, eds., *Sex Discrimination and Equal Opportunity* (New York: St. Martin's Press, 1984), p. 136.

31. Ministry of Finance, *Swedish Budget, 1986–87*, p. 75.

32. Siv Gustafsson and Roger Jacobsson, "Trends in Female Labor Force Participation in Sweden," *Journal of Labor Economics*, vol. 3 (January 1985), p. S266.

subsidized centers is relatively lavish but cheap from the point of view of most parents; the fee covers less than 9 percent of the cost of the care.[33] Not surprisingly, the centers are oversubscribed, and parents must typically wait several months for a place in the local center, although this delay has decreased as local governments raised their outlays on centers.

Paid parental leave and generous child care subsidies for working parents provide a strong inducement for Swedish women to enter the work force. Not only do these benefits reduce the burden on employed women with children, they are available only to families in which both parents are working, studying, or actively seeking work. From the point of view of a family in which the father already works, these benefits are equivalent to a sizable subsidy to the mother for becoming employed. The subsidy is particularly large for a woman who intends to have a child within one or two years.

The incentives are especially strong compared with those available to American families. Paid leave for childbearing is rare in the United States. Limited unpaid leave is provided by many employers, but no program of paid maternity leave is sponsored by the government. Absence caused by the illness of a child is often not compensated. Subsidies for child care are generally restricted to single-parent families with low incomes and may not always be available even to those families.[34] Although there is widespread grumbling about the lack of maternity and child care benefits in the United States, the coalition in favor of such benefits has historically been weak. The result is that the government-provided incentive for a woman of childbearing age to get a job is comparatively small.

Old-Age and Disability Pensions

A universal, means-tested pension system was introduced in Sweden as far back as 1913. The current system, established in 1948, provides old-age, survivors, and disability pensions. I will briefly outline the old-age and disability schemes because they affect the work behavior of older employees.

33. Ibid.
34. There is, however, a 20 percent income tax subsidy for child care expenses up to a low limit for single-parent families and two-parent families in which both parents work.

Old-age and disability pensions consist of two parts, a general pension (*folkpension*) and a supplementary earnings-related pension (ATP). The general pension is a flat monthly grant equal to 95 percent of the base amount for single pensioners and 145 percent of the base amount for pensioned couples. The general supplementary pension, established in 1960, is an earnings-related benefit determined in part by a worker's average pensionable income in the fifteen years of his or her highest earnings. Sickness pay and unemployment insurance as well as earnings are counted as pensionable income.[35] A worker whose income is less than the base amount in a particular year is not counted as having pensionable income in that year. Income in excess of 7.5 times the base amount is excluded in measuring pensionable income, although social insurance contributions on these excess earnings must nonetheless be paid by employers. Social insurance contributions on earnings above 7.5 times the base amount thus represent a pure tax; the worker's eventual social insurance benefits are in no way affected by these contributions. The earnings-related pension is also based on the number of years, up to thirty, in which counted pensionable income is received. Pensioners who have worked fewer than thirty years receive a benefit reduced by one-thirtieth for each year less than thirty worked.[36]

Low-income pensioners may also receive a pension supplement. Workers eligible for only a small earnings-related pension are guaranteed a minimum income equal to 140 percent of the base amount for single people and 245 percent for couples. For purposes of comparison, the combined supplemental security income (SSI) and food stamp benefit available to elderly low-income Americans is about 80 percent of the U.S. poverty line for single individuals and 95 percent of the poverty line for couples.[37] SSI and food stamps provide the equivalent of a guaranteed annual income to aged, blind, and disabled Americans. Because the U.S. poverty threshold is substantially higher than the

35. Olsson, "Welfare Programs in Sweden," p. 9; and Helen Ginsburg, "Flexible and Partial Retirement for Norwegian and Swedish Workers," *Monthly Labor Review*, vol. 108 (October 1985), p. 38.

36. Per Gunnar Edebalk and Åke Elmér, "Social Insurance in Sweden," in Lars Söderström, ed., *Social Insurance: Papers Presented at the 5th Arne Ryde Symposium* (Amsterdam: North-Holland, 1983), pp. 57–58. Transition rules for pensioners born before 1924 compensate for the recent start-up of the ATP system.

37. The poverty threshold for couples is a quarter higher than the threshold for single people. *Background Material and Data on Programs within the Jurisdiction of the Committee on Ways and Means,* Committee Print, House Committee on Ways and Means, 99 Cong. 2 sess. (Washington, D.C.: U.S. Government Printing Office, 1986), p. 476.

Table 6-2. *Swedish and U.S. Old-Age Pension Replacement Rates,*
Selected Years, 1969–80[a]

Category	Pension as percentage of gross earnings in year before retirement					
	1969	*1975*	*1977*	*1978*	*1979*	*1980*
Single worker						
Sweden	42	57	59	63	68	68
United States	30	38	40	41	41	44
Aged couple						
Sweden	56	73	73	79	79	83
United States	44	58	60	61	62	66

Source: Jonathan Aldrich, "The Earnings Replacement Rate of Old-Age Benefits in Twelve Countries, 1969–1980," *Social Security Bulletin,* vol. 45 (November 1982), p. 5.

a. Replacement rates of average wage earner in manufacturing after full working career.

Swedish base amount, the two countries in fact guarantee roughly comparable incomes to their aged populations.[38]

A full earnings-related pension replaces 60 percent of a retired Swedish worker's average pensionable income in the fifteen years of his or her highest earnings. Typical retirees probably do not receive the full pension, however, because pensionable income is not received in all of the required years. Nonetheless, the earnings-related pension combined with the basic general pension can provide a comfortable retirement income compared with wages typically received throughout a worker's career, particularly in the case of poorly paid workers.

It is instructive to compare retirement benefits in Sweden with those available in the United States. The U.S. Social Security Administration has computed the fraction of immediate preretirement earnings replaced by public retirement benefits in the two countries.[39] Gross earnings replacement rates are computed for an average wage earner during a full career in manufacturing. The trends in replacement rates are shown in table 6-2. Swedish replacement rates climbed rapidly from 1969 to 1980, reflecting the maturation of the earnings-related pension system. U.S. benefits rose nearly as fast, but from a lower base. By 1980 the replacement rate for a single worker was a third lower in the United States than in Sweden, while the replacement rate for an aged couple

38. See ibid., pp. 469–72; and Ministry of Finance, *Swedish Budget, 1986–87,* p. 83, to compare the income guarantees in the two countries.

39. Jonathan Aldrich, "The Earnings Replacement Rate of Old-Age Benefits in Twelve Countries, 1969–1980," *Social Security Bulletin,* vol. 45 (November 1982), pp. 3–11.

was a fifth lower. The table overstates the differences between the American and Swedish systems: Swedish pension benefits are fully taxable under the income tax system, while only a small proportion of U.S. social security benefits are subject to tax. The tax-free U.S. benefits consequently result in somewhat higher replacement rates on net earnings than on gross earnings. Full-time U.S. workers are also more likely to qualify for an employer-sponsored pension in addition to a social security benefit.[40] Private pensions are much rarer in Sweden. On the whole, however, the income incentives to retire are probably higher in Sweden than in the United States.

The age of eligibility for full social security retirement benefits—the normal retirement age—is 65 in both Sweden and the United States. The normal retirement age in the United States has been 65 since the creation of social security in 1935, although it is scheduled to rise to 67 in the next century as a result of legislation passed in 1983. The normal retirement age has moved in the opposite direction in Sweden. After remaining fixed at 67 for many years, it was reduced to 65 by legislation passed in 1974 and effective in 1976. Both Sweden and the United States also permit workers to draw actuarially reduced pensions if they choose to begin receiving benefits before the normal age. The earliest age for drawing pensions in Sweden is 60, down from 63 before 1976. Workers who begin receiving pensions at age 60 can receive 70 percent of the full pension obtainable at age 65. The earliest age for drawing U.S. social security pensions is 62; the benefit at that age is 80 percent of the full amount.

Older Swedish workers have a partial retirement option not available to U.S. workers. The partial pension permits a worker to reduce working hours between ages 60 and 64 and receive a pension that covers part of the resulting loss in gross earnings. Between 1976 and 1980 the partial pension covered 65 percent of lost earnings; since 1981 it has covered half. Unlike the early pension, the partial pension does not result in an actuarial reduction in the pension obtainable at age 65. If a 60-year-old worker reduces weekly hours by half—from, say, forty to twenty—the combined gross income from earnings and the partial pension drops by

40. For example, in 1980 the number of beneficiaries under American private pension plans was about 40 percent of the number under the social security retired worker program. Private pension payments amounted to about 35 percent of payments sent out under the old-age and survivors programs. See Alicia H. Munnell, *The Economics of Private Pensions* (Brookings, 1982), p.11; and *Social Security Bulletin*, vol. 45 (December 1982), pp. 20–22.

only 25 percent. Because of high marginal tax rates, the net income from earnings and the partial pension drops by even less, perhaps 15 percent.[41] This implies that the net return for working a marginal hour a week drops sharply when a worker turns age 60. Under the current program, the net wage drops by half; under the 1976–80 program, the net wage fell 65 percent. Not surprisingly, the partial pension program is popular. Just four years after its introduction in 1976, more than one out of four eligible workers participated. Even after the replacement rate was lowered from 65 percent to 50 percent in 1981, the participation rate remained above 20 percent.[42]

In both Sweden and the United States the disability insurance program is closely related to the old-age insurance system. Swedish disability pensions consist of a general, flat-rate pension and an earnings-related pension. Disability pensions are provided when a person's work capacity is reduced by at least half. The general disability pension is 95 percent of the base amount, and the earnings-related pension is computed according to rules similar to those used in calculating the earnings-related old-age pension. However, a projection formula is used to determine the amount of pensionable income the worker would have received by age 65 if he or she had not become disabled. The size of a Swedish disability pension also depends on the degree of work limitation: pensions are available for 100 percent, 65 percent, and 50 percent disabilities. The pension is proportionate to the disability.

A U.S. worker in poor health is eligible to receive social security disability insurance if he or she has accumulated enough work experience to be insured and is so severely impaired as to be unable to engage in substantial gainful activity for at least one year. There is no provision for partial disability in the program, nor are partial disability benefits available. As in the Swedish system, the disabled worker receives a benefit that corresponds roughly to the full old-age pension he or she would have received had earnings continued to age 65. A disabled worker with dependents is eligible for a substantial pension supplement. Table 6-3 shows after-tax replacement rates for disabled Swedish and American workers at various income levels. Swedish disability payments replace a much higher fraction of lost income, particularly in the case of workers

41. Ginsburg, "Flexible and Partial Retirement," p. 38.
42. Ibid., p. 39. The partial pension compensates 50 percent of the difference between reduced wages, on the one hand, and the minimum of previous wages or 7.5 times the base amount, on the other. Workers paid more than 7.5 times the base amount are consequently not treated as generously as average workers.

Table 6-3. *Swedish and U.S. Net Income Replacement Rates for Disabled Workers, by Income Level, 1968 and 1978*

	One-half median income		Median income		Twice median income	
Category	1968	1978	1968	1978	1968	1978
Sweden[a]						
Single person	105	117	73	88	55	66
United States[b]						
Single person	45	59	35	49	21	35
Person with three dependents	64	82	68	85	45	54

Source: Robert H. Haveman, Victor Halberstadt, and Richard V. Burkhauser, eds., *Public Policy toward Disabled Workers* (Ithaca, N.Y.: Cornell University Press, 1984), pp. 128–29.

a. General and earnings-related disability pension plus pension supplement, if any, for fully disabled worker. Median income levels for married men aged 45–49 in 1967 and 1977 are used as the base for the calculations.

b. Social security disability insurance. The insurance benefit is based on number of dependents as well as previous work experience and earnings.

with no dependents, although U.S. disability benefits have risen sharply since the late 1960s.

It should be emphasized that the generous Swedish disability benefits do not necessarily constitute a major work disincentive for those with impaired health. The Swedish state is not only generous in replacing earnings lost through disability but also zealous in attempting to bring disabled workers back into the work force through medical rehabilitation, retraining, subsidized employment, and sheltered workshops. This kind of combined health care and labor market policy can partly or wholly offset the work disincentive arising from high benefits, especially if the state exerts strong social and moral pressure on impaired workers to participate. Using a loose definition of disability programs in the two countries, analysts have found that a lower percentage of the potential work force receives disability transfers in Sweden than in the United States—8.7 percent versus 14.7 percent.[43] Part of the reason for the difference is that Swedish policy toward the disabled places greater emphasis on work and rehabilitation.

The work orientation of Swedish disability policy exempts one important group, the elderly. Since 1970 a worker over the age of 60 who is permanently laid off can claim a full disability pension. The worker's

43. The estimates refer to 1978. See Robert H. Haveman, Victor Halberstadt, and Richard V. Burkhauser, eds., *Public Policy toward Disabled Workers* (Ithaca, N.Y.: Cornell University Press, 1984) p. 84. For a more extended discussion, see Eskil Wadensjö, "Disability Policy in Sweden," in ibid., pp. 444–516.

age is considered sufficient proof of incapacity, and no further medical criterion is applied in determining benefits. Because members of insurance societies between the ages of 55 and 65 are eligible for up to ninety weeks of benefits after a layoff, a worker who is laid off shortly after his or her 58th birthday can receive jobless benefits for nearly two years and then apply for and receive a full disability pension starting at age 60. For lower-income workers in particular, the benefits from unemployment insurance and disability pensions replace enough income so that there is little net financial gain in finding another job. Because neither workers nor their employers pay for these benefits directly, there is no strong reason for either to resist the imposition of layoffs on older employees. This suggests that fluctuations in labor demand will be prominently reflected in changes in the unemployment or labor force participation rates of older experienced workers. But it should be recalled that Sweden extends strong legal job protection to experienced workers, especially older experienced workers. The older employee who genuinely wishes to continue working is in a powerful position to resist an unwanted layoff.

Theory of Labor Supply Response

Before evaluating recent trends in Swedish work effort, it is worth briefly considering the basic theory of work responses to taxes and transfers. I will distinguish between the responses of a worker (or a potential worker) within a single period, such as a month or a year, and the worker's labor supply behavior over the many periods of his or her entire life cycle.

Single-Period Framework

It is convenient to illustrate the single-period theory by reference to a simple diagram. Figure 6-4 represents the trade-off between hours of work, measured on the horizontal axis, and net income, measured on the vertical axis, under a simple progressive tax system. The straight line from the origin, $0E$, represents the trade-off between work and income in the absence of taxes and transfers; its slope is the worker's gross wage rate, including the employer's social security payroll contribution. The solid line ABC represents the worker's net income possibil-

Figure 6-4. *Work-Income Trade-Off within a Single Period*

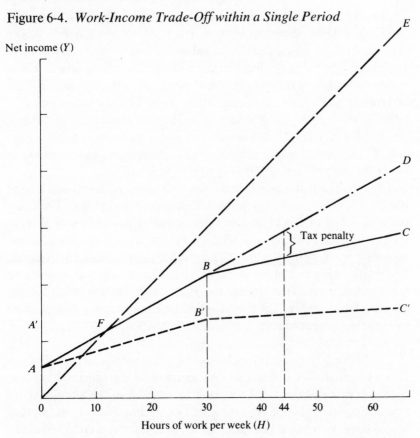

Net income (*Y*)

Hours of work per week (*H*)

ities at each level of work effort in the presence of taxes and transfers. Along the segment *AB* the worker is eligible to receive a transfer (equal to 0*A* at zero hours of work), but his earnings are taxed at a constant rate, thus reducing his net wage below what it would be in the absence of taxes and transfers. The slope of *AB* is therefore lower than the slope of 0*E*. Along the segment *BC* the worker's wages are subject to a higher income tax rate because of the presence of a progressive income tax formula. The slope of this segment is thus even less steep than that of *AB*. In the usual economic model, income, *Y*, is considered a "good" and hours of work, *H*, a "bad." Each worker has well-defined, convex preferences across all potential combinations of *Y* and *H*. Workers choose their level of work and income by maximizing utility over their attainable budget set, here represented by the combinations of *H* and *Y* below and to the right of *ABC*.

THE SWEDISH ECONOMY

The direction of the effect of taxes on labor supply is in general ambiguous. Only along the short segment *AF* does economic theory provide an unambiguous prediction about the effect of the tax-transfer system on labor supply. Work effort will decline among workers who would have chosen to locate on the segment 0*F* in the absence of taxes and transfers. Even this prediction depends on the assumption that time spent in leisure (the complement of time spent at work) is a "normal good," that is, a good that workers consume more of as their resources rise. To the right of point *F*, the tax-transfer system might either raise or lower the desired work effort of typical jobholders.

The effect of rising Swedish tax rates is shown by the broken kinked line *AB'C'*, which lies below the initial budget constraint *ABC*. The effect on work effort of this change in rates is ambiguous. At every level of hours along the new constraint the worker has a lower net wage, so the return for working has declined. The resulting substitution effect should lower labor supply. But the worker also has lower after-tax income, so the need to earn extra income has risen. This income effect should increase labor supply. The overall effect on labor supply will depend on the relative magnitudes of the income and substitution effects, which are unknown without detailed empirical analysis.

Even if the effect on labor supply is unknown, the sign of the efficiency effect is certain—it is negative. An increase in the marginal tax rate reduces the well-being of the worker by more than the additional tax revenue collected by the government. The minimum loss to the worker would have occurred if the same tax revenue had been collected under a head (or lump-sum) tax. The worker's loss in that case is exactly equal to the revenue raised. The economic distortion inherent in an income tax causes the worker to suffer an additional welfare loss, referred to as the "excess burden," deadweight loss, or efficiency loss of the tax change.[44] Many economists prefer to measure the consequences of taxes through estimating their efficiency effects rather than their direct effect on labor supply. Both measures ultimately depend, however, on the magnitudes of the income and substitution effects. If these effects are large, the efficiency loss is large; if they are small, the loss is small.

Several economists have pointed out that higher taxes not only reduce workers' wages but also finance a higher level of public spending, which

44. A derivation of measures of efficiency loss can be found in most public finance textbooks, such as Edgar K. Browning and Jacquelene M. Browning, *Public Finance and the Price System* (New York: Macmillan, 1979), pp. 288–92.

in turn affects labor supply.[45] Part of the spending is returned to workers in the form of higher transfers, and much of the remainder is used to finance services such as medical care or child care that workers would otherwise have to pay for themselves. The effect of higher public outlays can be analyzed in a straightforward way. Suppose that average extra public outlays and extra taxes for each worker amount to $A' - A$. If our representative worker values these outlays at their public cost, then budget constraint after a tax increase would originate at point A' in figure 6-4 and parallel constraint $AB'C'$. That is, the new budget constraint would be parallel to but above the constraint drawn as $AB'C'$. Note that the constraint after a tax increase actually lies above the constraint before an increase, ABC, at low levels of work effort. Because the public sector now provides a higher level of goods and services irrespective of a person's work effort, there is less need for work. Moreover, the increase in marginal tax rates has reduced the net reward to work. For many workers with low earnings before the tax increase, both income and substitution effects will thus tend to reduce work effort.

The value of public spending to workers is, however, unknown. Even if the cost of the additional public goods, services, and transfers received by a typical worker could be precisely measured, it is not clear that workers value these benefits at the public cost of providing them. If the benefits have no value to a particular worker, the budget constraint after a tax increase is precisely the one drawn in figure 6-4, $AB'C'$, and the tax increase could conceivably raise labor supply even for low-earning workers. Publicly provided benefits probably have some value to most workers, but their value is not exactly equivalent to a lump-sum cash transfer of the same direct cost.

Figure 6-4 can also be used to analyze the changing structure of Swedish taxes and the introduction of more generous child care and child-leave allowances. Before 1971 most married Swedish couples were subject to joint taxation of their combined earnings. For convenience, assume that the husband and wife earn the same hourly wage. Suppose a Swedish couple decides that the optimal level of family work effort under joint taxation is forty-four hours a week. Before 1971, no matter

45. Assar Lindbeck, "Tax Effects versus Budget Effects on Labor Supply," *Economic Inquiry*, vol. 20 (October 1982), pp. 473–89; Ingemar Hansson and Charles Stuart, "Taxation, Government Spending, and Labor Supply: A Diagrammatic Exposition," *Economic Inquiry*, vol. 21 (October 1983), pp. 584–87; and James Gwartney and Richard Stroup, "Labor Supply and Tax Rates: A Correction of the Record," *American Economic Review*, vol. 73 (June 1983), pp. 446–51.

212 THE SWEDISH ECONOMY

how this work effort was divided between the two spouses, part of the
family's earnings were subject to the high marginal tax applied along
budget segment *BC*. If there were fixed costs of working, such as
commuting and child care costs, the couple was better off if only one
spouse worked, because fixed costs for one wage earner were less than
those for two. So a system of joint progressive income taxation provides
an incentive for specialization in the supply of market work.

The tax incentives were dramatically altered when spouses were
permitted to file separate returns on their earnings. Figure 6-4 shows
that under separate taxation a two-earner family can have substantially
higher after-tax income than a single-earner family working the same
number of hours. If the tax schedule is left unchanged, a one-earner
family will owe the same taxes under separate and joint taxation. But
under separate taxation that family can significantly raise its net income
if the primary earner reduces workhours from forty-four to thirty a week,
while the second spouse raises weekly workhours from zero to fourteen,
because family work effort over thirty hours will be taxed at the low rate
applied on segment *AB* of figure 6-4 rather than at the high rate applied
on segment *BC*. Hence the family budget constraint under separate
taxation will be *ABD* rather than *ABC* if both spouses work.[46] The tax
penalty on single-earner families in comparison with two-earner families
is simply the vertical distance between the line segments *BD* and *BC*. If
the tax penalty is large compared with the fixed cost to a secondary
earner of becoming employed, the incentive for secondary earners to
join the work force will be strong. Note that the tax penalty grows as the
joint income of the family rises; the inducement for secondary earners
to join the labor force will thus be stronger for high-income than for low-
income families.

This powerful incentive for secondary earners to join the work force
has been strengthened by two other developments in Swedish public
policy. First, the shift from joint to separate taxation coincided with
rising marginal tax rates on the earnings of full-time workers.[47] This
trend probably increased the fraction of families for whom earnings-
splitting was attractive, since it increased the tax penalty on single-
earner families. Second, the growing availability and generosity of public

46. At sixty hours a week of joint labor supply the couple will begin to face the high
marginal tax rate applied along the segment *BC*.
47. In fact, the rising tax rates were virtually required to finance the tax reductions
for two-earner families.

day care has reduced the fixed and variable costs of working for an important group of secondary earners—married women with young children. Government policy thus has made employment more feasible for some secondary workers. At the same time, the more generous paid leave for new parents has furnished the equivalent of an earnings subsidy to secondary earners who contemplate having children. The more a secondary earner works, the greater is the value of the paid leave offered by the government.

On balance, the changing tax structure has introduced strong incentives for husbands and wives jointly to supply labor to the market. While it is unclear whether the increases in the average tax rate have raised or lowered the optimal level of total family work effort, it is obvious the reforms have encouraged families to substitute market work of secondary earners—predominantly wives—for that of primary earners—predominantly husbands. The explicit goal of the reforms was to bring about greater equality between men and women in the labor market. A possible efficiency gain arising out of the new policies is that they may encourage married women to maintain a more continuous level of participation in the job market. This is widely believed to be desirable from the point of view of maintaining and improving women's labor market skills. And in fact the differential between men's and women's hourly wage rates has shrunk.

But an offsetting efficiency cost of the policies is the disadvantage that they encourage families to disregard genuine costs associated with providing two earners to the market, and they substantially distort the marginal incentives for the two earners to work an additional hour. Safe, high-quality child care is expensive to provide. The annual cost of caring for children in a municipal center is well over $6,000 a child, though the typical parent is asked to pay only about 8 percent of that cost.[48] The tax distortion is somewhat more subtle. The discussion so far has assumed that the primary and secondary earners are paid the same hourly wage. Typically, however, the primary worker earns a higher gross wage, which presumably reflects a higher marginal social product. Yet under separate taxation, the after-tax wage of the primary worker can be substantially less than that of the secondary worker. In after-tax terms, Sweden strongly encourages families to substitute the work effort of a less productive worker for that of a more productive worker. Even

48. Gustafsson, "Equal Opportunity Policies in Sweden," p. 141.

if the total of family workhours is unaffected by this incentive, the output resulting from the work effort will be lower because a smaller share of those hours is supplied by the more productive worker. Given the popularity of the current Swedish system, it is conceivable that most Swedes are willing to pay the efficiency cost in exchange for the perceived equity gain. It is just as plausible, however, that many Swedes do not entirely understand the efficiency effects of their tax system.

Life-Cycle Incentives

The Swedish tax and transfer system provides clear incentives for workers to arrange their work effort in specific ways during their life cycles. Women of childbearing age are strongly encouraged to become employed before having children and to remain employed as their children grow up. Because of the very high marginal tax rates imposed on high annual earnings, well-paid men and women are encouraged to limit their labor supply in a particular year. In addition, old-age and disability pensions, in combination with the progressive income tax system, encourage older men and women to withdraw from the work force or to reduce weekly hours substantially when they attain age 60.

Figure 6-5 shows the relationship between a Swedish worker's gross monthly pension and the age at which he or she chooses to accept the pension. The pension's value is expressed as the ratio of the partial to the full benefit amount due at the normal retirement age. The lower solid line, originating at age 63 on the horizontal axis, represents the old-age pension schedule under the former pension law, the one in effect before 1976. The pension benefit rises from 70 percent of the full pension at age 63 to 100 percent of the full pension at age 67, the normal retirement age until 1976. Beginning in 1970, elderly workers on long-term unemployment were eligible to draw a full disability pension starting at age 60. The disability pension is indicated by the lightly drawn broken line to the right of 1.0 on the vertical axis. The old-age pension formula was significantly reformed in 1976 to permit workers as young as 60 to draw early retirement benefits. In the same year the normal retirement age was reduced from 67 to 65, and workers were given delayed retirement credits for earnings through age 70. The resulting pension schedule is shown as the heavily drawn broken line that originates at age 60 on the horizontal axis. The vertical distance between the pre-1976 and post-

Figure 6-5. *Swedish Old-Age and Disability Pensions in Relation to Age When Pensions Begin*

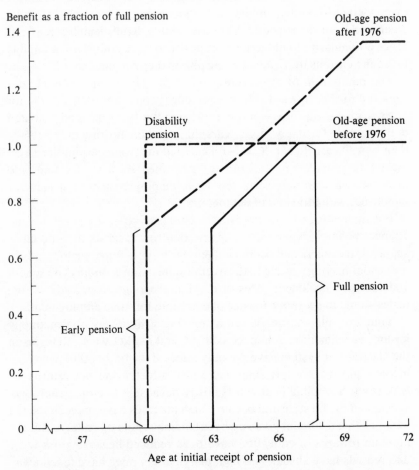

Benefit as a fraction of full pension

Age at initial receipt of pension

1976 pension schedules represents the value of the benefit increase implicit in the 1976 reform.

To understand the implications of figure 6-5 for work incentives, it is necessary to refer to figure 6-4, which shows the trade-off between net income and hours of work within a single period. The intercept term *A* in figure 6-4 represents the amount of nonwage income available to workers in a given period. Beginning at age 63 (before 1976) or age 60 (after 1976) workers are eligible to draw early old-age benefits. The intercept term *A* should reflect the value of these benefits to older workers. It is apparent from figure 6-5 that the 1976 pension reform significantly increased the money income available to older workers, thus shifting the budget constraint in figure 6-4 upward. The resulting income effect should unambiguously reduce desired work effort among older workers through age 67.[49] The availability of full disability pensions at age 60 similarly should reduce the desire to work among those eligible for such pensions by virtue of being placed on permanent layoff.

The maturation of the earnings-related (ATP) pension scheme has caused a further upward shift in the budget constraint in figure 6-4 for older workers. Because workers retiring in the 1980s have participated in the scheme for many more years than workers retiring in the 1960s, their benefits are higher. This is reflected in the rising earnings replacement rate provided by full old-age pensions. As a result, low- and moderate-wage workers can now leave employment in their early or middle 60s with little loss of net income.

It is interesting to speculate on the effects of tax-transfer reforms on younger people. Experience in other countries suggests that the labor supply of teenagers and people in their early 20s is sensitive to trends in the school-leaving age and to the overall state of the economy. As school and college enrollment rates rise, young people—especially young males—tend to postpone the age of entry into full-time employment.

Young people can be viewed as making a three-way choice among leisure, enrollment in school or college, and market work. Reforms in the tax-transfer system have not only affected the trade-off between net income and work effort, they have also affected the net returns on education. Schooling is now less costly because it is more generously subsidized by the state and because high tax rates have reduced the net earnings that a student gives up by attending school or college. But the ultimate rewards of education have been reduced because gross wage differentials have shrunk and high marginal tax rates have taxed away much of the remaining wage premium for Swedish workers with advanced schooling. It is not clear under these circumstances whether the attractiveness of schooling will rise or decline in comparison with that of market work.

---

49. The effect on workers older than 67 is not so clear. The 1976 reform for the first time gave these workers delayed retirement credits for postponing retirement from age 67 to 70. This reform implicitly raised the net return on labor as well as the nonwage income available to these workers. Conceivably, some workers remained employed longer as a result of the increased return on labor.

Labor Supply Trends, 1963–84

Trends in labor supply among several major population groups, defined by age and sex, are described below. For purposes of comparison I also include information about similarly defined groups in the U.S. population.

Trends among Prime-Age Workers

Figures 6-6 and 6-7 show labor supply trends among men and women who are between 25 and 64 years old. The upper panel in each case refers to Sweden; the lower panel to the United States. All trends are measured in relation to a baseline in 1963, which is defined as 100. For Sweden four measures of work effort are displayed. The broadest measure is the labor force participation rate. Labor force participation provides a rough measure of desired labor supply, but involuntary unemployment forces some workers to work less than they desire. The employment-to-population (E/P) ratio provides a closer approximation of actual labor supply. Swedish statistics also contain accurate information about the work status of labor force participants. Employed people who report being away from work during the entire survey week are classified as absent. Absenteeism rates have risen as Swedish employers and the Swedish state have offered more generous benefits for vacations, sick leave, and child rearing. To reflect these trends I display the ratio of people at work during the survey week to the total population (W/P). The difference between the E/P and the W/P ratios simply reflects the trend in absences from work. The most precise measure of average labor supply is total weekly hours at work divided by the total population. If the weekly hours of those actually at work remained constant, this variable would follow the same trend as the W/P ratio. But weekly hours of workers have fallen. Absenteeism within the week has risen. Standard full-time hours have decreased because of collective bargaining agreements between the major unions and employer groups. And, especially among women, the fraction of workers who are on part-time schedules has increased. For the United States it is possible to tabulate three of these four labor supply series. (Unfortunately, the W/P ratio is not available by age and sex groups.)

A cursory glance at figures 6-6 and 6-7 reveals that the trends in labor

Figure 6-6. *Labor Supply Trends among Swedish and U.S. Men Aged 25 to 64, 1963–84*

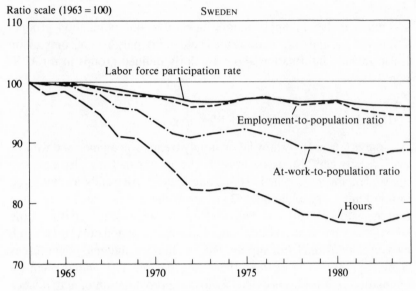

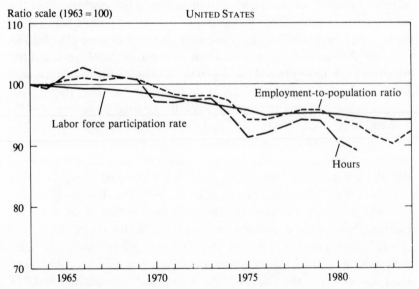

Sources: Author's tabulations of unpublished data from the Swedish government labor force surveys and U.S. Bureau of Labor Statistics.

Figure 6-7. *Labor Supply Trends among Swedish and U.S. Women Aged 25 to 64, 1963–84*

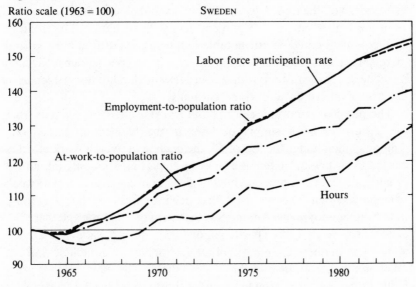

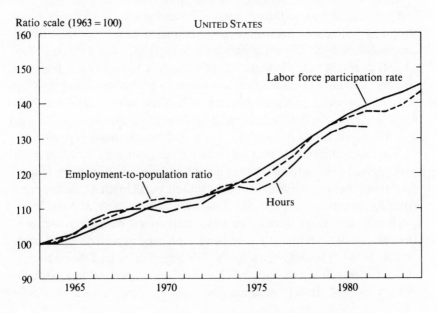

supply of men differ markedly from those of women in both Sweden and the United States. Male labor supply has fallen substantially in both countries, with the rate of decline in hours about twice as high in Sweden as in the United States—23 percent versus 11 percent.[50] The trend in both countries could be attributable to the upward drift in average and marginal tax burdens on full-time workers. The steeper decline in Sweden might be due to the faster rise in tax burdens and the shift toward separate taxation of husbands' and wives' earnings.

The possible importance of tax and transfer effects is evident from the pattern of labor supply declines in the two countries. Among American men under the age of 55, the decline in overall work effort is caused by a slow decline in the labor force participation rate (about 1.3 points a decade) and an equally slow decline in the average workweek of employed men. There is also a slow decline caused by the rising trend in U.S. unemployment. Among Swedish men of the same age there is a slower drop in labor force participation (0.7 points a decade) and a much slower rise in unemployment, but total labor supply nonetheless drops much more sharply than in the United States. The main reasons are a rising rate of absence from work and a shorter workweek for men who are at work. These two factors alone account for about 85 percent of the drop in labor supply among Swedish men aged 25 to 54. Men are not dropping out of Sweden's labor force; instead they are reducing their annual hours, possibly because of the extremely high tax rates imposed on their last hour of work. U.S. men show a greater tendency to drop out of the work force altogether, in part because nonparticipation is an eligibility criterion for the main transfer benefits available to prime-age American men, notably, disability and related compensation payments.

The most important source of decline in the labor supply of American men aged 25 to 64 is the decline in labor force participation rates of men 55 through 64. Between 1963 and 1984 their participation rate dropped from 86 percent to 68 percent, in part because of increased disability payments and early social security and private pension retirement benefits. However, among American men who remained employed, annual hours declined only slightly. For Swedish men of the same age participation rates also declined sharply, from 90 percent in 1963 to 76 percent in 1984. But, in addition, the rate of absence rose and weekly

50. The declines are measured as the percentage fall in average hours between 1963 and 1981. Detailed workhour data are not available in quite the same form for U.S. and Swedish workers. My unpublished data on U.S. hours end in 1981.

hours fell. These two factors accounted for more than half of the 35 percent decline in labor supply among men in this group.[51] As in the case of younger Swedish men, a large share of the decline in average work effort takes the form of reduced hours among those who remain employed. This provides indirect evidence that high marginal tax rates may affect work effort. But Sweden's work-oriented labor market and disability policies may tend to raise labor force participation and employment in comparison with the levels observed in the United States.

The same general pattern is repeated for the labor supply of women. Sweden is renowned for having one of the world's highest rates of female labor force participation. But U.S. women actually supply more hours to the market. Labor supply trends for the two countries are displayed in figure 6-7. Both Swedish and U.S. women registered large gains in employment between 1963 and 1984. In Sweden the employment-to-population ratio of women aged 25 to 64 rose from 52 percent to 79 percent. In the United States the ratio climbed from 41 percent to 59 percent, with much of the rise occurring among women aged 25 to 34. (The employment-to-population ratio nearly doubled among these younger American women.) On the whole, however, the rise in employment was greater among Swedish women. The 1984 employment rate of women in Sweden was a third higher than that of women in the United States.

Figure 6-7 makes clear that the employment rate and the labor force participation rate, by themselves, provide misleading indicators of effective labor supply among Swedish women. While weekly hours worked by employed American women fell only 3 percent between 1963 and 1981, weekly hours of employed Swedish women fell 19 percent. The Swedish decline was greater because the fraction of employed women with long-term absences, and the fraction of those on part-time schedules, increased, and because the standard workweek for women on full-time schedules fell. American women appear to have been largely immune to these trends. As a consequence, a typical American woman now works slightly longer hours than her Swedish counterpart. In 1963 the average work effort of American women aged 25 to 64 (including both the employed and nonemployed) was 14.3 hours a week. By 1981 average weekly hours had risen a third, to 19.0 hours a week. The weekly

51. Interestingly, there is little evidence that the partial benefit scheme caused the workweek of men aged 55 to 64 to drop any faster than that of the average male. Among 25- to 54-year-old men at work, the workweek dropped 12 percent between 1963 and 1984; among 55- to 64-year-olds it dropped 14 percent.

work effort of Swedish women rose from 15.6 hours to 18.8 hours during the same period, an increase of just 21 percent.

The relative labor market performance of Swedish and American women might seem perplexing to advocates of strong measures to encourage women to work. Sweden offers major incentives for women to become employed—separate taxation of earnings, generous child care subsidies, paid leave for childbearing and the care of sick children, and sweeping laws guaranteeing equitable pay. The United States is far less generous to families with two earners, providing almost no support for child care and imposing relatively high marginal taxes on the initial dollar of a second worker's earnings. Yet despite these contrasting incentives, Swedish and American women now work almost the same amount.

The explanation is that the Swedish incentive structure offers sizable rewards to women who become employed but only crumbs to those who work long hours. The U.S. system is much more generous to women who work long hours and comparatively less generous to women working short hours. In fact, because the U.S. government does not subsidize child care and other costs associated with working, women may have to work long hours simply to make a job worthwhile. Because America's income and payroll tax rates are more moderate than Sweden's, even at high levels of earnings, a much greater share of the rewards of working long hours is kept by the dual-income family. Since the private cost of entering employment is higher in the United States, fewer women do so. But among those who hold jobs, American women are much more likely to work full time.

It is worth briefly considering the trend in overall labor supply. The combined employment of Swedish men and women has clearly risen, because the employment rate of women climbed nearly 28 percentage points between 1963 and 1984, while that of men declined only 5 points. But the total annual hours of work supplied by a typical Swedish 25- to 64-year-old has actually dropped about 8 percent because the average workhours of men have fallen at about twice the pace that the average workhours of women have risen. By contrast, the average work effort of a 25- to 64-year-old American actually rose over the period, because the labor supply gains of women slightly outpaced the declines of men. (The labor supply gains would have been even larger if U.S. unemployment had not risen from the mid-1960s through the early 1980s.) In the early 1960s Swedish men worked more hours than American men, and Swedish women worked substantially more hours than American women.

By the early 1980s both Swedish men and Swedish women worked fewer hours than their American counterparts. It seems reasonable to attribute at least some of this reversal to the different tax and public spending policies of the two countries.

Trends among Older Workers

The differences between Swedish and U.S. trends narrow with respect to work effort of older workers. Figure 6-8 shows trends in the two countries for men and women aged 65 and older. (The Swedish statistics cover people between ages 65 and 74; the American figures cover all people aged 65 and older.) Clearly the work effort of older people has fallen in both countries, although the decline is far more dramatic in Sweden. Among older people who remain employed, the workweek has declined gradually and at about the same pace in both countries. The main reason for the decline in work effort is a steep decline in the rate of labor force participation. In 1963 the participation rate for Swedish men 65 to 74 years old was 43 percent, compared with a 28 percent rate among men aged 65 and older in the United States. By 1984 the rates in the two countries had declined to 11 percent and 16 percent, respectively. The decline in female labor force participation was far slower in the two countries, partly because the initial rates were so low.

The rapid declines in labor force participation among older men probably reflect changing tastes as much as they do changing incentives from taxes and transfers. For example, the participation rate of older U.S. men fell from more than 60 percent in 1900 to just over 40 percent in 1940. None of this decline is attributable to social security benefits, since the first benefits were not paid until 1941. However, careful analysis of recent U.S. retirement patterns indicates that at least some of the current decline is connected to rising benefit levels.[52] The more rapid decline in labor force participation in Sweden is probably the result of the drop in the official retirement age and the rapid maturation of the earnings-related pension scheme, which provided sharply higher retirement benefits during the late 1960s and 1970s. In addition, because Sweden is a far more homogeneous society than the United States, it is

52. See Jerry A. Hausman and David A. Wise, "Social Security, Health Status, and Retirement," in David A. Wise, ed., *Pensions, Labor, and Individual Choice* (University of Chicago Press, 1985), pp. 159–91; and Gary Burtless, "Social Security, Unanticipated Benefit Increases, and the Timing of Retirement," *Review of Economic Studies* (forthcoming).

Figure 6-8. *Labor Supply Trends among Older Swedish and U.S. Men and Women, 1963–84*[a]

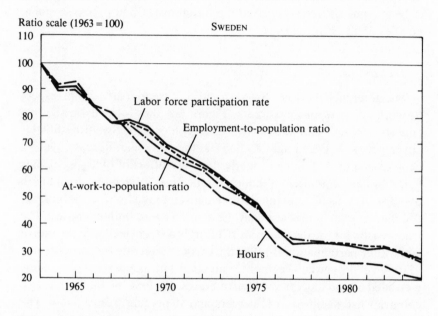

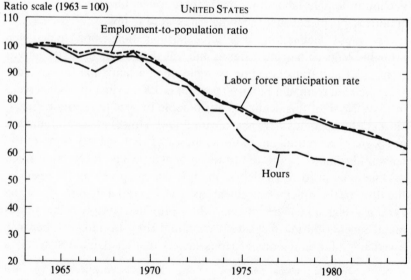

Sources: See figure 6-6.
a. The Swedish statistics cover people aged 65 through 74; U.S. figures cover people aged 65 and over.

likely Swedish workers and firms are more responsive to perceived changes in the socially sanctioned retirement age.

Supply Trends among the Young

Swedish men aged 16 to 24 have substantially reduced their work effort during the past two decades. Among men aged 16 to 19, total hours fell by half between 1963 and 1984; among those aged 20 to 24, work effort dropped nearly a fifth. Similar although somewhat smaller drops occurred among women aged 16 to 19 and 20 to 24. Presumably, much of the work effort at younger ages has declined because school enrollment rates in this population have risen. In the United States employment and labor force participation rates have steadily risen, especially for women.[53] The expansion in U.S. employment at younger ages has occurred despite sharply higher unemployment rates and rising school enrollment rates. A growing fraction of the U.S. youth population is combining employment with further education. This strategy may be more necessary for American than for Swedish youth, because higher education is less generously subsidized in the United States. Yet higher education is nonetheless attractive to Americans because of the substantial after-tax rewards available to workers with advanced degrees.

Effects of Taxes and Transfers on Swedish Work Effort

In this section I summarize a number of past studies of Swedish labor supply and statistically estimate the relationship between taxes and aggregate labor supply during the past two decades.

Past Studies

Several economists have attempted to estimate the effect of the Swedish tax-transfer system on work effort and net government revenues. One widely known study is a 1981 paper by Charles Stuart.[54] Stuart's goal was to determine how Swedish government revenue

53. Data on Swedish and American youth are from the sources cited in figure 6-6.
54. Charles E. Stuart, "Swedish Tax Rates, Labor Supply, and Tax Revenues," *Journal of Political Economy*, vol. 89 (October 1981), pp. 1020–38.

depended on the marginal and average tax rates levied on labor market income. He hypothesized that workers could freely substitute between market work and household production in their use of time. Untaxed home production could be substituted, though perhaps imperfectly, for goods and services purchased with after-tax earned income and transfer payments. To obtain estimates of the government revenue function, Stuart needed to make some assumptions about Swedish production functions in the home and in the market. In addition, he needed to assume a utility function describing how workers value output from home production compared with goods and services purchased in the market. Note that these assumed functions, particularly the utility function, were based only indirectly if at all on evidence about Swedish technology and preferences.[55] Stuart then computed the rate at which market labor and government revenue would decline as the marginal tax rate was raised 1 percentage point.

Stuart's calculations permitted him to compute the marginal tax rate, t^*, at which government revenue is maximized. Under the assumption that home production is perfectly substitutable for market purchases of goods and services, Stuart calculated that this rate is between 43 and 51 percent for Sweden. Under the assumption of imperfect substitutability, Stuart found that t^* lies between 69 and 73 percent. Because Swedish government revenue continued to rise well after the average marginal rate exceeded 51 percent, Stuart's first set of estimates appears far too low. Even the second set of estimates implies that by the mid-1970s the Swedish tax rate was in a range in which further increases would diminish government revenue.[56] Using the second set of estimates for t^*, we can infer from Stuart's results how much market labor supply falls as the average marginal tax rate rises 1 percentage point. At an average marginal tax rate of 65 percent, Stuart's estimate of the rate in 1969, market work effort is predicted to decline between 1.36 percent and 1.95 percent. This implies that the elasticity of overall labor supply with respect to changes in after-tax wages is between 0.48 and 0.68. My impression is that this

55. The parameter estimates in the model are calibrated using aggregate Swedish data for 1969. Stuart's model and simulation results, however, are in no way based on empirical evidence about the time-series or cross-sectional relationship between taxes and market work effort.

56. An identical conclusion was reached by Ulf Jakobsson and Göran Normann, "Welfare Effects of Changes in Income Tax Progression in Sweden," in Gunnar Eliasson, Bertil Holmlund, and Frank P. Stafford, eds., *Studies in Labor Market Behavior: Sweden and the United States* (Stockholm: Almqvist and Wiksell, 1981), pp. 313–38.

elasticity is high in comparison with empirical estimates reported in the literature.[57]

Stuart argues that his estimates provide good predictions of the trends in market work effort and output. For example, he points out that annual Swedish growth rates declined from 4.4 percent in the early and mid-1960s to 1.4 percent by the late 1970s. This evidence is far from persuasive, however, since virtually all of the decline was caused by a fall in total factor productivity, not to a fall in labor input.[58] Moreover, the sudden drop in productivity in the early 1970s was a worldwide phenomenon. While part of the decline might be indirectly attributable to higher taxes, such an effect does not automatically occur when labor input falls. In fact, the reverse is more likely, since the capital-labor ratio rises in the short run.

Stuart also contends that the trends in total Swedish labor supply correspond to predictions from his model. Labor supply per capita fell 1.6 percent yearly between 1964 and 1969 and 0.9 percent a year between 1969 and 1977. While the total decline is far below the amount predicted by his model, particularly during the 1970s, Stuart argues this shortfall is due to lags in response to tax changes and to growing disguised unemployment and underemployment. Unfortunately for this prediction, labor supply per capita has risen 0.1 percent a year since 1977, even as some marginal tax rates have continued to climb and workers have had additional time to respond to the high rates imposed in the past.[59]

More recently, Hansson and Stuart have written an interesting paper on a related subject.[60] Although this investigation, like Stuart's 1981 study, tries to estimate the marginal rate of taxation that will yield the most government revenue, the main focus is on estimating marginal "deadweight loss"—a measure of inefficiency—from an additional krona of taxes. The authors base their estimates on a more fully specified

57. A rise in taxes of 1 percentage point, from 65 percent to 66 percent, yields a 2.86 percent decline in after-tax wage rates, thus giving the elasticity estimates reported in the text. For a survey of empirical estimates, see Hansson and Stuart, "Tax Revenue and the Marginal Cost of Public Funds."

58. See table 2-1 in chapter 2 in this volume.

59. Stuart's estimates of the decline in labor supply are based on annual hours worked divided by the entire population aged 16 to 74. For evidence on the continued rise in overall marginal tax rates, see Ingemar Hansson, "Skattereformen och de Totala Marginaleffekterna," *Ekonomisk Debatt*, no. 1 (1983), p. 22.

60. Hansson and Stuart, "Tax Revenue and the Marginal Cost of Public Funds." See also Ingemar Hansson, "Marginal Cost of Public Funds for Different Tax Instruments and Government Expenditures," *Scandinavian Journal of Economics*, vol. 86, no. 2 (1984), pp. 115–30.

and defensible model of the economy than the one used by Stuart in 1981. In addition, they rely on empirical estimates of the production and labor supply functions in their simulations, rather than on assumptions. (The labor supply elasticities are taken from American and British rather than Swedish studies, however.) Hansson and Stuart estimate that between 1965 and 1979 Swedish labor supply in the taxed sector fell between 1.18 and 1.65 percent a year because of rising marginal and average tax rates.[61] We can infer that the response is substantially smaller than the one reported in Stuart's earlier study. This can be seen from the reported estimates of t^*. Low values of t^* indicate the work force is very responsive to variations in taxes, even at low rates; high values indicate the opposite. Hansson and Stuart estimate that t^* lies between 67 and 96 percent, considerably above the 43–73 percent range reported in Stuart's earlier paper.

Probably of greater interest to economists are the authors' estimates of the marginal rise in deadweight loss resulting from a slight rise in the marginal tax rate. Most economists prefer deadweight loss to actual labor supply reductions as a measure of the efficiency loss resulting from taxation. The estimate of marginal deadweight loss turns out to be highly sensitive to the authors' assumptions about labor supply elasticities. With high assumed substitution elasticities, the deadweight loss is very high; with low assumed elasticities, the loss is comparatively small, except at the highest marginal tax rates. At a marginal tax of 70 percent, the authors' preferred elasticity estimates imply the marginal deadweight loss is 1.29 times the extra revenue raised (in the case of taxes that are spent on income redistribution) or 0.69 times the extra revenue raised (for taxes spent on public goods). The authors interpret this to mean that a marginal krona spent on redistribution costs society Skr 2.29 while a marginal krona spent on public goods costs Skr 1.69. Most of this efficiency loss is caused by distortions in labor supply and labor alloca- tion. The major limitation of the Hansson and Stuart study is that the labor supply estimates used in the model are not based on observed Swedish behavior.

Only a few authors have tried to examine labor supply behavior using Swedish time-series data or evidence from surveys of a cross section of the population. One of the most thorough of the cross-sectional studies, by Gustafsson and Jacobsson, unfortunately cannot be used here because

61. Ingemar Hansson and Charles Stuart, "Laffer Curves and Marginal Cost of Public Funds in Sweden" (University of Lund, June 1982), p. 29.

it does not explicitly examine the relation between work effort and taxation.[62] Stig Tegle has completed an exhaustive study of the determinants of part-time work among men and women in which he considers the influence of taxes. But his time-series estimates of labor market behavior do not show a significant or systematic effect.[63] However, two of the empirical studies do deserve attention.

Axelsson, Jacobsson, and Löfgren examined the labor supply behavior of men and women aged 20 to 64 interviewed in the 1976 Income Distribution Survey.[64] They measured labor supply using an individual's "employed hours per year," defining this variable as the average weekly workhours multiplied by the number of weeks each year in paid employment. Because "weeks in employment" include time on vacation, on sick leave, and in other paid absences, the dependent variable excludes many sources of variation in actual hours worked. The sample includes only families in which the husband and wife each earn at least Skr 5,000 a year.

The authors' econometric specification is similar to one used in many early U.S. studies. Annual hours are assumed to be a function of the worker's gross hourly wage, the wage of his or her spouse, and the nonwage income available to the household. The empirical results imply that the labor supply function is backward bending for both men and women: higher wage rates reduce annual work effort. This would imply that tax increases will raise aggregate labor supply. While this result was obtained in many early U.S. studies of men, it is far less common among studies of American women.[65] To determine the influence of taxes on work effort, the authors enter a separate variable indicating the level of the proportional local (*kommunal*) income tax rate. The coefficient on this variable indicates that the work effort of a male falls by eight hours a year and the work effort of a female by thirty-one hours a year with every rise of 1 percentage point in the proportional tax rate. These

62. Gustafsson and Jacobsson, "Trends in Female Labor Force Participation."

63. Stig Tegle, *Part-Time Employment: An Economic Analysis of Working Hours in Sweden, 1963–1982* (University of Lund, Department of Economics, 1985). I have also profited from reading a preliminary report by Roger Jacobsson, "Three Papers on Estimation of Labor Supply Responses on Swedish Data" (University of Umeå, Department of Economics, October 1982). This research is not yet in final form, however.

64. Roger Axelsson, Roger Jacobsson, and Karl Gustaf Löfgren, "On the Determinants of Labor Supply in Sweden," in Eliasson, Holmlund, and Stafford, eds., *Studies in Labor Market Behavior*, pp. 269–300.

65. The authors in fact report that women respond more than men to increases in their gross wages. The wage elasticity of married women is -0.30; that of married men is only -0.025. Ibid., p. 288.

coefficient estimates are difficult for the authors to reconcile with their reported coefficients on the gross wage rate.

Two aspects of this study make the results difficult to generalize. First, the criteria for sample selection imply that the findings are applicable to only some husband-wife families. In particular, the results do not apply to single-earner families, nor can they be used to infer what factors influence the decision of single-earner families to become two-earner families. For example, the authors find that a rising gross wage rate for the husband has a strongly negative influence on the labor supply of wives. This finding apparently contradicts my suggestion above that high-income Swedish families would face the largest incentives to become dual-earner households as a result of progressive taxation and separate tax filing for spouses. There is no contradiction, however, because the results apply only to married women who earn at least Skr 5,000 a year. It is impossible to determine from the study whether these women are married to men whose marginal tax rates are greater or less than those faced by the husbands of women who do not work.

A second limitation is the study's failure to explicitly treat the progressive income tax structure faced by Swedish wage earners. Workers with high gross wage rates are subject to high marginal tax rates, even at fairly low levels of work effort. Their after-tax wages will consequently be far below their gross wages. In theory, workers should respond to the after-tax wage rather than the pretax wage in determining labor supply. Besides driving a wedge between gross and after-tax wages, the progressive income tax also provides an implicit "lump-sum transfer" to workers who face a progressive income tax rate on marginal increases in earnings. For example, the wage earner in figure 6-4 who works more than thirty hours a week can be viewed as responding to a tax system that implicitly pays a lump-sum transfer at zero hours of work and then, for every one-krona rise in gross income, imposes marginal taxes at a constant rate equal to the rate charged along the budget segment BC. (The lump-sum transfer, measured at zero hours of work, is simply the intercept of the continuation of the segment BC to the vertical axis. This intercept is sometimes referred to as "virtual income.") Relative to poorly paid workers, high-wage workers will typically face a net wage that is a smaller proportion of their gross wage and, in addition, will receive more implicit lump-sum transfers. Given this mathematical relation between gross wage rates on the one hand and net wages and virtual income on the other, it is not surprising if analysts find a negative statistical relation between gross wage rates and annual hours. But this statistical relation cannot be used to infer that reductions in net wages arising from an increase in tax rates will lead to an increase in aggregate labor supply.

The first study to carefully treat the issue of progressive taxation in Sweden was a 1983 analysis by N. Sören Blomquist. Blomquist adapted a procedure suggested by Burtless and Hausman to estimate the labor supply responsiveness of married men.[66] The rather complicated procedure takes full account of the mathematical relationship between gross and after-tax wage rates to estimate the exact statistical relationship between annual hours of work and both net wages and virtual income. Blomquist's results contrast strongly with those of Axelsson and others. Instead of finding a negative relation between wages and hours, he finds a strong and statistically significant positive relationship. The estimated elasticity of annual hours with respect to changes in the net wage is 0.08; the elasticity with respect to changes in virtual income is −0.04. Blomquist's estimates of wage elasticity lie in the upper part of the range of previous estimates, and his estimates of the income elasticity probably fall somewhere in the lower part of the range (in absolute value).[67] The most directly comparable estimates are those obtained by Hausman, who estimated the labor supply function of prime-age American men using essentially the same model. Blomquist finds a wage effect that is nearly eight times larger and an income effect that is roughly one-tenth as large as that found by Hausman.[68] If both sets of estimates are to be believed, Swedish labor supply preferences bear little resemblance to those in the United States.

Blomquist uses his estimates to predict the size of work reduction and deadweight loss resulting from Swedish income taxes in 1973, the

66. N. Sören Blomquist, "The Effect of Income Taxation on the Labor Supply of Married Men in Sweden," *Journal of Public Economics,* vol. 22 (November 1983), pp. 169–97; Gary Burtless and Jerry A. Hausman, "The Effect of Taxation on Labor Supply: Evaluating the Gary Negative Income Tax Experiment," *Journal of Political Economy,* vol. 86 (December 1978), pp. 1103–30; and Jerry A. Hausman, "Labor Supply," in Henry J. Aaron and Joseph A. Pechman, eds., *How Taxes Affect Economic Behavior* (Brookings, 1981), pp. 27–83.

67. See Hansson and Stuart, "Tax Revenue and the Marginal Cost of Public Funds," pp. 340–41.

68. Part of the difference might be due to the differing treatment of wives' net earned income in the two studies. Hausman disregards such income under the assumption that wives decide on their labor supply after husbands have determined theirs. Blomquist includes the wife's net earnings in his estimate of the husband's virtual income. The variation in virtual income should consequently be much higher in Blomquist's study.

year covered by his study. He finds that married men's labor supply is about 12 percent below what it would be in the absence of income taxation and 6 percent below what it would be under a strictly proportional tax system that raised the same amount of revenue. (This proportional tax rate would have been 34 percent in 1975.) The deadweight loss from the progressive income tax is about 19 percent of revenue raised, compared with only a 4 percent loss from a strictly proportional tax system. Of course, these estimates understate the implied work reductions and deadweight loss from the overall tax system. Payroll taxes and the value-added tax drive an additional wedge between the gross compensation paid to workers and the net wages they receive for their effort. If these taxes were taken into account, the work effort reduction would be somewhat larger and the deadweight loss far larger than the estimates reported by Blomquist. Moreover, tax rates have climbed significantly since 1973, suggesting that current losses from the system are larger still.

Time-Series Evidence

It is reasonable to ask whether the time-series pattern of Swedish labor supply supports the view that rising taxes and transfers have had a major effect on work effort. Three of the studies surveyed above suggest the response is so large that reducing current tax rates, at least on high-earning families, would actually increase tax revenues. A fourth study, by Blomquist, implies that the sensitivity of prime-age married men to taxation is high. Because prime-age men are usually considered among the least responsive to taxation, Blomquist's result has disturbing implications for total work effort. Yet the growing concern about the work effects of taxation seems a bit exaggerated when one reflects that Sweden enjoys an unusually high labor force participation rate and has experienced only modest declines in work effort among 25- to 64-year-olds during the past two decades, when the marginal income tax rate on an average full-time worker nearly doubled, the payroll tax quadrupled, and the rate of indirect taxation more than tripled.

Many economists argue that the loss of workhours does not concern them as much as the tremendous efficiency losses arising from high tax rates and generous income redistribution. When taxes in their present form are raised by Skr 100, taxpayers actually give up far more than Skr 100 in lost satisfaction because of the added distortion of their allocation decisions. Even if wage earners do not on average greatly reduce their work effort, there will be a loss in net satisfaction from the leisure and goods actually consumed. Taxpayers would be willing to pay far more than Skr 100 in lump-sum taxes to avoid the mischief that results from an additional Skr 100 of income, payroll, or value-added taxes. What economists do not always acknowledge, however, is that available estimates of efficiency loss ultimately rest on estimates of labor supply responsiveness. If that responsiveness is low, the efficiency loss from taxation may be small.[69] For that reason the time-series relationship between taxes and total work effort is worth considering.

There are two ways to view trends in Swedish labor supply. Trends can be compared with those in a country where taxes and the rate of tax growth have been lower. If the two countries are otherwise similar, the difference in labor supply trends might provide a crude measure of the impact of faster tax growth. A second estimate can be obtained by determining the time-series correlation between taxes and total work effort. Neither estimate is a substitute for careful econometric analysis of cross-sectional evidence, such as that recently performed by Blomquist, but the aggregate time-series evidence does provide a simple check on the results from cross-sectional studies.

A comparison between Swedish and U.S. trends can be performed using statistics described above. I will compare trends between 1963 and 1981. (The earlier year is the first with detailed Swedish labor supply data; the latter is the most recent for which I have comparable U.S. data.) Table 6-1 shows the growth of tax burdens in the two countries. If "labor taxes" are defined as the sum of individual income taxes, contributions to social security, and general consumption taxes, Swedish labor tax burdens can be seen to have grown from about 21½ percent of gross domestic product in 1963 to slightly more than 41 percent of GDP in 1981. Using a comparable definition, labor taxes in the United States have grown from roughly 13½ percent in 1963 to 21½ percent in 1981. During the same eighteen-year interval, Swedish labor supply among people aged 25 and older fell by 17 percent; U.S. labor supply in the same population fell 2 percent.[70] Much of the supply reduction in both countries was due to withdrawals from the labor force of men and women

69. This relationship is demonstrated in Hansson and Stuart, "Tax Revenue and the Marginal Cost of Public Funds."

70. Labor supply is measured as total annual workhours of the population divided by the number of people in the population. Data available for the Swedish population are restricted to men and women aged 25 to 74, inclusive, whereas U.S. population data include all people aged 25 and older.

aged 65 and older. If the work reductions of the elderly are ignored, labor supply fell 11 percent in Sweden and rose 1 percent in the United States between 1963 and 1981.

This pattern might suggest that Sweden has paid a high price in lost hours of work for rising tax burdens and public expenditures. Some allowance should be made, however, for the more advanced state of the U.S. economy in the early 1960s. Real U.S. incomes were higher and the average workweek of full-time employees was shorter than in Sweden. It is therefore likely that Swedish workhours would have declined after 1963 even if taxes and public spending had not increased.[71] Furthermore, labor force participation rates of older American men were initially well below those of comparable Swedes, so Swedish participation rates would probably have tended toward the U.S. levels regardless of increases in taxes and social security retirement benefits.[72] Even making adjustments for these factors, however, the more rapid rise in Swedish taxes and government spending has probably contributed substantially to the more rapid decline of work effort. A plausible estimate is that labor supply has fallen 5 to 9 percent among people aged 25 through 64, and 7 to 12 percent among all people aged 25 and older, as a result of faster growth in taxes and transfers.

One shortcoming of these estimates is the implicit assumption that labor supply trends in Sweden would have been similar to those in the United States in the absence of differing growth rates in taxes and government spending. This cannot be safely assumed without better knowledge about comparative Swedish and American work preferences. If Swedish and U.S. preferences differ, there is no assurance that the trends would have been similar. As reported above, Blomquist found

71. The standard workweek appears to fall with rises in real wages and incomes, even in the absence of particularly high tax rates. The workweek of full-time male employees in U.S. manufacturing fell to forty hours by the late 1940s, and it has fallen only slightly since. Most of the decline in the workweek therefore occurred some time before typical workers paid substantial taxes on earnings. See "Worktime: The Traditional Workweek and Its Alternatives," in *Employment and Training Report of the President, 1979* (Washington, D.C., U.S. GPO), p. 77. Even in the early 1960s many full-time Swedish employees continued to work a standard week of forty-six or forty-eight hours. These long hours would probably have fallen with higher real incomes, regardless of the trend in taxes and transfer payments.

72. Robert Moffitt has found that most of the time-series trend in the labor supply of older men in the United States can be attributed to factors other than the rise in social security benefits—for example, rising levels of real income and wealth and changing population tastes. See Robert Moffitt, "Life Cycle Labor Supply and the Effect of the Social Security System: A Time-Series Analysis," in Gary Burtless, ed., *Work, Health, and Income among the Elderly* (Brookings, forthcoming).

substantially different preferences among Swedish men than Hausman found among comparable American men.

It is possible to obtain a crude estimate of Swedish preferences with aggregate time-series data. Using Stig Tegle's computations of income tax burdens on representative Swedish workers, I have computed before-tax and after-tax real wages as well as real tax burdens from 1963 through 1982. Ordinary least squares (OLS) is then used to regress these real wage and tax variables on aggregate labor supply to measure the sensitivity of work effort to taxation. Interpreting the results of this type of regression requires caution. The time-series evidence usually does not permit reliable identification of the aggregate labor supply function. Year-to-year movements in observed gross wages and aggregate labor supply reflect movements in the equilibrium of price and quantity—that is, movements of the intersection of the supply and demand functions, not movements along one function or the other. In this case, however, I am regressing supply on the after-tax wage paid to labor. Much of the variation in the after-tax wage arises from exogenous shifts in government tax policy. These shifts might conceivably be enough to identify the supply function. The identification is nonetheless problematical, and the results should be interpreted accordingly.

Because there are only a few degrees of freedom, I have adopted an extremely parsimonious specification of response, but a specification that captures some of the main features of labor supply response described above. The econometric specification for men is as follows:

$$(6\text{-}1) \qquad H_m = \beta_0 + \beta_1 VR + \beta_2 w_m (1 - t') + \beta_3 w_m t' \\ + \beta_4 [w_m (1 - t') - w_w (1 - t)],$$

where H_m is annual average weekly hours of work per male in the population, VR is the vacancy rate measured as a percentage of the labor force, w_m and w_w are the average hourly wages of men and women in industry (measured in constant 1980 kronor), t' is the marginal income tax rate imposed on an average full-time male worker in industry, and t is the average tax rate on a twenty-hour-a-week female worker in industry. Because the dependent variable is actual rather than desired hours of work, the vacancy rate, VR, is included to control for the effects of demand fluctuations on actual hours. Note that w_m and w_w are not equal to the factor prices of male and female labor. The full factor price would include social insurance contributions paid by employers, which are omitted from w.

The independent variable $w_m(1 - t')$ is simply the net real marginal wage of a full-time male worker. The overwhelming majority of prime-age men were employed both at the beginning and end of the period under study. The response of men to taxes probably takes the form of marginal increases or decreases in annual hours. The marginal net wage seems the most appropriate variable to capture the influence of real wages on work effort. The tax variable $w_m t'$ directly captures the effect of rising marginal taxes on behavior. If men respond only to net wages in setting their labor supply, the coefficient on this variable should be zero. As Lindbeck and others have pointed out, however, revenue raised through taxation largely returns to workers in the form of transfers and public goods. Hence increases in $w_m t'$ should be associated with reduced hours if public spending substitutes for private spending of workers. The last variable, $[w_m(1 - t') - w_w(1 - t)]$, is the difference between the net marginal wage of a full-time male worker and the average after-tax wage of a part-time female worker. A fall in this difference, either because of a rise in w_w relative to w_m or a fall in t relative to t', should encourage husbands in married-couple families to reduce their work effort relative to that of their spouses.

The econometric specification for women's labor supply is similar to that for men's:

$$(6\text{-}2) \qquad H_w = \gamma_0 + \gamma_1 VR + \gamma_2 w_w(1 - t) + \gamma_3 w_w t$$
$$+ \gamma_4[w_m (1 - t') - w_w(1 - t)],$$

where H_w is annual average weekly hours of work by each woman in the population and other variables are defined as above. Equation 6-2 differs from equation 6-1 only in the tax used to measure the after-tax wage and tax burden. The most significant trend in women's labor supply is the growth in labor force participation and employment, rather than the shrinkage in workhours among women who were employed at the beginning of the period. The average after-tax wage seems more relevant than the marginal wage to the decision to participate.

The results of performing these regressions are reported in tables 6-4 and 6-5, which show coefficient estimates for men and women, respectively. Separate results were obtained for 20- to 24-year-olds and 25- to 64-year-olds of each sex. No regressions were estimated for the very young (16- to 19-year-olds) or those older than 65; the young are influenced by trends in schooling and the elderly by trends in retirement benefits in addition to trends in taxes. For each group covered in the

Table 6-4. *Regression for Work Responses of Swedish Men to Income Taxes, by Age, 1963–82*[a]

Variable	Coefficients for:			
	Ages 20–24		Ages 25–64	
Constant	51.02	51.54	52.01	53.65
	(13.95)	(15.17)	(9.48)	(29.17)
VR	3.06	2.48	2.53	0.72
	(4.11)	(3.30)	(2.27)	(1.76)
$w_m (1 - t')$	−0.78	−0.80	−0.51	−0.58
	(−4.70)	(−5.21)	(−2.04)	(−6.92)
$w_m t'$	−0.71	−0.61	−0.52	−0.22
	(−3.98)	(−3.55)	(−1.95)	(−2.29)
$[w_m(1 - t') - w_w(1 - t)]$	−0.18	−0.17	0.09	0.13
	(−0.92)	(−0.92)	(0.32)	(1.37)
Time trend	. . .	−0.12	. . .	−0.39
	. . .	(−1.87)	. . .	(−10.97)
$\overline{R}^2$	0.90	0.92	0.91	0.99
Durbin-Watson statistic	1.30	1.63	0.65	2.03
Addendum: Simulation results				
Percent change in 1980–82 hours				
without tax increase[b]	−12	−18	4	−10
Percent change in 1980–82 hours				
without social security rise[c]	−43	−48	−12	−25

Sources: Tax rates are from Stig Tegle, *Part-Time Employment: An Economic Analysis of Weekly Working Hours in Sweden, 1963–1982* (University of Lund, Department of Economics, 1985), pp. 76–77; wages are from Siv Gustafsson and Petra Lantz, *Arbete och Löner* (Stockholm: Almqvist and Wicksell 1985), p. 223; hours are from Sveriges officiella statistik, *Arbetskraftsundersökningarna (AKU)* (Stockholm: Statistiska centralbyrån) [Official Statistics of Sweden, *The Labor Force Surveys* (Stockholm: Statistics Sweden)], various issues.

a. Numbers in parentheses are *t*-statistics.

b. Income tax rate assumed held constant at 1963 level.

c. Income tax and social insurance contribution rates assumed held constant at 1963 rates.

tables, I estimated two equations, one including a trend variable and one without. An argument against including a time trend is the desire to assign as much of the total variance as possible to economic variables. Some variables, such as the average and marginal tax and the difference between men's and women's net wages, have an important trend component, as does the dependent variable, H. Excluding the trend term presumably permits the independent variables to explain a larger fraction of the variation in H. This should yield upper-bound estimates of their influence on behavior.

Most of the reported coefficients possess the expected sign, and a great many are statistically different from zero at conventional significance levels. The vacancy rate, as expected, has a positive effect on

Table 6-5. *Regression for Work Responses of Swedish Women to Income Taxes, by Age, 1963–82*[a]

Variable	Coefficients for:			
	Ages 20–24		Ages 25–64	
Constant	34.05	33.73	18.76	18.37
	(9.60)	(12.40)	(5.69)	(10.54)
VR	0.58	1.84	−0.95	0.55
	(0.93)	(3.05)	(−1.65)	(1.41)
$w_m(1 - t)$	−0.58	−0.57	−0.16	−0.15
	(−3.66)	(−4.68)	(−1.09)	(−1.89)
$w_m t$	−0.22	−0.68	0.24	−0.30
	(−1.61)	(−3.97)	(1.87)	(−2.74)
$[w_m(1 - t') - w_w(1 - t)]$	−0.38	−0.21	−0.23	−0.04
	(−3.49)	(−2.21)	(−2.34)	(−0.63)
Time trend	. . .	0.28	. . .	0.33
	. . .	(3.40)	. . .	(6.30)
$\overline{R}^2$	0.45	0.67	0.77	0.94
Durbin-Watson statistic	1.52	2.75	0.77	1.58
Addendum: Simulation results				
Percent change in 1980–82 hours				
without tax increase[b]	−23	−12	−17	−21
Percent change in 1980–82 hours				
without social security rise[c]	−46	−38	−21	−11

Sources: See table 6-4.
a. Numbers in parentheses are *t*-statistics.
b. Income tax rate assumed held constant at 1963 level.
c. Income tax and social insurance contribution rates assumed held constant at 1963 rates.

labor supply. When vacancies are high, the cost of securing a job is small, and more men and women should enter the work force. In the equations in which it is entered, the trend variable also has the expected sign—positive for women and negative for men. There is consistent evidence of supply curves that are backward bending in net real wages for both men and women. The coefficient on the net marginal wage is always negative for men, and the coefficient on the net average wage is similarly negative for women. This sign simply indicates that on average the negative income effect from rising real wages offsets the positive substitution effect. By implication, a rise in marginal and average tax rates should *increase* aggregate labor supply.

This effect is partially or wholly offset by the return of taxes to workers in the form of transfers and public goods. The coefficients on the marginal and average tax variables are negative, with one exception, indicating that rising tax burdens and government spending act to depress labor supply as predicted by Lindbeck and others.

The effects of the changing tax structure are captured by the coefficient on $[w_m(1 - t') - w_w(1 - t)]$, the difference between men's and women's after-tax wage rates. This variable's effect on male labor supply appears to be small and poorly determined in the data. Only for men aged 25 to 64 does it possess the predicted positive sign. The variable is a far more significant determinant of women's labor supply, indicating that the working woman is indeed sensitive to the difference between her own and her husband's ability to earn after-tax income.

The overall effect of taxes on labor supply can be inferred from differentiation of equations 6-1 and 6-2:

(6-3) $$\frac{dH_m}{dt'} = (-\beta_2 + \beta_3 - \beta_4)w_m + \beta_4(w_w)\frac{dt}{dt'};$$

(6-4) $$\frac{dH_w}{dt} = (-\gamma_2 + \gamma_3 + \gamma_4)w_w - \gamma_4(w_m)\frac{dt'}{dt}.$$

To see the effects of taxes on male work effort, consider the third column of table 6-4. The effect of an increase of 1 percentage point in t', assuming t remains fixed, can be computed as $(0.51 - 0.52 - 0.09)w_m = (-0.10)w_m$. If t' rises so that the difference in male and female net wages remains constant, the effect on work effort is only $(0.51 - 0.52)w_m = (-0.01)w_m$.

Two simulations show the effects of rising taxes since 1963. In the first, I hold t and t' constant at their 1963 levels and predict the average change in 1980–82 labor supply as a percentage of actual labor supply in those years. In the second, I hold t and t' constant at their 1963 levels and, in addition, impute higher gross wage rates, w_m and w_w, to reflect a reduction in 1980–82 social security contribution rates to the 1963 level. The results of these simulations are presented in the bottom two rows of tables 6-4 and 6-5. Nearly all the simulation results indicate that labor supply would have been *lower* if tax rates had been held to their 1963 levels. The explanation for this is straightforward. The Swedish time-series evidence is at least weakly consistent with backward-bending supply curves for prime-age men and women. This evidence suggests that if Swedish workers had been permitted to keep a larger share of wages from their market work, they would have felt less need to work long hours. Total labor supply would have dropped even faster than it actually did.

Clearly, this time-series evidence is inconsistent with the cross-sectional results in Blomquist's study. It is also at variance with the

comparative time-series evidence about Swedish and U.S. behavior
described above. The two pieces of time-series evidence do not, however, directly contradict one another. The disparate trends of Swedish
and U.S. labor supply may be attributable to a variety of national
differences besides taxes and government spending. The most obvious
possibility is a difference in tastes. It is not so easy to reconcile the cross-
sectional and time-series evidence for Sweden. I turn to this problem in
the final section.

Conclusion

This chapter has considered several strands of evidence about how
taxes and transfers affect the supply of labor in Sweden. Undoubtedly,
the most reliable evidence about work preferences would be produced
in randomized experiments, such as the American negative income tax
studies. Because experiments are rarely feasible, however, and have
never even been attempted in Sweden, economists have been forced to
rely on observations of naturally occurring variations within a given
population or across time. The detailed cross-sectional evidence assem-
bled by Blomquist is probably the best available for Sweden. The data
set provides many degrees of freedom and permits a detailed specification
of the relevant economic variables. Blomquist's study is limited, however, by its focus on only a single population group, one that is widely
believed to be the least responsive to taxes and transfers. Cross-sectional
studies could be improved by subjecting their findings to verification,
either by reestimating the identical model using cross-sectional evidence
from a different period or by attempting to predict the aggregate time-
series pattern of labor supply. No labor supply model, either in Sweden
or the United States, has yet been subjected to these tests.

In my opinion aggregate time-series evidence by itself is less convincing than cross-sectional data as a basis for inference. Time-series data
sets typically offer too few degrees of freedom to allow much confidence
in parameter estimates. (The regressions in this study are based on only
twenty observations, for example.) The restriction on degrees of freedom
severely limits the number of economic variables that can be included
in the analysis. Defining the relevant economic variables is also difficult
using aggregate data because different members of the population are
subject to markedly different incentives. Finally, investigators can

seldom have much assurance that aggregate labor supply functions are reliably identified in time-series data. Despite these shortcomings, time-series results are probably somewhat more reliable than predictions based on behavior in another country. For that reason, I am slightly less confident about estimates that rely on simple comparisons between trends in two countries or—perhaps more imprudently—on the belief that estimated behavioral patterns in one country can be assumed to apply in another.

Allowing for these uncertainties, several pieces of evidence indicate that total labor supply in Sweden has been reduced by high tax rates and generous redistribution. The most reliable cross-sectional study shows that prime-age married men work 6 percent less under the current income tax than they would under a strictly proportional system that raised the same revenue. If the income tax were eliminated altogether, men would work 12 percent longer than under the current system.

A comparison of labor supply trends in Sweden and the United States supports this conclusion. Male labor supply has dropped much more sharply in Sweden than in the United States, while female labor supply has failed to rise as fast. These differences can be plausibly attributed in large part to differing rates of growth in taxes and public spending. With a few adjustments for obvious dissimilarities between the two nations, I estimate that in the twenty years after 1963, the labor supply of prime-age men and women in Sweden fell 5 to 9 percent because of rising taxes and government spending. That is, if tax and spending growth had been limited to U.S. rates, Swedish labor supply in the early 1980s might have been 6 percent to 10 percent higher. This inference is reinforced by recent studies designed to measure how variations in the total tax rate affect Swedish earnings and government revenues. The studies rely on estimates of behavioral response drawn from American and British empirical research. Given the Swedish tax rates now in effect, nearly all the estimates imply that aggregate hours have been reduced.

One piece of evidence points in the opposite direction, however. Time-series data on the relationships among total hours, real net wages, and taxes suggest the aggregate supply function of Swedish labor is backward bending. During the past two decades, labor supply has fallen as real after-tax wages have risen. Income tax, payroll tax, and value-added tax increases during the past quarter century have severely constrained the rise in after-tax wages received by workers, especially males. Because the aggregate supply function is negatively sloped, the tax increases might, on balance, have slowed the decline in total labor supply. Although I find the aggregate time-series evidence to be weak compared with other available information, it cannot be dismissed out of hand. Swedish labor supply fell faster in the late 1960s and early 1970s, when real after-tax wages were rising, than it has fallen in more recent years, when after-tax wages have been stagnant or declining. Any plausible model of Swedish work behavior must be capable of explaining this pattern.

It could be argued that the direction of the labor supply effect of taxes and transfers is irrelevant. Economists and voters should be concerned with the efficiency or deadweight losses associated with taxes and government spending, not with the absolute magnitude of the work response. Even if higher taxes stimulate workers to increase their labor supply, the distortion in economic behavior reduces their well-being, and it is this loss in welfare that society should focus on. This argument is true but misleading. The loss in economic welfare caused by high taxes and transfers is intimately related to the size and direction of the labor supply response. If the net response to a large tax change is a small change in work effort, the efficiency cost of the tax is probably modest. More technically, if the income and substitution effects arising out of the tax change are small, the efficiency loss is small. If economists are uncertain about the size and direction of work responses to taxes, they are equally if not more uncertain about the welfare costs of taxes.

On balance, the evidence in this chapter suggests that current Swedish labor supply is below what it would be if tax burdens and government spending were closer to those in the United States. The efficiency cost associated with the loss in work effort could be large. I do not conclude from this that taxes and outlays should be lowered. Presumably most Swedes believe, at least implicitly, that the equity and welfare gains from the current level of spending are worth the efficiency and labor supply costs, especially since those costs are uncertain. When the amount of loss is unknown, but the gain in equity is clear and palpable, it should hardly be surprising if voters are reluctant to tamper with a system they have become used to. Yet an uncertain loss is not the same thing as a small loss. The uncertainty of the efficiency cost should not be used to excuse inaction on tax and spending policy. It should be used instead to spur action to measure these costs and take account of them in policymaking.

Comments by Assar Lindbeck

Gary Burtless concentrates on the effects of taxes and public spending on hours of work in the official labor market (that is, on the sum of income and substitution effects on labor supply). Even though these effects constitute an interesting research topic they are, of course, not a reliable indicator of distortions and welfare losses caused by tax wedges; such distortions are instead related to the substitution effects of the marginal tax rates. To cite an extreme example: a large tax increase for financing an expansion of public administration may so impoverish households (that is, create such a strong positive income effect on labor supply) that both husbands and wives will have to work longer hours. An observer who believes that negative consequences for hours of work is an appropriate measure of tax distortions may incorrectly conclude that no distortions for labor have been generated.

Instead of quarreling about details in Burtless's study, I would like to say a few words about what is not discussed, namely the losses in efficiency and welfare caused by the high marginal tax rates on labor in Sweden.

The easiest way to clarify the issue is perhaps to give an example. If an individual has a marginal tax rate of 70 percent and earns, for instance, Skr 100 an hour before taxes, including payroll taxes, in the taxed sector, he or she has incentives to allocate time to the tax-free sector (leisure, household work, and so forth) to the point where private and social marginal return is as low as Skr 30 an hour, assuming that workers are paid according to marginal product. Hence for an hour that would hypothetically be reallocated from the tax-free sectors to the taxed sector, total output would rise by Skr 70, which then measures the tax distortion at the margin.

This type of distortion exists regardless of whether a tax increase actually increases or decreases hours of work in the market. This point is in fact easily demonstrated in figure 6-9. Let the lines $0E$ and $0D$ denote the relation between hours of work and income before and after a proportional income tax, respectively. To demonstrate that welfare losses occur even if the income effect dominates the substitution effect of an isolated income tax increase, let the chosen position of the household after the tax increase be point b while the initial position is

Figure 6-9. *Economic Distortion of an Income Tax*

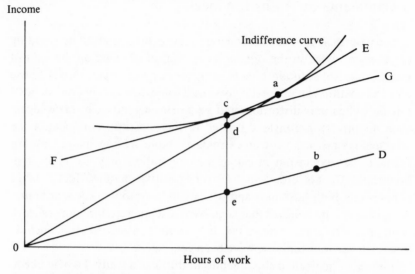

point *a*. The household, to be compensated for the welfare loss from the tax distortion, has to be paid transfers of the size *ce,* requiring a parallel shift of the budget line from 0*D* to *FG.* Hence in the new optimum position the household has to be compensated for the higher income tax payments, *de,* by the extra amount, *cd,* which then is a measure of the utility loss due to the economic distortion introduced by the income tax wedge (in fact the Hicksian "compensating variation").

Similar distortions occur for other types of decisions concerning the allocation of labor, such as work effort, striving for promotion, labor mobility, investment in human capital (if the tax system is progressive), and emigration (though in the last case it is the average rather than the marginal tax-benefit rates that matter). Unfortunately, these effects are so difficult to measure that we are still unable to quantify them in a reasonable way.

However, I would hypothesize that the greatest worries among many citizens, including some economists like myself, are connected with features that are even more difficult to measure, like the frustration of people when the high marginal tax rates prevent them from increasing their living standard much by their own effort in the official labor market—so-called learned helplessness. Indeed, because of high tax rates it is extremely difficult to support a family in Sweden with only one income earner. This helps explain the high labor force participation rate for married women—in addition to the explanation provided by separate tax returns for couples and the high subsidies to public services such as municipal daycare centers that are close substitutes for household work by married women.

Other worrisome and difficult-to-measure effects might arise from the high tax on honesty—that is, there is a great temptation to cheat on taxes. It is also evident that many citizens worry about the new types of income differentials that have popped up not because of different levels of productive effort in the official labor market but because of differences in the demographic composition of the household, luck in getting subsidized public services, and willingness or ability to exploit various asymmetries in the tax system. Indeed, it could be argued that from the point of view of rewarding productive contributions it is largely the wrong type of people that become rich in Sweden. I do not, of course, blame Burtless for not trying to quantify these types of effects. However, if economists shy away from issues like these, we could be ridiculed by reference to the standard story in statistics textbooks, in which the researcher looks for the lost key under the lampost in the street even though he knows very well that the key was lost somewhere out in the dark.

Comments by Ingemar Hansson

Gary Burtless provides a competent description of the Swedish tax and transfer system and an interesting comparison with that of the United States. The fundamental question of the chapter is: to what extent do higher taxes and more generous distribution policies yield a lower labor supply?

This question is extremely important both from a Swedish and an international perspective. Taxes on income are the major source of tax revenue. In Sweden, direct or indirect taxes on labor income, including consumption taxes, constitute 95 percent of total tax revenue. A welfare state of the Swedish type requires high taxes on labor income. If such high rates can be achieved with small distortions, the Swedish model of a welfare state may be an interesting option for other countries. Even Sweden has the option to develop it further by, say, higher and more progressive taxation. If, however, taxes on labor at the Swedish level involve major efficiency losses, the model may offer a less attractive option for other countries, and Sweden may have reached the limit of taxation in the sense that further increases may be associated with very high indirect costs owing to additional distortions.

Now, how does Burtless attack the crucial question of how taxes affect labor supply in Sweden? He reviews different pieces of evidence, including some original contributions, and provides a summary evaluation based on this evidence. This is an attractive approach, even considering that each piece of evidence is subject to a substantial source of error and often yields mixed results.

I will review and comment on three conceptually different types of empirical evidence. First, however, I would like to comment on the measures of labor supply used in the chapter. Burtless measures labor supply by labor force participation rates or hours of work per person. Labor force participation rates provide a very poor basis for measuring the potential distortionary effect of taxes, however. A redistribution of a given number of hours among more individuals does not necessarily involve fewer distortions. I am surprised that Burtless uses this measure. For the many readers that read the first page only, the impression is conveyed that Swedish taxes and transfers involve no major distortions since labor force participation is high.

The more eager reader discovers that Burtless later uses hours of work per person as his preferred measure. Even this measure is, however, inadequate in many respects. If we are interested in distortions, we should try to measure labor supply in efficiency units rather than in terms of reported hours of work. This involves several potentially important adjustments. First, changes in hours of work should be weighed according to their marginal productivity, which may be represented by the wage rate in the absence of more exact measures. This adjustment may be important for an evaluation of the Swedish experience, since under a system of progressive taxation, the substitution effect may be larger for people with high wage rates. Also, a system of individual taxation encourages households to even out their labor income among their members, even if productivity differences as expressed by the wage rates suggest specialization. Such distortions are not incorporated in the measured hours of work per person.

Also, this measure does not catch the intensity of work or the effective hours of work. High marginal tax rates involve an incentive for employers to increase the effective wage not by increasing fully taxed wages but rather by letting people, say, make private telephone calls or go to restaurants or engage in other activities unrelated to work during their reported hours of work. More generally, high marginal taxation of labor income discriminates against all types of organizational changes (in a very broad sense) that promote production. With a current marginal tax on labor income of about 70 percent, the benefit to the employer of an increase in effort must be three or four times the after-tax compensation required by the worker in order to be implemented. Analogously, the employer and employee directly involved carry only 30 percent of a productivity decline associated with a corresponding decline in gross labor earnings. Such effects on labor supply, measured in terms of efficient labor per hours of work, may be important.

Keeping these limitations in mind, I now turn to consider the three methods used to examine the effects of taxation on labor supply, measured as hours of work per person.

The most challenging piece of evidence presented in the chapter involves a comparison of the trend in labor supply in Sweden and the United States for 1963–81. Hours of work for each person aged twenty-five or older fell by 17 percent in Sweden and by 2 percent in the United States. During the same period, total labor taxes as a share of GDP increased by 19.5 percentage points in Sweden and by 8 percentage points in the United States. Can the excess 15 percentage points of decline in labor supply in Sweden be due to the extra 11.5 percentage points of increase in labor taxes? (The difference is somewhat smaller, 12 percentage points, for persons aged 25 to 65.)

Burtless discusses this question briefly, and argues that two additional factors may help explain the more rapid decline in labor supply in Sweden. First, real wages and real incomes were higher in the United States in the initial year, 1963, which may contribute to a lower initial level of hours. Second, labor force participation by older U.S. men was initially well below the levels in Sweden. Apparently, these two observations provide Burtless a rationale for adjusting the 15 percentage point discrepancy to a 7 to 12 percentage point discrepancy that is attributed to faster tax increases in Sweden.

My main objection here is that Burtless provides no convincing empirical basis for this adjustment. If real gross wages have grown faster in Sweden, this can be measured and the likely quantitative importance could be discussed based on different values for the wage elasticity of labor supply. The potential quantitative importance of an initial difference in the labor force participation of older men could also have been examined.

In addition, factors likely to act in the opposite direction could have been picked by anyone who wanted to provide larger rather than smaller numbers. Unemployment increased much less in Sweden than in the United States during this period, which suggests that labor supply decreased relatively more.

The second type of evidence Burtless uses is taken from cross-section estimates and simulations for Sweden. The most advanced econometric study is Sören Blomquist's estimate of the labor supply for married men. His study suggests that the income tax reduces their labor supply by 12 percent of which 6 percent is due to the progressive features of the tax system. Since the labor supply of men is normally found to be much less sensitive to wage rates than that of women, this represents a fairly large effect.

Burtless also cites some simulation studies by Stuart published in 1981 and by me and Stuart published in 1985. He is critical of the weak empirical basis of Stuart's first paper, and I (and Stuart) agree; indeed this was the major reason for our second paper. An earlier, but unfortunately too long, version of the latter paper included some results that would be relevant here. The experiment was to replace the actual tax rates in 1979 by the tax rate of 1965 for 1979 preconditions and calculate the two general equilibrium solutions. According to these calculations, the tax hikes from 1965 to 1979 have decreased labor supply in the taxed sector by 15 to 20 percent.

The lower bound of this interval is approximately equal to the decrease in actual hours of work per person during this period. As Burtless notes, this model uses U.S. and British estimates on labor supply because of the few available estimates for Sweden. If Blomquist's estimates had been used in the model, the magnitude of the simulated decline in labor supply would have increased.

Burtless obtains a third piece of evidence from annual time series data on supply for 1963–82. But the specification incorporates no virtual-income variable, in conflict with standard theory. Also, standard econometric problems arise since it is a single-equation model. Furthermore, it is doubtful that each single year really represents an equilibrium for labor supply. I think that the responses are slow and that temporary involuntary underemployment and overemployment are important here.

In spite of these problems, Burtless's results deserve serious consideration, especially since they are so inconsistent with the earlier reported results. Income and social security tax increases between 1963 and 1983 are estimated to have actually increased labor supply, essentially from backward-bending labor curves. This result may partly be caused by the absence of a virtual-income variable that could have captured the disincentive effects of increased transfers and increased progressivity. Anyhow, the results are a sharp contrast to those reported earlier and, again, emphasize that the evidence is quite mixed.

In his summary, Burtless puts only modest emphasis on the time series estimation, and I share this judgment. Instead, he concludes that Swedish labor supply is substantially lower than it would be if tax burdens and government spending were closer to the U.S. situation. The evidence suggests that a best guess of the net effect of tax hikes in Sweden since the early 1960s would be in the range of 10 to 15 percent, in spite of the opposite results from the reported time-series estimate. I agree with Burtless that this best guess is associated with a high degree of uncertainty and that further empirical work is required to reduce the sources of error.

7

Rethinking the Role of the Public Sector

EDWARD M. GRAMLICH

SWEDEN has one of the most extensive welfare states in the world. By 1982 the consolidated expenditures of all levels of government amounted to two-thirds of the country's GDP. Public expenditures covered all the usual items—defense, police and fire protection, schools, roads, health, unemployment insurance, old-age pensions, and occupational injuries. Expenditures also covered many items that would raise eyebrows in other countries—an extensive public employment program that guarantees near full employment, tuition-free higher education, highly subsidized public day care, large industrial subsidies to bail out failing firms, child-rearing allowances, government-paid parental leave, and many more.

Although the negative incentive effects from such a large public sector are well known and widely advertised, for years the Swedish economy grew at rapid rates, spurred by a very high ratio of investment to GDP. But beginning about 1970 the rosy statistics became harder to find. Sweden's real growth rate was sliced in half; its investment-GDP ratio fell by one-quarter. Indicators of labor mobility showed a downward trend. Anecdotal evidence of a flourishing "gray market" of activities to avoid the tax collectors became widespread. Polls reported large majorities of Swedes feeling that taxes were unfair, and there were brief tax revolts.

Swedish economists jumped on the bandwagon too. After a series of laudatory tracts on the Swedish model in the 1960s, modern bookshelves have been filled with such attention-getting titles as *The Welfare State in Crisis: The Case of Sweden,* "Work Disincentives in the Welfare State," "Emerging Arteriosclerosis of the Western Economies: Consequences for the Less Developed Countries," "The Swedish Welfare State in Trouble: Transition to Socialism or Enhancing Private Ownership," and "The Rise and Fall of the Swedish Model."[1]

Very recently signs of recovery have appeared. Since a successful devaluation in 1982, the annual growth rate of real GDP is up slightly, the government deficit has been reduced, and the share of output devoted to capital formation has increased slightly. The share of GDP devoted to government expenditures has declined, and marginal income tax rates have been cut. Is this the spring following a long Swedish winter?

In this chapter I will examine the development of Swedish budget policy and its impact on the economy. I begin with a short factual summary to show how remarkable the Swedish experiment is. In its level of public spending and commitment to full employment and income redistribution, Sweden differs dramatically from the United States and other countries in the Organization for Economic Cooperation and Development (OECD).

The second section focuses on the budget deficit: its magnitude, why it developed, and its impact on the economy. Looking backward, one sees that deficits increased, or public-sector saving decreased, because of very rapid growth in the noninvestment components of public spending from 1970 to 1982. Looking forward, one sees that Sweden now has an urgent need to increase its public-sector saving. The consequent growth in outstanding debt and interest payments is making it increasingly difficult for Sweden to control deficits.

The chapter next examines Sweden's tax system, made extensive to finance expenditures amounting to two-thirds of GDP. Sweden has a 19 percent value-added tax (VAT), a 36 percent payroll tax, a 52 percent corporate tax, a personal income tax with marginal rates rising to 70 percent, excise taxes, wealth taxes, inheritance taxes, and user fees.

1. See Per-Martin Meyerson, *The Welfare State in Crisis: The Case of Sweden,* (Stockholm: Federation of Swedish Industries, 1982); Assar Lindbeck, "Work Disincentives in the Welfare State" in *Nationalökonomische Gesellschaft Lectures 79–80* (Vienna: Manz, 1981); Assar Lindbeck, "Emerging Arteriosclerosis of the Western Economies: Consequences for the Less Developed Countries," *India International Centre Quarterly,* no. 1 (1982); Gunnar Eliasson, "The Swedish Welfare State in Trouble: Transition to Socialism or Enhancing Private Ownership," working paper (Stockholm: Industriens Utredningsinstitut, April 1984); and Erik Lundberg, "The Rise and Fall of the Swedish Model," *Journal of Economic Literature,* vol. 23 (March 1985), pp. 1–36.

With so many taxes imposed at such high rates on so many forms of activity, it is hard to see how public-sector saving could be increased by raising taxes further, as is advocated for the United States. But modest changes could definitely improve the Swedish revenue system. Since interest deductions outweigh taxable capital income, Sweden manages to lose revenue by taxing capital income. One way to increase public-sector saving would be to limit these interest deductions. Another change that would increase economic efficiency without obvious cost in terms of equity would be to shift revenues from the income tax to the VAT.

The next section examines expenditures. Given the infeasibility of increasing public-sector saving, these spending programs are examined with an eye to seeing which ones could be cut without serious equity problems. The most eligible programs in this sense are subsidies for low-cost consumption, transfers to failing firms, certain kinds of social insurance transfers, and various types of grants to local governments. In aggregate, possible cutbacks in these eligible programs add up to much more than a generous estimate of the public-sector saving deficiency. In a word, Sweden can resolve its public-sector saving deficiency entirely on the spending side, with an increase in economic efficiency and no obvious losses in equity.

Overview

A central government, some social insurance funds financed through payroll taxes, and a large number of local government units provide Sweden's public services. The central government carries responsibility for national defense and transfers to households, firms, and local governments. The social security funds, which finance retirement, unemployment, and health insurance payments, are often shown separately from the other central government funds in budgetary presentations.

Sweden is divided into 23 counties, covering the entire country except Gothenburg, Malmö, and the island of Gotland. These counties are responsible for providing medical services (though there is a small group of private doctors). Two hundred and eighty municipalities have responsibility for most other public services—education, nursing homes, day care, housing allowances, relief aid, transportation, sewage, and various cultural and recreational facilities. As recently as 1950 there were 2,500

Table 7-1. *Tax and Spending Levels for the Consolidated Government Sector, 1982*
Billions of kronor

Item	Central	Social security funds	Local	Total
Expenditures	241.8	46.4	134.6	422.8
Consumption	52.2	2.8	130.5	185.5
Investment	5.6	. . .	18.8	24.4
Interest	37.7	−19.4	. . .	18.3
Grants, local	44.0	. . .	−44.0	. . .
Grants, social security	5.4	−5.4	. . .	. . .
Transfers	97.0	68.4	29.4	194.6
Revenues	182.4	65.0	135.6	383.0
Direct taxes	41.2	. . .	97.4	138.6
Indirect taxes	89.4	. . .	. . .	89.4
Social security contribution	29.1	57.5	. . .	86.6
Other	22.6	7.5	38.2	68.3
Net financial saving	−59.4	18.6	1.0	−39.8
Addendum: contribution to capital formation	−53.8	18.6	19.8	−15.4

Source: Ministry of Finance, *The Swedish Budget* (Stockholm, various years).

municipalities, but the central government has forced them to consolidate to their present number. With these mergers have come increased responsibilities—in 1950 local governments accounted for about half of Sweden's public consumption; today they account for three-quarters.

Some numerical detail is given in table 7-1, showing tax and spending levels for the three types of government bodies in 1982, the year when both expenditures and the budget deficit peaked as a share of GDP. For the consolidated governmental sector, expenditures totaled about Skr 423 billion (a krona is worth about $0.13), two-thirds of Sweden's GDP. The central government makes most of the transfers (including social security); the local governments account for most of the public consumption and investment. The central government still levies most of the taxes, the only significant local tax being a proportional individual income tax at a rate that averages 30 percent.

Although many of the social welfare programs date from the turn of the century, most of the growth in spending has occurred within the last two decades.[2] As late as 1960, just before a new contributory old-age

2. The development of the Swedish welfare state is discussed in Lundberg, "Rise and Fall of the Swedish Model."

Figure 7-1. *Total Public Expenditures as a Percent of Gross Domestic Product, Selected Countries of the Organization for Economic Cooperation and Development, 1960 and 1981*[a]

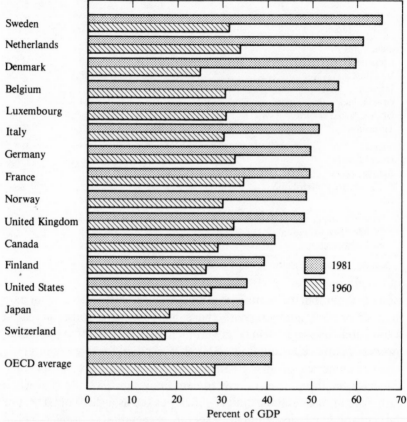

Source: Organization for Economic Cooperation and Development, *Historical Statistics 1960–1982* (Paris: OECD, 1984), p. 64, table 6.5.

a. Total expenditures include current disbursements plus gross capital formation and purchases of land and intangible assets. Luxembourg expenditures shown at 1980 level (1981 level not available). Switzerland expenditures include current disbursements only.

pension plan was introduced, Sweden's public expenditures were only 31 percent of GDP, roughly average for OECD countries (see figure 7-1). From then until the early 1980s the public sector grew rapidly. While it is claimed that part of the reason for the rapid growth in the public spending share is that GDP growth slowed in the 1970s, the main reason is the straightforward one that public spending just grew at extraordinary rates during this period. By 1981 the share of GDP devoted

Table 7-2. *Consolidated General Government Accounts for Sweden and the United States, 1983*
Percent of GDP

Expenditures	Sweden	United States	Difference
Total	61.0	36.4	24.6
Consumption	28.5	19.3	9.2
Defense	3.0	6.8	−3.8
Health[a]	7.3	1.2	6.1
Welfare	4.9	0.7	4.2
Education[b]	5.9	4.7	1.2
Other	7.4	5.9	1.5
Social security	14.8	7.8	7.0
Subsidies	5.2	0.7	4.5
Other transfers	5.6	4.5	1.1
Net interest	1.9	3.0	−1.1
Net investment[c]	5.0	1.1	3.9

Source: Author's calculations based on Organization for Economic Cooperation and Development, *National Accounts, 1971–1983*, vol. 2: *Detailed Tables* (Paris: OECD, 1985).
a. In total public and private spending for health, the United States outspends Sweden, 9.9 percent of gross domestic product (GDP) versus 8.2 percent of GDP.
b. In total public and private spending for education, the United States outspends Sweden, 6.0 percent of GDP versus 5.9 percent of GDP.
c. Investment here includes depreciation expense because the *National Accounts* do not elsewhere include depreciation as a current expense.

to public spending had become higher than for any other OECD country, 24 percentage points above the OECD average, 30 percentage points above that in the United States.

To see how meaningful the differences are, table 7-2 provides a comparison of public expenditures for Sweden and the United States for 1983.[3] The gross difference, equal to 24.6 percent of GDP, illustrates the disparate approaches to public policy in the two countries, with Sweden obviously much more inclined to finance services publicly and to provide a wider range of transfer payments.

To interpret the table, one should keep two special factors in mind. On the one hand, as a percentage of GDP the United States spends more on national defense than does Sweden. In this sense, the table underestimates proclivities for public spending—were Sweden saddled with a defense burden as large as that of the United States (as a percentage of GDP), its public sector would no doubt be even larger than it now is. On the other hand, the apparent difference in health spending overstates the

3. The data are compiled on a common basis by the Organization for Economic Cooperation and Development. There are slight discrepancies between these numbers and those published by the governments of both Sweden and the United States.

true difference. In Sweden virtually all health spending is financed by the public sector, while in the United States private health insurance bears most of the costs. But even though private health insurance is important in the United States, many of the supposed advantages (care provided below cost to the poor and aged) and disadvantages (inadequate incentives to economize on care) of public provision of health care seem as prevalent in the United States as in Sweden. As the footnote to table 7-2 suggests, the share of GDP devoted to spending on health is even higher in the United States.

In other areas, however, the data indicate real differences in approach between the two countries. While total spending on education as a share of GDP is again almost identical in the two countries, the United States finances less of it in the public sector. Spending on welfare and social security is proportionately much higher in Sweden because of a stronger commitment to income redistribution. Subsidies are also a much more significant component of the budget. The most striking difference between the two countries is the emphasis in Sweden on expenditure programs that reflect strong concerns about equity. Two fundamental objectives have guided development of the so-called Swedish model from the beginning: full employment and income redistribution.

The Swedes have constructed an ambitious set of labor market programs, public employment programs, and regulations to hold down unemployment. Since World War II "open" or official unemployment has never been very high in Sweden. It averaged less than 2 percent between 1960 and 1980, and only lately has it risen to 3 percent—still only 40 percent of the average OECD unemployment rate for 1983. However, the official unemployment rate is held down by a wide range of labor market programs, such as relief work, sheltered workshops, and vocational training. In 1983, while 150,000 workers were reported as unemployed (3.5 percent of the labor force), another 165,000 (3.9 percent) were enrolled in these labor market programs. The cost of the labor market programs in 1983 was about 4 percent of GDP. An additional 1 percent of GDP was paid out in unemployment compensation, and another 2 percent in industrial subsidies to prevent unemployment.[4] It is certainly unique for a country to devote resources on this scale to ensuring full employment.

The Swedish commitment to income redistribution is even more

4. Jan Johannesson and Inga Persson-Tanimura, *Labour Market Policy under Reconsideration* (Stockholm: Arbetsmarknadsdepartementet, 1984), pp. 11, 14, 47.

remarkable. The importance of this objective is most evident in the statistics on the distribution of income. A Lorenz curve–Gini coefficient calculation does not show complete equality for Sweden; but as Assar Lindbeck points out, the standard way of presenting the figures is misleading when the tax-transfer system is as focused on vertical inequities as it is in Sweden.[5] Lorenz curves and Gini coefficients rank households from bottom to top based on whatever income concept is being studied: factor income, disposable income, or some other. In Sweden the redistribution is so extensive that it totally rearranges households in the income distribution. Although equality is not perfect when all these public rearrangements have been made, there is also relatively little correspondence between pre- and postpolicy incomes. The income redistribution policies eliminate much of the vertical inequality but then introduce some horizontal inequality.[6] In such a case, it is only meaningful to examine distribution measures when families are ranked by their original factor income. To begin with, the system of "solidaristic" wage bargaining, described in chapter 5 in this volume, results in a more equal distribution of factor incomes, even before taxes and transfers come into play, than in the United States. But figure 7-2 shows that taxes and transfers also do significant equalizing. Households in the bottom decile have essentially no factor income, in the second decile a slight amount, and in the top decile sixty-six times as much as in the second decile.[7] Taxes and transfers bring the ratio of the top to the second decile down to 4 to 1. Since the number of earners (and consumers) for each household rises with income, it may be more meaningful to do the calculations for each consumer unit. When this is done, the ratio becomes 2.2 to 1.

Many further adjustments could be made. Since individuals in the lower-income groups spend less time working, Lindbeck does a further calculation in terms of hours of work and reaches the remarkable conclusion that the hourly wage rate, after adjusting for taxes and transfers, declines in the upper-income brackets.[8] Another study that

5. Assar Lindbeck, "Interpreting Income Distributions in a Welfare State: The Case of Sweden," *European Economic Review* (May 1983), pp. 227–56.
6. Vertical equity refers to the after-tax incomes of individuals with different pretax incomes; horizontal equity refers to the after-tax incomes of individuals with equal pretax incomes.
7. This distribution is heavily influenced by the inclusion of the retired, who have little or no factor income.
8. Lindbeck, "Interpreting Income Distributions," p. 253.

Figure 7-2. *Income Distribution in Sweden, Deciles of Factor
Income, 1979*

Thousands of kronor

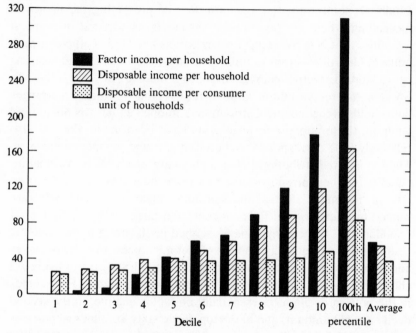

Source: Assar Lindbeck, "Interpreting Income Distributions in a Welfare State: The Case of
Sweden," *European Economic Review* (May 1983), p. 232.

attempts to take account of the distributional benefits of government
consumption programs showed even more equalizing tendencies.[9]

Whether one examines Sweden from the point of view of its high level
of public expenditures, commitment to full employment, or extensive
degree of equalizing tax and spending measures, the natural question
that arises is whether too much economic efficiency is being sacrificed
for the sake of the equity goals. What are the costs of the Swedish welfare
state?

Deficits

When public expenditures rise rapidly and hit high levels, budget
deficits often result. It is, after all, easier to administer to voters the

9. Thomas Franzen, Kerstin Lövgren, and Irma Rosenberg, "Redistributional Effects
of Taxes and Public Expenditures in Sweden," *Swedish Journal of Economics,* vol. 77,
no. 1 (1975), pp. 31–55.

sugar of public services than the salt of taxes. Indeed, referring again to table 7-1, Sweden clearly has a budget deficit problem. In 1982 the net financial deficit of the central government reached Skr 59 billion, 9.5 percent of GDP; and despite the recent efforts to reduce it, the deficit was 5.7 percent of GDP in 1985.

During the 1970s the growth of the budget deficit was defended on the grounds that fiscal stimulus was required to maintain employment, and concern about unemployment continues to inhibit efforts to reduce deficits. It may be a mistake, however, to place so much emphasis on the employment benefits of large budget deficits. One reason is that in modern, open economies, fiscal policy has very weak impacts on aggregate demand. For a small country such as Sweden it is not clear whether large deficits will raise, lower, or leave unchanged unemployment, inflation, and interest rates. Furthermore, continuous structural budget deficits will ultimately result in a lower national saving rate, less Swedish-owned capital stock, and lower Swedish living standards.[10] Hence any short-term employment benefits of large and continuing government deficits are likely to be offset by their longer-term adverse impact on the accumulation of wealth in the Swedish economy.[11] The numbers in table 7-1 can be rearranged to show this impact better.

First, on a consolidated basis the government deficit is smaller than that of the central government deficit alone because the trust funds have a consistent surplus. Thus the consolidated deficit in 1982 was Skr 40 billion compared with a central government deficit of Skr 59 billion.[12] Second, some of the Swedish expenditures go for public-sector capital

10. These statements follow what are by now standard postulates in the macroeconomics literature. The point about short-term open economies follows a model first laid out by Robert A. Mundell, "Capital Mobility and Stabilization Policy under Fixed and Flexible Exchange Rates," *Canadian Journal of Economics and Political Science,* vol. 29 (November 1963), pp. 475–85. The observation about long-term effects follows a whole series of models of the economic growth process by Robert M. Solow. Paul N. Courant and Edward M. Gramlich summarize the entire argument in "Fiscal Responsibility: The Nerds are Right," in *The Economic Outlook for 1985: Papers Presented to the Economic and Social Outlook Conference* (Ann Arbor: University of Michigan, 1984), pp. 325–70.

11. In keeping with the improved performance on budget deficits, the official rhetoric on economic goals now contains a much stronger statement linking budget deficits to reduced capital formation. See, for example, Ministry of Finance, *The Swedish Budget, 1986–87* (Stockholm, 1986), pp. 7–12.

12. In fact, it was even slightly less than this amount, for Swedish budgets do not correct for capital gains on government debt when exchange rates change. I have not made this correction either because, to be consistent, one must also recompute interest payments for capital gains with domestic inflation, as in Robert Eisner and Paul J. Pieper, "A New View of the Federal Debt and Budget Deficits," *American Economic Review,* vol. 74 (March 1984), pp. 11–29.

formation. The government's contribution to capital formation is more accurately measured by excluding public investment from the measure of government expenditure. When this is done, the deficit for 1982 is much smaller—Skr 15.4 billion, or 2.5 percent of GDP.

The focus on a single year, however, ignores the historical importance of the government as a major source of saving in the Swedish economy. The government's contribution is most evident within the national income accounting identity, by which economywide gross investment, public and private, must equal the sum of private saving, foreign capital inflow, and the government's contribution to capital formation. In symbols,

$$(7\text{-}1) \qquad\qquad I + I_g = S + (M - X) + (T_g - C_g),$$

where I is gross private investment, I_g is gross public investment, S is gross private saving, $M - X$ is the current account foreign trade deficit, or the net inflow of capital from foreign sources, T_g is all taxes less all transfers, C_g is public consumption, and $T_g - C_g$ is the government's contribution to capital formation.

In figure 7-3 these magnitudes are plotted for 1950 through 1985. The top line shows gross fixed public and private investment, the left side of equation 1, as a share of GDP. Both the numerator and denominator are measured in constant 1980 dollars; inventory investment has been removed from the investment series to eliminate erratic movements. The bottom line shows the government contribution to capital formation, the number in the bottom righthand corner of table 7-1.[13] As is made clear by equation 7-1, the difference between the top line $(I + I_g)$ and the bottom line $(T_g - C_g)$ equals the sum of private saving (S) and foreign capital inflows $(M - X)$.

Figure 7-3 illustrates three, or perhaps two and a half, broad epochs of change in the Swedish economy. From 1950 to 1967 the share of GDP devoted to capital formation generally increased from 18.7 percent to a peak of 24.8 percent. At that point, things went into reverse, and the share dropped back to 18.5 percent by 1982. The share recovered to 19.5 percent in 1985.

Most important, figure 7-3 highlights the strong correlation between

13. Because there is no available price deflator for total government expenditures and taxes, government's contribution to capital formation is measured as net financial saving in nominal terms divided by gross domestic product (GDP) in nominal terms, plus the ratio of real public investment to real GDP.

Figure 7-3. *Gross Investment and Government Contribution to Capital Formation Relative to GDP, 1950–85*

Percent of GDP

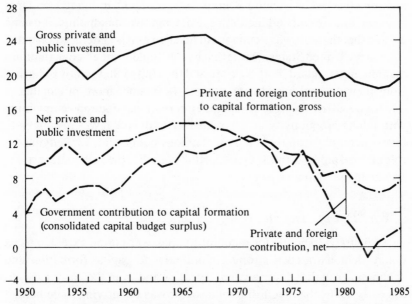

Source: Ekonomifakta Databank (1985); and Hans Tson Söderström, "Imbalances in the Swedish Economy from a Financial Perspective," *Skandinaviska Enskilda Banken Quarterly Review*, no. 2 (1984), p. 47.

domestic investment and fiscal policy. The government's contribution to capital formation was 3.9 percent of GDP in 1950, 12.8 percent in the peak investment year of 1971, −2.5 percent in 1982, and has now recovered to 3.6 percent in 1985. When the government contributed more, as it did in the 1950–70 and 1982–85 periods, net investment as a share of output rose. When the government contributed less, as it did from 1970 to 1982, the net investment share fell. In this period Sweden followed a progressively more consumption-oriented fiscal policy, diverting resources from future-oriented investment and toward present-oriented consumption.[14]

14. The correlations are not perfect for several reasons well known in the macro-economics literature. For one thing cyclical effects operate differently on total investment and the budget contribution. For another, depreciation allowances form a component of gross investment but not of the budget contribution. Third is the open economy offset—as the budget contribution rises, foreign capital flows out and the current account trade deficit decreases. A fourth is the interest effect—as the budget contribution rises,

Of course, the key question here is whether it was appropriate to divert resources from investment to consumption, as was done in Sweden in the 1970s and the United States in the 1980s. The question is hard to answer objectively because it involves a trade-off in living standards between the present and the future. But from two standpoints, it can be argued that the shift was as unwise in Sweden as it is generally conceded to be in the United States. One is that by the "golden-rule" consumption-maximizing standard, both Sweden and the United States moved farther from their optimal investment ratios.[15] A second, more pragmatic, is that for countries trying to compete in international trade and contending with falling productivity, it is not healthy to devote fewer resources to investment, particularly in high-technology equipment. Remedying the role of fiscal policy in this saving shortfall underlies the policy suggestions I make in the following pages.

Why Did the Deficits Rise?

As figure 7-3 shows, for much of the postwar period Swedish fiscal policy demonstrated a strong commitment to capital formation and economic growth.[16] Over a twenty-year period from the early 1950s to the early 1970s the Swedish public sector was the driving force behind an accelerating rate of capital formation. If nothing else, this record puts the lie to the claim that countries with large public sectors are intrinsically unable to generate capital.

But things did fall apart in Sweden in the early 1970s. The 1972–82 period was a disaster for the government's contribution to capital formation; twenty years of increased accumulation was more than undone in only ten. The turnaround in the mid-1980s has managed to restore only about one-third of what was lost in the prior decline.

The enormous expansion of government expenditures stands out as the most evident cause of the growth in the budget deficit. From 1970 to 1982, when deficits grew, nominal GDP grew at an annual rate of 10.8 percent. But as table 7-3 shows, those government expenditures that do

---

interest rates fall and there is less private saving. A fifth is the Ricardian equivalence effect—as the budget contribution rises, farsighted and altruistic households may save less.

15. The golden-rule standard, if maintained for a long period, leads to the highest standard of living in a country. Edmund S. Phelps worked out the logic of the rule. See "The Golden Rule of Accumulation: A Fable for Growthmen," *American Economic Review,* vol. 51 (September 1961), pp. 638–43.

16. In doctrine as well as in fact. One early Social Democratic deputy finance minister who worried much about growth and capital formation was Dag Hammarskjöld.

Table 7-3. *Growth in Swedish Public Consumption Expenditures, Selected Years and Periods, 1970–86*

				Annual growth rate	
Expenditures	1970	1982	1986	1970–82	1982–86
	Billions of kronor				
Expenditures detracting from capital formation	64.3	398.4	562.2	15.2	8.6
Local government consumption	22.9	130.5	187.1	14.5	9.0
Central government transfers, households	11.6	61.6	82.4	13.9	7.3
Central government transfers, business	2.3	31.0	34.8	21.7	2.9
Social security transfers	6.0	68.4	108.8	20.3	11.6
Interest	1.2	18.3	36.5	22.7	17.3
All other	20.3	88.6	112.6	12.3	6.0
	Percent of GDP				
Expenditures detracting from capital formation	37.3	63.5	61.1	4.4	1.0
Local government consumption	13.3	20.8	20.3	3.7	0.6
Central government transfers, households	6.7	9.8	9.0	3.2	2.1
Central government transfers, business	1.3	4.9	3.8	11.1	6.4
Social security transfers	3.5	10.9	11.8	9.5	2.0
Interest	0.7	2.9	4.0	11.8	8.0
All other	11.8	14.1	12.2	1.5	3.6

Source: Ministry of Finance, *The Swedish Budget,* various years.

not contribute to capital formation grew at an annual rate of 15.2 percent, rising from 37.3 percent of GDP in 1970 to a peak of 63.5 percent in 1982.

Of course, whenever deficits grow relative to GDP, there is a possibility that the "cause" will not be in excessive expenditure growth but in taxes (if tax rates have been cut) or reduced growth of GDP, which could have grown less rapidly. In Sweden, however, taxes also rose sharply, from 48 percent of GDP in 1970 to 61 percent in 1982. Yet the government contribution to capital formation still declined by 13 percent of GDP. And while the real GDP growth rate did dip by 2 percentage points after 1970, had it continued its former growth, the expenditure share would still have increased by 2.2 percent annually between 1970 and 1982, rising above 50 percent of GDP. Hence it is impossible to avoid the conclusion that the fall in capital formation occurred primarily because of the rapid rise in public noninvestment expenditures.[17]

17. One may also ask whether real noninvestment expenditures grew at a faster rate

The categories of expenditures that grew most rapidly are also shown in table 7-3. Local government consumption, central government transfers to households and business, social security transfers, and interest payments rose sharply as a share of GDP from 1970 to 1982. These five items, representing 68 percent of total expenditures in 1970, accounted for more than 90 percent of the increase in the share of GDP represented by government spending.[18]

The Interest Burden

One of the five rapidly growing items in table 7-3 is the net interest payments of the consolidated public sector. These rose from 0.7 percent of GDP in 1970 to 4.0 percent of GDP in 1986. Interest payments have played a critical role in the development of the budget deficit, both because they are uncontrollable in the short run and because of the dynamics of the link between past budget deficits, the outstanding debt, and future interest payments. The cumulative buildup of debt creates the potential for explosive growth in future deficits.

The role of debt accumulation can be illustrated with a slight rearrangement of the definition of the budget deficit to separate interest expenses from other government outlays:

$$(7-2) \qquad\qquad dD = E' - T + rD,$$

where dD is the change in the outstanding debt, E' is government expenditures other than interest payments, T is taxes, and rD is the average interest rate on government debt.[19] The difference between E' and T is often referred to as the primary deficit, and it is a measure of the extent to which taxes are sufficient to cover the current level of public services. Dividing equation 7-2 by D, and rearranging terms yields

$$(7-3) \qquad\qquad \frac{dD}{D} = \frac{E'-T}{D} + r = r + z,$$

---

in the 1970s than previously. The answer is yes. From 1970 to 1982 real noninvestment spending grew by about 7 percent a year, about 25 percent faster than in the previous decade.

18. This calculation is done as follows: had noninvestment expenditures remained at 37.3 percent of GDP in 1982, they would have totaled Skr 234 billion. In fact, they totaled Skr 398 billion, an excess of Skr 164 billion. The increase in the share of GDP accounted for by the five items represented Skr 150 billion, 91.5 percent of the total.

19. This formulation ignores non-interest-bearing debt, such as money creation, but since money creation was small relative to the deficit, the simplification has no effect on the basic analytical points.

where z equals the ratio of the primary budget deficit to the outstanding debt. If Sweden's capital market is open to international flows, as it almost certainly is in the long run, the nominal interest rate on government debt can be viewed as exogenously determined by world markets.[20] In that case, elimination of the primary deficit implies that the public debt will grow at the nominal interest rate, and the interest burden relative to GDP, rD/Y will grow if the nominal rate of GDP growth falls short of the nominal interest rate.

The dynamics of the relationship between the growth in the public debt and the interest burden for 1974–84 are shown in figure 7-4.[21] The numbers are taken from a recent International Monetary Fund report on Sweden that shows consistent debt, interest rates, and interest payments since 1974.[22] The top line in figure 7-4 gives the nominal rate of growth of interest-bearing debt, the left side of equation 7-3. The growth in debt has exceeded the nominal interest rate, implying consistent primary budget deficits. However, the nominal rate of growth of GDP (dY/Y) fell below the nominal interest rate in the early 1980s. In theoretical growth models dY/Y should be less than r for countries that are undersaving, as Sweden has been in recent years. Since the growth of debt is greater than r and the rate of growth of nominal GDP is less than r, it is obvious that D/Y will rise over time. If r does not decline, the interest burden, rD/Y, will also rise. That it has can be observed by the bottom line in figure 7-4.

Figure 7-4 highlights the difficulties of bringing the budget deficit under control in Sweden. Even if it were possible to eliminate the primary budget deficit, the outstanding debt, and thus the interest burden, would continue to increase as a share of GDP because the growth of income is less than the rate of interest. In future years an increasing portion of

20. This condition is only true when Sweden's inflation rate is approximately equal to that of its major trading partners, but the impact of my simplification is slight. If nominal interest rates are given by world capital markets but they are variable, the question becomes more complicated because any induced change in r should be factored in. And if r is determined in a capital market sealed off from foreign capital flows, the question becomes still more complicated because now higher deficits might influence r, and the higher income of domestic bondholders would return new tax revenue to the Treasury.

21. All the numbers in the figure are averaged over three-year periods from 1974 to 1983 to smooth out erratic variation.

22. The report identifies Sweden as one of the countries with the worst interest payment growth problem. See Martin J. Fetherston, "Aspects of the Growth of Budgetary Interest Payments," working paper DM-85-2 (Washington, D.C.: International Monetary Fund, 1985), p. 11.

Figure 7-4. *Dynamics of Interest Growth, Three-Year Averages, 1974–84*

Percent

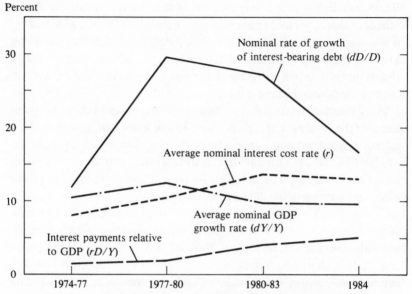

Source: Martin J. Fetherston, "Aspects of the Growth of Budgetary Interest Payments, 1974–81," working paper DM-85-2 (Washington, D.C.: International Monetary Fund, 1985), p. 11.

taxes must be diverted from financing current public services to pay interest on old debt. Were it not for the growing interest burden, Sweden's recent progress in reducing deficits would have been much more noticeable. The problem will only get worse unless the deficit is cut even further.

The Ownership Question

I have argued that Sweden's fiscal policy could be, and should be, altered to promote more capital formation. Since a high share of the requisite saving is generated by the public sector, and since Sweden has a long history of debate on the split of income shares between labor and management, it is perhaps inevitable that the issue of capital formation gets confused with the issue of ownership. If there is going to be more capital, do workers or capitalists get to own it? This issue is a red herring. There is no intrinsic reason why either group should own whatever stock of capital exists, and however this ownership issue is resolved, the debate about it should not be allowed to prevent the desired accumulation in the first place.

In principle the government's contribution to capital formation could be used in either of two ways. The government could run a surplus, retire government debt, and provide new funds for privately owned capital. Or the surplus could be used to create publicly owned capital. Indeed, at any point the government can sell or buy capital and privatize or socialize the existing stock with no impact on the national income accounts budget. Logically, the accumulation issue and the ownership issue are totally separate. Any rate of accumulation can be consistent with any ownership pattern.

Accumulation and ownership have also been totally separate in practice. Figure 7-3 shows that most of Sweden's net saving has been generated by the public sector. But most new capital has been owned by the private sector. Private investment, I, was three-quarters of total investment, $I + I_g$, in the peak years around 1970, about 78 percent in the trough year 1982, and 85 percent in 1985.

Although the issue is a red herring from both a logical and empirical standpoint, confusion over it may have done some damage. It is sometimes alleged that a political stalemate over ownership has reduced accumulation—conservatives have opposed government investment and liberals have opposed private investment. If this is so, it is a regrettable example of unresolved political disputes in the present diverting resources from the future.

Summary

While it may be stretching things to describe the growth of the budget deficit as a crisis, one cannot help but view the Swedish fiscal policy during the 1970s with some concern. In 1970 Sweden's investment share was high, its fiscal policy promoted capital formation, and there was no problem of an interest burden. In the space of a decade, all these advantages were squandered. In making budget decisions about spending, taxation and ownership, a regrettable tendency to load the costs of political disagreements onto the future recurred. Recently, Sweden has started on the road back, but the road is harder because a large potential increment to the capital stock has been lost in the meantime and because the interest burden has grown. One can admire the Swedes for making the turnaround, much more established and advanced than the still incipient U.S. fiscal turnaround, but regret that the consumption binge in both countries made the road so much harder.

Taxes

By international standards Swedish taxpayers face a truly enormous annual tax bill, 61 percent of GDP. Total revenues have grown from 24 percent of GDP in 1950 to their present level; and while the greatest growth has been in social insurance payroll taxes, all types of taxes have increased greatly as a share of GDP.

Most of the controversy over tax policy concerns the high marginal rates embedded in the income tax and the distorting influences it has had on the Swedish economy. A study by Ingemar Hansson found that the marginal rate for the average Swedish wage earner rose from 31 percent in 1955 to 55 percent by 1980 (30 percentage points of that 55 percent go to local governments).[23] Figure 7-5 provides cross-sectional estimates of marginal tax rates that vary between 30 percent and 70 percent for the income tax alone, between 60 percent and 70 percent when means-tested spending programs are added, and between 70 percent and 80 percent when the payroll tax and the VAT are included.[24] Marginal rates can surely not be any higher for such a large share of the population anywhere else in the world.

While marginal tax rates seem incredibly high now, a short time ago they were even higher. In 1985 the government completed a three-year tax reform package that, among other things, lowered marginal tax rates for most taxpayers. Whereas in 1982 almost half of all taxpayers faced marginal tax rates of 80 percent (and more than that when the other taxes were considered), by 1985 the share was down to 10 percent. A further reform will lower the top bracket rate to 75 percent.

Incentive Effects

The natural question that arises about these high tax rates is their effect on incentives for work, saving, paying taxes, and even living in

23. Ingemar Hansson, "Skattereformen och de Totala Marginaleffekterna," *Economisk Debatt,* no. 1 (1983), p. 19.
24. Assar Lindbeck, "How Much Politics Can Our Economy Take?" Unpublished manuscript, 1986.

Figure 7-5. *Marginal Tax Rate of Income Taxes and Benefits*
(Tenant without Income of Capital)

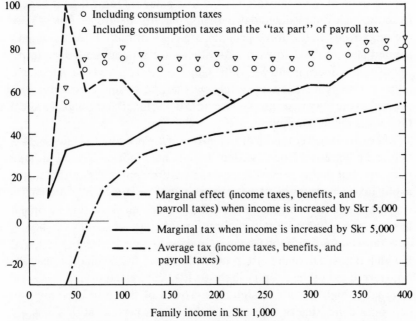

Marginal rates (%)

Family income in Skr 1,000

Source: Assar Lindbeck, "How Much Politics Can Our Economy Take?" Unpublished manuscript, 1986.

Sweden. As Gary Burtless points out in chapter 6, the effect on labor supply is complex because of offsetting provisions in the tax laws. The antiwork provisions, by and large, come into full force for those workers already in the labor force. The high marginal tax rates that emerge from the tax and transfer system do discourage long hours of work. The average number of hours worked each year is low in Sweden compared with hours worked in the United States. The disincentives are also reflected in increased absenteeism. Between the early 1960s and the late 1970s, paid absenteeism increased from 8 percent to 14 percent for male employees, from 11 percent to 18 percent for females, and from 14 percent to 28 percent for women with children under seven years of age.[25] Furthermore, all firms must grant five weeks of vacation. There

25. Lindbeck, "Work Disincentives in the Welfare State," p. 48.

may be many other subtle effects on intensity of work, willingness to gamble on a new profession or work in a new region, and so forth.

But along with these disincentives are very strong incentives for people to be in the labor force in the first place. Parents do not benefit from the highly subsidized day care and parents' insurance unless both are employed. Labor force programs make it attractive for the handicapped and disabled to work. And there are programs for teenagers. Spouses considering entry into the labor force are given one additional fillip—earnings are taxed separately, with an added child-care deduction, to prevent the lower-earning spouse from being taxed at the high marginal rate of the higher-earning spouse.

There are other potential disincentives. One possibility is that of tax-induced emigration from Sweden. People have not emigrated in large numbers, but that is partly because the government makes it difficult to avoid taxes by leaving. It is presumed that an emigrant's income is subject to tax for five years, unless the person can show that he or she has no strong link to Sweden, such as relatives or a summer home. Several well-known public figures, however, have emigrated to avoid the high taxes. There are also reports that up to Skr 3 billion a year are transferred out of the country in the form of capital exports.

Finally, high taxes can stimulate growth of the gray economy, an economy consisting of transactions that are either illegal or semilegal and are inspired by the desire to avoid taxation. If the size of the gray economy could be easily measured, taxes could be collected on it, so it is almost intrinsic that estimates of its size will range widely. Many believe it is not very large. Tax cheating is difficult in Sweden because all returns are audited, income and payroll tax returns are compared, and individuals' social security numbers are used in almost all transactions—for bank loans, rent contracts, subscriptions, and so forth.

But some economists have come up with larger estimates that challenge the conventional wisdom. One is based on a theoretical model built by Ingemar Hansson.[26] Hansson has two sectors, one producing measured (taxable) and the other unmeasured (untaxed) output, with taxes causing resources to flow from the former to the latter. In equilibrium, after-tax earnings are equal in the two sectors; but because of the tax wedge, the productivity of factors is higher in the taxed sector.

26. Ingemar Hansson, "Marginal Cost of Public Funds for Different Tax Instruments and Government Expenditures," *Scandinavian Journal of Economics,* vol. 86, no. 2 (1984), pp. 115–30.

Hansson then inserts parameters in the model that fit Swedish data in 1979 for all observable variables and elasticities, the key ones being the response of labor supply to after-tax wages and the response of capital (saving) to after-tax interest rates. His model implies that Swedish income tax rates are very close to the point at which a further increase in rates actually reduces tax revenue because of the shift of output to the gray economy.

A second empirical attempt to measure the gray economy comes from Edgar Feige.[27] He notes that despite the growth of a very advanced mechanism for settling accounts in Sweden, currency demand has increased sharply since 1972 (before then it had fallen, when controlled for other independent factors). He then develops a model to estimate how much this unexplained rise would have raised effective transactions in the quantity theory identity, arriving at a residual of about 25 percent of GDP. While there is no direct proof that the residual is entirely or even largely caused by the growing gray economy, Feige makes the attribution. Given the differences in productivity between the measured and unmeasured sectors, Feige's estimate implies that even more than 25 percent of resources, as opposed to output, is employed in the underground economy.[28]

Whatever the accuracy of these estimates, much productive activity could be diverted from the market either to illegal activities or to legal but less productive, or at least untaxed, activities. Rather than relying on comparative advantage and working in the market in their most productive professions, Swedish workers have a powerful incentive to work for themselves as, for example, household repair persons. Impersonal transactions such as household repairs are thus diverted from the market to the home. Lindbeck cannot resist pointing out that what goes with this is a movement of very personal activities such as child rearing from the home to subsidized public services, a bizarre possible manifestation of the welfare state.[29]

Because of this diversion, Hansson's model suggests that a clear gain in economic efficiency would result from reducing the maximum marginal

27. Edgar L. Feige, "The Swedish Payments System and the Underground Economy" (Stockholm: Industriens Utredningsinstitut [Industrial Institute for Economic and Social Research], 1985).
28. No allowance of this magnitude is made for underground activity in the Swedish national accounts. Thus, by implication, Feige believes that the standard of living in Sweden is even higher than that implied by international comparisons of GDP per capita.
29. Lindbeck, "Work Disincentives in the Welfare State," pp. 44–45.

tax rate from, say, 80 percent to 50 percent. The estimates of revenue loss are not large, only about Skr 5 billion to Skr 7 billion, and the revenue could be recovered with a rise in the VAT rate to 20.5 percent. While there would be a loss of vertical redistribution for those now in the tax base, the figures indicate that overall redistribution would still be extensive.

Finally, another kind of redistribution should be considered—between the evaders not in the tax base and those unwilling or unable to evade. When evaders earn income in the gray market and spend in the real market, they pay only the VAT rate of 19 percent. When full taxpayers earn income they are subject to tax rates of 70 to 80 percent. If marginal income tax rates were reduced and the VAT increased, the gap between the two groups would be reduced and the tax system would be much fairer.[30]

Capital Income

Sweden now taxes income from capital in several ways. In the personal income tax, capital income received by high-income families is added to the income of the highest-earning spouse and taxed at that marginal rate. At lower ranges capital income is treated just like labor income. As in the United States, nominal income from dividends and interest is fully taxable, and 40 percent of nominal income from long-term capital gains is taxable. The rules for interest deductions are complicated; most interest income is now deductible, but only at a maximum rate of 50 percent. In one interesting contrast to U.S. procedures, Sweden taxes the imputed income from owner-occupied homes, though at a low rate. Most homeowners are assumed to earn imputed income equal to 2 percent of their homes' value, with a higher rate being used for expensive houses.

Sweden has a corporate tax that looks much like that in the United States. As in the United States, it does not raise very much revenue (only 1 percent of GDP in recent years). Corporations pay the national tax at a 52 percent rate, but, after a recent change, no local corporate

30. A recent paper by Jonathan R. Kesselman discusses all of this with regard to Australia where similar suggestions have been made. See "The Role of the Tax Mix in Tax Reform," paper prepared for the Conference on Changing the Tax Mix, Monash University, Melbourne, Australia, 1985. Kesselman points out that the horizontal equity claim is overstated if the flow into evading activities lowers returns there (though of course there would still be an efficiency gain from raising the VAT).

tax. Firms are allowed to deduct dividends on new shares for twenty years following the new issue to reduce the double taxation of income from dividends. Historical cost accounting is used to measure both capital gains from inventory and capital depreciation. But to prevent inflation-induced increases in tax rates, firms are allowed to deduct up to 60 percent of the value of inventories purchased, and as in the United States accelerated depreciation rules are generous.

The Swedish tax system has other interesting components. An investment fund system is intended to stabilize investment over the business cycle. Each year a firm can deduct up to half of its taxable profits for an investment fund, depositing half this amount interest-free at the Central Bank and being allowed to use the other half for any purpose. The central government then releases these investment funds in recessions, and firms are allowed to withdraw funds equally from the Central Bank and non-Central Bank reserve for investments.

A second component affects Sweden's wealth tax. Individuals are taxed on their wealth at nominal rates that go from 1 percent at the bottom to 2.5 percent at the top. The wealth tax is not deductible within the income tax. There is also a tax on inheritances and gifts.

In the aggregate, taxes on labor income totaled 49 percent of GDP in 1982. In contrast, aggregate taxes on capital barely yield positive revenues, only 1 percent of GDP. The corporate income tax brings in 1 percent of GDP, and the personal income tax on capital income actually loses as much revenue as wealth and inheritance taxes gain. The net tax on capital income is low because firms and individuals deduct interest expenses at high rates while most of the interest income accrues to tax-exempt institutions. In addition, individuals are able to borrow funds, deduct the interest expenses at high marginal tax rates, and invest the proceeds in lightly taxed assets such as housing and capital gains. One striking result is that the government would actually gain revenue by not taxing the capital income of individuals, provided that the interest deduction was also eliminated.

Despite the low overall tax on capital income generated within Sweden, the income tax imposes a large penalty on the incentive for households to save. Users of borrowed funds receive generous tax deductions, while savers must pay large taxes on interest and dividend income. This is particularly true when inflation is high because the income tax base is not indexed. In recent years there have been attempts to promote saving by creating accounts in which taxes on interest are deferred. As with U.S. individual retirement accounts, however, individuals are not prevented from shifting previously existing assets into these accounts, and they do not necessarily add to personal saving at the margin. Moreover, because of the interest deduction, it is possible to borrow funds to deposit in the tax-free account, claim an interest deduction, and hence thwart the purpose of the tax deferral.

On the investment side, the most salient feature of the Swedish tax structure is that it has a highly distorting effect on the allocation of capital. Because of the investment credit and depreciation provisions, the tax rate is lower on equipment than on structures and inventories. Because nominal interest is deductible, debt-financed investment is taxed at lower rates than new equity-financed investment. Because of the new share dividend deduction, equity-financed investments are taxed at a lower rate than investments financed from retained earnings. Because new firms cannot carry over all their eligible deductions for interest and depreciation, investment in old firms is subsidized more than investment in new firms. All of these distortions get worse with inflation, because most capital income is not indexed. A study by Jan Södersten and Thomas Lindberg found variations in effective tax rates on different types of investment in 1980 that ranged from −52 percent to 105 percent.[31] The exact numbers and features of the tax system are different from those in the United States, but the general inefficiencies in taxing income from capital are serious in both countries.

In evaluating proposals for tax reform it is important to take account of the increasingly open structure of Swedish capital markets. If savers are free to invest in a world capital market at world rates of interest and investors are free to borrow in that same world market, wealth accumulation in Sweden depends only on the sum of private and government saving. Any changes in private investment are offset by changes in the trade balance, leaving domestic wealth accumulation unaffected even in the short run. In such a world, investment subsidies make very little sense. The government is, in effect, diverting saving that could be invested at the world real interest rate to subsidized investment in Sweden that pays less than this rate. Or it is compensating foreign savers to invest in Sweden at returns less than the world real interest rate. In

31. The results of the study can be found in Mervyn A. King and Don Fullerton, eds., *The Taxation of Income from Capital: A Comparative Study of the United States, the United Kingdom, Sweden, and West Germany* (University of Chicago Press, 1984), pp. 87–148.

general, tax-induced distortions in capital allocation generate dead-weight losses without affecting the overall supply of wealth that determines long-run living standards.[32]

In view of the undesirability of capital income subsidies, an obvious remedy would be to abolish the personal income tax on capital income, and along with it the personal interest deduction. The most extreme version of such a change would be a thoroughgoing consumption tax, and indeed that has been suggested.[33] Without repeating that proposal, which among other things requires reform of the corporate tax, there is a simpler alternative that accomplishes many of the same ends: prohibit taxpayers from deducting more interest than the amount of capital income of all sorts that they claim. According to numbers from Krister Andersson, aggregate revenue and aggregate saving would rise by about 0.5 percent of GDP under such a measure, and that estimate may understate the true effect on aggregate saving if the disappearance of arbitrage opportunities increases the impact on personal saving of the tax-deferred accounts. Andersson also shows that such a measure would improve the distribution of income because for low-income people capital income taxes exceed interest deductions, while for high-income people it is the reverse, particularly for the very rich.[34]

Summary

Four major conclusions emerge from this brief overview of the Swedish tax system. First, the taxation of labor income has increased to the point that it is imposing major costs on the economy in lost efficiency. It is distorting the allocation of labor, promoting the growth of a gray economy, and undermining public support of the tax system. These grounds alone constitute a powerful argument for continuing the rollback of marginal income tax rates.

Second, the taxation of capital income generates very little net revenue, yet it has had major distorting effects on the allocation of capital

32. There is one slight exception to this statement. High investment taxes on foreign investment could deter capital inflows. This point is likely to be relevant in a high-tax country like Sweden, because even if Swedish taxes are credited against host country taxes, they may exceed host country taxes.

33. See Sven-Olof Lodin, *Progressive Expenditure Tax—An Alternative?* Report of the 1972 Government Commission on Taxation (Stockholm: Liber Förlag, 1978).

34. Krister Andersson, "The Swedish Tax System," (University of Lund, 1986), p. 45.

among sectors of the economy. The distortions result from the failure to adjust the taxable income base for inflation, inconsistencies in the treatment of interest as an expense and as income, and tax preferences granted to specific types of investment, such as housing.

Third, Swedish policymakers need to rethink the issue of capital income taxation in what is becoming an increasingly open world capital market. In such circumstances, subsidizing investment in Sweden is inefficient in replacing foreign investments yielding higher returns with domestic investment yielding lower returns. On the other side, excess taxation of capital employed in Sweden is also counterproductive, as it drives investment abroad. There is an urgent need to undertake a thorough reform of the whole system of capital income taxation, including the corporate and individual income tax and the wealth tax.

Fourth, while tax reform is important, that reform is unlikely to yield either a significant increase in tax revenues or generate significant improvement in savings and investment. To a large extent reform will mean a shift in emphasis among different taxes, such as lower income tax rates financed by an increase in the VAT or removals of various kinds of distortions. Most significant efforts to reduce the budget deficit must focus on expenditures.

Expenditures

One could examine Sweden's extensive expenditures from a positive standpoint. Why are expenditures so high? Why have they grown so rapidly? Does either their level or growth reflect the true tastes of Swedish voters or the many types of political distortions that have been pointed out in recent years?[35] While each topic could make for a fascinating discussion, my main focus is on controlling spending. I argued earlier that deficits should be cut; I have also argued that at least certain tax rates should be cut. Hence I will not adopt the positive approach here but instead follow the more normative approach of

35. There are many such theories. Some involve the motives of bureaucrats and politicians and how these lead to growth in public consumption; some involve political bribes and how these lead to growth in either transfers or public wages. It is ironic that most theories have been developed by U.S. economists and tested, with only indifferent success, with U.S. data. One suspects that should the researchers focus on Sweden, they could claim more convincing successes for their theories.

examining the list of spending programs to find those with particularly
tenuous rationales.

In principle one should search for these dubious spending programs
everywhere on the spending side of the budget, but I will follow the
further simplification of focusing on the rapid-growth items identified in
table 7-3 as primary causes of the rising deficits. Four of these programs—
the three types of transfers and local consumption—are discretionary.
It makes sense to focus on them for possible cutbacks: they are where
the big money is, and a short time ago, when the Swedish economy was
growing more rapidly, they were much less extensive. It also turns out
that each of these programs is large by world standards.

Transfers to Households

Two of the transfers listed in table 7-3, those from the central
government and those from the social security trust funds, go to
households. These more than doubled as a share of GDP between 1970 and
1986, growing from 10.2 percent of GDP to 20.8 percent sixteen years
later. From a programmatic standpoint it makes sense to discuss the two
together, because the largest of each type of transfer is a pension payment
for the aged. From a fiscal standpoint, spending cuts will have differential
effects. The 10.9 percent of GDP devoted to social security transfers is
financed by payroll taxes paid into trust funds that have been running
surpluses. Cuts here will result in payroll tax reductions over a long
period of time, with little short-term impact on the deficit. The 9.0 percent
of GDP devoted to central government transfers to households is only
partially financed by payroll taxes of the central government. Should
spending be cut here, with no change in payroll tax rates, there will be a
cut in the deficit.

The oldest of these programs, known as the basic pension, was
enacted in 1913. Benefits are paid by the central government at a flat rate
that is now about 32 percent of average disposable income for single
people and 50 percent for couples, with this flat rate being adjusted as
income grows. On top of this basic pension there is a national supplementary pension (ATP) paid by the social insurance fund and financed
by payroll taxes on a pay-as-you-go basis. Initially, benefits were tied to
the individual's prior contributions, but in recent years the tie to prior
contributions has been frayed, and the program incorporates some

redistribution.[36] Perhaps because of this, Sweden is beginning to see growth in private pensions.

That Sweden funds the future liabilities of the ATP system through current taxes explains some of the budgetary trends discussed earlier. To qualify for the maximum ATP benefit (60 percent of pensionable income over a person's highest-paid fifteen years in the labor force), a worker has to have employer contributions made for thirty years. Hence the system does not fully reach maturity until the mid-1990s. That is also the period in which, given Sweden's demographics, the expenditures will peak as a share of GDP.[37] In the meantime, the payroll contributions are running ahead of benefit payments, and the system is in substantial surplus.

The obvious policy change recommended by those who write about pension programs in Sweden is to reduce the generosity of the system.[38] There are numerous ways in which this could be done: replacement rates could be lowered, disability provisions could be tightened, retirement ages could be raised, and the discount for early retirement could be increased. Depending on how these cuts were distributed among the programs paid for by the central government and by the social security funds, and on what was done to payroll tax rates, such changes could either cut deficits or cut payroll tax rates. In either case the changes would simultaneously increase the work incentives for older workers.

The social security fund also includes two other significant social insurance programs. One affects health insurance. Health insurance benefit payments are not very large in Sweden, only about 2.5 percent of GDP, because the main health costs occur elsewhere in the budget. The municipal governments run all the hospitals and clinics. What is meant by health insurance is thus only a payment for income losses when not working because of sickness, and for a "parental insurance" program. Both programs have obvious rationales, but neither contains any cost-cutting incentives. Tax rates under the sickness plan do not depend

36. Additional details are provided in chapter 6 in this volume. Complete descriptions of these and other programs are provided by Per Gunnar Edebalk and Åke Elmér, "Social Insurance in Sweden," in Lars Söderström, ed., Social Insurance: Papers Presented at the 5th Arne Ryde Symposium (Amsterdam: North-Holland, 1983), pp. 53–79; and Sven E. Olsson, "Welfare Programs in Sweden," in Peter Flora, ed., Growth to Limits—The West European Welfare States Since World War II (New York: W. de Gruyter, 1986).

37. Ann-Charlotte Stahlberg, "Transfereringar Mellan den Förvärvsarbetande och den Äldre Generationen" (Stockholm: Institutet för Social Forskning, 1984). See also the chapter by Gary Burtless for a more detailed discussion.

38. Ibid.

on an employer's experience, and there is no incentive for employers to police claims. The parents' insurance plan, introduced in 1974, gives payments to new parents for up to one year based on a measure of income loss for days taken off because of infant care. This is one of the programs that complicate the work incentive issue. There is a large incentive to be in the labor force and collect the benefits if one expects to become a parent.

The other major program is for unemployment insurance. The main program is financed by a payroll tax. As with the other transfers, unemployment compensation payments are taxable, and the effective replacement rate is about 85 percent of after-tax wages.[39] The most interesting features of the unemployment insurance program are the long length of the benefit period—up to sixty weeks for those less than age fifty-five and ninety weeks for those older—and again the lack of any experience rating in setting employer tax rates. There is also a small program, financed through general revenue, with much lower wage replacement rates (about 50 percent) for new and disadvantaged workers who have not worked in covered employment long enough to qualify for regular benefits.

Obvious savings could be made in this part of the budget: introducing experience rating into the tax for the unemployment and sickness plans and trimming the extremely generous parents' insurance plan. Perhaps the budget savings would be small in the short run because of the quasi-contractual nature of these benefits, but the savings would increase over time.

Transfers to Business

While household transfers grew relative to GDP, much of that growth could be explained by demographic changes and the maturation of the large Swedish pension. Transfers to business also grew sharply, from just 1.3 percent of GDP in 1970 to 4.9 percent of GDP by 1982, but without the rationales.

Slightly more than half of the total includes price subsidies, regular continuing payments to hold down the cost of some consumption item. They illustrate the tendency in Sweden to pile redistributional programs

39. Greater detail on effective tax rates is provided in Anders Björklund and Bertil Holmlund, "Unemployment Compensation in Sweden" (Stockholm: Industrial Institute for Economic and Social Research, 1984).

on top of one another—to the point that today they create horizontal inequities rather than increasing vertical equity.

One such payment is an interest subsidy for housing. Because subsidies are based on nominal interest rates, they have grown sharply (from zero in 1970), and they magnify the distortions already present in the uneven set of capital income taxes. Drugs, medical and dental care, and public transportation in Stockholm all receive hefty subsidies. And although the cost is not large, in some ways the most curious subsidy of all is for daily newspapers. The point of the subsidy is to keep alive different political points of view, a goal that, while laudable, seems grossly inconsistent with the fact that Sweden does not permit private television channels.

The other major category of business transfers has evolved out of Sweden's industrial policy: subsidies of losses, investment grants, and other special transfers for struggling firms. A large share of the subsidies went to the shipyards, steel, and forest product industries located in the sparsely populated north of Sweden, which produces for the export market. Before 1975 such subsidies were almost nonexistent. But since then the standard Swedish full-employment guarantee has apparently been supplanted by a more ambitious regional full-employment guarantee.[40] If a wage agreement, movement in terms of trade, change in technology, or something else threatens large-scale layoffs in particular firms, the government has simply bailed out the firm with large transfers. These subsidy programs became very costly, reaching 2 percent of GDP in 1982. The consequences for promoting wage discipline were harmful. The redundancy of government subsidies is again exemplified in the response to unemployment. Sweden not only has an unemployment compensation system with very complete coverage, which includes a costly and extensive set of programs for training unemployed workers and giving them public employment, but the government also bails out failing firms.

As table 7-3 shows, these transfers to business have been reduced as a share of GDP in recent years, and the magnitude of the industrial subsidies has been cut in absolute amount. Subsidies for steel plants and forestry products have disappeared entirely from the budget, subsidies for mining are down to less than Skr 0.5 billion, and the subsidies for shipbuilding, about Skr 3 billion a year, are being phased out.

40. Lundberg, "Rise and Fall of the Swedish Model."

Local Government Consumption

By most political standards Sweden's governmental system would not be described as highly decentralized. But ironically, the general level of public spending has become so large that in terms of some basic considerations, such as the importance of local spending, grants, and taxes, Sweden's local governments play a bigger role in the economy than do the local governments in other countries with much more decentralized systems.

Central government consumption of goods and services, as opposed to transfers, has declined as a share of GDP since 1970. Local consumption, now 74 percent of the total, has more than taken up the slack, being one of the main areas of spending growth identified earlier. This growth reflects a large expansion in all the domestic functions under the responsibility of local governments, even though there has been an offsetting trend within each of these functional areas to shift responsibility from local governments to the central government.[41]

Spending by local governments has not attracted the attention of Swedish economists, and very little analysis is available in English.[42] The 23 county governments make about 36 percent of the consumption expenditures, mainly to operate the large Swedish health and hospital systems, to provide some social welfare services, and occasionally to run county high schools (table 7-4). The 280 municipal governments do just about everything else—they oversee the public schools, day care centers, housing, recreation, public safety, roads, and so forth.

While consumption by local governments is now more than 20 percent of GDP, there are various ways in which the central government restricts local decisionmaking. For one thing, the central government has merged many local governments out of existence. There were 2,500 municipalities in 1950, and now there are only 280. The reason given for these combinations, worked out by city planners and geographers, was that the municipalities needed to be strengthened to take on their big responsibilities, or that there were certain economies of scale in running school systems and the like. However, in the earlier period, the many municipalities had developed extensive networks for sharing the costs

41. Richard Murray, "Central Control of the Government Sector in Sweden" (Stockholm: Industrial Institute for Economic and Social Research, 1984).
42. There are Swedish papers on this topic, but the only one I could find in English, as of now unpublished, was the one by Murray.

Table 7-4. *Local Government Consumption and Grants, 1983*[a]
Billions of kronor

Level of government	Local consumption	Grants	
		General purpose	Special purpose
Total	146.3	7.4	39.0
Municipalities[b]	93.5	4.3	31.5
Counties[c]	52.8	3.1	7.5

Source: *National Accounts, Appendix 1.*
a. Disaggregated data are not available for 1982.
b. General responsibility for education, social welfare, housing and community amenities, public safety, business promotion, culture and recreation, sewage, roads, and public utilities.
c. General responsibility for health and hospitals, with some high schools and some social welfare services.

of certain public services. It is not clear whether the resulting economies of scale have outweighed one new deadweight loss. Diverse tastes are submerged into a common level of public spending as governmental units get larger.

The next limitation on the freedom of action of local governments lies in an extensive system of mandating. Murray has calculated that about 44 percent of the expenditures of local governments are obligatory, for activities such as supporting a public school system; about 25 percent of expenditures are voluntary but in some way regulated, such as housing allowances; and the remaining activities, such as town planning, parks and recreation, and public transportation are voluntary.[43]

Finally, the central government controls the financing. Local governments cannot run deficits and can impose virtually no indirect taxes. Their revenue comes from income taxes, grants, and user fees, as table 7-1 shows. The proportional income tax raised Skr 97 billion, more than twice as much as the income tax raised for the central government. Although local governments set their own tax rate, the central government determines the tax base, collects the tax, and redistributes the revenue (with a two-year delay).[44] In recent years the central government has raised the minimum taxable income and removed corporations from the local income tax base.

43. Murray, "Central Control of the Government Sector."
44. There is one point of interest in light of the recent U.S. debate on tax reform. The U.S. federal income tax permits the deduction of state and local taxes. President Ronald Reagan proposed eliminating this deductibility as a means of broadening the tax base. The change was largely successfully resisted, in part because of fears that eliminating deductibility would reduce state and local spending. It may be reassuring to those holding such fears to note that in Sweden, where local spending exploded in recent years, local income taxes are not deductible.

Further details on Sweden's grant system are given in table 7-4. In 1983 special purpose grants constituted 84 percent of all grants; the remainder were general purpose grants. The general purpose grants are supposed to be redistributive, but, as in the United States, many question exactly how redistributive, because of problems in defining local tax bases. Since these are general purpose grants, they have no marginal effect on prices facing local governments.

The special purpose grants are given out for functions such as education and day care on a per student or per worker basis. Since they depend on numbers of students, they are not open-ended with respect to spending per student and usually have no price effect on spending for public services.[45] This is just as well because the normal justification for such grant-induced price reductions—benefit spillovers across community lines—is probably as absent in Sweden's remote communities as it is anywhere in the world.

Since the usual rationales for central government grants—externalities and community income differences—seem not to be germane in the Swedish context, one might wonder why these grants should not be cut back, perhaps drastically. Were this to be done, it might be possible to improve local decisionmaking by increasing accountability, for at least three reasons.

Rather than having outside grants finance one-third of local consumption, communities would have to foot a greater share of the bill. They would then be more economical in their use of tax dollars and more vigilant in guarding against spending programs that could not pass a public choice test. These political incentives to economize would be increased still more if localities were to start collecting their own income taxes.

The second source of greater accountability is at the level of the individual. If grants were reduced, there would be pressure either to reduce uneconomic expenditures or to increase user fees. To the extent that user fees were increased, gains would be likely in both efficiency and horizontal equity. At present, for services such as health care, day care, and nursing homes, user fees are low, and there are large and often

45. Grants are referred to as open-ended when the central government matches a constant share of local spending, thus lowering the price of those services to local government. Grants are closed-ended when central government matches local spending only up to a point and after that forces the local government to pay the entire cost of the added service. I am arguing here that both types of grants operate like closed-ended grants without price effects.

unsatisfied demands for services. These unsatisfied demands lead to horizontal inequalities and long queues—queues that could be cut back were the price system to do more rationing.[46] A commonly stated reason for not raising user fees is the impact on vertical equity, but this rationale seems particularly weak. For one thing, other redistributional policies are already so extensive that further efforts are redundant. For another, the existence of queues raises the possibility that scarce slots will be allocated to the rich and powerful by factors other than prices.[47]

A third way cutting back grants could improve accountability and efficiency is that it would encourage governments to seek out cheaper sources of supply of public services. One possibility is to permit competition by licensing, for example, parents' cooperatives to run day care centers. Another is through a voucher system. Under such a scheme, consumers are given a voucher that can be spent either at public agencies or at licensed private suppliers. Consumers could be required to pay a portion of the cost of the voucher.

There are still other possibilities. In the United States one promising solution to burgeoning health costs is the health maintenance organization, in which consumers pay, or are given a voucher for, a predetermined premium, and there is an economic incentive for the supplier to maintain the consumer's health as cheaply as possible.[48] Another possibility is for explicit contracts with private suppliers for trash collection, cleaning parks, and so forth. Unlike the permanently franchised public agencies, the private suppliers have an incentive to keep costs down in order to renew their franchise.

Summary

This discussion of expenditures can be summarized numerically. The analysis of deficits, particularly in figure 7-3, showed that Sweden's public contribution to capital formation is now 2 percent of GDP, about 8 percentage points less than in the high-saving days between 1962 and

46. Marten Lagergren and others, "Care and Welfare at the Crossroads" (Stockholm: Secretariat for Futures Studies, 1982).
47. If vertical equity were still a serious concern, it would always be possible to differentiate the user fees so that lower-income groups could consume public services at a lower price.
48. Ingemar Ståhl, "Can Equality and Efficiency Be Combined? The Experience of the Planned Swedish Health Care System," in Mancur Olson, ed., *A New Approach to the Economics of Health Care* (Washington, D.C.: American Enterprise Institute, 1981), pp. 172–95.

1977. The analysis of taxes showed that the most that could be recovered on the tax side, by the limitation of interest deductibility, was about 0.5 percent of GDP. That leaves about 7.5 percent of GDP to be made up by spending cuts. Of course, in a high-tax country like Sweden there is independent justification for spending cuts. Even if deficits were not cut at all, spending cuts might arguably increase efficiency, as Hansson and others have been saying.

I have discussed a few of the possible spending cuts. All can be defended on grounds of efficiency, and most would appear feasible with little or no cost in terms of equity. Central government transfers now amount to 9 percent of GDP, 4 percent of GDP more than the social security transfers levied to pay for them. There does not, of course, need to be exact pay-as-you-go financing for these transfers, but it is still true that many of them seem generous by world standards, and the share of effective general revenue financing is large. Business subsidies have been cut sharply in recent years, but they still amount to 4 percent of GDP, and further cutbacks would seem to make sense. Grants to local governments do not seem to fulfill the usual rationales for such grants; they amount to 7 percent of GDP, and they could be trimmed as well. Were this to be done, local governments would be forced by their budget limitations either to cut spending or raise fees, resulting in more public-sector saving in the consolidated accounts. These three numbers alone indicate that there is much scope for achieving the desired reductions in spending.

Conclusion

Since World War II the Swedes have constructed a very ambitious welfare state. The goals are laudable—to even out income distribution, provide for full employment, give effective social insurance for unforeseen and damaging events, and provide a full menu of public services. But there are also costs in tax distortions, redundant subsidies, and declining public saving. It is not clear that the dire predictions of some Swedish economists are in order, but certain things need fixing to combat some of the economic problems that Sweden is now having.

Deficits should be reduced, marginal taxes on earned income should be lowered, local accountability should be increased, transfer programs should be experience rated, redundant transfers and capital subsidies should be eliminated, and user fees should be increased. The distinguishing feature of these remedies is that they are reasonably straightforward: the problems caused by the inappropriate policies are well known, and the remedies can be implemented without big sacrifices in the distributional and employment goals that have guided Swedish policy. Indeed, in recent years some of the necessary actions have been taken.

This analysis suggests that what is really needed, in Sweden as elsewhere, is a willingness to think about and experiment with policies from a broader perspective. To solve the problem of deficits, the political debate must move beyond the budgetary stalemate to a recognition that if changes are not made, serious burdens will be placed on future generations, and the economic growth that has made the Swedish model work will be threatened. In rethinking their policy on marginal tax rates, the Swedes should consider what equitable redistribution really means when vertical redistribution is already extensive and horizontal redistribution haphazard, and when the status of those able and not able to avoid income taxes is compared. Transfer programs are evidence of the problem of redundant subsidies. It is not necessary to have more than one systematic program to protect against social ills. The focus on public consumption must take account of efficiency as well as equity and of the fact that expenditures cannot keep rising at past rates, or even stay at past levels, without causing serious distortions in both taxes and expenditures. Particular policies can readily be changed if these broader perspectives are taken and if the more subtle and long-term costs can be made part of the debate.

Comments by Michael Sohlman

This chapter covers many important issues related to the role of the public sector in the Swedish economy: the role of the government budget deficit in national capital formation, the dynamics of the deficit problem, and allocational and distributional aspects of both taxes and expenditures.

The budget deficit is discussed from two angles: the contribution of government to capital formation and the dynamics of interest payments on government debt.

The discussion of capital formation begins with the dramatic deterioration of the national saving ratio in the latter half of the 1970s and the beginning of the 1980s, and the need to improve the share of investments and net exports in GDP. Even before 1982 the opposition drew attention to the dismal writing on the wall for Sweden represented by the saving ratio. And as Edward Gramlich reasons, it is in the central government budget that the correction has to take place. But how much capital formation should rise, and in which sectors, is a not unimportant question.

Here Gramlich is not conclusive, but he does imply that a return to the record high investment shares of the 1960s, including that of the public sector, is necessary. Two circumstances, however, reduce the extent of the required capital formation: first, Sweden will not have any housing boom of the kind it had in the 1960s, and second, the growth of public consumption has slowed, with accordingly lower investment requirements. In the *1984 Medium Term Survey* the overall investment share in 1990 was estimated to be almost unchanged compared with 1983.[49] The share of manufacturing and basic industries was supposed to almost double, however, whereas that of the public sector and housing clearly fall back. As for the dynamics of the ratio of debt to GDP and the development of the interest burden, here the well-known objective is to stop the rise of the interest burden as a share of GDP. Gramlich examines the experience up to 1984, and based on the 1974–84 trend he is understandably worried. But if he had included the developments of the past three fiscal years the situation would look much less catastrophic. I have extended the data from figure 7-3 to include the 1986–87 budget. My calculations show that growth in interest paid as a share of GDP has been halted and even reduced in recent years. This is not to say that the present restrictive fiscal policies could or should be relaxed, but the unavoidable path to state bankruptcy that was commonly predicted only a few years ago seems to have lost its immediate relevance.

One factual correction with considerable importance is that Gramlich's analysis ends with 1985, when public sector savings was -3.6 percent of GDP, and on that ground describes the results as slow. The figure for 1986, however, is around 1 percent of GDP. This is quite respectable both in comparison with other countries and in relation to the starting point for the decline, 6.5 percent of GDP in 1982. A closer analysis of this development and a certain shift of the focus of the description to the more recent past would be desirable. On taxes the

49. Ministry of Finance, *The 1984 Medium Term Survey of the Swedish Economy* (Stockholm, 1984).

chapter naturally draws heavily on the local literature, including even anecdotal evidence about the decreasing loyalty to the tax system. However, some important empirical aspects are missing.

One is the difference between nominal and effective tax rates. For corporate taxes the difference is strong—the effective rates are around 20 percent and nominal rates 52 percent. For personal taxes the effective tax rates have also been reduced through deductions and loopholes.

This in turn has great importance in judging the degree of progressivity of the tax system. Very large capital gains have been generated by the combination of low or negative real interest rates, full deductibility of interest payments, and rising prices of real estate.

With respect to personal taxes, Gramlich could have mentioned the tax proposal for 1987 and 1988 recently voted by the Riksdag, which will lead to a lowering of marginal rates and closing of some loopholes. It will also include an element of a tax-based incomes policy in order to dampen inflation.

Gramlich discusses the need for a norm in budget policies and how difficult it is to find a suitable one. Here the recently restored norm that the government should not borrow abroad merits mention. This norm has the advantage of being automatic. A shortfall of saving in a cyclical upturn is immediately checked by an increase in interest rates. Administrative borrowing by the state abroad has been an important way to conceal the fall in the national saving ratio. As a foreigner, Gramlich sees things that should be obvious but that we Swedes seldom think about. One such observation is that the system of taxes and transfers contains not only the well-known negative incentives for labor supply but also very strong positive ones. Another is how surprisingly little economic analysis has been done on the huge local government sector. Finally, it is a consoling revelation to read that Sweden is de facto the most federal country in the world—this immediately makes the sometimes irrational relationship between our central and local governments more noble and respectable.

8

Political Foundations of Swedish Economic Policy

R. KENT WEAVER

UNTIL the mid-1970s, observers considered Sweden's economic and political systems tremendously successful. They admired the economy for its steady and rapid growth and the political system for its ability to provide a comprehensive welfare state and facilitate economic growth in a highly consensual manner. But the verdict in the past decade has been much less favorable. Economic growth has declined. Unemployment, much of it in disguised forms, has risen. Budget deficits, fueled in large part by government transfer payments, have reached extraordinary levels.

The concern of this chapter is how political constraints have influenced these outcomes, and what the effect of politics is likely to be on future economic performance. The analysis assumes that just as Swedish firms must generally allow their prices to be dictated by world markets, so the Swedish government's economic policy must respond to changing economic conditions in ways that promote rather than hinder economic adjustment. This response will often require that Sweden's government impose, or at least acquiesce in, losses suffered by specific individuals and groups—notably jobs lost because of firm closures and income lost because of inflation. At the same time, however, a government must be responsive to its political constituents, in particular to demands that losses suffered in the short term be avoided, diffused, or transferred to others at the expense of long-term adjustment.

This chapter explains and evaluates the changing capability of the

Swedish state to promote long-term economic adjustment rather than short-term political responsiveness when the two goals come into conflict. The ability of the government to promote adjustment deteriorated in the 1970s as it was increasingly confronted with performing tasks for which its structure and evolution had not prepared it. Meanwhile, public expectations, especially of full employment and a comprehensive welfare state, had become relatively fixed, leaving the government little room to maneuver as it pursued its economic growth objectives. These expectations now drive the policymaking process, and the government has been forced to commit whatever resources are required to maintain those employment and welfare objectives.

This is not to say that constraints on policy are absolutely inflexible. Nor is it to say that there is no viable development path for Sweden. But certain development paths are less viable than others: in particular, a policy of nonaccommodation similar to that of West Germany, with inflation brought down by increasing open unemployment to near double-digit figures, does not seem politically feasible.

This chapter develops these arguments in five steps. First, it discusses the preconditions for a successful adjustment policy. It then briefly outlines the fundamental constraints that have shaped the politics and policies of the "Swedish model" since World War II. After showing how political and economic changes led to serious problems with that model in the 1970s, the chapter discusses the implications of these developments for future Swedish economic policy, comparing the feasibility of socialist and nonsocialist policy paths. Finally, it suggests some changes in the Swedish political process to improve its ability to promote economic adjustment under the new economic and political conditions.

A Political Analysis of Economic Adjustment

Governments may, broadly speaking, respond to economic change in three ways.[1] First, they may pursue protectionist policies, seeking to delay, disguise, or diffuse the costs of industrial adjustment. They may use tariffs, import quotas, operating subsidies, and other instruments to rescue failing businesses and maintain employment in declining sectors.

1. For a further elaboration of this analysis, see R. Kent Weaver, *The Politics of Industrial Change* (Brookings, 1985), chap. 1.

But protectionist policies impose significant economic costs by misallocating capital and labor, crippling overall economic competitiveness, and draining government resources. Still, the political appeal of protectionist policies is strong because they directly aid those who would otherwise suffer concentrated losses while the costs of the policies are spread broadly.

Two other governmental responses take a more positive attitude toward industrial change. Market-oriented policies rely heavily on market signals, but they also attempt to lower the political and economic barriers to change. Unemployment insurance and retraining programs attempt to make workers more willing to leave jobs in declining industries rather than raise their collective political voice to force protectionist measures. Government can provide tax incentives for saving and investment to promote capital formation without directing it into specific sectors. But market-oriented policies nonetheless require governments to acquiesce as groups within declining sectors suffer severe losses.

Accelerationist policies attempt to anticipate and guide market forces as well as simply to respond to them. In this approach to industrial adjustment, governments choose specific sectors and firms to promote and others to phase out, using subsidies, contracts, state enterprise, and other mechanisms to create winners and losers. But if market-oriented policies require governments to acquiesce in concentrated losses, accelerationist policies require governments to impose losses. And that is a very sensitive political task.

For each of these methods of industrial adjustment there are left and right variants. Proponents of the left variant assign the state greater power vis-à-vis the private sector—for example, by nationalizing instead of subsidizing troubled firms—than do those of the right. They are also less willing to impose the costs of adjustment on industrial workers, relying on retraining and public employment programs rather than tolerating open unemployment.

For the moment, however, I will focus on the three broad means of industrial adjustment. These economic policy choices are not made in a political vacuum, and political pressures generally seem to favor protectionist policies. What conditions, then, and what kinds of decisionmaking procedures are conducive to market-oriented or accelerationist policies in a democratic, densely organized society like Sweden?

Several such conditions can be outlined. If the economy is expanding, politics becomes a struggle over shares of a growing pie. An expanding economy allows the state to compensate losers by means of economic growth without intense opposition from those who gain from adjustment (and who must indirectly pay the bill for compensation). Economic growth also makes the victims of economic adjustment less afraid of risk and more willing to rely on market solutions (finding a new job, for example) instead of seeking political ones.

Governments are also more likely to be able to take a long-term, adjustment-oriented perspective when they have substantial autonomy. In a democratic society, autonomy depends on a relatively secure electoral mandate. Insecure governments will be particularly leery of actions that impose losses on the electorate or a particular segment of it when electoral divisions are close, when voters are volatile in their political preferences, or when an election is near (and hence losses suffered are fresh in the minds of voters).

Finally, a long-term perspective is most likely to be attainable when the leaders of economic, cultural, and religious organizations and voting blocs cooperate to produce mutually beneficial outcomes and are able to convince their followers, who are likely to bear the brunt of short-term sacrifices, to accept the compromises the leaders have worked out.

Sweden enjoyed these conditions during much of the time since World War II. Its economy was expanding, its government had a reasonably secure mandate, and business, labor, and political leaders were noted for their cooperative approach to problems. These attributes were the foundation for what became known as the "Swedish model." In the past fifteen years, however, each of these conditions has significantly deteriorated.

Political Foundations of the Swedish Model

During most of the postwar period, the Swedish government attempted to promote economic adjustment through left variants of accelerationist and market-oriented policies. Policy choices reflected Sweden's particular balance of social and economic forces and were intended to advance the interests of the Social Democratic party's constituents while keeping political conflict within acceptable limits.

The central feature of the Swedish model was a set of agreements to limit conflict between capital and labor.[2] Space does not permit a detailed discussion of how these agreements evolved. I will instead focus on the internal logic of the model: the forces that made it possible and the way it was supposed to (and to a large extent actually did) function.[3]

The development of the Swedish model stemmed in large part from two fundamental characteristics of Swedish life: a small, open economy and a powerful trade union movement.[4] Sweden's dependence on international trade fostered an awareness among both business and labor leaders of the importance of international competitiveness. Thus while the ultimate goals of the two might differ, they realized that neither could achieve its objectives without an accomodation that kept prices competitive and promoted production by limiting disruptive industrial disputes.

The Swedish political system was not unique in its emphasis on achieving agreement. Indeed, such an emphasis has been a common feature of small, open European economies.[5] Accomodation among classes can take place on a variety of terms, however. In Sweden, a high degree of organizational cohesion by industrial workers, combined with divisions among business and agricultural interests, helped workers to reach an accomodation on terms favorable to their own interests in the 1930s, at the same time that labor movements among many other European workers were in retreat.[6] More than one-third of Sweden's wage earners were unionized by 1930. Equally important, organized labor was not divided along religious or ideological lines as in many other

2. James Fulcher, "Class Conflict: Joint Regulation and Its Decline," in Richard Scase, ed., *Readings in the Swedish Class Structure* (Oxford: Pergamon Press, 1976), pp. 51–97; and Walter Korpi, *The Working Class in Welfare Capitalism* (London: Routledge and Kegan Paul, 1978).

3. For a further discussion of the history and ideological origins of the Swedish model, see Erik Lundberg, "The Rise and Fall of the Swedish Model," *Journal of Economic Literature,* vol. 23 (March 1985), pp. 1–36.

4. While not denying that distinctive Nordic values and historical experiences have influenced the evolution of the Swedish state and public policy, this chapter focuses on more proximate causes in the economy and society. On the impact of Scandinavian political culture, see for example, Arne Ruth, "The Second New Nation: The Mythology of Modern Sweden," in Lennart Arvedson and others, eds., *Economics and Values* (Stockholm: Almqvist and Wiksell, 1986), pp. 51–75. On political history, see Timothy A. Tilton, "The Social Origins of Liberal Democracy: The Swedish Case," *American Political Science Review,* vol. 68 (June 1974), pp. 561–71.

5. Peter J. Katzenstein, *Small States in World Markets: Industrial Policy in Europe* (Ithaca, New York: Cornell University Press, 1985), p. 10.

6. Peter Alexis Gourevitch, "Breaking with Orthodoxy: The Politics of Economic Policy Responses to the Depression of the 1930s," *International Organization,* vol. 38 (Winter 1984), pp. 95–129.

European countries. About 80 percent of organized workers in 1950 belonged to unions affiliated with the blue-collar Swedish Confederation of Trade Unions, or Landsorganisationen (LO).[7] And LO was able to maximize its political clout through its close links with Sweden's Social Democratic party (Socialdemokratiska Arbetareparti, or SAP).[8] In 1938 LO and the Swedish Employers' Confederation (Svenska Arbetsgivareföreningen, or SAF) signed a basic agreement to limit strikes and other disruptions of production. In 1956 LO and SAF began centralized national bargaining on wage issues. These agreements between capital and labor to cooperate to promote economic growth while leaving production decisions in the hands of management, were the central elements of Sweden's historic compromise.[9] In addition, the Social Democrats signed a "red and green" compact with the Agrarian party in 1932–33 that gave the Social Democrats stable control of the government. Indeed, during the past half century, the Social Democrats have dominated political life in Sweden more than in any other West European country.

It is not simply the size of the Social Democratic vote but its stability that is amazing. Figure 8-1 shows the popular vote for each of the major parties in Riksdag elections since 1914. Since the end of World War II, support for the Social Democrats has varied within an extraordinarily narrow band. Under Sweden's proportional representation system, the Social Democrats have always been near, if they did not achieve, a parliamentary majority and have invariably polled about twice as many votes as their nearest foe. The party has thus been the "natural" one to form Sweden's governments, holding power (sometimes with coalition partners) almost continuously from 1932 to 1976. Indeed, the broad acceptance of the growth of Sweden's welfare state, often attributed to an all-party consensus, can more accurately be laid to the Social Democrats' electoral dominance.

The story has been very different for the three "bourgeois" parties: the Conservatives (now officially known as the Moderates, or Moderata samlingspartiet), the Liberals (now officially the People's party, or

7. Gøsta Esping-Andersen, *Politics Against Markets: The Social Democratic Road to Power* (Princeton, N.J.: Princeton University Press, 1985), p. 64.
8. Donald J. Blake, "Swedish Trade Unions and the Social Democratic Party: The Formative Years," *Scandinavian Economic History Review*, vol. 8, no. 1 (1960) pp. 19–44.
9. Walter Korpi, "The Historical Compromise and Its Dissolution," in Bengt Rydén and Villy Bergström, eds., *Sweden: Choices for Economic and Social Policy in the 1980s* (London: Allen and Unwin, 1982), pp. 124–41.

Figure 8-1. *Distribution of Popular Vote in Riksdag Elections, 1914–85*

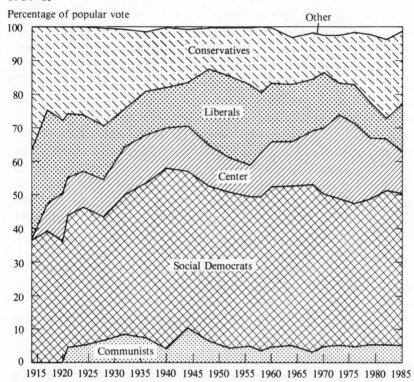

Source: M. Donald Hancock, *Sweden: The Politics of Postindustrial Change* (Hinsdale, Ill.: Dryden Press, 1972), pp. 116–17; Sveriges officiella statistik, *Statistik årsbok för Sverige 1986* (Stockholm: Statistika centralbyrån, 1985) [Official Statistics of Sweden, *Statistical Abstract of Sweden, 1986* (Stockholm: Statistics Sweden, 1985)], p. 389; Christopher Mosey, *The Times* (London), September 17, 1985; and Bo Särlvik, "Voting Behavior in Shifting 'Election Winds': An Overview of the Swedish Elections 1964–1968," in *Scandinavian Political Studies*, vol. 5 (Oslo: Universitetsforlaget; and New York: Columbia University Press, 1970), p. 243.

Folkpartiet), and the Center (Centerpartiet, formerly the Agrarian party). While overall support for the bloc has remained relatively constant, support for individual parties has fluctuated wildly. Moreover, the furthest right of the parties, the Conservatives, has been relatively small and isolated both from power and from the other nonsocialist parties.[10]

10. On the importance of the role of parties of the Right, see Francis G. Castles, "How Does Politics Matter? Structure or Agency in the Determination of Public Policy Outcomes," *European Journal of Political Research*, vol. 9 (June 1981), pp. 119–31.

Characteristics of the Swedish State

Political systems, like economic systems, have comparative advantages and disadvantages that make them better at performing some tasks than others. Economic systems differ in their endowments of natural resources and human capital, shaping their ability to produce specific goods and services. Political systems differ in their ability to compel agreement, to impose losses on some groups in society when necessary, and to implement decisions once they have been made.

Neither form of comparative advantage is immutable. Comparative advantages may evolve gradually as a result of changing resource bases, shift dramatically because of a crisis, or be manipulated through substantial investments. There is one major difference between the comparative advantages in economic and political systems, however: when a society has a comparative economic disadvantage in producing a specific good or service, it can trade for it, attempt to develop substitutes, or simply suppress or have unfulfilled demand for it. When governmental institutions have disadvantages in producing needed policies, the first of these options is likely to be absent altogether, and the second two may be very limited.

The Swedish state has some well-recognized attributes. First, policymaking has traditionally been highly organized and deliberative.[11] Much of the formulation of public policy is delegated to temporary royal commissions, which incorporate representatives from the civil service, interest groups, experts, and the Riksdag.[12] Further opportunities for group influence are present in the *remiss* procedure, in which proposed legislation is circulated to interested parties before its introduction in the Riksdag. Thus participation is both limited and structured. Only recognized groups are likely to have effective influence on government decisions, and their participation in formal decisionmaking provides an opportunity for government to co-opt those groups.

This organized, deliberative system has both advantages and disadvantages. Decisionmaking is well adapted to achieving consensual

11. The classic formulation of this view is Thomas J. Anton, "Policy-Making and Political Culture in Sweden," in *Scandinavian Political Studies,* vol. 4 (Oslo: Universitetsforlaget; and New York: Columbia University Press, 1969), pp. 88–102.

12. See, for example, Hans Meijer, "Bureaucracy and Policy Formulation in Sweden," in *Scandinavian Political Studies,* vol. 4, pp. 103–16; and Rune Premfors, "Governmental Commissions in Sweden," *American Behavioral Scientist,* vol. 26 (May-June 1983), pp. 623–42.

outcomes, although more agreement has been achieved in some policy sectors (for example, defense) than in others (taxation or the labor market).[13] The system is poorly adapted, however, to achieving rapid change, and is susceptible to paralysis. As one observer has noted, Swedes "go to great lengths to avoid having a losing side at all. . . . The typical result is a settlement in which winners and losers are virtually indistinguishable, because everybody wins something."[14] In political conflicts, winners are expected to compromise; losers are expected to acquiesce in the compromise. In short, the system is organized to promote so-called positive-sum outcomes, and it works best when such outcomes are attainable.

This is not to say that the Swedish system is incapable of imposing losses altogether, but rather that such losses are likely to be disguised and broadly diffused. Thus upper-income groups have seen their share of national income decline substantially under Social Democratic rule. But these losses have been gradual and have been taken largely out of a growing pie—that is, they have been relative rather than absolute. This type of conflict resolution can be maintained only as long as positive-sum outcomes remain achievable, however. In recent years this has not been possible.

A second attribute of the Swedish state is its reformist and statist momentum. After forty-four years of uninterrupted Social Democratic government from 1932 to 1976, it is not surprising that strong support for Social Democratic objectives remains within the bureaucracy. Equally important, once created, bureaucracies and programs take on lives and interests of their own. Once a specific definition of a policy problem and a reponse to it have been adopted, those in charge of administering that response are likely to be suspicious of attempts to take a dramatically different approach. For them, the costs of a different approach are likely to be very real. In day care, housing, and health care, for example, proposals from the political right that the private sector be allowed greater participation threaten the job security of those administering current programs. This situation is not, of course, unique to Sweden. What is unusual is the size of the Swedish bureaucracy and hence its political strength.

13. Olof Ruin, "Sweden in the 1970s: Policy-Making Becomes More Difficult," in Jeremy Richardson, ed., *Policy Styles in Western Europe* (London: Allen and Unwin, 1982), p. 142.
14. Thomas J. Anton, *Administered Politics: Elite Political Culture in Sweden* (Boston: Martinus Nijhoff, 1980), p. 173.

Again, this attribute of the Swedish state has both advantages and disadvantages. While reformist momentum facilitates the Social Democrats' redistribution objectives, the statist momentum makes it difficult to turn the state toward austerity and a lesser role for government.

Policy Mechanisms and Policy Outcomes

In the sustained economic growth following World War II, political debate primarily centered on how to facilitate economic growth and how to allocate the fruits of that growth. The Social Democrats generally favored a greater role for the state; the nonsocialists favored a lesser role. The Social Democratic party was able to use its control of the state to push the terms of political debate slowly and steadily to the left.

Capital did not fare too poorly. Ownership of industry remained primarily in private hands. Public-sector budget surpluses encouraged an adequate supply of investment funds, and the government provided strong incentives to invest at low points in the business cycle. More importantly, economic policy attempted to encourage the flow of investment into growing, highly productive sectors of the economy. The mechanisms chosen were largely market-oriented rather than accelerationist—the state generally did not attempt to favor individual firms or sectors. Instead, it reinforced existing market trends and eased the costs to workers of leaving jobs in declining sectors. Exit of inefficient firms was speeded by squeezing their profits through taxation and minimizing wage differentials among firms for employees doing similar work. Policies that subsidized retraining and relocation encouraged labor mobility. Centralized wage bargaining restrained wage demands and inflation rates so they would not compromise the country's international competitiveness. This policy mix, it should be noted, was developed largely at the initiative of LO economists and with the full cooperation of the trade union federation.

At the same time, the trade union federation and the Social Democrats used a variety of state and nonstate mechanisms to equalize income. Unemployment rates were kept very low. High marginal tax rates and such universal social programs as pensions, child benefits, and health care directly redistributed income. In addition, LO's policy of bargaining for wage solidarity in centralized negotiations attempted to lessen wage differentials among occupations, industries, and firms.

The Social Democratic program certainly was not adopted without conflict. Most notably, the creation of a national income-related pension fund in the 1950s, which gave the state enormous potential power over investment funds, provoked bitter opposition from the bourgeois parties.[15] But because the Social Democrats were careful to make social programs universal, rather than targeted on their core working-class constituency, the programs have won broad support. Dismantling them and replacing them with private alternatives has become increasingly impractical.

Changing Constraints and the Swedish Model

In the late 1960s a number of serious problems with the Swedish model became evident. Some were relatively short-term; others must be considered more or less permanent. These challenges can be broken down into five components: external shocks, changing domestic conditions, internal tensions generated by the model, changes in the Swedish state, and increasingly inflexible policy outcomes.

External Shocks and Slow Growth

The early 1970s brought two serious disruptions to the Swedish economy. The oil price shocks of 1973–74 hit Sweden particularly hard, and new international competitors in steel and shipbuilding helped create immense overcapacity on world markets for two of the country's most important heavy industries. These developments, which are described in other chapters of this volume, were exacerbated by government policies that attempted to bridge what was expected to be a relatively short world recession by maintaining domestic demand. The result was a serious decline in Sweden's competitiveness and a halt to economic growth. Increasingly, politics became a zero-sum game.

Changing Domestic Constraints

In addition to adverse international developments in the 1970s, the Swedish government confronted changing domestic conditions that influenced policymaking.

15. Hugh Heclo, *Modern Social Politics in Britain and Sweden* (New Haven, Conn.: Yale University Press, 1974), chap 5.

The loss of the Social Democrats' stable electoral base and mandate has been the most important political development of the past twenty years. This development has several roots. Changes in Sweden's employment structure have weakened the role of manual workers, the party's voting base, in the electorate. Class voting in general has declined during the past two decades, especially among younger voters.[16] In addition, the growing white-collar labor federations, while they cooperate with LO and the Social Democrats on specific issues, do not have formal links with either. Hence they do not perform the tasks of socialization and political organization for the Social Democratic party that LO does, and their members support the party at much lower rates than LO members.[17]

The Social Democrats have attempted to weather this decline in blue-collar unionized support in part by building a new political base among public employees. The party has also stressed that it seeks to build a common "wage-earner front" with white-collar workers.

New issues such as opposition to nuclear power and protection of the environment further disturbed existing party loyalties, especially during the 1970s.[18] These issues were often seen by their partisans as matters of principle and not subject to negotiation and compromise at the margin. Environmental and regional issues were exploited with particular success by the Center party after it decided that collaboration on a regular basis with the Social Democrats was no longer in its interests. The Center party's growth in the early 1970s and its movement toward cooperation with the other two bourgeois parties helped make a non-socialist government possible. Moreover, politics has become more

16. John D. Stephens, "The Changing Swedish Electorate: Class Voting, Contextual Effects, and Voter Volatility," *Comparative Political Studies,* vol. 14 (July 1981), pp. 163–204; and Henrik Jess Madsen, "Social Democracy in Postwar Scandinavia: Macroeconomic Management, Electoral Support and the Fading Legacy of Prosperity" (Ph.D. dissertation, Harvard University, 1984), chap. 5.

17. Nils Elvander, "In Search of New Relationships: Parties, Unions, and Salaried Employees' Associations in Sweden," *Industrial and Labor Relations Review,* vol. 28 (October 1974), pp. 67–70. In the 1979 Riksdag election, for example, 68 percent of LO members voted for the Social Democrats, compared with 37 percent of the Salaried Workers' Confederation (Tjänstemännens centralorganisation, or TCO) members and only 13 percent of the members of the Swedish Confederation of Professional Associations (Sveriges akademikers centralorganisation, or SACO) and the State Salaried Workers' Confederation (Statstjänstemännens riksforbund, or SR): see Andrew Martin, "Wages, Profits, and Investment in Sweden," in Leon N. Lindberg and Charles S. Maier, eds., *The Politics of Inflation and Economic Stagnation* (Brookings, 1985), p. 423.

18. Donald Granberg and Sören Holmberg, "Political Perception among Voters in Sweden and the U.S.: Analyses of Issues with Explicit Alternatives," *Western Political Quarterly,* vol. 39 (March 1986), pp. 7–28.

polarized in recent years, with the once-isolated Conservatives becoming the largest nonsocialist party in the late 1970s.[19]

Declining economic performance also increased electoral volatility in the early 1970s. The Social Democratic party had built its political base on full employment and a comprehensive welfare state, and studies of public opinion show that the unemployment rate is still the most important economic influence on party popularity.[20] But by the early 1970s, economic decline was causing voters to question whether a socialist government was in fact the best guarantor of full employment.[21] The nonsocialist parties did not fare much better in voters' minds. The four governments formed by those parties between 1976 and 1982 were widely perceived to be ineffective—in large part, no doubt, because they too were unable to solve Sweden's economic problems.[22]

The tendency toward increased electoral volatility is evident in table 8-1, which shows the voting patterns of vote switchers, new voters, and previous nonvoters in general elections from 1960 to 1976. The Social Democrats' retention rate—the percentage of voters in the previous election who remained with the party—dropped in the 1960s and 1970s, as did the party's share of new voters. Defections to the bourgeois parties—especially the Center party—increased.

19. According to surveys by the Swedish Institute for Opinion Research (SIFO), the Conservatives passed both the Liberal and Center parties in voter preference in 1979. The Liberals then passed the Conservatives following their unexpectedly strong showing in the 1985 election, but the gap between the two had narrowed to 1 percentage point (18 percent for the Liberals, 17 for the Conservatives) again by May 1986; see *Skånska Dagbladet* (Malmö), June 1, 1986, p. 6.

20. A substantial literature exists on the influence of various macroeconomic developments on party standings in Sweden. The preponderance of evidence suggests that unemployment rates do exert a significant influence on party popularity, although this relationship is unstable over time and also declines with the age of the voter. The effects of other economic variables—notably inflation and economic growth rates—are weak or nonexistent. See Lars Jonung and Eskil Wadensjö, "The Effect of Unemployment, Inflation and Real Income Growth on Government Popularity in Sweden," *Scandinavian Journal of Economics*, vol. 81, no. 2 (1979), pp. 343–53; Johan A. Lybeck, "A Simultaneous Model of Politico-economic Interaction in Sweden, 1970–82," *European Journal of Political Research*, vol. 13 (June 1985), pp. 135–51; Lars Jonung and Eskil Wadensjö, "Rational, Adaptive and Learning Behaviour of Voters," Institutet för Social Forskning, *Meddelande 3/1986*; and Lars Jonung, "Business Cycles and Political Changes in Sweden," *Skandinaviska Enskilda Banken Quarterly Review*, no. 2 (1985), pp. 1–15.

21. SIFO, "The Swedish Election 1985," *Indikator*, no. 4 (September 2, 1985), p. 10. See also Madsen, "Social Democracy in Postwar Scandinavia," chap. 5.

22. On the declining perception of the bourgeois parties' effectiveness, especially with respect to economic management, see SIFO, "The Swedish Election 1985," pp. 10–11; and Hans L. Zetterberg, "The Return of the Swedish Social Democrats," undated SIFO memorandum, pp. 4–5.

Table 8-1. *Effects of Electoral Movements on the Vote for the Social Democratic Party in Swedish National Elections, 1960–76*
Percent

Year	Social Democratic party retention rate[a]	Shift in vote to (+) or from (−) Social Democrats[b]			Voters supporting the Social Democratic party	
		Left Party Communists	Center party	Liberal and Conservative parties	Previous nonvoters	New voters
1960	93	+0.2	0	+0.5	56	65
1964[c]	88	−0.8	−0.7	−0.2	50	52
1968	87	+0.9	−0.1	+0.3	58	57
1970	85	−0.9	−1.8	−0.2	44	46
1973	86	−0.6	−2.3	−0.3	50	36
1976	82	+0.2	−0.7	−1.2	49	41

Sources: Henrik Jess Madsen, "Social Democracy in Postwar Scandinavia: Macroeconomic Management, Electoral Support and the Fading Legacy of Prosperity" (Ph.D. dissertation, Harvard University, 1984), p. 373.

a. Share of Social Democratic voters at election t who voted for the party at election $t + 1$.

b. Percentages are based on voters who voted at the first election, all of whom also voted at the subsequent election.

c. Vote shifts in 1964 refer to shifts between the municipal elections in 1962 and the general elections in 1964.

The extent of these changes in voter loyalty should not be overstated. The decline in support for the Social Democrats has been relatively modest: in the six elections since 1970 the party's support has ranged from a low of 42.7 percent in 1976, when the socialists lost power for the first time in forty years, to a high of 45.6 percent in 1982.[23] Vote switching across the socialist-nonsocialist divide has remained relatively modest.[24] But the socialist and nonsocialist blocs have been so closely matched in the past fifteen years that a very modest change in voter preferences can result in a change of government.

The decline in the Social Democrats' base of support has not resulted

23. This compares to an average Social Democratic vote in national elections of 49 percent in the 1940s, 46 percent in the 1950s, and 48 percent in the 1960s. See Francis G. Castles, *The Social Democratic Image of Society* (London and Boston: Routledge and Kegan Paul, 1978), p. 6.

24. In the 1982 election, for example, only 3 percent of voters who had voted for the Social Democrats in 1979 switched to support one of the three bourgeois parties. Three percent of Conservative (Moderate) voters switched to the Social Democrats or the Left Party Communists, along with 9 percent of Center party voters and 11 percent of those who voted for the Liberals in 1979. See Sveriges officiella statistik, *Statistik årsbok för Sverige 1986* (Stockholm: Statistiska centralbyrån, 1985) [Official Statistics of Sweden, *Statistical Abstract of Sweden, 1986* (Stockholm: Statistics Sweden, 1985)], p. 387.

Table 8-2. *Electoral Performance of Governing Parties, 1968–85*

Year	Governing[a] party or coalition	Percentage of vote in previous election	Percentage of vote in current election	Difference
1968	S	42.3	50.1	+7.8
1970	S	50.1	45.3	−4.8
1973	S	45.3	43.6	−1.7
1976	S	43.6	42.7	−0.9
1979	L	11.1	10.6	−0.5
	L,Ce,Co[b]	50.8	49.0	−1.8
1982	L,Ce	28.7	21.4	−7.3
	L,Ce,Co[c]	49.0	45.0	−4.0
1985	S	45.6	44.9	−0.7

Sources: Bo Särlvik, "Recent Electoral Trends in Sweden," in Karl H. Cerny, ed., *Scandinavia at the Polls: Recent Political Trends in Denmark, Norway, and Sweden* (Washington, D.C.: American Enterprise Institute, 1977), pp. 74, 116; Svante Ersson and Jan-Erik Lane, "Polarisation and Political Economy Crisis: The 1982 Swedish Election," *West European Politics,* vol. 6 (July 1983), p. 288; and Christopher Mosey, *The Times* (London), September 17, 1985.

a. S = Social Democratic party; L = Liberal (People's) party; Ce = Center party; Co = Conservative (Moderate) party.

b. At the time of the 1979 election, a Liberal minority government was in office after the breakup of a Liberal-Center-Conservative coalition. However, the three parties were considered part of the same nonsocialist bloc. Thus figures for both the Liberals separately and the entire bloc are given.

c. At the time of the 1982 election, a Liberal-Center minority government was in office after the breakup of a Liberal-Center-Conservative coalition. As with the 1979 election, figures for the entire nonsocialist bloc are given for comparative purposes.

in a stable gain for the nonsocialist parties, either singly or collectively. In a major realignment to the right one would expect to see a breakthrough by those parties, consolidated in later elections by an increasing share of votes. This has not occurred. But another very clear pattern does emerge: in each election since 1970 the party or parties in government have won a smaller share of the vote than they had in the the previous election (table 8-2). In short, voter loyalties, at least in a small (and perhaps shifting) portion of the electorate, seem to have been overlaid by negative retrospective judgments about the performance of the government. Parties (in their platforms) and governments (in their actions) have been increasingly forced to allocate uncertainty and losses. In strictly political terms the challenge for parties and governments has been to choose policies that would maintain the support of their political bases without alienating the few marginal voters needed to win or maintain control of the government. This has proved exceedingly difficult.

The legislative consequences of increased electoral volatility have been magnified by Sweden's constitutional revisions of 1970 and 1974.

A new electoral system eliminated the Riksdag's indirectly elected chamber, established a shorter (three-year) term of office, and put in place a system of proportional representation that more precisely reflected the parties' percentages of the total popular vote. Electoral rules are never neutral in their effects, and the new system has had some profound consequences.[25] By ending the bonus of Riksdag seats for the largest political parties (notably the Social Democrats), the new electoral system has made minority or coalition governments very likely and has made alternation in government between the socialist and nonsocialist parties more likely as well. The system's cutoff for representation in the Riksdag (a minimum of 4 percent of the national popular vote or 12 percent in one of the multimember electoral districts) contains a compensating tilt toward the Left: the Left Party Communists (Vänsterpartiet Kommunisterna, or VPK) could generally be expected to meet the cutoff and lend their support to the Social Democrats when required; the smaller Christian Democratic party (Kristen Demokratisk samling or KDS), however, has consistently been denied independent representation in the Riksdag.[26] This effect is particularly important in the current Riksdag, where the Social Democrats depend on VPK votes to maintain a Left majority in the legislature. More generally, the cutoff has tended to prevent the growth of antisystem parties and the fragmentation of existing parties.

Constitutional reform has also eliminated incentives for the bourgeois parties to unite: there is no bonus in seats to be won by doing so. Maintaining three parties has both electoral advantages and disadvantages for the nonsocialists. It offers a broader range of choices to voters who might be wooed away from the Social Democrats. Voters who might not consider voting for the Conservatives, for example, might be willing to vote for the Center party or the Liberals. But the division among the parties also conveys an image of division and conflict to voters, while the Social Democrats still project an image of relative strength and unity.

The impact of the continuing division within the nonsocialist bloc has thus probably varied over time: when one of the parties has been able to mobilize additional support on the basis of a single issue—as the Center party did in 1976 with its opposition to the further development of nuclear

25. On the effect of electoral rules generally, see Douglas W. Rae, *The Political Consequences of Electoral Laws,* rev. ed. (New Haven, Conn.: Yale University Press, 1971).

26. The Christian Democrats did win Riksdag representation in the 1985 election through an electoral coalition with the Center party.

power—division has probably increased the nonsocialists' overall support; when such mobilization has not occurred, division has probably hurt them. The minimization of incentives for the bourgeois parties to unite has also kept alive the possibility that the Social Democrats might be able to woo one (or more) of those parties as a coalition partner for a Social Democratic minority government or, more likely, as a supporter of specific pieces of legislation on an ad hoc basis. Finally, the continued existence of three bourgeois parties means that when they do control the government, as they did between 1976 and 1982, there is likely to be continued jockeying for power among them, as each party seeks to improve its relative position in the coalition for the next election.[27] This jockeying was very much in evidence between 1976 and 1982. In 1978, for example, the Liberals refused to serve in a cabinet with the Conservatives after the Center party quit the government over the continued development of nuclear power: the Liberals believed that to do so would link them too closely in voters' minds with the rightists. And in 1981 the Liberal and Center parties chose to reach an agreement with the Social Democrats over tax reform, even though this resulted in the collapse of their coalition with the Conservatives.[28]

Declining adherence to traditional partisan allegiances has had a counterpart in nonelectoral organizations. Increasingly, leaders of Sweden's highly centralized organizations have been challenged by their member organizations and the rank and file. No longer is there an assumption that decisionmaking by a cartel of elites is in everyone's interests; those who have power in specific economic and political markets are increasingly willing to use it to advance their own cause. This declining organizational cohesion makes it more difficult to reach agreements and more difficult to stick to them once they are reached.

27. Two other effects of the constitutional revision are worth noting briefly. First, the revision was seen by the Social Democrats as a way of improving their chances of winning communal elections because they are now held simultaneously with the national elections. Lower-class voters are less likely to turn out for elections, especially those at the subnational level. A second effect of the new electoral system is to minimize the prospect that the Riksdag will be dissolved and a new election held, since holding a midterm election does not restart the clock for a new parliamentary term. If a special election is held two years after the previous one, the regularly scheduled election will nevertheless have to be held in another year. Parties are understandably reluctant to untertake this expense and uncertainty. There has been no special election since the new constitution was enacted, despite the collapse of several coalitions during the period of bourgeois party rule.

28. See Stig Hadenius, *Swedish Politics During the 20th Century* (Stockholm: Swedish Institute, 1985), pp. 148–54.

The lack of cohesion is evident in labor markets, where wildcat strike activity, lockouts, and "wage drift" (agreements negotiated at the plant level that vary from national wage agreements) have increased. The inability of the employers' federation to come to an agreement on negotiating a national wage agreement in 1984 was a further manifestation of this trend.

Declining organizational cohesion has resulted in part from changes in the domestic labor market. The growth of the service sector has increased the importance of white-collar unions, notably those in the Salaried Employees' Confederation (Tjänstemännens Centralorganisation, or TCO). These unions were less committed to LO's solidaristic wage policy, which guided centralized wage bargaining.[29] The growth in public-sector employment and unionization has meant that a growing proportion of workers is no longer directly concerned with international competitiveness. And the increasing entry of women into the paid labor force has meant that there are more two-income families with a substantial economic stake in a particular locale. Thus workers are less willing to be geographically mobile in the wake of job loss or to take advantage of new job opportunities.

Serious tensions are also evident within the Social Democratic party and in the relationship between the party and LO. The party's national leadership faced serious discontent among the rank and file (the so-called War of the Roses) over its austerity-oriented 1986–87 budget. And the party and LO have clashed over the issue of implementing wage-earner funds, which LO leaders back for reasons of ideology and organizational maintenance, but which pragmatic party leaders believe will cost the party votes.

Conflicts within the Model

So far I have addressed changes that can be considered exogenous to the Swedish model. But the development policies pursued by Social Democratic governments have themselves produced effects that have

29. While LO unions continued to grow as a percentage of the labor force from 1960 to 1980 (from 45.8 to 50.2 percent), this growth was dwarfed by that of TCO, which grew from 12.1 percent to 24.6 percent of the labor force. LO's share of the organized labor force declined from over 75 percent to about 62 percent. There were also changes in the balance of power within LO, as the local government workers' union passed the Metalworkers' union as the largest member of LO. See Andrew Martin, "Trade Unions in Sweden: Strategic Responses to Change and Crisis," in Peter Gourevitch and others, *Unions and Economic Crisis: Britain, West Germany, and Sweden* (London: Allen and Unwin, 1984), p. 345.

undermined the model's political and economic basis. Foremost among these policies was the one that squeezed corporate profits. This policy was intended to force a reallocation of capital and labor to more productive sectors. The policy also had a political purpose: convincing the LO rank and file that the organization was doing all it could to defend their interests. But in the 1970s it became increasingly clear that squeezing corporate profits also meant Swedish industry was not receiving adequate investment funds.

The solution favored by LO to resolve this problem has been the so-called wage earner funds, a tax on corporate profits that was to be used to buy equity in Swedish firms, with the several regional funds eventually achieving a controlling position in some.[30] Unfortunately for LO and the Social Democrats, the proposed program prompted a lukewarm response from workers and outrage from the business community. Although a small wage earner fund program was enacted after the Social Democrats' return to power in 1982, it was a watered-down version of LO's original proposal. Even so, the funds provoked so much conflict that the party is reluctant to raise the issue again by expanding existing funds or creating new ones when the current ones reach their maximum intended size.[31] Yet no other answer has emerged that simultaneously meets the political needs of LO and the need to provide additional investment capital.

Changes in the Swedish State

Parliamentary systems like Sweden's concentrate authority in the executive. It has generally been argued that this arrangement allows

30. On the wage earner funds, see Rudolf Meidner, Anna Hedborg, and Gunnar Fond, *Employee Investment Funds: An Approach to Collective Capital Formation* (London: Allen and Unwin, 1978).

31. Polls by the Swedish Institute for Opinion Research in 1985 reveal both the lack of support for wage earner funds and the Social Democrats' success in burying the issue as that year's election approached. Supporters of the nonsocialist parties overwhelmingly favored abolition of the funds (93 percent of Conservatives, 86 percent of Liberals, and 83 percent of Centerites). Social Democrats were far from united in supporting the funds: 20 percent believed that they should be abolished, 45 percent that they should be retained, and 36 percent did not know. Only 6 percent of voters, however, saw the funds as the most important issue in the election: see SIFO, "The Swedish Election 1985," *Indikator,* no. 4 (September 2, 1985), pp. 4–9. On public opinion toward the funds, see also Torsten Österman, *Vad Hände i valet?* (Stockholm: Tidens Forslag, 1983), pp. 39–47; and Henrik Jess Madsen, "Class Power and Participatory Equality: Attitudes Towards Economic Democracy in Denmark and Sweden," *Scandinavian Political Studies,* vol. 3, no. 4 (New Series, 1980), pp. 277–98. On the conflict over adoption of the wage-earner funds, see Erik Åsard, *LO och Löntagarfondsfrågan: En studie i Facklig Politik och Strategi* (Stockholm: Rabén & Sjögren, 1978); and Åsard, *Kampen om Löntagarfonderna: Fondutredningen Från Samtal Till Sammanbrott* (Stockholm: P.A. Norstedt & Söners Förlag, 1985).

governments to be more responsive to changing economic conditions because they need not worry about multiple "veto points" within government. But while responsiveness may be increased in a period of sustained economic growth, the concentration of authority is less clearly advantageous during periods of uneven growth or stagnation in which governments must allocate losses.[32] Just as parliamentary systems concentrate authority, so they also concentrate accountability and blame. Unless the party or parties in power have a very secure electoral mandate, they will be very reluctant to impose losses on current or potential supporters.

This reluctance has been exacerbated by slow economic growth that has reduced the government's ability to compensate losers through expanding the economic pie. Moreover, the electoral system introduced in 1970 narrowed the window for government actions that acquiesce in or impose concentrated short-term losses on groups within the society. With only a three-year term of office for the Riksdag, the chances increase that voters will remember such actions. The government now has a very limited ability to resist short-term pressures, knowing that elections are never far away, the partisan division is extremely close, and that the party or parties in power can be clearly identified as the source of painful outcomes.

Fear of retrospective judgments by voters is not the only difficulty faced by Swedish governments in choosing policies. Minority and coalition government has become the norm since 1970. Thus interparty negotiation has increasingly been required not just to obtain broad support for legislation but to pass it at all. The situation has at times reached absurd proportions: between 1973 and 1976 the Social Democrats and their Left Party Communist allies were exactly tied with the bourgeois parties in the number of Riksdag seats they held (175 each). Passage of legislation had to be decided by lot if one or more of the nonsocialist parties could not be wooed to support it. (The number of seats in the Riksdag was later changed to 349 to prevent a repetition of this phenomenon).

Clearly, these developments have had a major impact on the Swedish state's traditional attributes of reformist, statist momentum and organized, deliberate decisionmaking. The disadvantages of those attributes have become much more salient. Stalemate and paralysis have become

32. For an elaboration of this argument, see R. Kent Weaver, "Are Parliamentary Systems Better?" *Brookings Review,* vol. 3 (Summer 1985), pp. 16–25.

real threats, and the incentives to seek additional statist solutions to diffuse and disguise losses (largely through higher state expenditures) have increased.[33] Organized, deliberative decisionmaking has been partially supplanted by crisis decisionmaking, which is called into action when the party or parties in power face pressures on specific issues from concentrated constituencies. Rather than slow, careful, consensual decisionmaking by fairly autonomous bureaucracies, it is characterized by direct, politically motivated interventions by elected officials. This new channel has not displaced the old model, but coexists with it. Crisis management has been particularly noticeable in industrial policy decisions involving large firms that are failing.[34]

Declining Policy Flexibility

In the long run, perhaps the most serious adverse development in Sweden is the rigidification of additional constraints on economic policymaking. The earlier, highly fixed constraints (an open economy and trade union strength) clearly influenced the overall direction of Swedish policy. By the 1970s specific policy outputs and outcomes had become inflexible as well. The critical elements here are full employment and an inclusive welfare state. In both cases the political need to maintain these features of the system in the much less hospitable economic environment of the 1970s and 1980s has required a huge infusion of government resources. The political unacceptability of open unemployment rates greater than 3 percent has led to dramatically increased expenditures to support the labor market—public employment, training, and unemployment compensation—as well as increased aid to failing companies.[35] In

33. Andrew Martin, "Economic Stagnation and Social Stalemate in Sweden," in Joint Economic Committee, *Monetary Policy, Selective Credit Policy, and Industrial Policy in France, Britain, West Germany, and Sweden,* 97 Cong. 1 sess. (U.S. Government Printing Office, 1981), p. 146.

34. See Kjell Lundmark, "Welfare State and Employment Policy: Sweden," in Kenneth Dyson and Stephen Wilks, eds., *Industrial Crisis* (New York: St. Martin's Press, 1983), pp. 220–44.

35. There is very weak evidence, however, that Swedish governments have successfully carried out a political manipulation of the business cycle to engineer booms during election years. In a recent survey of research on political business cycles, Lars Jonung concludes that "the politicians in power appear therefore to have had the will but not the ability to control the business cycle" and that "economic policy has probably been focused if anything on broadly and permanently keeping open unemployment at a low and constant level." See "Business Cycles and Political Changes in Sweden," p. 14. Governmental manipulation of the business cycle is of course more difficult in a small, open economy than in a larger one. See also Lybeck, "A Simultaneous Model of Politico-economic Interaction in Sweden."

addition, LO sought and in the mid-1970s secured laws that restrict the power of firms to dismiss workers.

Income transfers have also increased dramatically, with a high percentage of the payments indexed for inflation. Transfer payments are provided not just to the unemployed and those who are in danger of losing their jobs but also to broad categories of citizens—the aged, families with children—that make up most of the populace and electorate. Health care is provided by the government to all. This dominance of universal rather than means-tested programs has had three predictable consequences: the programs enjoy wide public support; they are very expensive; and they are very hard to cut, even at the margins. The broad popularity of universal benefit programs is not surprising. What is more important is the relationship between attitudes on taxing and spending: would Swedes be willing to get fewer services and transfers in exchange for lower taxes? Public opinion surveys suggest the answer is no. While taxes, and in particular high marginal tax rates, are very unpopular when viewed independently, most Swedes believe their tax burden is reasonable given the benefits they derive from the state.[36]

Policy Rigidity in a Troubled Economy

Many developments in the past twenty years have had serious repercussions for the ability of the Swedish government to carry out a policy oriented toward economic adjustment. The decline of economic growth has made it more difficult to avoid imposing absolute economic losses on some groups in the society, and changes in the labor market have made individuals more reluctant to take risks. The end of Social Democratic electoral hegemony combined with a shorter term of office has meant that no matter which party or parties are in power, their mandate and sense of security in office is very weak. And the multiplication of political cleavage lines and organizations has meant that leaders have more difficulty in delivering the support of their followers for any policy agreement.

36. Axel Hadenius, "Citizens Strike a Balance: Discontent with Taxes, Content with Spending," *Journal of Public Policy,* vol. 5 (August 1985), pp. 349–63. In a 1985 survey asking "Which government do you think would be best at establishing a good system of *taxation*—a Social Democratic or a nonsocialist government?" the nonsocialist parties were favored by only a narrow margin—39 percent to 34 percent—over the Social Democrats, with 28 percent not knowing or perceiving no difference. See SIFO, "The Swedish Election 1985," pp. 11–12.

A push for budget austerity or economic rationalization now creates severe problems for either a socialist or a bourgeois government. Nonsocialist governments have invariably had a tenuous hold on power and thus have been reluctant to impose losses on groups that could create a margin of victory for the Left in the next election. A Social Democratic government might in theory have greater latitude in imposing losses on its own supporters—they are presumably unlikely to vote for the nonsocialists, who might be expected to treat them even more harshly—but this advantage is offset by several other factors. First, parties are unlikely to wish to hurt their own supporters. Second, aggrieved Social Democratic voters may have real alternatives. They can move to support the Left Party Communists, further increasing the Social Democrats' dependence on that party for a majority in the Riksdag.[37] They may also move to the Liberals, who have pledged under their current leader to maintain the welfare state. The Center party, too, could hold some appeal because it has emphasized defending the interests of smaller, declining communities. Or disgruntled Social Democrats can simply abstain from voting. The important point is that electoral loss is a credible threat in response to any austerity move by a Social Democratic government. Moreover, the Social Democrats cannot be seen entirely as free agents: the leaderships of LO and the party are closely intertwined, and policy changes with a direct impact on LO membership would almost certainly be subject to direct negotiation between the two.[38]

It is not surprising, then, that Swedish economic policy took on an increasingly protectionist cast in the 1970s under both Social Democratic and bourgeois governments. And economic outcomes, exacerbated by these protectionist policies, became increasingly unsatisfactory. Most of these changes are discussed in detail in other chapters and can simply be summarized here. To maintain the goal of low open unemployment, labor-market expenditures were drastically increased. Unemployment rose anyway, although rates were far lower than elsewhere in Western Europe. Selective interventions in industry—both subsidies and state takeovers—were used to bail out failing firms. Inflation seriously weak-

37. On the Left Party Communists as a safety valve for disgruntled Social Democratic voters, see Olof Petersson, "The 1973 General Election in Sweden," in *Scandinavian Political Studies*, vol. 9 (Oslo: Universitetsforlaget; and Beverly Hills: Sage Publications, 1974), p. 223.

38. On relations between LO and the Social Democrats, see Elvander, "In Search of New Relationships," pp. 60–74; and Martin, "Trade Unions in Sweden," pp. 189–359.

Table 8-3. *Swedish Government Expenditures and Revenues,*
1982–83 to 1984–85, and Projected to 1986–87
Billions of current kronor unless otherwise indicated

Item	1982–83	1983–84	1984–85	1985–86 (estimated)	1986–87 (draft budget)
Revenues	191.3	221.2	260.6	273.3	286.7
Expenditures (excluding interest on national debt)	229.7	237.9	253.9	254.0	264.6
Surplus (deficit) of current spending over current revenue	38.4	16.7	(6.7)	(19.3)	(22.1)
Interest on national debt	48.2	60.4	75.2	71.5	71.0
Surplus (deficit) of total spending over revenue	(86.6)	(77.1)	(68.5)	(52.2)	(48.9)
Surplus of total spending over revenue as a percent of GDP	13.0	10.3	8.3	5.9	5.2

Source: Ministry of Finance, *The Swedish Budget 1986–87* (Stockholm, 1986), p. 37.

ened Sweden's international competitiveness. Industrial investment dropped dramatically. In Sweden's highly constrained political environment, maintaining international competitiveness increasingly depended on devaluation, a government action that had the political advantage of distributing short-term costs fairly broadly and indirectly while stimulating employment. But relying on devaluation risks fueling an inflationary cycle as labor seeks to compensate for the income losses of past devaluations and to anticipate the effects of future ones.

Sweden's central budget deficit reached the astonishing level of 13 percent of GDP in 1982 (table 8-3), in large part because of expanded industrial and labor-market expenditures. Total public-sector savings (including pension fund activity) turned negative, forcing the government to borrow heavily abroad. Indeed, the Swedish experience shows that there are limits to the argument in public choice theory that governments have a political incentive to run deficits to provide more benefits to their publics than they are currently raising in taxes. Deficit spending ostensibly allows governments to create the illusion that taxpayers are getting more for their money than is in fact the case, while it shifts the burden of paying for those expenditures to future generations of taxpayers.[39]

39. James M. Buchanan and Richard E. Wagner, *Democracy in Deficit: The Political Legacy of Lord Keynes* (New York: Academic Press, 1977), chap. 9.

There are of course limits to this strategy, notably limits on a government's ability to borrow, the potential crowding out of private investment, and balance-of-payments problems. There is an additional economic constraint: when interest rates are high, the interest paid on high deficits rises so fast that a government may find itself unable to keep current benefits (expenditures other than interest payments) higher than tax intake, even if it continues to run huge deficits. Moreover, this situation can develop fairly quickly.

This is precisely the situation in which Sweden found itself by the early 1980s. Budget deficits first passed 5 percent of GDP in 1977. But by the 1984–85 fiscal year, debt service requirements forced the government to raise more in revenue than it spent on current benefits (see table 8-3).[40]

Sweden's economic performance has improved substantially since the 16 percent devaluation imposed in 1982 by the newly elected Social Democratic government. Economic growth has rebounded and competitiveness has improved. A broad-based austerity program has cut budget deficits significantly, although they are still huge. The government has attempted both to make higher profits acceptable to its constituency and to revive centralized bargaining as a means of restraining inflation. But as previous chapters have pointed out, the stimulus from devaluation has been largely exhausted. Sweden still has very serious economic challenges to face—most notably, curbing public- and private-sector nominal wage increases, further reducing public-sector deficits, and ensuring adequate investment in a politically acceptable manner.

New Rules of the Game?

Political and economic developments of the past fifteen years have weakened agreement on the historic compromise in Sweden and weakened the capability of the government to promote market-oriented or accelerationist economic policies. Obviously, the prospects for the

40. These figures are of course only crude estimates of the perceptions that taxpayers may in fact have of the costs and benefits of various fiscal policy choices. These perceptions may be distorted by the "fiscal illusion" of hidden taxes (payroll taxes paid by employers, value-added taxes, corporate taxes). Benefits may also be misperceived—for example, through undercounting collective benefits such as national defense.

Swedish economy depend in large part on whether these new constraints are temporary or permanent.

Prospects are better for reversing some of these trends than for others. The international economic environment will probably not produce shocks of the same magnitude as those of the early 1970s, although certain sectors such as pulp and paper and steel will continue to have problems. But trends toward increasing voter volatility and decreasing organizational cohesion show few signs of being reversed very soon. Strong popular support for low unemployment and an inclusive welfare state also appears firm. And the recent nuclear accident at Chernobyl is almost certain to have sustained political fallout in Sweden by rekindling debate on phasing out the use of nuclear power plants. This issue could be especially disruptive for the Social Democrats.

Changes in voter loyalties have not increased the political feasibility of any alternative to current policies. Instead they have made it more difficult to implement either socialist or bourgeois development paths. Consider the prospects for a major shift toward a right (nonaccommodationist) variant of a market-oriented model. Such an approach would rely on an increase in unemployment to bring down wage demands. It might also include a decline in marginal and overall rates of taxation, decentralization of wage bargaining, a drop in transfers and overall government spending, decreased government regulation, and privatization of such services as day care and some aspects of health care that are now performed by government.

Even for the nonsocialist parties the political constraints on a nonaccommodationist strategy are real. A substantial cut in government transfers would be particularly difficult to enact. As noted earlier, the Liberals and the Center party have each made commitments that limit their ability to support such cuts. Moreover, the bourgeois parties can only hope to form a government by winning away marginal Social Democratic voters who are likely to share most of that party's views on the welfare state. Because so much of Sweden's GNP is redistributed through state mechanisms, any efforts to streamline that apparatus would undoubtedly impose losses on some groups, redounding to the political credit of the Social Democrats and further undermining the prospects of the bourgeois parties. And with their large electoral base, the Social Democrats are almost certain to regain power. This certainly lowers the incentive of the bourgeois parties to make major policy departures, such as dismantling some programs, that the Social Democrats would very likely reverse when they won office again.

An anti-inflation strategy based on increased unemployment would also face severe difficulties. Even if it could be engineered, it is doubtful whether it would work, because after three years it almost certainly would lead to the fall of the government imposing it, and the policy would be reversed before most of its beneficial effects could be felt.

A major realignment in policy cannot take place without a significant realignment in electoral behavior to provide a secure mandate for a bourgeois government. But as noted earlier, there is little evidence that such a realignment is occurring or will occur in the near future. Of course, an immense economic crisis could promote such a realignment, but it is instructive to remember that the crises of the 1970s did not bring about such a change. Indeed, the bourgeois parties have not even been able to agree on a common election platform. And it probably is not in their interests to do so: any effort to write such a program would almost certainly cause public squabbles over its content and result either in a document full of platitudes or a statement that would drive away potential supporters of one or more of the parties. Yet without such a common program, voters are likely to continue to see the three parties as divided—which, of course, they are.

The adjustment path proposed by the Social Democrats is not without political problems of its own. The decline in the relative power of LO and other changes in the domestic market, and the reluctance of employers to cooperate in centralized bargaining mean that such bargaining will probably be a much less effective tool for restraining wage hikes than it has been in the past. The Social Democrats will need to rethink how to control wage demands in this new environment. The party's relationship with LO will also lead to serious tensions. In particular, the use of the wage earner fund to provide capital needed for investment without increasing wage differentials does not appear to be expandable beyond its current level. The Social Democrats must thus either come up with a more acceptable mechanism to create public savings or acquiesce in increased private savings, which presumably implies increased income inequality.

Suggestions for Change

Political scientists are generally more reluctant than economists to prescribe changes in the "reality" they study. They are all too aware that institutional arrangements are built upon societal interests and that these interests are difficult to change. But a few tentative prescriptions would seem to be in order.

The most important political reform needed is to increase the government's ability to resist short-term pressures so that it can achieve long-term objectives in economic policy. That, obviously, is not easily accomplished given the current trends toward electoral volatility and faltering organizational cohesion. But a change to a longer parliamentary term—perhaps four years—could allow more latitude for actions (or nonactions) that impose or acquiesce in losses by some groups in Swedish society.

Second, the industrial policy experiences of the 1970s and early 1980s suggest that selective accelerationist interventions in industrial change, especially those that focus on firms rather than workers, are dangerous and likely to fail. Where such interventions are politically unavoidable, the government should at least choose responses that minimize the long-term costs of short-term responsiveness. The elements of such a second-best policy of responding to irresistible pressure in the least harmful way possible can be seen in the government's recent decisions to close Sweden's last two shipyards, in Uddevalla and Malmö. Rather than continue to subsidize the yards, as the local unions demanded, the government put together packages of aid featuring the construction of new auto plants—Volvo in Uddevalla, Saab in Malmö. In each case the effect of the package was at least as much political as economic. The lag time between the closing of the shipyards and the opening of the auto plants makes it unlikely that many shipyard workers will obtain employment in the new plants. But the government's aid packages have been widely perceived as both responsive and fair, a perception that has stifled local protest and kept it from spreading. Although it would be an exaggeration to see these aid plans as successful cases of picking winners, they have at least made it politically possible for the government to end bailouts to an industry that was a certain loser, while giving a boost to an industry that is currently very competitive in world markets.[41]

Third, the government's insistence that devaluation will not be used as an adjustment mechanism is neither credible nor beneficial. The reason for this insistence—a reluctance to ease pressures for restraint in

41. The packages are not without potential costs, however. They could be viewed as government subsidies for auto exports, prompting retaliatory action by the United States.

domestic wage negotiations—is understandable. But devaluation has proved one of the few successful mechanisms for adjustment in Sweden in recent years, in part because of its political attributes: it spreads costs broadly and relatively indirectly, and it can be sold as a mechanism to create employment. Instead of eschewing devaluation entirely, the government should make it clear that it is an option that will be considered, but only in combination with strong, painful restraints on wages and transfer payments.

Finally, Sweden's political and economic leaders need to seek a new and revised historic compromise. Given the political infeasibility of either a strongly left or right variant of market-oriented adjustment policy, a softening of the lines between the bourgeois and socialist blocs would appear both inevitable and beneficial. There are precedents for ad hoc cooperation between the Social Democrats and the middle parties (the Center and Liberals) on specific issues such as tax reform. A more regularized cooperation would not be easy: it would threaten cherished images and interests on both sides. For the Social Democrats it would mean surrendering the image that they are the only true defenders of the welfare state, an image that probably works to their electoral benefit. Moreover, it would mean that adjustment policy would take a more centrist course, which would certainly cause internal dissent in both the party and LO. For the Center party and the Liberals, regularized cooperation with the Social Democrats would threaten their electoral images as clear alternatives to that party as well as their own ideological commitments, for the Social Democrats would inevitably be the largest group in any partnership.

Despite the adverse trends of the past twenty years, Sweden's political system does not impose insuperable obstacles to successful economic adjustment. But the system does limit the form those policies can take. The virtual standoff between socialist and nonsocialist parties means that far left or right variants of adjustment policy are unlikely to be adopted. The decline in organizational cohesion that has taken place in recent years means markets will almost certainly be increasingly important in wage bargaining. Sustained public support for the welfare state means that governments cannot expect to free up substantial revenue from this source. And the need to increase savings and investment in a way acceptable to both labor and capital will inevitably lead to continuing conflict. Whether Swedish leaders can fashion a new Swedish model out of these constraints remains to be seen.

Comments by Leif Lewin

Like most foreign observers, R. Kent Weaver admires the traditional consensual manner by which Sweden has for a long time reached political decisions. This style of compromise instead of confrontation is the so-called Swedish model. His argument is that consensual decisionmaking could be more effective for solving the economic problems our country faces. Compromises and consensus between parties seem to him a necessity: "a softening of the lines between the bourgeois and socialist blocs would appear both inevitable and beneficial."

I would like to comment on three aspects of Weaver's presentation of the Swedish model: its historical development, its economic consequences, and the causes of the decline of the model.

It is most common to trace the roots of the Swedish model to the compromise between the Social Democrats and the Agrarian party in the early 1930s, or to the replacement of labor market tensions by better relations in the late 1930s. Others cite the policy realignment and reconciliation between the political parties after the election of 1948, or the later consensus and cooperation inspired by the new, active labor market policy during the 1950s.

However, I think it is useful to go back a little further not only to see the origin of the model but also to understand better the significance of this decisionmaking procedure.

I would go back to a famous political science debate seventy years ago about parliamentarism, that is, the idea that the government should spring from Parliament rather than from the king and that the majority party in Parliament should have the governmental power. Parliamentarism had not yet been introduced into Sweden. Instead our country was ruled by the king, who appointed his government. But because the king was dependent on Parliament for taxes, he had an incentive to compose a government that had the confidence of Parliament. This meant a lot of maneuvering in order to get the right balance in government among different interests. This politics of compromise was the style in Sweden for fifty years—roughly 1866 to 1917—and is often associated with the father of the constitution of 1866, Prime Minister Louis De Geer.

But then parliamentarism arose. The idea was inspired by Britain, and the prerequisite for this procedure was a functioning two-party system as in Britain. This majority rule was the favorite idea of Liberal party leader Karl Staaff.

Parliamentarism was adopted in 1917, but Sweden did not get a clear, well-functioning version. A conservative government succeeded in introducing a proportional method of representation that preserved the multiparty system, and as a consequence Sweden did not get majority rule but minority parliamentarism, with many minorities dealing with each other in various coalitions. In reality, De Geer's politics of compromise prevailed.

After the crisis of majority rule versus parliamentarism during the 1920s, the Social Democrats, having become the biggest party, took over the heritage of De Geer by implementing his politics of compromise. There followed forty-four years of Social Democratic rule characterized by various logrollings and compromises with the nonsocialist parties, including two periods of formal coalition governments.

Now let us look at these two methods of making decisions, De Geer's politics of compromise and Staaff's majority rule, from a theoretical point of view. The idea behind De Geer's politics of compromise is that a decision should mirror the preferences of as many of those involved as possible. All preferences are counted, not only the first preference of the majority. If one does not get what one wants most, at least one gets one's second or third wish. Everyone gets at least something and everyone is happy. The idea behind Staaff's majority rule is that the decision should express only the first preference of the majority in all issues. The opposition gets its chance in the future, when it comes to power.

What are the economic consequences of these two models? Weaver argues in this chapter for a new Swedish model of compromise, which would reduce short-term pressures and allow the government to impose a strict economic policy. But is this the way it would function?

In the politics of compromise all those involved are paid for their support. How much money, for example, have the Social Democrats paid the Agrarians in all their logrolling over the years? Isn't majority rule more effective at keeping costs low, since one never pays opponents off and never gives anything away?

I would have liked to see this reasoning developed a little further. From a normative point of view—and Weaver does come up with policy recommendations—suggestions on how to make majority rule more likely in this country would probably be more useful for the economic

policy he would like us to implement than suggestions of how to renew
the political art of compromise, the Swedish model.

What have been the causes of the decline of the Swedish model?
Weaver describes the decline of the model as a mistake, something that
happened against the will of the politicians. That is only partly true.
Most Social Democrats, I am sure, regret this development. What I think
is an especially fine analysis in this chapter is the short section entitled
"Conflicts within the Model."

The solidaristic wage policy that LO applied meant that all unions
should take more or less the same wage from the employers, even if that
led to difficulties for the less profitable firms and even if not everything
possible was actually taken from the more profitable firms. This led to
increased income equality in Sweden.

But what happened to the money that remained in the profitable
branches? Well, large private fortunes were made. To achieve equality
in wealth as well, LO suggested wage earner funds. The labor movement
was supposed to become an owner of capital. From an ideological point
of view this meant that the Social Democratic party went back to its
theories from before the historic compromise in the early 1930s, again
making capital ownership a political issue. This was the final step in the
decline of the politics of compromise. The nonsocialists saw a revival of
old-fashioned orthodox socialism and attacked the fund idea vigorously.
Most Social Democrats were unhappy about the idea because it began a
new era of confrontation in Swedish politics.

But for the nonsocialists, the fall of the Swedish model was not so
deplorable. The model had allowed the Social Democrats to manipulate
various minorities, form winning coalitions, and thus maintain governmental power regardless of their electoral losses and minority share of
the vote. After 1971 the nonsocialists changed strategy. They oriented
themselves away from the politics of compromise to form a majority
alternative. With many exceptions and irregularities, the mainstream in
nonsocialist strategic thinking during the past fifteen years has been
cooperation against the Social Democrats. What I miss most in this
chapter is a discussion of the development of this strategy, which
succeeded in 1976 with the formation of a nonsocialist three-party
government. The decline of the Swedish model and of the politics of
compromise was not an unforeseen mistake. It was, at least to some
extent, the result of a considered strategic calculation by leading nonsocialist politicians.

Finally, I have three minor points.

The influence of the electoral system on economic policy is discussed many times in the chapter, using arguments we have heard before. However, there is another constitutional peculiarity in Sweden that better explains subsidies to pressure groups. These subsidies are granted by Parliament, and not, as in many other issues, by a politically more remote administrative agency.

Second, I disagree with Weaver's description of what he calls "declining organizational cohesion" and a new inability among leaders to convince their followers. No data are presented to support these statements. This is typical of Sweden's critics. Journalists often gave this picture of Sweden during the 1970s. But in studies made of internal democracy in organizations and parties, little evidence has been found to verify this description. The dominance of elites is still a striking phenomenon in Swedish politics.

Third, Weaver talks about the "rigidification" of policy alternatives and mentions full employment as an example. But that is not a new condition for Swedish decisionmaking. Full employment has been an "inflexible" goal, if you would like to use this word, for the Social Democrats since 1932 and for the nonsocialists since 1945.

Comments by Daniel Tarschys

The key issue that Weaver addresses, namely the role of government in economic development, is difficult, interesting, and very controversial. What is the net effect of politics on economic growth? Does it accelerate or does it retard, does it reinforce or does it undermine the forces of expansion? This issue is hotly debated at many different levels. There is an ideological dispute between the interventionists and those who would leave hands off. Always and everywhere there is a political dispute between government and opposition in which the government claims credit for good economic performance and places the blame for bad economic performance on its predecessors or the world market, while the opposition praises itself or blames the government. Finally there is a wide-ranging discussion among economists and political scientists about the impact of political decisions on decisions in the economy.

Weaver's argument, slightly simplified, is that Sweden's good eco-

nomic performance was linked to good political performance and that
the weaker economic record of the past ten to fifteen years can be linked
to weakening political capability. Previously, he argues, Swedish economic policy was market oriented or accelerationist, but lately it has
turned more protectionist. This shift has been caused not only by external
pressures from the world economy but also by significant changes in the
domestic political system: the end of Social Democratic hegemony, the
new constitution, increased volatility in the electorate, decreased organizational cohesion, and increasing rigidities in social and economic
legislation. One of the main consequences is that the political system
has become excessively responsive to short-term pressures and therefore
too constrained. To overcome these problems, Weaver argues that
Sweden should try to make the political system more immune to the
demands of various interest groups and strive for a national consensus
encompassing both sides of the political spectrum, the socialists and the
so-called bourgeois parties.

I find a lot of sound judgment and perceptive analysis in this chapter.
But before succumbing to the idea that declining political performance
breeds declining economic performance, it might be worthwhile to
consider some competing perspectives.

The first one is centered on changing values. One possible interpretation of the shift in economic growth is that in the 1950s and 1960s the
political system promoted rapid growth because there was a strong
demand for rapid growth; but in the 1970s the appetite of the electorate
had simply changed in the direction of nonmaterial values. A whole
school of sociologists—Inglehart and others—has argued that generations take different attitudes toward economic growth. Though economists point to the 1970s and early 1980s as an era of decline, one could
take the opposite view—that this period produced things that are not
adequately reflected in the GNP: more leisure (the introduction of a fifth
week of paid holiday, for instance), protection of the environment, aid
to the handicapped, and other things bearing on the quality of life. Not
that zero growth turned out to be quite as beautiful and harmonious as
people imagined, and perhaps Sweden is now in the midst of a reaction,
with economic growth again being placed on the agenda. But there was
at least for some time a declining interest in economic growth: in terms
of the Maslow ladder, people had satisfied certain basic needs and were
asking for something else. If this observation is correct, one ought not
to be so harsh on the political system. It might very well be that it

produced economic expansion when expansion was in demand, and a slowdown when there was popular demand for other values. I am not saying that Sweden did particularly well at either stage, but it could at least be argued that the political system was equally responsive to popular aspirations throughout the period. If it is true that the taste for economic growth varies over time, changes in GDP can hardly be an adequate indicator of success for the political system.

Another perspective, perhaps closer to Weaver's analysis, is to look at the declining growth rates as a consequence of the aging of the welfare state. When Mancur Olson and many others argue that advanced industrial societies are entering into sclerotic rigidification, they emphasize cartelization, the mobilization of interest groups, the emergence of what David Riesman once called veto blocks, and so forth. What strikes me very much as a policymaker is the phenomenon of sedimentation in the evolution of the welfare state. New legislation is passed not to replace old legislation but to supplement it; new agencies are often set up in addition to old ones; one reform is stacked on top of another. And many of these programs contain very strong escalator effects. What we have seen in recent years in Sweden is not so much growing bureaucracies as rapidly expanding transfer systems. Just as human beings pass through certain critical stages during their life cycles, there seem to be certain critical stages in the development of subsidies, social security systems, and other benefit programs. Pension systems, for instance, tend to be very cheap in the first few decades after passage, but payments soar when they reach maturity. This, then, may be a somewhat different explanation of Sweden's economic performance in recent years: to find the reason for declining growth rate, one should not so much look to the nuts and bolts of the political system as to the policy heritage, the geological sediments of the policy aspirations of many different political generations.

To return to Weaver's picture of Swedish political development, I have only minor objections. Some of the trends strike me as somewhat exaggerated in his presentation: I do not see a decline in the electoral base of the Social Democrats, I do not think organizational cohesion has suffered as much as he claims, and I find the discussion of declining state autonomy a bit overdone. But these are minor quibbles. What evokes more fundamental skepticism is his final recommendation to make the political system less responsive and more autonomous. Underlying that prescription must be a certain faith in enlightened despotism that is not entirely convincing—essentially it suggests that democracy would be an excellent system of government were it not for the stupid oafs that constitute the people. The point is not to make the government less responsive to the people but to make it more responsive to the broader interests of the people as opposed to their narrow interests, and more concerned about long-term consequences as opposed to short-sighted concerns. Perhaps this is also what Weaver has in mind, but then he should have said so.

Conference Participants

Dan Andersson
Swedish Trade Union Confederation

Krister Andersson
University of Lund

Villy Bergström
Trade Union Institute for Economic Research

Anders Björklund
Industrial Institute for Economic and Social Research

Barry P. Bosworth
Brookings Institution

Gary Burtless
Brookings Institution

Lars Calmfors
Institute for International Economic Studies

Jan Olof Carlsson
National Board for Technical Development

Sten Carlsson
Uppsala University

Klas Eklund
Swedish Cabinet Office

Gunnar Eliasson
Industrial Institute for Economic and Social Research

Karl-Olof Faxén
Swedish Employers' Confederation

Kjell-Olof Feldt
Ministry of Finance

Robert J. Flanagan
Stanford University

Edward M. Gramlich
University of Michigan

Hans-Olof Hagén
National Industrial Board

Carl Hamilton
Institute for International Economic Studies

Ingemar Hansson
University of Lund

Lars Heikensten
Ministry of Finance

Bertil Holmlund
Trade Union Institute for Economic Research

Eva Christina Horwitz
National Board of Trade

Ulf Jakobsson
Swedish Employers' Confederation

Lars Jonung
University of Lund

Robert Z. Lawrence
Brookings Institution

Leif Lewin
Uppsala University

Assar Lindbeck
Institute for International Economic Studies

Erik Lundberg
Skandinaviska Enskilda Banken

Nils Lundgren
PKbanken

Johan Lybeck
Swedebank

Per-Martin Meyerson
Federation of Swedish Industries

Clas-Erik Odhner
Swedish Trade Union Confederation

Thomas Olofsson
Ministry of Finance

Joseph A. Pechman
Brookings Institution

Inga Persson-Tanimura
University of Lund

Alice M. Rivlin
Brookings Institution

Irma Rosenberg
National Institute of Economic Research

Sven H. Salén
Salénia

Claes-Henric Siven
University of Stockholm

Michael Sohlman
Ministry of Finance

Ingemar Ståhl
University of Lund

Ann-Charlotte Ståhlberg
University of Stockholm

Bo Södersten
Swedish Parliament

Hans Tson Söderström
Studieförbundet Näringsliv Och Samhälle

Daniel Tarschys
Swedish Parliament

Eskil Wadensjö
University of Stockholm

R. Kent Weaver
Brookings Institution

Lars Werin
University of Stockholm

Sten Westerberg
Skandinaviska Enskilda Banken

Per Magnus Wijkman
National Board of Trade

Staffan Viotti
Stockholm School of Economics

Lars Wohlin
Urban Mortgage Bank of Sweden

Index